PAUL D. SANSONE, O.F.M.

The traditional demographic regime of ancient Greece and Rome is almost entirely unknown; but our best chance for understanding its characteristics is provided by the three hundred census returns that survive on papyri from Roman Egypt. These returns, which date from the first three centuries AD, list the members of ordinary households living in the Nile valley: not only family members, but lodgers and slaves. *The demography of Roman Egypt* has a complete and accurate catalogue of all demographically relevant information contained in the returns. On the basis of this catalogue, the authors use modern demographic methods and models in order to reconstruct the patterns of mortality, marriage, fertility, and migration that are likely to have prevailed in Roman Egypt. They recreate a more or less typical Mediterranean population as it survived and prospered nearly two millennia ago, at the dawn of the Christian era.

The material presented in this book will be invaluable to scholars in a wide variety of disciplines: ancient historians—especially those working on social and family history; historical demographers, papyrologists, and social historians generally.

The demography of Roman Egypt

Cambridge Studies in Population, Economy and Society in Past Time 23

Series editors

PETER LASLETT, ROGER SCHOFIELD, and E. A. WRIGLEY
ESRC Cambridge Group for the History of Population and Social Structure

and DANIEL SCOTT SMITH
University of Illinois at Chicago

Recent work in social, economic and demographic history has revealed much that was previously obscure about societal stability and change in the past. It has also suggested that crossing the conventional boundaries between these branches of history can be very rewarding.

This series exemplifies the value of interdisciplinary work of this kind, and includes books on topics such as family, kinship and neighbourhood; welfare provision and social control; work and leisure; migration; urban growth; and legal structures and procedures, as well as more familiar matters. It demonstrates that, for example, anthropology and economics have become as close intellectual neighbours to history as have political philosophy or biography.

For a full list of titles in the series, please see end of book.

The demography of Roman Egypt

ROGER S. BAGNALL

Professor of Classics and History, Columbia University

and

BRUCE W. FRIER

Professor of Classics and Roman Law, University of Michigan

CAMBRIDGE
UNIVERSITY PRESS

Published by the Press Syndicate of the University of Cambridge
The Pitt Building, Trumpington Street, Cambridge CB2 1RP
40 West 20th Street, New York, NY 10011–4211, USA
10 Stamford Road, Oakleigh, Melbourne 3166, Australia

First published 1994

Printed in Great Britain at the University Press, Cambridge

**Publication of this book has been aided by the
Stanwood Cockey Lodge Fund of Columbia University.**

A catalogue record for this book is available from the British Library

Library of Congress cataloging-in-publication data

Bagnall, Roger S.
The demography of Roman Egypt / Roger S. Bagnall and Bruce W. Frier
  p.   cm. (Cambridge studies in population, economy, and
society in past time : 23)
Includes bibliographical references and index.
ISBN 0 521 46123 5 (hardback)
1. Egypt—Population—History. 2. Egypt—Census—History.
I. Frier, Bruce W., 1943– . II. Title. III. Series.
  304.6′ 0932—dc20   93-32406 CIP

ISBN 0 521 46123 5 hardback

AU

O I perceive after all so many uttering tongues,
And I perceive they do not come from the roofs of mouths for nothing.

I wish I could translate the hints about the dead young men and women,
And the hints about old men and mothers, and the offspring taken soon
    out of their laps.

Walt Whitman, Song of Myself 6

Contents

Figures

Tables

Foreword

Bagnall and Frier have performed two extraordinary labors in their construction of this book. First, they have assembled about 300 original returns from censuses in Roman Egypt during the first to the third centuries. It has been possible to collect these returns in usable form because they were inscribed on papyrus. After assembling these records (literally assembling them in some instances of crumbled documents), they have put them in order, and translated the inscriptions. Second, they have applied to this body of data the set of modern methods of inferring basic demographic characteristics from incomplete and inexact information. These techniques have been devised in recent years to enrich our knowledge of the characteristics of historical populations and the populations of contemporary less developed countries. This combination of the skills of outstanding classical historians with the most refined techniques of modern demography is indeed unusual; the result is a clear picture of the age composition, marriage customs, fertility, and mortality in Egypt at the height of the Roman Empire. It is not a completely clear picture because of the limited size of the sample, and because of various kinds of bias in what is written on the returns, but still an exciting increase in our knowledge.

Ansley J. Coale
Office of Population Research
Princeton University

Preface

During the early Roman Empire, the provincial government of Egypt conducted a periodic census of all residents. Among the tens of thousands of documentary papyri from Roman Egypt, there survive just over three hundred census returns filed by ordinary Egyptian declarants. Extant returns run from AD 11/12 down to the last known census in 257/258, but the vast majority date to the second and early third centuries. Their state of preservation varies: some are scraps, but many contain complete or nearly complete registers of Egyptian households. In all, nearly eleven hundred registered persons can now be made out, of whom sex is known for more than a thousand, and age for more than seven hundred. About three-quarters of surviving returns come from the Arsinoite and Oxyrhynchite nomes (administrative districts), which lay in Middle Egypt to the south-west of the Nile Delta; other nomes are represented only intermittently.

Although the Egyptian census returns are not free of the flaws that beset all pre-modern censuses, their surprisingly high demographic quality has long been recognized. Early discussion of them from this standpoint culminated in Marcel Hombert and Claude Préaux's classic *Recherches sur le recensement dans l'Egypte romaine*, published in 1952. Since then, however, research has been spasmodic. The only major demographic contribution is Keith Hopkins's 1980 article on "Brother-Sister Marriage in Roman Egypt." Hopkins devoted much of this article to exploratory demographic comments on the census returns, which he argued "are far from perfect, but . . . the best data we have" for ancient populations. Hopkins was the first historian who applied to the returns the sophisticated modelling techniques that modern demographers use when analyzing imperfect data.

In 1988, the co-authors of this book decided to extend Hopkins's approach in a more sustained and comprehensive manner. Our aim was to examine what we both consider a fairly typical example of the ancient demographic regime, especially as it was experienced by quite ordinary individuals situated far beneath the Roman Empire's social and political elite: farmers, laborers, soldiers, scribes, weavers, doctors, goldsmiths, gardeners, stone-cutters, ropemakers, donkey-drivers, and their families and households, all persons commonly met with in the Egyptian census returns. We set ourselves two goals. The first was to collect all known returns, to verify their texts, and to publish demographically relevant information in a uniform catalogue. The second was to employ modern methods in reconstructing the long-term demographic characteristics that the census returns can most probably be held to support for Roman Egypt. Roger Bagnall took primary responsibility for the first part of the project, and Bruce Frier for the second; but at every stage we commented at length on each other's drafts, and the resulting book is entirely collaborative.

Demography, as a social science, examines an extremely important aspect of human experience through an intellectual framework largely specific to it as a discipline. Although the techniques employed in this book may seem exotic to many ancient historians, all are in everyday use among modern historical demographers. We intend our study to be as "user-friendly" as possible; therefore we carefully set out and explain the methods we use, but avoid congesting the text with equations and formulas that might confuse or intimidate. However, we also provide bibliographic references to elementary and more advanced demographic manuals describing these techniques, in the hope that interested readers will not only check our results, but also extend these methods to other sources. Throughout we try to be as clear as possible in defining technical terms, and more generally in explaining the conceptual framework of demographic research. Readers who remain baffled may wish to consult a standard introduction such as Colin Newell's *Methods and Models in Demography* (1988), a wonderfully lucid exposition we draw on heavily.

Modern demography makes frequent use of models in order to evaluate imperfect statistical evidence about past populations. In our experience, these models can be a source of confusion in their own right. Models such as the ones we use are not infallible guides to demographic truth, and they have sharply limited historical worth independent of empirical data to which they are applied. Instead, models are simply "tools of the trade," the purpose of which is to provide a well-established basis for analyzing raw facts in terms of what might reasonably be expected (Newell, pp. 117–119). Since any given population is likely to combine both normal and unusual demographic features, demographers constantly balance the anticipated against the unanticipated, in a delicate effort to reconstruct, within the limits of available evidence, a unique historical population that is at once realistic and plausible.

As will emerge, this approach calls for discernment. Although demography may seem at times a rigorously statistical and hence ineluctable discipline, scholarly taste and judgment inform it at every stage, and such subjective factors assume greater consequence when, as is true of Roman Egypt, surviving data are incomplete and poorly preserved. In this respect, the demography of Roman Egypt does not differ from any other historical study of the ancient world; scanty surviving evidence is pressed to its limits, and at times doubtless a bit beyond. We consider it essential that the seeming precision of our statistics not of itself induce false confidence in the result. On the other hand, the census returns present historians with extraordinary opportunities, which it would be unfortunate to lose simply because the subject matter is unpalatable or numbers arouse suspicion. Even an approximate reconstruction of the major demographic functions for Roman Egypt has value, since so little is otherwise known about these functions in the ancient world; but the fine balance between mortality and fertility was certainly as fundamental to Greek and Roman civilization as to all other societies before the modern demographic transition.

As to demographic method, this book raises different issues: how well do modern techniques work when applied to an historical population known only through evidence that is of reasonably high quality, but sparse and scattered? Do these techniques continue to yield generally credible results? Although the Egyptian census returns are, in this respect, virtually a limiting case, the techniques appear to hold up well. Modelling alone cannot eliminate all defects in the evidence; indeed, it often brings defects into sharper focus, thereby establishing the limits of our knowledge. Nonetheless, as we hope to show, the modern approach can still considerably deepen our understanding of a population in the distant past.

Beyond models, there is now also a large body of comparative evidence against which to test the plausibility of hypotheses about Roman Egypt. Benchmarks are, especially, Mediterranean Europe in the eighteenth and nineteenth centuries, and Egypt in the nineteenth and early twentieth; but early data are now also available for India and rural China, which in some respects may resemble Roman Egypt closely.

In the course of preparing this work we have been helped by numerous individuals and institutions. The many persons who aided Bagnall in the pursuit of the originals and photographs of three hundred census declarations are listed in the introduction to the Catalogue (below, p. 179). We repeat here our thanks for generous assistance without which this entire project would not have been possible. Bagnall is also indebted to the John Simon Guggenheim Memorial Foundation for a fellowship in 1990–91 during which much of the examination of the papyri took place, and to Columbia University for a sabbatical leave that year and continued research support from the office of the vice president for Arts and Sciences.

Frier's portion of the manuscript was largely written during his sabbatical in 1992–93 at Institute for Advanced Study in Princeton; this sabbatical was underwritten by the Institute, the National Endowment for the Humanities, and the University of Michigan, to all of whom he is grateful. He also owes a large debt for help received from the Population Studies Center at Michigan and the Office of Population Research at Princeton University. In particular, Ansley Coale, former director of OPR and one of the world's foremost experts on reconstructing imperfectly known populations, took a lively interest in our project and offered much useful advice on technical points; he also read the completed manuscript and provided a foreword to it. His generous aid was of immense value.

Both of us would like to thank Academic Press, Inc., and Professor Coale for permission to reproduce copyrighted life tables from A. J. Coale and P. Demeny, *Regional Model Life Tables and Stable Populations* (2nd ed., 1983); and also Michael Meckler, a graduate student at the University of Michigan, who prepared the stemmata in the Catalogue.

In December, 1992, at its Christmas meetings in New Orleans, the American Philological Association mounted a special seminar on the preliminary results of our project. Diana Delia and Sarah Pomeroy organized this seminar, which included comments by Keith Bradley, Keith Hopkins, and Richard Saller; all participants provided thoughtful comments that were of considerable help to us. On a more advanced draft, Ann Hanson, Dominic Rathbone, and Richard Saller made dozens of detailed and perceptive observations; their help was invaluable in the final stages of writing, though they must not be implicated in the result. Finally, we are grateful to the editors of this series for accepting our book in it; to Pauline Hire and Karl Howe at Cambridge University Press, for help at every stage of the passage from manuscript to book; and to our copy-editor, Henry Maas, for surefooted but lighthanded improvement of a complex manuscript.

December, 1993

A note on references and abbreviations

Modern works cited more than once are included in the Bibliography and indicated by author's name, short title, and date of publication; those cited only once are normally given in full at their appearance. Abbreviations for journals and standard works may be found in *L'Année Philologique* and the *American Journal of Archaeology*; deviations should be transparent. Papyri and related works are cited according to J. F. Oates *et al.*, *Checklist of Editions of Greek and Latin Papyri, Ostraca and Tablets*, 4th ed. (*BASP* Suppl. 7, 1992). Papyrus references are to volume (roman numerals) and papyrus (arabic numerals), except where references to page numbers are specifically so indicated. Critical work on papyri published up to about 1986, as recorded in the various volumes of the *Berichtigungsliste der griechischen Papyrusurkunden aus Ägypten*, is indicated with *BL* plus volume and page number; critical work since 1986 is cited in full.

1

The census returns

1. The documents and the history of the census

This book is a study of the population of Egypt in the first three centuries of Roman rule. Its central questions concern the size and structure of Egyptian households, the population's age and sex distribution, and the patterns of mortality, marriage, fertility, and migration that are likely to have prevailed in Roman Egypt. The basis for all of this inquiry is a body of about 300 census declarations, of which the earliest dates to AD 12 and the latest to AD 259 (but survives only in a later copy, perhaps from around 266). These declarations are by no means the only evidence for the ages of the residents of Egypt in this period, but they are the only sizable corpus of evidence that at least purports to provide complete rosters of particular households, whatever the age, sex, or status of their members. The problems inherent in constructing statistics from any assemblage of ancient data are considerable. It has been our view that these problems could best be mitigated by a firm exclusion of all texts that could not with reasonable certainty be taken to be census declarations, copies of declarations, or full extracts of the lists of persons from declarations. That is not to say that all problems are thus removed. Chapter 2 is devoted to an assessment of the quality of these data from the point of view of demography.

Before we come to that assessment, however, the reader needs to understand the process by which these texts were created. To this end, Chapter 1 is given over to a description of the origins and end of the census, the geographical and chronological distribution of the surviving evidence, the process by which the census returns were drawn up and compiled into official registers, the form of the declarations, and the uses made of the census data by the Roman government of Egypt. For the most part, these questions were dealt with forty years ago by Marcel Hombert and Claire Préaux in their classic monograph on *Le recensement dans l'Egypte romaine*, and much of what follows is a summary of the still-valid conclu-

1

sions that they reached.[1] These are modified or extended to the extent that
new evidence or reconsideration of old evidence dictates, but the
scrupulous scholarship and sound judgment of Hombert and Préaux have
stood up well in most matters of procedure and diplomatics.[2]

The origins of the census

There is sufficient evidence to demonstrate that census declarations were
submitted for the years 33/34, 47/48, 61/62, and all years at 14-year intervals thereafter through 257/258.[3] Nor are there any surviving declarations
attributable to any year outside the 14-year cycle later than 33/34. The
small number of surviving declarations before 33/34, however, has meant
that it is not possible to demonstrate that the cycle itself was intended as
early as that year. The coincidence of the 14-year intervals makes it likely
at the least that 61/62 was chosen because the interval since 47/48 was the
same as that between 33/34 and 47/48. That, in turn, suggests that there
were no full censuses between 33/34 and 47/48, or else the interval would
not have been meaningful. That view conforms to the absence of intervening declarations. The registers of taxpayers were periodically updated during the interval between those two years, but there is no evidence that taxpayers were asked to submit new declarations during that interval.[4] None
of this, however, tells us anything about official intentions in the 30s and
40s. The coincidence of the interval of 14 years between censuses with the
minimum age at which poll tax was paid may point to an early decision to
use this interval in the census cycle (cf. below, p. 27).

When we come to look at the pre-33 evidence, there is great obscurity.
The earliest Roman texts with any resemblance to census declarations are
documents of 19 and 18 BC in which a royal farmer from Theadelphia, one
Pnepheros son of Phanemieus, reports himself in what he describes as a
ὑπόμνημα.[5] Pnepheros describes himself as 63 in the first declaration and

---

[1] Because the volume has been out of print for many years and may be unavailable to many
readers, their conclusions are summarized in more detail than would otherwise be needed.

[2] Individual papyri are cited throughout this book by the household numbers they are given
in the Catalogue, in which the first element is the first julian year of the Egyptian regnal
year in which the census was announced, the second is a two-letter code for the nome, and
the third is a sequence number within the year and nome. For example, 103-Ar-3 is the
third household in the Arsinoite nome for the census proclaimed in 103/4. A list of the
two-letter codes for the nomes may be found on p. 7.

[3] The discussion of M. Hombert and C. Préaux, *Recherches* (1952) 47–53, is still the fundamental treatment of the 14-year cycle. They showed that there was no persuasive evidence
for a 14-year cycle under the Ptolemies, and that none of the pre-33/4 Roman evidence
was sufficient to demonstrate such a cycle either.

[4] This whole question will be treated by Ann Ellis Hanson in her forthcoming work on *The
First-Century A.D. Tax Archive from Philadelphia*, where she will reedit *P.Mich.* X 578.
See also preliminarily her remarks in *P.XV Congr.* 13.6n. (pp. 65–66).

[5] *W.Chr.* 200 = *P.Grenf.* I 45 and 46.

64 in the second; he does not include any other members of his household in his report, and there is no external evidence to tell us if any existed. These apparently annual reports are of uncertain purpose and have neither predecessors nor successors.[6] They may represent an early attempt at a generalized census, but the absence of other family members suggests that self-declaration as a royal farmer may have been the object (as S. L. Wallace thought).[7] It is also possible that they were a form of annual updating of an existing register of taxpayers liable to the poll tax, something that must have existed in order to allow the introduction of that tax, which certainly was in place before 24 BC.[8]

Two texts have generally been invoked with reference to a supposed census of AD 19. One, *P.Oxy.* II 254 (19-Ox-1), preserves neither any reference to a year of the census nor a date for the declaration itself. Grenfell and Hunt, who supported an early introduction of the 14-year cycle, dated this declaration to the census of 19/20 on the basis of the fact that it is addressed to Eutychides and Theon, *topogrammateis* and *komogrammateis*, a pair known to them also from *P.Oxy.* II 252, dated to 19/20, a notice of the flight (*anachoresis*) without property of the declarant's brother. The same pair, but with the names in reverse order, are the addressees of *P.Mich.* X 580, a similar declaration of *anachoresis* in the [. . .]του year of Tiberius. The editor refrained from restoring the numeral (3rd, 4th, 5th, 6th, 9th, and 10th are all possible), evidently on the grounds that these offices had a five-year term. The term is in fact unknown, but a minimum of six years is attested in one and perhaps both of the only other known pairs of officeholders, all Oxyrhynchite.[9] Dating *P.Oxy.* II 254 to 19/20 is thus an economical, but not necessary, hypothesis, since a date within six or more years on either side of 19/20 would also be acceptable.[10]

---

[6] See M. Hombert and C. Préaux, *Recherches* (1952) 51–52, on this matter.

[7] S. L. Wallace, "Census and Poll-Tax under the Ptolemies," *AJP* 59 (1938) 432. Curiously enough, Wallace does not cite these papyri in his *Taxation* (1937).

[8] See A. Bowman and D. Rathbone, "Cities and Administration" (1992) 113; D. Rathbone, "Egypt, Augustus and Roman Taxation" (1993) 86–88, who attributes the revolt of 26 BC to the introduction of the poll-tax.

[9] Apollonios and Didymos are known in *P.Oxy.* XXXIII 2669 (41–54) and *P.Mich.* III 170 (49); if the Didymos and [ ] known in *P.Oxy.* II 251 (44) and 255 (48) are the same, a span of at least 44 through 49 would be attested. Apollophanes and Diogenes are attested at least from 62 (*SB* XII 10788B) through 63/4 (*P.Gen.* II 94) and 65 (*PSI* VIII 871) to a date that at earliest can be 66/7 and may well be as late as 72/3 (*P.Genov.* I 12, cf. H. C. Youtie, *ZPE* 24 [1977] 138–319 = *Scriptiunculae Posteriores* I 400–401), since it involves a royal scribe whose (apparent) predecessor is attested through 65/6 and who is himself attested in 72/3.

[10] G. M. Browne, in the introduction to *P.Mich.* X 578, argued that the census list published there referred to a census in 19/20, thus strengthening the argument for dating *P.Oxy.* 254 to that year. A. E. Hanson's reedition (above, n. 4) will present an argument that the list in fact refers to the census of 47/48; but removing that prop to the argument does not help to establish any particular date for the Oxyrhynchos declaration.

The other text is a declaration of the reign of Augustus, of which the upper part has long been known as *P.Mil.* 3 (11-Ar-1). It is only with the discovery of its lower part as P.Col.inv. 8, however, that the full usefulness of the text can be seen.[11] Giving a date to year 41 of Augustus, Tybi [?2]6, or 22 January 12, the Columbia fragment justifies fully the views of Hombert-Préaux and Montevecchi that there was a census in the year 11/12.[12] Without having the exact date available to her, but pointing to the mention in *P.Oxy.* II 288.35 of an ἐπίκρισις (*epikrisis*) of the 41st year (11/12), which was the basis of a list of persons with their ages, and a succeeding mention ἐξ ἀπ[ογραφῆς κω]μογραμματέων μβ (ἔτους), Montevecchi had proposed that a census was held in 11/12, with declarations due in 12/13, and that the Milan declaration refers to this census.[13] It is now clear, however, that the declarations were filed in year 41 itself.[14]

There are references elsewhere to an *epikrisis* in year 34,[15] which therefore seem likely to signal a similar operation during that year, seven years earlier. A tantalizing clue to the earlier history of the census is now offered by the descriptions in the declaration of AD 12 of the two men listed there. The declarant is (before his age is given) listed as "20th year," and the 9-year old son is similarly described as "6th year." There is no indication whether inclusive or exclusive reckoning is meant. Since we know that a registration took place seven years before year 41, in year 34, it is an attractive hypothesis that in the case of the son we are to take 6th year as exclusive reckoning, meaning that he was first registered in year 34. It may follow, then, that these indications refer to registration in a periodic or occasional (rather than annual) census, since otherwise he would presumably have been registered at least a year earlier. Two points about the father's registration year now demand attention. First, the interval between his figure and his son's is 14. Secondly, his first registration would have been in year 20, when, according to the present declaration, he

---

[11] It is published in R. S. Bagnall, "Beginnings" (1991) with full commentary.

[12] And not at some earlier date. Cf. most recently the confused discussion in Nicolet, *Space* (1991) 135 (with 147 n. 55), where he propounds both AD 5/6 and 6/7, basing himself upon a long (and now demonstrably wrong) discussion by J. Modrzejewski, "Entre la cité et le fisc," *Symposion 1982* (Valencia 1985) 241–280, reprinted in *Droit impérial et traditions locales dans l'Egypte romaine* (Aldershot 1990) chapter 1.

[13] O. Montevecchi, "Censimento" (1976) 73–74.

[14] Rathbone, "Egypt, Augustus and Roman Taxation" (1993) 89–90 argues that 12/13 should be regarded as the actual census year, but his arguments (cf. 90 n. 27) seem to us very weak. There is no other instance where declarations were collected in advance of a census, and the mention of *epikrisis* in both years 34 and 41 seems to us decisive; this term was not yet at this point specialized to refer to status checks but could refer to the entire census process.

[15] A register compiled in the 34th year of Augustus (4/5) is mentioned in several Oxyrhynchite documents, cf. *Aegyptus* 54 (1974) 29 and see below.

would already have been 34 years old. Since it now seems probable that there was a 7-year interval between one census (in year 34) and the next (that of year 41), it is a reasonable guess that two such intervals explain the 14-year difference between father and son, and that there were also censuses in years 27 (4/3 BC) and 20 (11/10 BC), but not before that year (or else Harthotes would have been registered in an earlier one). By implication, then, there were four general censuses held under Augustus at 7-year intervals, for three of which (all except that of year 27) there is some direct evidence.

There are as yet too few points of evidence to make this reconstruction more than suggestive. But it has a reasonable claim to explain the scanty evidence and does not contradict any of it. It is equally evident, however, that some significance must be attached to the year following 41, mentioned as that of the "declarations of the *komogrammateis*" in *P.Oxy*. II 288.42–43. Even if this is not, as Montevecchi proposed, the year when the individuals' declarations were filed, it must have some significance. It is possible that the officials proceeded in the following year to draw up their registers on the basis of the declarations. That hypothesis would help explain *P.Köln* V 227, an official journal recording transfers of katoikic land, which in line B.1 appears to be dated to year 42 of Augustus. Moreover, in B.5 there is a reference to the volume and *selis* in the records of year 35 of Augustus where a particular parcel was recorded. That would suggest that the same procedure was followed in 4/5 and 5/6 as in 11/12 and 12/13: declarations in the first year, official registers compiled in the second and then used for reference until the next register. There is no evidence for any such general collection of data before year 34 on the basis of the previous censuses we have hypothesized, and it is possible that these compilations did not begin until 5/6. But evidence may yet turn up to show that the process antedates that year. *If* there was a census in 19/20 (which remains to be demonstrated), the choice of that year (if not purely fortuitous) may have depended on the interval since the last compilation of registers. But nothing at this point entitles us to claim that any such census was held, let alone that it followed any regular pattern.

We append a table of what we suppose to have been the major instances of registration under Augustus:

Regnal year	Julian years	Event
20	11/10 BC	Declarations
27	4/3 BC	Declarations
34	4/5	Declarations (ἐπίκρισις)
35	5/6	Establishment of registers
41	11/12	Declarations
42	12/13	Establishment of registers

Distribution of the finds

The hazard of discovery confronts us with a body of declarations very unevenly distributed over the years between the early first century and the middle of the third. The entire first century, in particular, is poorly represented, with the result that many key aspects of the census in that period are unclear. The incomplete preservation of most of the surviving first-century declarations makes matters still more obscure. Generalizations useful in the second century may not be valid in the first. For example, the mention of the edict of the prefect ordering the census appears for the first time in 89-Hm-1 and 89-At-1. That does not mean that there was no such order before the census of 89, but there is no surviving reference to it.

Another interesting example is the absence of regularity before 89 in the date of filing of returns.[16] All three of those for 89 were filed in 90/91, but for earlier censuses no such pattern is found. For the previous census, 75-Ox-1 was apparently filed in 76/7, but the year number in the date is uncertain. For 75-Ar-1, 75-Ar-2, and 75-Ar-3, there is no indication that the census year is past, nor is the exact date preserved. Both declarations for 61 were filed during 61/2 itself. The only declaration for 47 was filed early in 48/9. 33-Ox-2 was filed during 33/4 itself, as were 33-Ar-1 and 33-Ar-2. The earliest declaration was filed in the census year itself. The other early declarations, discussed above, preserve no dates of filing. These scattered data do not offer any obvious pattern, but filing during the census year itself seems prevalent at least through 61/2 and perhaps through 75/6, after which filing in the following year becomes standard (cf. also below).

The general contours of the distribution can be seen in Tables 1.1 and 1.2 (pp. 7–8). Geographically, the Arsinoite alone represents three-fifths of the returns, the Arsinoite and Oxyrhynchite together three-quarters. The only other substantial mass is the Brussels group of Prosopite declarations. The rest is a scatter. The declarations are proportionately more urban than the country, with 49 percent of them coming from nome metropoleis. Since all urban areas together are unlikely to have contained more than about 35–40 percent of the population,[17] the cities are overrepresented. We have calculated many of our figures separately for the two and corrected the weighting in totals; see p. 57. On the other hand, there is no particular reason to believe that these Middle Egyptian nomes were on the whole significantly different from the rest of the country in demographic characteristics. There is certainly no evidence on the basis of which one could correct for any bias. But the possibility of such bias should be remembered.

---

[16]Even the term κατ᾽ οἰκίαν ἀπογραφή is not found before 60, cf. O. Montevecchi, "Censimento" (1976) 74 n. 8. On the general subject of the date of filing, see below, p. 16.

[17]See D. W. Rathbone, "Villages" (1990); and below, p. 56.

Table 1.1. *Source of returns with data on households*

Census	An	Ap	Ar	At	Be	He	Hm	Ly	Me	Oa	Ox	Pr	XX	Total
11			1											1
19											1			1
33			2								2			4
47											1			1
61			1											1
75			3								1			4
89			1				1							2
103			11											11
117		8	11								1			20
131			8	1	4				1		15	1		30
145			17		2			1	1	1	3	1		26
159			21			3			3					27
173			14						3			14		31
187	2		29				1		1		2			35
201			8								2			10
215	1		7			3	3							14
229			1				1	1						3
243			4								1			5
257			1											1
???			4						1		1			6
Total:	3	8	144	0	1	9	9	2	10	1	30	16	0	233

Key to abbreviations

An	Antinoite	Ly	Lykopolite
Ap	Apollonopolite	Me	Memphite
Ar	Arsinoite	Oa	Great Oasis
At	Antaiopolite	Ox	Oxyrhynchite
Be	Berenike (Red Sea)	Pr	Prosopite
He	Herakleopolite	XX	Unknown
Hm	Hermopolite	???	Year unknown

Table 1.2. *Source of all returns*

Census	An	Ap	Ar	At	Be	He	Hm	Ly	Me	Oa	Ox	Pr	XX	Total
11			1											1
19											1			1
33			2								2			4
47											1			1
61			1								1			2
75			3								1			4
89			1	1			1							3
103			14											14
117		9	11								2			22
131			11		1	5			1		16	1		35
145			25			2	1	1	1	1	3	1		35
159			27				3		3		1			33
173			20						3			18		41
187	2		37				1		1		6			47
201			12								3			15
215	1		8			3	3				1			16
229			2			1	2	1			2			8
243			4								3			7
257			1											1
???	1		5						1		2		1	10
Total	4	9	184	1	1	11	11	2	10	1	45	20	1	300

Chronologically, the distribution is—if not more even—at least less idiosyncratic. Figure 1.1 (p. 9) shows the numbers plotted by census year and adds as a control the average number of datable papyri for the fourteen-year period up to the filing year (i.e., the year after the census year).[18] It can be seen that we have a somewhat exaggerated version of the same curve. If a few archival masses are subtracted from the census declaration totals, the peaks of the second century are significantly lowered, and the contours resemble the general shape of papyrus documentation even more closely.[19]

[18] The numbers were counted from the Heidelberg data base of datable documents, thanks to the courtesy of Dieter Hagedorn in making it available over the Internet. We have excluded from the count those papyri dated only to a decade or where the possible range exceeded the fourteen-year period in question.

[19] Those that could be so eliminated are the Tanyaithis declarations of 117, the Oxyrhynchite declarations of 131 in *PSI* I 53, the Brussels roll from the Prosopite (173), and the Berlin mass of Arsinoite declarations from 187.

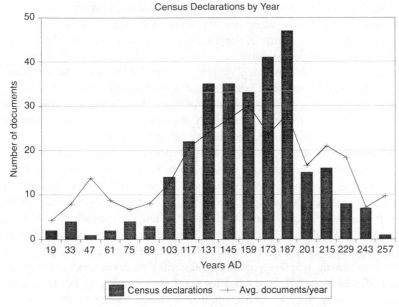

Figure 1.1. *Chronological distribution of returns*

The end of the cycle

The disappearance of periodic census declarations after the census of 257/8 certainly cannot be attributed simply to the chance of discovery. Although the middle of the third century is not a well-represented period, the latter decades of the century are heavily documented.[20] No further declarations even for 257/8 have been discovered since Hombert and Préaux wrote. They concluded their brief discussion of the end of the cycle[21] by asking "s'il n'est pas vain d'imaginer que les opérations du recensement se soient déroulées régulièrement pendant la période si troublée de la fin du IIIe siècle." More recently, Orsolina Montevecchi has put forth a candidate for the precise cause of the end of the censuses, namely the occupation of Egypt by the Palmyrenes just at the time when the edict would normally have gone out for the next census.[22] She argues further that the troubles of the ensuing years would have made a resumption difficult.

Another suggestion, by S. L. Wallace, was to connect the end of the census cycle with the disappearance of requests for *epikrisis* after 250.[23]

---

[20] For the documentation of the late third century, see R. S. Bagnall and K. A. Worp, "Papyrus Documentation in the Period of Diocletian and Constantine," *BES* 4 (1982) 25–33.

[21] M. Hombert and C. Préaux, *Recherches* (1952) 52–53.

[22] O. Montevecchi, "Censimento" (1976) 77–84.

[23] Cf. M. Hombert and C. Préaux, *Recherches* (1952) 53.

But this is certainly incorrect. In general, population lists were definitely maintained for purposes of examining status and entitlements after 250, even after 257/8. The entire Oxyrhynchite grain dole at the end of the 260s (*P.Oxy.* XL) rested on the existence of such records, and there is a request for *epikrisis* as late as 274/5 or 280/1.[24] The need to maintain records classifying the population into Romans and non-Romans, however, and to administer the many restrictions set forth in the *Gnomon of the Idios Logos*, had ended with the Constitutio Antoniniana in 212, which conferred Roman citizenship on most Egyptians and other provincials.

The continued maintenance of classified population lists into the 270s suggests that the administration was, even in these difficult times, able to maintain some level of normal operations. It may well be that disarray in Alexandria is in fact the culprit for the failure of the census for 271/2 to take place as anticipated. But in that case it is not obvious why the Roman government would not have taken a new census once its control was restored, perhaps in 274 with Claudius Firmus in office as *corrector*.[25] It is thus worth asking whether something else may be responsible, if not for the specific lapse in 271/2, at least for the failure to pick up later on. Specifically, it seems logical to ask whether a change in the taxation system may not have removed the *raison d'être* of the census still earlier.

Hombert and Préaux in fact invoke Diocletian's restructuring of the tax system at the end of the century as a possible occasion for drastic changes in the census, and they point to the two known early fourth-century census returns, very different in character from those studied here, as possible offspring of this reform. But, as they point out, these declarations (*P.Sakaon* 1 and *P.Cair.Isid.* 8, dated 309 and 310) do not seem to have any relationship to the quinquennial tax cycle that preceded the introduction of the 15-year indiction cycle (based on 312). Any connection is thus hypothetical.

It is commonly agreed that the census had a close connection with the system of capitation taxes, and there is considerable evidence in the first-century Philadelphia archive that accurate lists of men liable to the poll tax and other capitation levies were indeed at least one of the principal uses to which census data were put (cf. below, p. 27). One may naturally ask what the history of these taxes in the third century was. The last receipt for *laographia*, the poll tax, is dated to 248.[26] There is a reference to *laographia* in an Oxyrhynchite petition to a phylarch dated to 267, where it

---

[24] *P.Turner* 38; see O. Montevecchi's commentary there. *PSI* V 457, the next latest, dates to 269. P.Yale inv. 1360 (*ZPE* 96 [1993] 221–222) is assigned by its editor to the reign of Probus on slender grounds, but the period must be approximately right.

[25] Cf. O. Montevecchi, "Censimento" (1976) 81–82.

[26] *Pap.Lugd.Bat.* XIX 14; cf. the commentary for other third-century receipts.

is not clear whether it refers to the tax or more generally to a population survey or register. Evidence for the poll tax thus ends before the next census in the 14-year cycle would have been due (for 271/2). Only a more comprehensive study of third-century taxation, however, could show if tax changes could in fact be the grounds for the discontinuance of the regular census cycle. But the Oxyrhynchite petition suggests that some regular census records were being maintained as late as 267.

2. The census process

The edict of the prefect

Many of the declarations from 89 and later, though by no means all, refer to an edict of the *Praefectus Aegypti* in accordance with which the census is being carried out.[27] Since no example of such an edict for the population census has yet appeared, scholars have been reduced to speculation in discussing it.[28] Because the census is described as being of a particular year, it is reasonable to suppose that the edict was issued during that year. It was certainly not issued later than that year, as one can tell from the existence of declarations dated to that year. On the other hand, without any knowledge of the edict's contents we are completely unable to say what lapse of time between edict and declarations is to be anticipated. Since the time of filing, as will be seen, seems to be a matter of local circumstances and bureaucratic decision, it is impossible to establish any general rule in the matter. Montevecchi has argued that it was normal for the edict to be issued during the summer, but there is insufficient evidence to say if this is correct.[29]

Who was subject to the census?

When Hombert and Préaux wrote, a near-complete absence of census declarations in Greek drawn up by Roman citizens seemed to authorize their statement, "On n'a, en effet, jamais trouvé avant 212 de Romain auteur d'une κατ᾽ οἰκίαν ἀπογραφή grecque."[30] They did point to *PSI* 1183, a declaration in Latin, as suggesting that Roman citizens nonetheless had to register; and they admitted (with Wilcken) that this declaration may have been submitted on the occasion of the census of 47/8. The careful formulation of their statement took account of 145-Ar-7, in which the slave of two women who are apparently Roman citizens filed a return, and 131-Ar-5, in which the *phrontistes* (agent) of a Roman citizen woman files on her

---

[27] See M. Hombert and C. Préaux, *Recherches* (1952) 76–77.
[28] M. Hombert and C. Préaux, *Recherches* (1952) 53–56, 76–77.
[29] O. Montevecchi, "Censimento" (1976) 76–77.
[30] M. Hombert and C. Préaux, *Recherches* (1952) 56.

behalf. In both of these instances, only property is declared, with no persons registered in it.

Since Hombert and Préaux wrote, further instances of property with no registered occupants have occurred: 61-Ox-1, 145-Ar-16 (apparently) and 173-Ar-1. In the latter two, it is not the owner who actually files the registration but the *phrontistes* (145-Ar-16) or son (173-Ar-1). In the last case, however, the filer is himself a Roman citizen (or at least has the proper *tria nomina*). And in 61-Ox-1, the filer is the owner, a Roman veteran whose citizenship is clear (he gives his tribal affiliation). Still more telling, however is 173-Ar-10, in which the declarants are two sisters, evidently citizens. Although the text breaks off before a list of persons, Petronia Gaia indicates that she is registering the two women and her children. This would be, then, the first clear example of a declaration *by* a Roman citizen before 212 in which Roman citizens (and not only their property) are declared. It is certainly true that the names are not by themselves sufficient evidence of citizenship, but the use in this context of the *ius trium liberorum* suggests that these really are citizens. It is, moreover, likely that 159-Ar-6 is a declaration by a Roman citizen, but the property there appears to belong to a minor for whom the declarant is tutor.

The fact that Roman citizens were exempted from the capitation taxes that were based on the lists derived from census declarations is no argument against their having had to file these declarations, since women and children (as well as the elderly) were also exempted but had to be registered all the same. Women and Romans are in fact handled in the same fashion in the synopsis of households in Philadelphia published as *P.Lond.* II 257–259 (pp. 19–42). They are listed as proprietors but their ages are not given; ages are given only for men of taxpaying age. Because the synopsis gives every sign of having been compiled from census declarations, it is hard to escape the conclusion that Romans had to file declarations. It appears, then, that the entire population of Egypt was registered, whatever their status.[31]

It is difficult to derive universally applicable rules about the unit of filing and the person responsible for filing.[32] It appears generally true that pro-

---

[31] For a general description of the London text see M. Hombert and C. Préaux, *Recherches* (1952) 136–138; we are indebted to Ann Hanson for helpful comments on the text, which appears to represent in fact a single document concerning the village of Philadelphia (for AD 94), in which men added to and subtracted from the rolls are enumerated separately. D. Rathbone, "Egypt, Augustus and Roman Taxation" (1993) 89 argues that because Romans and Alexandrians were not *laoi* and thus subject to the *laographia* they were exempt from the census. This view construes the purposes of the census too narrowly, as we shall argue (below, p. 26), as well as being contradicted by evidence.

[32] See M. Hombert and C. Préaux, *Recherches* (1952) 57–62, for details. They note their surprise (59) at "la diversité des procédés employés dans la déclaration des biens possédés en commun." There is in fact a large element of variation in the entire matter of definition of the household and the person responsible for declaration, not all of which need be gone into here.

prietors were liable to file for all of their house property, including vacant lots.[33] The unit of filing was not always the house, for there are numerous declarations of fractions of houses.[34] As Hombert and Préaux say, "ce n'est pas au bien dans son existence matérielle que s'attache l'obligation de déclarer, mais au droit de propriété." It was not unusual for individuals to own fractions of several properties. These might be listed at the end of the person's principal declaration, usually in the form of a statement like "And I also own a fourth of a house and courtyard at . . ." But there are a number of declarations by persons who describe themselves as "registered through another declaration" for pieces of property "in which no one is registered" (or similar). It is not evident why these were not listed at the end of the principal declaration.

A special problem is posed by registrations of households composed entirely of tenants. Many Egyptian households included lodgers, usually described by the Greek word ἔνοικος (*enoikos*). These were listed along with the members of the family with whom they lodged, rather than in a separate declaration, and we have included them as such. But there were also entire households of tenants, occupying the entirety of an identifiable property (house or part thereof) as a unit. In some cases these are declared (in a separate declaration) by the landlord. In others, particularly in Memphis, they file their own declarations (but with an indication of the landlord's knowledge).

The position of women in the process of declaration is still more complex. We find cases in which house property belonging to a married woman is noted at the end of the declaration by her husband, but we also find separate declarations of such property. Most women before the Constitutio Antoniniana are accompanied by a *kyrios*, or legal representative, but this is apparently not true in the Prosopite Nome and was perhaps by no means so universal as has been assumed.[35] It seems likely that the government did not lay down rules concerning the capacity of women to declare property, the matter being of little importance in this particular context.

In general, then, we can say that the unit of declaration was the household,[36] but that every property right to houses and lots had to be

---

[33] Productive land was registered by an entirely different process.

[34] And in *P.Lond.* II 257–259 there are numerous entries for οἰκί(ας) μέρο(ς), part of a house.

[35] M. Hombert and C. Préaux, *Recherches* (1952) 60–61. Alternatively, one might suppose that the Prosopite declarations simply do not mention the presence of the *kyrios* even though one was actually involved.

[36] A term referring to one or more individuals operating as a unit (cf. below, p. 55). The statement of M. Hombert and C. Préaux, *Recherches* (1952) 57 that the declaration "comporta[it] tous les habitants d'une maison" is inaccurate. A house often included more than one household.

declared as well. The name of the census, the κατ᾽ οἰκίαν ἀπογραφή, refers to the government's interest in seeing that every physical house was enumerated; but the declarations do not give addresses or descriptions of the houses themselves, and it is evident that no register of the houses could have been compiled from these declarations without the assistance of other lists or declarations. The declarations of property without persons therefore presumably have the function of assuring the government that there are no persons to be registered outside of those listed in the sum total of household declarations. We shall see that this assurance was in some degree false, at least as regards males, but the complete enumeration of persons, listed by household, was clearly the object. Registration was, it should be remembered, compulsory, and there were stiff penalties for non-compliance.[37]

The place of filing[38]
There is ample evidence to support the instinctive modern notion that people must have submitted their census declarations in their legal domiciles, an idea reinforced of course by the Lucan narrative of Jesus' birth, in which "everyone went to register, each to his own city" (ἐπορεύοντο πάντες ἀπογράφεσθαι, ἕκαστος εἰς τὴν ἑαυτοῦ πόλιν, Lk 2:3).[39] The fragmentary Edict of Vibius Maximus from 104, ordering Egyptians to leave Alexandria to register, preserves in part the relevant passage:

τῆς κατ᾽ οἰ[κίαν ἀπογραφῆς ἐ]νεστώ[σης] ἀναγκαῖόν [ἐστιν πᾶσιν τοῖς καθ᾽ ἥ[ντινα] δήποτε αἰτ[ίαν ἀποδημοῦσιν ἀπὸ τῶν] νομῶν προσα[γγέλλε]σθαι ἐπα[νελ]θεῖν εἰς τὰ ἑαυ[τῶν ἐ]φέστια, ἵν[α] καὶ τὴν συνήθη [οἰ]κονομίαν τῆ[ς ἀπο]γραφῆς πληρώσωσιν καὶ τῇ προσ[ηκού]σῃ αὐτοῖς γεωργίαι προσκαρτερήσω[σιν]

The house-to-house census having started, it is essential that all persons who for any reason whatsoever are absent from their nomes be summoned to return to their own hearths, in order that they may perform the customary business of registration and apply themselves to the cultivation which concerns them.[40]

---

[37]Cf. M. Hombert and C. Préaux, *Recherches* (1952) 97–99, for a description.

[38]M. Hombert and C. Préaux, *Recherches* (1952) 63–76.

[39]The relationship of this narrative to the Egyptian evidence is most recently discussed by S. R. Llewelyn, *New Documents Illustrating Early Christianity* 6 (Macquarie University 1992) 112–132, with extensive bibliography and a general description of the filing process.

[40]*P. Lond.* III 904.18–38 (p. 125) = *Sel. Pap.* II 220. The date is not preserved, but the edict stands on the second column of a papyrus with other official correspondence dated to Epeiph 24 and Mesore 14 of year 7 of Trajan. The edict mentions a month beginning in epsilon (theta's cross-bar in this hand is lower) in line 38, qualified as 'present' (ἐν]εσ[τ]ῶτος), making it likely that the edict dates from Epeiph of year 7, or June-July, 104, near the end of the official census year.

Extensive modern scholarship has been devoted to the question of the general applicability of the edict, which many have sought to restrict to residents of the *chora* who were currently present in Alexandria (for whose special needs subsequent clauses provide).[41] There is no doubt that this particular edict does refer to country people in the capital, but there is also no reason to question its stated motive, namely to facilitate the operations of the census. Nor is there any reason to suppose that *only* those in Alexandria were expected to report home for the census.

The real difficulty arises in understanding the term ἐφέστιον, for which most of the parallel evidence is centuries later. Hombert and Préaux argue persuasively that for the rural population it is equivalent to the term ἰδίᾳ found in many contexts, and that for city residents it is equivalent to the subdivision of the metropolis in which they are 'registered,' for which the technical term is ἀναγράφεσθαι. "Fiscal domicile" is perhaps the most straightforward translation.

The notion of domicile, however, is anything but simple, and definition is probably not the most profitable strategy. Modern jurisdictions tend to use a series of criteria, not all of which will necessarily coincide for a given household. For Roman Egypt, "fiscal domicile" is not necessarily straightforward, since (as Hombert and Préaux observed) one might well have tax and even liturgical obligations in more than one place as a result of landholdings. It appears, actually, that domicile was defined circularly as the place given in the records as one's domicile. Changing it required an application to the authorities.

For the most part, residence, domicile, and place of filing census declarations coincided for village residents. The order to return to the legal domicile, in fact, makes good sense under the circumstances outlined below, in which village declarations were all drawn up and submitted within a narrow time-frame while the requisite officialdom visited the village. But persons resident in one place owning property in another commonly file declarations in the places where they own property. We do not have complete enough documentation to describe procedures in detail, but it appears that in such cases the declaration in the non-domiciliary village was a second or subsequent declaration, not the primary one for the person. It is hardly necessary to imagine that there was a single, universal procedure applied in all cases with juridical precision, and much of the scholarly discussion on the subject (particularly in connection with the account of Luke) suffers from a lack of realism about the circumstances of the Egyptian countryside.

[41] A discussion with bibliography can be found in H. Braunert, *Binnenwanderung* (1964) 168–171, who accepts the notion that it is limited to Alexandria.

In the cities, on the other hand, the circumscription (ἄμφοδον in the case of our main provenance, Arsinoe) given as place of record (ἀναγραφόμενος ἐπὶ . . .) is not usually that of residence. The documents contain some instances of declarations filed in the place of record, some in the *amphodon* where the property is located, and (when declaring tenants) some in the *amphodon* where the tenants were previously registered. There is no rule, conclude Hombert and Préaux, to which exceptions cannot readily be found. Either there was no rule at all, or else the administration routinely transmitted information among the *amphoda* so that it simply did not matter where one deposited the information into the system.

We must before leaving the question of place of filing discuss briefly one problem to which we have no solution but that has significant implications for the treatment in Chapter 8 of migration and the difference in sex ratios between metropoleis and villages. This is the extent to which the place of filing may generally be treated as that of physical residence, and particularly how far we may assume that those registering in metropoleis actually lived in the metroplis and those registering in a village actually lived in a village. In some cases (e.g., 159-Ar-15/17) the declarant says explicitly that he or another member of the household is living elsewhere. But can we rely on the assumption that statements were routinely made when that was the case?

In a number of instances, houses "in which no one is registered" are declared. Are we to imagine that all of these were truly vacant? Or were they the country residences of metropolitans who filed their declarations in the metropolis? Conversely, could and did villagers who moved to a metropolis change their *idia* and register thenceforth in the metropolis? The hypothesis (in Chapter 8) that the difference in sex ratio between metropolis and village exhibited by the declarations can be explained by migration depends on an affirmative answer to the last question, for otherwise even those who migrated would show up in the *apographai* as living in the village of origin. We see no way of telling what percentage of the population overall is affected by such questions, nor any means of settling what answer to give to these questions for most of those people. The reader should bear these uncertainties in mind in the discussion that follows.

The date of filing

Hombert and Préaux, building on earlier work by A. Calderini and V. Martin, gave a list of declarations by filing date and a careful analysis of these data.[42] They noted that there are no known declarations dated before Pauni of the designated census-year (as indicated in the declarations by the phrase τὴν τοῦ —— ἔτους κατ᾽ οἰκίαν ἀπογραφήν), and that most are dated

[42]M. Hombert and C. Préaux, *Recherches* (1952) 77–84.

in the following year. There are, however, none dated *after* the following year. This apparent demonstration of administrative efficiency and control was in their view an argument in favor of the hypothesis that the census in the villages was carried out by travelling teams of officials.

General conclusions are made more difficult by the peculiar skewing of the evidence in place and time described above. Hombert and Préaux note that almost all Arsinoite declarations after the first century are dated in the last three months of the Egyptian year after the official date of the census ('year 2'), but that elsewhere hardly any declarations fall into that zone. The overwhelming majority of Oxyrhynchite declarations, however, do fall in year 2. In the limited sample from other nomes, considerable variation can be found within a single nome or city for a given census.

A striking phenomenon observed by Hombert and Préaux is the concentration of the declarations from individual villages within a narrow chronological zone. The most salient example is precisely the Brussels roll they published, containing sixteen declarations from the Prosopite village of Thelbonthon Siphtha all dated to 19 July 174, except for one dated to the 20th (173-Pr-3 to 18). But there are other instances as well. 173-Pr-1/2, both from Theresis in the Prosopite, are three days apart (21 and 24 June). Of the nine declarations of 117 from Tanyaithis (117-Ap-1 to 9), four have surviving exact dates, all to 15 or 16 May. The two Tebtunis declarations from 147 fall on 3 and 18 July. Four declarations from Karanis in the same year fall between 7 (or 10) and 24 July. In the next census, the Karanis declarations all fall between 7 and 17 July. Theadelphia the same year has one declaration on 27 May, then five others on 25 July to 4 August. Talei's two declarations are dated 25 and 29 April. We have five declarations from Soknopaiou Nesos in 217, all dated 28 August.

As Hombert and Préaux acutely noted, this pattern might in part be explained by the fact that such clusters of documentation usually result from the preservation of groups of declarations glued together in a τόμος συγκολλήσιμος or kept together archivally. They rejected this as a sufficient explanation, however, citing the Brussels roll's extreme compression of the filing season. A stronger argument is that similar concentrations, even from *tomoi*, from the metropoleis do not show the same pattern. The dated declarations from *PSI* I 53 (131-Ox-1 to 12) are spread from 15 November to 28 April, though mostly falling in November and December. The numerous Arsinoite metropolitan texts of 189, as far as dates are preserved, stretch from 26 May to 28 August. They do seem rather clustered at the starts and ends of months, but otherwise they occupy a three-month span. If archival preservation determined the known span of dates, the villages and cities might be expected to show the same pattern.

This difference between city and village may then be taken to demonstrate that the preserved pattern of dates is not simply a figment of preservation.

It seems most plausible to attribute it to a fundamental difference in method of operation. In the villages, the officials necessary (and perhaps the scribes who knew the formula) were present only for a limited time, which no doubt varied according to the size of the village. In the cities, there were permanent public offices, which were probably open at least for an extended season if not throughout the census years. Hombert and Préaux, following Wilcken, cite Aristotle (*Ath.Pol.* 40) for the natural human propensity to put off such declarations as late as possible.

The drafting of the returns

A number of factors make it certain that declarations were drafted and written by professional scribes. The Brussels roll from Thelbonthon Siphtha in the Prosopite contains 16 declarations, of which 13 are in a single hand, 2 by another, and 1 by a third. These are originals, which wound up in an official *tomos* (cf. next section). The very high degree of formulaic character found among declarations from a particular area and period would have been impossible without the dissemination of officially sanctioned standard forms, and it is unlikely that anyone except a professional would have had any means of learning these standard document types. Moreover, the handwriting of the bodies of the declarations is consistently professional, generally a fast cursive. There are exceptions, but these can in the main be explained as private copies, sometimes after the fact. Those declarations that can be identified as originals submitted to officials are almost all written in trained hands characteristic of the work found also in professionally written contracts. The contrast with the signatures (see below) is often striking.

This professionalism has a number of consequences for the editor and user of the declarations. One useful result is that the formula of the declarations can in many cases be reconstructed even from exiguous remains, allowing a fairly high degree of certainty about the extent of lost text and how it will have run. The relatively good local consistency in the size and shape of declarations also contributes to this ease of reconstruction. Another is that we may expect a fair degree of competence and accuracy, not to mention the ability to read copies of previous declarations which the declarants may have possessed, thus allowing the verification of ages, or at least their consistent reporting.

The professional handwriting does, however, have at least one important negative consequence. Such hands are readily legible when they are writing the expected and formulaic, but they were meant to be read, if at all, by eyes accustomed to the writing, the language, and the formulas. When they deviate from standard formulas, they are often extremely difficult for the modern reader, lacking much of this context, to decipher. Rapid sawtooth writing may also leave some names unreadable. It should be said, however, that the scribes went to great pains to write ages clearly, often in larger numerals readily distinguishable from the ordinary handwriting.

Official handling of the returns[43]

No ancient document explicitly describes the initial processing of the declarations, and the surviving declarations themselves provide only very limited insight into this matter. For nomes other than the Oxyrhynchite and Arsinoite, in fact, the data are insufficient to say much more than that the surviving examples are all addressed to a single recipient. This does not mean, however, that only one copy was made and only one official received it. In the Arsinoite the contrary was certainly the case. Good luck has preserved one splendid illustration, the declaration of a household (159-Ar-13) which survives in six copies, all in the same hand and identical except for the address, addressed to the *strategos* (in duplicate), to the *basilikos grammateus*, to the *komogrammateus* of Soknopaiou Nesos (in duplicate), and the *laographoi* of that village. None bears any sign of receipt or official handling, and none was ever made part of a composite roll. It is entirely likely that they were for whatever reason never submitted.

"Chaque fois qu'on s'efforce de tracer avec quelque précision les règles suivant lesquelles l'administration traitait les déclarations, on aperçoit de multiples exceptions, qui rendent toute généralisation aléatoire." So Hombert and Préaux. But they discern some *normal* procedures all the same. Some exemplars of each declaration, whether original or copy, were retained in administrative offices and glued together into composite rolls (τόμοι συγκολλήσιμοι), in which sheets were numbered sequentially (from left to right, as we read them). These *tomoi* were certainly made up by village, but that tells us little; some villages must have required multiple *tomoi*, and the order within the *tomoi* also needs definition. Hombert and Préaux suggest date of filing as one organizing principle, which they see at work in the Brussels roll. But there can have been others. *P.Mil.Vogl.* III 193-194, with four declarations altogether, certainly belonged to the same roll; all four are declarations from currently unmarried female heads of household.[44] There is no reason to imagine that all village officials classified declarations in the same way.

The subsequent use of the declarations by officials will be considered below. They were certainly checked against existing records and used to bring the latter up to date. At least one set was kept permanently (however long that was), probably that in the nome capital in the *bibliotheke*, and it

---

[43] M. Hombert and C. Préaux, *Recherches* (1952) 129-135.
[44] These are 145-Ar-1 to 4.

is certain that in the case of villages another set, or at least a summary of another set, was kept in the village archives not only until the next census but for some extended period beyond. Whether the declarations themselves were still available, their data were still in official use for at least two and probably three cycles, as can be seen from *P.Lond.* II 257–259.

It is very difficult to say if the declarants received any proof of submission from the officials. There are no known receipts, at least in the sense of separate texts drawn up like tax receipts in the form "I have received from you the census declaration for your household for the census of the 7th year" or something of that sort. There are, however, some declarations with official markings at the bottom, which *may* in some cases be official acknowledgments for the benefit of the declarant—or may not. These are discussed below, p. 26. The low incidence of age-rounding in the declarations suggests that declarants generally were not guessing when they declared their ages, and there are certainly some cases in which households clearly possessed copies of previous declarations. It seems more likely that people had copies of their own previous declarations than that they consulted official registers—not always well preserved or easily searchable—to determine their ages. The exceptionally low Whipple's Index for the metropoleis (below, p. 46) points to ready accessibility of previously declared ages there, and even in the villages the index is not high by the standards of modern countries with probably comparable illiteracy rates.

3. The form of the returns

The form of the census declarations was studied with great care by Hombert and Préaux, in the hope that the detailed description of matters "qui, en soi, sont d'un intérêt minime," would be useful to future editors.[45] Though much new documentation has accumulated in the intervening years, only details in their treatment require alteration. Our purpose in describing them here is not to replace that account, but to provide a foundation for assessing the nature and quality of the evidence. In particular, the damaged state of many of the declarations is such that one might well despair of extracting any useful data from them, were it not for the highly regularized (though not fully uniform) character of the formulas and physical disposition of the declarations. Since many reconstructions of such texts and the households declared in them, as they are listed in the Catalogue and used in our discussions, depend on these diplomatic characteristics, at least a general description will be useful to the reader who wishes to test the data.

---

[45]M. Hombert and C. Préaux, *Recherches* (1952) 99.

The address[46]

We have already alluded to the exceptional case of household 159-Ar-13, the declaration of which survives in six examples, two addressed to the *strategos*, one to the *basilikos grammateus*, two to the *komogrammateus*, and one to the *laographoi* of the village of Soknopaiou Nesos. Parallels to all of these exist severally in other declarations, and this list describes well the normal recipients of surviving village declarations. (In cities, the city or *amphodon* secretaries replace the village secretary and *laographoi*.)[47] But, as Hombert and Préaux pointed out, this process of addressing identical texts to several different officials is not the only one known.[48] There are also declarations addressed simultaneously to several officials. In most cases, of course, only one example survives, so that we cannot say what a complete set looked like. The paucity of information for nomes other than the Arsinoite makes it particularly difficult to generalize.

Hombert and Préaux showed that declarations from Arsinoe addressed to several officials do not form part of *tomoi*, the official records; they are never originals; they never bear the signature of the declarant. All those with preserved lower parts bear the signatures of officials showing the registration of the document. This situation may be explained either by the hypothesis that these declarations were returned to the declarants as receipts or by supposing that they remained in the lowest level of officialdom to aid in the composition of registers. In the case of declarations from Arsinoite villages, on the other hand, at least some of the preserved texts addressed to multiple officials did form part of the administrative archives in the form of *tomoi*. Once again, however, we find that they do not (as far as preserved) contain signatures, but that they do have official subscriptions. No hypothesis for their essential character (retained officially or returned as receipts) seems quite to account for all of the documents. The Arsinoite circulating multirecipient declaration is apparently unique to that nome.

With declarations addressed to a single official, on the other hand, the situation is different. Some have signatures from the declarant, but none has any official subscription at the bottom. The evidence thus suggests that they were intended to be kept in the archives of the official addressed. The declarations from other nomes are in the main addressed to a single recipient, and they appropriately have signatures but no official subscriptions.

---

[46]See generally M. Hombert and C. Préaux, *Recherches* (1952) 84–97, 101–102.

[47]The changes over time and place in the organization of the municipal governments produce some variation. We find the amphodarchs on occasion; in Antinoopolis the nomarch and a three-person board for each tribe seem to have been the normal recipients. Village *presbyteroi* occur in 89-Ar-1.

[48]M. Hombert and C. Préaux, *Recherches* (1952) 85–86.

Declarant
The name(s) and title(s) of the recipient(s), in the dative, were followed by
the name of the declarant in the genitive, introduced by παρά.[49] Some
declarations give only the name and patronymic of the declarant, but most
add the paternal grandfather's name, the mother's name, and her
patronymic, e.g., παρὰ Ἰσιδώρου Ἀπίωνος τοῦ Ἰσιδώρου μητρὸς Ἀπίας
τῆς Χαιρήμονος. Although our sample of first-century declarations is
small, it is noteworthy that more names are given as time goes on, a
process paralleled in the official registers.[50] Occupations are rarely given at
this point, except for that of priest, which forms part of the legal self-
description of the person. (Occupations are, however, given more commonly in the list of persons.) There follows generally an indication of the
origin of the person and in some cases of status. For villagers, normally the
phrase ἀπὸ κώμης NN (perhaps with a following indication of district) is
generally sufficient.

Metropolitans, however, tend to give more detail, mainly because there
was a more complex array of statuses available to them. These include
λαογραφούμενος (despite the name, this refers in the case of metropolitans
to those paying laographia *at a reduced rate*), κάτοικος (in the Arsinoite, a
member of the defined group of descendants of Greek settlers), ἀπὸ
γυμνασίου (a term of similar significance elsewhere), and ἀργός (at
Memphis, perhaps a privileged class of those without a manual trade).
Only κάτοικος, however, figures in the initial statement of the declarant's
identity, the others being reserved for the body of the list. Metropolitans
also generally indicate their circumscription of registration (*amphodon*).
Women typically, though not uniformly, indicate their legal representative
(*kyrios*) or agent (*phrontistes*).

The initial self-identification of the declarant, then, gives us in most cases
a fair amount of information, particularly about family connections. It does
not, however, include the age (always given in the list of persons), and
thus if the list is lost, the age cannot be recovered. Moreover, it does not
indicate whether the declarant is in fact declaring himself or herself in this
particular declaration. It is only subsequently that we are informed if this is
a declaration for a piece of property other than the domicile of the
declarant, inhabited by lodgers or by no one.

Declaration of persons and property
Once the declarant has identified himself, there follows a section in which
the notions of declaration and possession are set forth. The formulas in
which this is done vary considerably from time to time and place to

---

[49] See M. Hombert and C. Préaux, *Recherches* (1952) 102–108 on the filers.
[50] A point we owe to Ann Hanson.

place.[51] They typically contain a mention of the census itself and its year, often accompanied by a reference to the prefect's edict (κατὰ τὰ κελευσθέντα or something similar). In the Arsinoite, the formula generally begins with a statement of ownership of property, "there belongs to me . . ." (ὑπάρχει μοι . . .), with a description of the property. There then follows a statement that the declarant is registered in the property, sometimes in the fuller form "in which I reside and register" (ἐν ᾧ κατοικῶ καὶ ἀπογράφομαι). In cases where the property is not the domicile, a phrase like "in which no one registers" (ἐν ᾧ οὐδείς sc. ἀπογράφεται) is found, indicating that the declarant has filed another declaration for his place of domicile. A variant found in Arsinoite villages takes the form of "I register myself and my family in the house belonging to me in the village of X" (ἀπογράφομαι ἐμαυτὸν καὶ τοὺς ἐμοὺς ἐν τῇ οἰκίᾳ ὑπαρχούσῃ μοι ἐν κώμῃ NN). In most other nomes, the verb ἀπογράφομαι precedes information about ownership of the property.

The amount of detail given about the property varies considerably. In many cases no more than "house" or "part of a house" is referred to. In others, an extensive description appears, enumerating the house, courtyard, lightwell, accessory buildings and unbuilt lots, and so on. In no case, however, does the declarant give what we would consider an address, i.e., a description of the precise location of the property. Despite the official designation of the process as the "house-by-house registration" (κατ᾽ οἰκίαν ἀπογραφή), then, the contents of the declarations would not have provided the authorities with the information necessary to construct a survey-list of houses in any kind of topographical order. Such registers did exist; *P.Oslo* III 111 is a good example. It includes a list of persons living in the houses, but only males, gives no ages, and does not date from near the time of a census year—the declarations are from February 235, and the last census declarations would have been submitted in 231. It is not obvious just why many declarations are so explicit about listing small shares of property, particularly just for the sake of indicating that no one is registered in them, when the declarations would not have allowed the authorities to identify the properties in question.

The listing of persons
The heart of the declaration, both from the point of view of the Roman government and for our demographic purposes, is the listing of persons in the household headed by the declarant.[52] This is introduced in most cases by some brief phrase like καί εἰμι or εἰμὶ δέ, which varies by locality. There is also local variation in the extent and order of information given

[51] Cf. M. Hombert and C. Préaux, *Recherches* (1952) 108–113.
[52] A detailed analysis is given by M. Hombert and C. Préaux, *Recherches* (1952) 113–123.

about individuals and in the order in which they are listed. In reconstructing families in the numerous damaged or hard-to-read declarations, careful attention to the appropriate details is all-important. Hombert and Préaux remarked that metropolitan declarations tend to be fuller of detail than village ones. The fullest listings provide names, status, profession, age and physical description (scars or absence thereof). In most cases there is some indication of the relationship of each person to the declarant or to some other declared person. There may also be a mention of a previous declaration, or (in the case of a young child) the fact that someone has not been previously registered; absent persons may be specifically indicated.

Arsinoe: Metropolitan declarations from Arsinoe characteristically give information about status, which is normally absent from village declarations. The terms given mostly concern tax privileges, such as λαογραφούμενος (ἐπικεκριμένος), accompanied by an occupation or ἰδιώτης (indicating a private person, i.e., an adult, male citizen without a trade); κάτοικος (with various fuller phrases); and the quarter of registration. Slaves or freedmen, on the other hand, are indicated as such, with the name of the owner or patron and sometimes of the natural mother. Male children are normally described as having been declared at birth or as not having been so declared, whereas girls are not. A variety of occupations also appears in the Arsinoite declarations, particularly those in the textile industry, which (as Hombert and Préaux pointed out) were subject to special taxes.

Arsinoite villages: Most of the complicating elements of the metropolitan declarations are absent in the villages, where persons of special status were not registered (even though some of them certainly lived there). Even occupation is not given in most cases, with the single exception of priests, for whom it constituted an important status conferring in many cases a reduced rate of taxation. Public farmers are occasionally indicated as such.

Oxyrhynchite: The most interesting peculiarity of declarations from the Oxyrhynchite is the habit of listing all men first, then all women. Reconstruction of households has to take this characteristic into account. Oxyrhynchite declarations are much less full than metropolitan Arsinoite ones of information about the fiscal status of individuals, but they do use the term ἄτεχνος for many individuals where one would expect an occupation, very much in the same manner that ἰδιώτης is found at Arsinoe and ἀργός at Memphis, but like the latter not restricted to adult males. All no doubt refer to the same phenomenon, that of individuals not registered to any craft or trade, but presumably living from their landed revenues (or the proceeds of lending, perhaps).

Other nomes: As Hombert and Préaux observed, the numbers of declarations elsewhere are too small to allow much generalization. Metropolitan texts do tend, as at Arsinoe and Oxyrhynchos, to contain more information about privileged status, which is not surprising.

Apart from the Oxyrhynchite habit of putting males as a group before females as a group, it is difficult to establish general rules about the order in which names appear, which is one of the most critical elements of the listing from the point of view of reconstructing households. The listing is constructed from the viewpoint of the declarant, which means that his or her immediate family will generally be listed first in any complex household. An order of declarant-spouse-children-others is normal; children are usually given in descending order of age, but boys may be listed as a group before girls. Lodgers, freedmen, and slaves are at the end of the listing of the family. Where multiple couples with children form part of a single household for declaration purposes, these may be listed seriatim, i.e., with each nuclear family completed before the next is started. But other patterns are also possible.

Concluding elements[53]

Arsinoite declarations generally add after the list of persons, "thus I make my declaration," διὸ ἐπιδίδωμι. Except for a couple of early texts, they do not include an oath formula here, as the declarations from all other nomes except the Prosopite do routinely. The reasons for this local variation are unknown.[54] Where it is found, the oath may be by the emperor or his τύχη, as well as by local divinities. The oath asserts the truthfulness and completeness of the declaration, with varying degrees of fullness. It aims above all to certify that no one has been omitted, the point of principal interest to the authorities.

Complete, submitted declarations included both a signature of the declarant and a date, although many surviving declarations lack one or both elements, either by virtue of damage to the papyrus or because what we have is a copy. Signatures, in which the operative verb is usually ἐπιδίδωμι (mostly in the perfect), are almost always in a different hand from that of the body of the text; exceptions are attributable to the text's being a subsequent copy of the submitted declaration. The signature need not be that of the declarant, of course; in most cases it is that of someone writing for the declarant. Hombert and Préaux reckoned that of the sufficiently complete cases they listed, 15 of 47 were by the declarant, or 32 percent, with the rest by someone else because of illiteracy on the part of the declarant.[55]

---

[53] See generally M. Hombert and C. Préaux, *Recherches* (1952) 123–129.

[54] Cf. M. Hombert and C. Préaux, *Recherches* (1952) 124–125 for discussion, rightly rejecting Seidl's attempts to assign some legal or bureaucratic significance to the divergence.

[55] M. Hombert and C. Préaux, *Recherches* (1952) 128–129. Subsequently published declarations are in general less well preserved, so they have added only about ten to the total of signatures; the proportions remain about the same, a third signing for themselves.

The subscriptions are of importance for our purposes principally because
they preserve the declarant's names in a number of cases where upper parts
of the text are lost.

Official subscriptions[56]
The outlines of official handling of submitted declarations have already
been traced above. Those copies with official subscriptions form a minority
of the whole; whether they were for the benefit of the declarant or of the
bureaucracy, they are in broad outline consistent in content though variable
in wording. The commonest phrases involve a form of καταχωρίζω, most
normally κατεχωρίσθη, followed by an office in the dative, and its equivalent ἔσχον τὸ ἴσον. In both cases, the effect is an acknowledgment that a
particular office has had an exemplar of a declaration filed with it. It is
common, but not universal, for more than one of these to be found on a
single text, i.e., for more than one office to acknowledge receipt. Other
variants include ἀπεγράφη, verbs of signature like σεσημείωμαι, and
variants of number in the ἔσχον phrase.

4. Government uses of the returns

Neither any imperial order, nor prefectural edict, nor internal correspondence of the Roman government assists us in understanding why the
census was ordered or what use it was put to by the authorities. Barring an
unexpected find, we will never know by direct statement just why it was
carried out in the manner it was. But a number of surviving documents
show what uses the census data had both for the government and for private
individuals, and it may be legitimate to infer that the governmental uses
represent the underlying purposes. Our understanding of the register-
making and taxation practices of Roman Egypt is of course very incomplete, given that these practices stretch across several centuries and the
entire span of Egypt, while the surviving papyri are unevenly distributed in
time and heavily concentrated in a few nomes. The habits visible in the
Philadelphia tax archive of the first century, for example, may not have
been the same as those in the third-century Hermopolite, let alone in nomes
for which there is no surviving evidence.

---

[56]M. Hombert and C. Préaux, *Recherches* (1952) 129–135, survey the whole question of
official handling of the declarations. Among the more recently published texts with useful
indications of such handling are 117-Ar-8, 117-Ox-1, 159-Ar-24, 187-Ar-3, 187-Ar-37,
and 201-Ar-4.

Taxation and tax lists

Much of the evidence surviving for the use of the census data concerns the importance of this information as the base for tax lists and taxation itself, and modern scholars have generally seen this purpose as the central focus of the entire census. Whether the Romans actually made such distinctions among their purposes remains obscure, but there can be no doubt that the full collection of taxes on persons was very important. It should be remembered, however, that if this had been the *only* purpose of the census, it would not have needed to include females or men past the age at which the capitation taxes ceased to be due (sixty-two). The comprehensiveness of the declarations can be explained only by broader purposes. On the other hand, the 14-year cycle coincides so exactly with the age at which boys became liable to poll tax that it is difficult to suppose that the two are not connected.

Listmaking began with lists as comprehensive as the declarations themselves, omitting the repetitious formulaic elements and extracting only the list of persons with data about them.[57] These included both sexes and all ages and statuses. Such lists were in general kept up to date with information from declarations of birth and death, as can be seen for example in *P.Oxy.* VI 984. It is certain that they were composed anew with each census, but checked against existing lists and recent declarations of additions and subtractions. Those on previous lists who had failed to register this time and who were not known to have died were added. These lists will at least have saved the authorities the trouble of referring frequently to the *tomoi*, which were cumbersome to use, and will thus have served as a handy reference tool.

Their composition was contracted for by the government with appropriate scribal personnel. An example of such a contract has survived as *P.Mich.* XI 603, where nine scribes agree with the secretaries of the metropolis both for these lists and for derivatives: "apart from the house-by-house registration [conducted during 132/3 for the census of 131/2], to draw up single copies of the population lists arranged person-by-person, lists of *katoikoi*, and lists of minors and of those excluded from the tax estimate . . .[and] single copies of population lists in summary." All of these are to be drawn up current for the year 133/4, i.e., for the year after that in which declarations were submitted, just as had been the case under Augustus.

Tax lists for everyday use, like *P.Lond.* II 257–259, needed only to record males subject to taxation, i.e., between the ages of 14 and 62. The giving of ages allowed the authorities to remove the small minority who passed the end of tax liability by surviving to old age. It was also essential

---

[57]On the various lists derived from the declarations, see M. Hombert and C. Préaux, *Recherches* (1952) 135–147.

(as the scribes' contract shows) to maintain lists of those under 14 who would become liable when they reached that age, so that each year the year's cohort of 14-year-olds could be added to the main list of taxpayers. These lists accounted carefully for every taxpayer, to the point sometimes of giving *tomos* and sheet number references for their declarations in previous censuses. From these lists could be computed the numbers liable in each tax category and thus the amount to be collected.

Given the role of age in both the beginning of liability and its termination, the correct recording of the age will have been much more important in tax lists than elsewhere. Obviously there was some incentive to underreport the age of boys younger than 14, in order to delay the onset of taxation. But this will have been of limited use, because anyone reported in the census at all will of necessity be at least 14 by the time of the *next* census, no matter what age was reported. The maintenance of lists against which declarations were checked meant that inconsistent reporting of age on a subsequent declaration was likely to be caught. More profitable, but also more risky, would be omission of boys altogether. That might succeed if the boy was not at home, but (for example) working in Alexandria or some other sizable city where he might go unnoticed.

For demographic purposes, however, the crucial facts are that the authorities had records by which they could and did check census reports for consistency with birth declarations and previous census declarations, ensuring that statements of age did not rest simply either on the memory of the declarant or on the judgment of the census-taker. In the case of our declarations, however, as opposed to the official records derived from them, it should be remembered that the effect of these official capabilities is to be seen only in whatever accuracy may have been induced by the fear of their application, as there is no reason to believe that any of the *surviving* declarations have actually been checked by officials.

Control of the population

The gathered declarations, glued together in *tomoi*, remained on file in government archives. They were a basic source of authoritative information concerning the identity, parentage, status, and age of individuals, and they were thus sometimes copied for private purposes, whether in short extracts or in full copies.[58] This information might be required to help establish eligibility for *epikrisis* as a member of a privileged class, or to show entitlement to inherit. Beyond the surviving copies of declarations or parts of them, there are many references to the information they contained. We should not suppose that the declarations thus copied were always decisive, however. A rescript of Gordian III from AD 239 stated firmly what was no

---

[58]See M. Hombert and C. Préaux, *Recherches* (1952) 144–47.

doubt not a new idea, that "failure to register children does not render them illegitimate if they are in fact legitimate, nor do entries in the registers, if they were indeed made, introduce outsiders into the family."[59] The same was no doubt true of matters other than legitimacy. A dramatic example concerning legitimacy is provided by the pair of Prosopite declarations (131-Pr-1 and 145-Pr-1), discussed by Herbert Youtie in his classic article on illegitimacy, in which a woman is declared as the daughter of a man and his wife. These texts were copied out onto a single papyrus years later (March, 161) and followed by a statement by the woman's brother that she was his sister only by their mother, not by their father.[60] No doubt the matter had for some reason (perhaps inheritance) come to have importance. The brother asserts that he has documents to prove his statement.

The government did, however, consider the accuracy of the information in the declarations to be of vital importance, and the *Gnomon of the Idios Logos* has a number of provisions punishing severely any omissions or falsehoods.[61] It is not difficult to see why, given the vigor with which the Roman administration sought to maintain a rigidly fixed social structure, in which Romans, citizens of Greek cities, metropolitans, and other Egyptians (not to mention freedmen and slaves) were kept clearly distinct and barred by a complex set of rules from many forms of interaction. Accurate records were the basis of this type of social control, and accurate records were formed in the first instance by accurate census declarations, supplemented by birth and death registrations.[62] Obviously for this purpose some types of information were more important than others—filiation and status more than age or scars, particularly. But the overall result of official concern with status will have been insistence on making the census as complete and accurate as possible.

It is entirely possible that both taxation and control of the population were among the government's motives from the beginning of the periodic census. Both the poll tax and the rigid status system characteristic of the principate in Egypt were introduced early in Augustus' reign, presumably on the basis of existing records brought up to date through some process.[63]

---

[59] *P. Tebt.* II 285.

[60] See H. C. Youtie, "ΑΠΑΤΟΡΕΣ" (1975) 723–725.

[61] See M. Hombert and C. Préaux, *Recherches* (1952) 97–99.

[62] Bowman and Rathbone, "Cities and Administration" (1992) 113 take a more limited view: "It should be noted that the function of the Roman provincial census in Egypt was to register liability to taxation on the person and to liturgic service. It was quite distinct from the land survey and, although status was recorded, control and registration of status were effected through separate procedures and reviews." This claims more than we know about intentions and is only partly correct; the census declarations were demonstrably the principal source of evidence for most claims about status and relationships. Liturgies *per se* became a factor only later when compulsory service became more widespread, but corvée labor certainly was important from the start.

[63] See Rathbone, "Egypt, Augustus and Roman Taxation" (1993) 86–90.

It is reasonable to suppose that in both cases the government soon found the existing records inadequate, and that in both cases the periodic census made it possible to maintain the new policies more effectively. It is also possible that the symbolic value of the poll tax, representing subjection to Roman power, extended to the census itself—that the census itself was a means of demonstrating Roman control of the world.[64]

[64]A point both D. Rathbone, "Egypt, Augustus and Roman Taxation" (1993) and C. Nicolet, *Space* (1991) make, though the latter has a confused notion of what the Egyptian census entails (p. 135, "Deeds to the building had to be provided, specifying its location . . .").

2

The census returns as demographic evidence

1. The scientific study of human populations

Demography is commonly defined as "the scientific study of human populations, primarily with respect to their size, their structure and their development."[1] This definition brings out three essential aspects of the discipline. First, its primary concern is with aggregate populations, large groups of people historically bounded by geography and time; a "population" is the basic unit of study.[2] Second, the mode of study is "scientific" in that demographers seek to understand a population objectively, above all through statistics that describe it. Third, a demographic description of a population focuses especially on the numerical size of a population, its composition, and its change over time. What demographers isolate are objective explanations for gross population trends.

There are two main demographic approaches. First, we may look at a given population, like that of the Roman Egypt in the first to third centuries AD, as an entirety, and ask, for instance, how many persons this population had, whether it was growing, how it was geographically distributed, and so on.[3] Second, we may instead study the more basic demographic functions that bring about population change: mortality, the rate at which persons leave the population by dying; fertility, the rate at

---

[1] E. van de Walle, *Multilingual Demographic Dictionary, English Section* (1982) 101. For good general introductions to demography, see G. W. Barclay, *Techniques of Population Analysis* (1958); P. R. Cox, *Demography* (1976); D. Yaukey, *Demography* (1985); and esp. C. Newell, *Methods* (1988). For those with some knowledge of calculus, N. Keyfitz, *Introduction to the Mathematics of Population* (1968) and *Demography* (1985), are highly recommended. T. G. Parkin, *Demography* (1992), is an introduction to demography written specifically for Roman historians. W. Suder, *Census Populi: Bibliographie de la démographie de l'antiquité romaine* (1988), is useful but not exhaustive.

[2] C. Newell, *Methods* (1988) 9–10.

[3] See Chapter 3, Section 1, on Roman Egypt's population.

31

which persons enter the population through birth; and migration, the rate at which persons enter or leave the population by physically relocating.

The second approach is more interesting because it incidentally raises issues of great social importance. These issues include the level of overall welfare in a given society, its structures of family life, the emphasis it places on bearing and rearing children, its treatment of women and the elderly, and so on. But a purely demographic study casts limited light on such issues. For example, a demographer can use statistics to determine the probability that a woman aged 25 has already married and borne children, or that her children will die before reaching age 5. But if, as is true for Roman Egypt, these probabilities are high, we are still far from understanding the woman's experience; we need also to know, especially, how early marriage and childbirth, or infant mortality, are viewed and evaluated from a social and cultural standpoint. Further, these more subjective phenomena are part of the larger culture of a society, and they play a very heavy role in causing or even determining objective phenomena such as the likelihood of early marriage and childbirth.[4]

It may seem tempting to move immediately from statistics to the larger social dimensions of demography. However, as we shall see, demographic "facts" can be difficult to establish and slippery to interpret, and overhasty explanations of them are all too often founded on air. For purposes of this book we therefore deliberately restrict our vision, leaving to other scholars, or to other occasions, the larger task of integrating demography within a comprehensive historical account.

Model life tables
Modern approaches to demography make extensive use of statistical models and modelling, particularly for populations, such as that of Roman Egypt, where surviving information is fragmentary and not fully reliable.[5] One set of models we often use in succeeding chapters are the Coale-Demeny model life tables, developed by Ansley Coale and Paul Demeny to assist in the study of historical and modern populations.[6]

---

[4] See J. T. Noonan, "Intellectual and Demographic History," *Daedalus* 117.3 (1988) 119–141. Demographers often distinguish between demography as statistical analysis, and "population studies" as broader research into the relationship between demographic reality and its social, economic, and cultural context. See, e.g., W. Petersen, "Thoughts on Writing a Dictionary of Demography," *Population and Development Review* 9 (1983) 677–687; compare R. A. LeVine and S. C. M. Scrimshaw, "Effects of Culture on Fertility: Anthropological Contributions," in *Determinants* II (1983) 666–695.

[5] On the nature and purpose of demographic models: C. Newell, *Methods* (1988) 117–119; also J. A. Menken, "Current Status of Demographic Models," *Population Bulletin of the United Nations* 9 (1978) 22–34; United Nations, *Manual X* (1983) 11–26.

[6] A. J. Coale and P. Demeny, *Life Tables* (1983). For a non-specialized introduction to life tables: C. Newell, *Methods* (1988) 62–81, 130–166; also T. G. Parkin, *Demography* (1992) 72–84. Problems with model life tables for high mortality populations are discussed below and in Chapter 5, Section 4 (at notes 43–44).

A life table describes the mortality conditions in an actual population at a given time; it offers a kind of snapshot of that population from a very particular perspective. Model life tables, by contrast, depict the mortality conditions in *typical* populations at various levels of mortality. Because female and male mortality differ significantly in most populations, separate life tables are always provided for each sex. The Coale-Demeny models are arrayed by female life expectancy at birth, with the lowest life table for females with a life expectancy at birth of 20.0 years (Level 1) and successive tables at 2.5-year intervals up to a life expectancy of 80.0 years (Level 25). Each female life table is accompanied by a male life table giving the levels of male mortality that are commonly, but not invariably, associated with various levels of female mortality.[7]

The Coale-Demeny model life tables rely upon a large number of accurate life tables from many historical populations, though the bulk of the evidence comes from Europe.[8] The authors acknowledge, however, that one set of model life tables did not entirely suit even all European populations. Accordingly, they offer four "geographic" sets (West, North, East, and South). Of these, Model West is the most generalized and has by far the broadest statistical foundation; further, Model West also produces the most reliable results for populations with very high levels of mortality.[9] Since Roman Egypt was undoubtedly such a population, we use Model West exclusively in this study. Model West also produces a much closer "fit" for the Egyptian data than other Coale-Demeny models.[10]

---

[7] C. Newell, *Methods* (1988) 138. The Coale-Demeny models may not adequately express the changing historical relation between male and female mortality as overall mortality declines; see D. Yaukey, *Demography* (1985) 86-87, 130-135. This is a major issue in Chapter 5 below.

[8] However, all the empirical life tables had life expectancies at birth higher than 35 years, see A. J. Coale and P. Demeny, *Life Tables* (1983) 24-25. Models for lower life expectancies use extrapolation, a source of possible error that the authors acknowledge (pp. 24–25). The problem is that populations with very high mortality have rarely if ever produced accurate life tables. See in general T. H. Hollingsworth, *Demography* (1969) 341-344; also below, note 10.

[9] A. J. Coale and P. Demeny, *Life Tables* (1983) 25 ("We would suggest utilizing the 'West' family in the usual circumstances of underdeveloped countries"), 33 ("There is some reason for believing that the 'West' stable is the most likely choice at . . . a high level of mortality"). United Nations, *Manual X* (1983) 16 ("If little is known about the population under study, the West model is recommended, simply on the grounds of generality"); also pp. 15–16 on criteria for choosing other models.

[10] Experiments with Model South were not successful; Model South (despite its name) is used mainly for populations in which infants are known to suffer unusually high levels of malnutrition or gastroenteritis. The other well-known set of model life tables, from the United Nations, do not include life expectancies at birth below 35 years: United Nations, "Model Life Tables for Developing Countries," *Population Studies* 77 (1982). The Egyptian data are insufficiently robust for more complex "relational" models; see C. Newell, *Methods* (1988) 151-165. "Relational" models are preferable for high-mortality populations (like Roman Egypt) because they provide for a wider range of mathematical relationships between juvenile and adult mortality.

Table 2.1. *A life table for Model West, Level 2, females*

Age	Probability of death: $q(x)$	Cohort decline: $l(x)$	Expectation of life: $e(x)$
0	0.33399	100,000	22.500
1	0.23760	66,601	32.608
5	0.06657	50,776	38.346
10	0.05205	47,396	35.920
15	0.06744	44,930	32.750
20	0.08385	41,899	29.930
25	0.09369	38,386	27.431
30	0.10558	34,790	24.998
35	0.11511	31,117	22.642
40	0.12227	27,535	20.249
45	0.12967	24,168	17.708
50	0.16518	21,034	14.959
55	0.20571	17,560	12.404
60	0.29144	13,947	9.943
65	0.37188	9,833	7.964
70	0.49858	6,214	6.130
75	0.63720	3,116	4.640
80	0.75601	1,130	3.398
85	0.87919	276	2.429
90	0.95785	33	1.709
95	1.00000	1	1.187

This important issue merits a digression. Some demographers now believe that for populations with extremely high mortality, the applicable Coale-Demeny models may *both* overstate typical infant mortality in relation to adult mortality *and* inadequately reflect the normal variation in infant mortality; for a good discussion, see P. N. Mari Bhat, in *India* (1989) 73–118, with T. Dyson's critical comments on p. 3. Whether these demographers are correct is, at present, uncertain; see J. D. Willigan and K. A. Lynch, *Sources* (1982) 46–48. In any case, for several internal reasons, the Egyptian census returns do not yield reliable infant mortality rates, and so are unhelpful on this subject. Therefore we adopt the Coale-Demeny infant mortality rates as printed. But readers should be warned that infant mortality is important in estimating both life expectancy at birth and general mortality and fertility rates; our discussion in Chapters 4 to 7 *may* therefore be somewhat inaccurate for this reason (though whether our infant mortality estimates are too high or too low is not determinable), see the following section. A good example of the practical difficulties this problem creates for historical demography is early modern France: A. Bideau, J. Dupâquier, and H. Gutierrez, in *Population française* II (1988) 222–238. On causes of variation in pre-modern infant mortality, see M. Livi Bacci, *Population* (1991) 72–78.

Our Table 2.1 is a brief version of Coale-Demeny Model West, Level 2, in which females have a life expectancy at birth of 22.5 years;[11] we selected this life table for discussion because, as will emerge in Chapter 4, it approximates the female mortality levels probably prevailing in Egypt during the early Roman Empire. The life table gives three columns of statistically interlinked figures for exact ages 0, 1, 5, and thereafter at five-year intervals until age 95.

The leftmost column of figures is *q(x)*, probability of death, representing the likelihood that persons aged exactly *x* will die before the next indicated birthday.[12] Thus, for instance, in this model newborn females have about one chance in three of dying before their first birthday, girls aged 1 have just under one chance in four of dying before their fifth birthday, and so on. As in all historical populations, mortality declines sharply after infancy, only to rise again exponentially during adulthood. The "bounding curve of mortality," a standard element of all life tables, is illustrated in Figure 2.1 (p. 36), which shows *q(x)* for model female life expectancies at birth of 22.5 and 50.0 years. The two curves display the normal mathematical relationship between various levels of mortality, a relationship that makes it possible to calculate model life tables. Rates for probability of death converge in old age, as natural human life span is reached.[13]

The second column of figures, *l(x)*, shows the impact that such mortality has on a representative "cohort" of 100,000 females born simultaneously. In Model West, Level 2, about a third of newborn females die before their first birthday, nearly half by age 5, more than nine-tenths by 65, almost 99 percent by 80.

The third column of figures is *e(x)*, average life expectancy at age *x*, the mean number of years that females aged exactly *x* will live, under these mortality conditions, during the remainder of their lives.[14] In this model, life expectancy at birth is 22.5 years; but for females who survive infancy, average life expectancy rises to 38.3 years at age 5 and 35.9 years at age 10,[15] only to fall back gradually through the remainder of life.

[11] A. J. Coale and P. Demeny, *Life Tables* (1983) 42.

[12] Probabilities are always a decimal value between 0.0 (no probability) and 1.0 (certainty). Probability of death is distinct from the central mortality rate, which is *m(x)*. On the mathematical relation of mortality functions to one another: N. Keyfitz and W. Flieger, *Population: Facts and Methods of Demography* (1971) 127–143; C. L. Chiang, *The Life Table and Mortality Analysis* (1978), and *The Life Table and Its Applications* (1984). For a brief discussion of statistics, see our Appendix on "Statistical Methods."

[13] H. S. Shryock and J. S. Siegel, *Methods* (1980) 433: "Life span appears to be about 100 and may not have changed in historical times"; also T. G. Parkin, *Demography* (1992) 106. (But this subject is controversial.)

[14] Average life expectancy is measured from exact age *x*. Distinct is *median* life expectancy, the number of years until half the persons aged *x* are dead; this figure is not important for demography. On calculating average life expectancy, see Chapter 4, Section 1.

[15] Life expectancy at birth is heavily influenced by infant mortality; especially for high-mortality populations, demographers often use life expectancy at age 5 or 10 as a more reliable

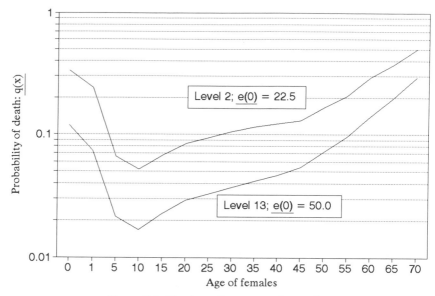

Figure 2.1. *The bounding curve of mortality:*
Model West, females

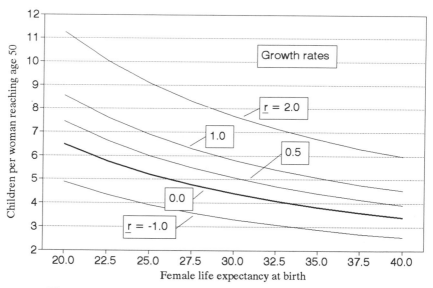

Figure 2.2. *Intrinsic growth rates related to mortality and fertility*

---

overall indicator of general mortality levels. A. J. Coale and P. Demeny, *Life Tables*
(1983) 21. This is the strategy we pursue in Chapters 4 and 5.

Mortality and fertility

Before the demographic transition of the past three centuries, human populations experienced a normal life expectancy at birth of between 20 and 40 years, with most probably falling in the lower half of this range.[16] From a modern viewpoint, such populations resemble each other because all have comparatively high mortality rates. But their apparent similarity is misleading, and so particularly for their fertility rates. Since this issue is pivotal for the demography of Roman Egypt, we introduce it here.

Figure 2.2 (p. 36) shows the relations between two variables:[17] female life expectancy at birth in the Model West life tables from Level 1 ($e(0)$ = 20.0) to Level 9 ($e(0)$ = 40.0), and the number of children borne by a woman who survives from age 15 to 50 and who bears children at an average yearly rate for women her age.[18] At issue is the number of children such a woman bears at various rates of intrinsic annual population growth r, ranging from -1.0 percent per year (rapid population decline) to +2.0 (very swift growth).

As Figure 2.2 shows, populations with very high mortality, if they are to survive, need considerably higher fertility rates than those with lower (but still quite high) mortality. At the extremes of Figure 2.2, simple replacement of the population (r = 0.0) requires about 6.5 children at Level 1, but only 3.4 at Level 9; and a population at Level 9 can grow very swiftly while experiencing a fertility rate lower than that required for simple replacement at Level 1. Therefore, in principle, a population at Level 9 can tolerate considerably more individual freedom in fertility than can a population at Level 1. As E. A. Wrigley observes,[19] "At, say, level 1 Model West a population could hardly allow private choice since it must mobilize maximum fertility if it is to survive at all."

---

[16]E.g., K. H. Weiss, *Models* (1973) 49; M. Livi-Bacci, *History* (1992) 21, with 100–131 describing the transition. (The range often cited by Roman historians, 20 to 30 years, is much too narrow; numerous counterexamples are known.) On early modern Europe: J. Vallin, "La mortalité en Europe de 1720 à 1914: tendances à long terme et changements de structure par sexe et par âge," *Annales de Démographie Historique* (1989) 31–54. On Germany: A. E. Imhof, *Lebenserwartungen in Deutschland von 17. bis 19. Jahrhundert* (1990). In question here is what *a priori* assumptions we should have about ancient life expectancy.

[17]Figure 2.1 is adapted from A. J. Coale, in *Decline of Fertility* (1986) 3; see also M. Livi-Bacci, *Population* (1991) 9, and *History* (1992) 21–24.

[18]This statistic (the Total Fertility Rate) is discussed further in Chapter 7 (at notes 9 to 16); it is estimated as 2.05 times the Gross Reproduction Rate (for daughters only). Figures for the GRR are taken from A. J. Coale and P. Demeny, *Life Tables* (1983) 55–63, who suppose a mean age of mother at childbirth of 29; this figure is too high for most pre-modern societies, but the effect on GRR is modest for present purposes.

[19]E. A. Wrigley, *People* (1987) 209. However, this observation must be qualified; see Chapter 7, Sections 1 and 2 below.

Before the modern demographic transition, most human populations had long-term intrinsic growth rates that lay between 0.0 and 0.5 percent per year. That is, *irrespective of their relative mortality levels*, the birth and death rates of these populations were usually closely balanced, and population therefore grew slowly. In Europe between 1200 and 1700, for example, the average annual rate of growth is thought to have been barely 0.13, though with sizable fluctuation both by date and region.[20]

In the chapters that follow, and particularly in Chapters 4 and 5, we analyze the age structure of Roman Egypt as it emerges from the census returns. Age structure is the distribution of a population by age. If migration is ignored, age structure is determined by mortality and fertility rates over time. Although at any single moment in time short-term variations in mortality and fertility may strongly influence age distribution,[21] they have much less effect when data are spread over an extended period of time, as is the case with the Egyptian census returns. The data then reveal longer-term "normal" patterns of mortality, fertility, and population growth. Such longer-term patterns are the subject of our book.

2. Data bases

For this study, we created two computer data bases.[22] The first, called PERSONS, contains twenty-nine pieces of information for each person listed in the Catalogue as the resident of a household.[23] Included are the following:

---

[20]M. Livi-Bacci, *Population* (1991) 1–22, esp. 3 (also noting that "Europe was able, in the absence of serious crisis, to maintain an annual rate of increase of 3 per thousand," or 0.3); and *History* (1992) 22, 101 (also 1–8 on the demographic theory of pre-transitional population growth). F. Hassan, *Demographic Archaeology* (1981) 234–235, reconstructs similar long-term rates (0.04 to 0.13 percent per year) for most ancient states, but notes spurts of up to 1 percent growth especially during the emergence of regional states; see also J. N. Biraben, "Essai sur l'évolution du nombre des hommes," *Population* 34 (1979) 13–24. Low population growth is undoubtedly linked to low economic growth; but how traditional populations achieved and maintained such "homeostasis" remains among the most controversial topics in demography.

[21]This is a recurrent theme in R. Sallares, *The Ecology of the Ancient Greek World* (1991), e.g., 89–90, 120–121; but Sallares exaggerates its significance, see G. W. Barclay *et al.*, "Reassessment" (1976) 621–624.

[22]Principal software: *dBase III Plus* (copyright 1985, 1986, 1987 Ashton-Tate) for data bases; *Quattro Pro 4.0* (copyright 1991, 1992 Borland) for graphs and spreadsheet analysis; *Minitab Release 8* (copyright 1991 Minitab) for statistical analysis.

[23]We occasionally include persons declared as non-resident, especially if their age is given. Thus the three fugitive slaves in 187-Ar-30 are catalogued, as are the married daughter and her slave in 201-Ox-1, and the man in tax flight (*anachoresis*) in 173-Ar-9; but the three non-resident daughters in 145-He-2, and the two daughters in 201-Ar-6, are not, since their ages are not given. However, permanently absent persons are not used in determining household structure.

(1) the papyrus number in the Catalogue (e.g., 11-Ar-1), plus a description of the apparent completeness of the household it describes (complete, virtually complete, or incomplete);

(2) if known, the name of the person, a person number identifying him or her within the household, the person's legal status (free, freed, or slave), the person's age[24] or approximate age, sex, and occupation or other description;

(3) if known, the current ages of the person's mother and father, as well as their ages when the person was born;

(4) whether the person is married or formerly married, and if so, whether the spouse is close-kin, plus the spouse's age, the difference in their ages, and the number and age of known offspring from this or prior marriages;

(5) a brief formal description of the household in which the person lives, the number of persons in the family, and whether the family owns or rents the dwelling or is lodging in another's household (slaves are included in the household of their owner);

(6) the location of the household, and whether it is metropolitan or village;[25] and

(7) any comments on unusual aspects of the entry.

When this data base was closed in September, 1993, it contained 1,084 personal entries. Although the computer file is bulky (just over 210,000 bytes), it has proved sufficiently flexible; information, especially statistical information, is easily retrieved.

The second data base, called OWNERS, contains one entry for every census return in our Catalogue, including those for which no information on residents survives. The following data are given:

(1) the papyrus number in the Catalogue, whether it contains useful information on residents, whether the household is complete, the date on which the return was filed, and a cross-reference to standard editions of the papyrus;

(2) the owner (or owners) of the house, his or her age, sex, and legal status, and a description if any survives;

---

[24] Age, crucial throughout our discussion, is entered as it appears in the census return, even if scribal error has probably occurred (as with Family Member 1 in 145-Pr-1: 52 for 59). In a few cases we use an exact age reconstructed from internal evidence or other sources (e.g., Family Member 2 in 103-Ar-7); 187-Hm-1 is the most heavily restored return (see the Discussion). Approximate ages, and ages in which only one digit remains (e.g., Family Member 3 in 173-Me-3: 4[.]), are not used in statistical calculations based on age.

[25] Twenty-four census returns cannot be certainly assigned to a location; all are treated as village returns, as most seem to be. The twelve unassignable returns with information on residents are: 117-Ar-11; 131-Pr-1; 145-Ar-22; 145-Pr-1; 159-Ar-19; 173-Ar-11; 187-Ar-23 and 36; 187-Ox-4; 201-Ar-12; 215-Ar-7; ???-Ar-2.

(3) if different from the owner, the declarant and his or her relationship to the owner;

(4) the location of the dwelling, whether it is occupied by the owner or by renters, whether it is metropolitan or village, a brief description of the form of the principal family, and the number of principal family members, lodgers, slaves, and total persons attested in the household (these numbers may be incomplete, depending on the state of the papyrus); and

(5) any comment on unusual aspects of the household.

When this data base was closed, it contained 300 entries, of which 233, or 78 percent, had useful information of even the most minimal kind on one or more persons resident in the household. The remaining returns either were too fragmentary to yield any data on household residents, or declared habitable property with no current residents.

Throughout both data bases, when the Catalogue expresses uncertainty about a piece of information but provides a "best reconstruction," we adopt this reconstruction for purposes of the data base, but note the uncertainty in the comment or elsewhere in the entry.

3. Demographic quality of the census returns

Census returns, and statistics derived from them, are among the most frequently used of all demographic sources. Demographers have developed sophisticated methods both for assessing the quality of census returns as documents of a population, and for analyzing the statistics that returns provide.[26] These methods are particularly important for our study because the Egyptian census returns are both very sparse in number (by modern demographic standards) and scrappily preserved. What we need to know is whether and to what degree these returns should be trusted as demographic registers. Problems of quality concern both the completeness and the accuracy of census records.

Completeness

Egyptian census returns are adventitiously preserved. We have only a tiny sampling of all returns, and this sample is neither wholly random nor representative of the entire Egyptian population in the early Empire.[27] First, it is geographically restricted; about three-quarters of the returns are from the Arsinoite and Oxyrhynchite nomes, with other nomes represented

---

[26]See esp. H. S. Shryock and J. S. Siegel, *Methods* (1980), the standard work. "The measurement of births, deaths, migrants and population size is a very imprecise and error-prone process, even in highly developed societies." C. Newell, *Methods* (1988) 8.

[27]In this respect K. Hopkins, "Brother-Sister" (1980) 314–315, was unduly sanguine.

sporadically except for spectacular chance discoveries like the set of returns from Tanyaithis (117-Ap-1 to 9) and that from Theresis and Thelbonthon Siphtha (173-Pr-1 to 18). There are no returns at all from the great city of Alexandria; on the other hand, the single metropolis of Arsinoe contributes nearly a third of our data. Second, surviving returns cover a series of censuses from the early first century AD (11-Ar-1) to the mid-third century (257-Ar-1); but they are chronologically concentrated in, especially, the second and early third centuries. The data base that surviving returns provide is so exiguous that its statistical reliability decreases substantially when only portions of it are examined. For this reason it is almost never possible to quantify chronological changes in basic demographic functions.

Beyond these large obstacles, there is virtually no way to discover how thorough Egyptian administrators were in collecting returns. Certainly they regarded themselves as thorough, as is shown by the lengthy lists of tax-paying males they prepared on the basis of the census returns.[28] An impression of exactitude is also created by their practice in small villages, which were normally registered in one sweep within a few days.[29] Nonetheless, modern experience in less developed countries suggests the probability of substantial omissions;[30] we return to this question below.

As to the individual returns, there is no *a priori* reason to believe that declarants were less than normally diligent in reporting residents of their households. Still, the amount of information required of them was large, and omissions or mistakes probably did occur, just as in modern censuses.[31] A likely case of an omitted person is from a family from Hermopolis that is registered in returns from three censuses.[32] In 187-Hm-1, a declarant aged [47] reports his wife aged [51]; his sons Hermeinos aged [21], Isidoros aged 13, and Theognostos aged [8]; and his daughter Isidora aged 0. Twenty-eight years later, in 215-Hm-1/2, the apparent survivors are Hermeinos now aged 49, Theognostos aged 36, and Dioskorous aged 30, described as the full sister and wife of Theognostos. In 229-Hm-2, Theognostos aged [50] is still living with Dioskorous aged 44. Dioskorous therefore ought to have been two years old in the census of 187/188; her name was apparently omitted.[33]

[28] These lists are discussed in Chapter 1, Section 4, and Chapter 5 (at notes 32–34).
[29] See Chapter 1, Section 2.
[30] For example, the Egyptian census of 1882 (the first modern census) appears to have undercounted the Egyptian population by about 10 percent, and there are evident undercounts also for 1897 and 1917: A. R. Omran, *Egypt* (1973) 9–15.
[31] On census returns as sources for demography, see J. D. Willigan and K. A. Lynch, *Sources* (1982) 79–104; also H. S. Shryock and J. S. Siegel, *Methods* (1980) 102–111.
[32] The ages in the three returns are heavily restored; we indicate these restorations below. 187-Hm-1 is not yet published, and the restored ages are therefore provisional.
[33] There are two other possibilities: Dioskorous is identical with Isidora, who however was reported as two years younger than Dioskorous would have been; or Dioskorous was born after the census of 187–188, and her age is slightly exaggerated in the later returns. Either

As will emerge in Chapter 4, this case may not be isolated; for reasons that are obscure, metropolitan declarants may in fact have failed to report some girls, especially those less than 5 years old.[34] Much more serious is the evidence, discussed in Chapter 5, that declarants often either concealed young males from the census takers, or listed them with ages lower than their actual ones, in an effort to evade the poll tax levied on adult males aged 14 up to 62. Their failure may be the single most significant source of undercounting in surviving returns; and it is important to remember, in this connection, that the information in surviving returns had not yet been checked or corrected by government officials (see Chapter 1).

As a rule, however, the returns are internally consistent. Declarants provide so much information about their households that, whenever papyri are well preserved, family stemmata are now easily reconstructed.

Accuracy

It is usually impossible to check the accuracy of information, especially ages, reported in the census returns. Very occasionally, internal or external evidence suggests that information is correct or incorrect.[35] 131-Pr-1 and 147-Pr-1 are returns from the same family transcribed in a document of 161; they contain two evident errors on age that doubtless result from particularly sloppy copying.[36] More significantly, however, in both returns Thamistis is described as the full sister of Anikos, but in the cover letter she is alleged to be his half-sister on the mother's side and *apator* (illegitimate); here the original returns were probably erroneous.

A few very early or very late births give rise to suspicion of error in reporting ages. Leaving aside the mother at 9 years in 131-Pr-1, there is also a mother at 13 years in 201-Ar-12.[37] The next earliest births are to women aged 15 (seven cases). Even more suspicious is the father aged 26 with a son aged 13 in 187-Ar-4, implying that the father married by 12 and

---

[34] possibility also involves declarant error.
Table A suggests that metropolitan declarants were especially likely not to register girls aged 0–4.

[35] A good example of probable declarant error is 145-Ar-20, where the patronymic of Stotoetis age 55 was apparently muddled; see the Discussion. Similar is 173-Pr-3, see Discussion. The age of Sarapias in 187-Ar-32 accords with her age in *P.Fam.Tebt.* 48 from AD 202/203. On the other hand, Harthotes in 11-Ar-1 is 55 in 11/12, but 40 in A.D. 1 (*P.Oslo* II 32); one or both ages are rounded. Similar mistakes occur in lists derived from census returns; e.g., *P.Lond.* II 259.87–91 (mother's name), *P.Thmouis* I 159.1–160.22 (patronymics).

[36] In 131-Pr-1, a woman of 29 has a son of 20, which yields an impossible age at childbirth. 131-Pr-1 lists the age of Thenthnoupis as 45; but in 145-Pr-1 he is 52, not 59. Further, several ages are omitted in 131-Pr-1. See the Discussion on these returns.

[37] She is now 16, her child 3. But this text is also a later extract from a return; further, the parties' relationship is not certain. On age at marriage, Chapter 6, Section 1.

was 13 at his son's birth; the next youngest fathers are 17 (131-He-4) and 18 (117-Ar-2; 173-Pr-15). At the other end of the female fertility range is a woman who has just given birth at age 51 in 187-Hm-1; however, her age is restored and may well be slightly exaggerated.[38] In general, though, attested ages at childbirth appear to be credible; they lend themselves readily to demographic analysis, as we shall see in Chapter 7.

A check of a different sort is provided by several instances in which we have returns from the same family in successive censuses; here we can test for internal consistency in the ages. Generally the ages correspond. The outstanding example is the series 89-Ar-1, 103-Ar-8, and 117-Ar-4, where four persons have consistent ages (two of them across all three censuses).[39] But consistent also is the age of Aphrodous from 117-Ar-1 to 131-Ar-3; Tausiris and Pnephoros from 131-He-2 to 145-He-1; and, as noted above, Dioskorous from 215-Hm-2 to 229-Hm-1.

If (as we argue in Chapter 1) a family's prior census return frequently served as the basis for its subsequent returns, such correspondence is easily explained: declarants (or the census takers) simply added 14 to the age previously reported for household members. An error in math might then account for the one glaring discrepancy: Zosime is 22 in 159-Ar-1, but 38 in 173-Ar-3; but this discrepancy could also result from age misreporting in either census.[40]

The census returns offer a further clue that Egyptians were not always absolutely accurate in reporting ages. The returns provide at least twelve instances, perhaps as many as fifteen, of "twins": full siblings, or even half-siblings, reported as having the same age.[41] In human populations, twins are born in slightly more than one percent of all deliveries, so the Egyptian figure is more than suspect.[42] In four papyri (145-Ar-17; 145-Ox-1; 173-Ar-9; 187-Ar-4), declarants describe siblings as twins. Some

---

[38] This papyrus is still unpublished, and it is unclear how the woman's age was established. The next youngest births are at 49 (159-Hm-3 and 173-Pr-5), also probably exaggerated. Compare H. S. Shryock and J. S. Siegel, *Methods* (1980) 474: "Currently in the United States birth reports with ages below 13 are queried and those with ages 50 or over are rejected outright." On age exaggeration among the elderly, see also Chapter 5, Section 4.

[39] Consistent across all three censuses are Horos and Horion; across the first two, Peteuris; across the second two, Thenatymis.

[40] Another age discrepancy is explained as scribal error in note 36.

[41] These returns are 33-Ar-1; 117-Ar-2 (probably); 131-Ox-1 (different mothers); 145-Ar-17 and 19 (possibly); 145-Ox-1 (see Discussion); 159-Ar-5; 173-Ar-9 and 16; 187-Ar-4; 201-Ar-9 and 10 (*bis*); 215-Ar-4 (different mothers); 243-Ox-1 (probably). It is, of course, just possible that siblings are the same age without being twins; but such close spacing is very rare, see H. S. Shryock and J. S. Siegel, *Methods* (1980) 519–520.

[42] H. S. Shryock and J. S. Siegel, *Methods* (1980) 480; the number of twins in the census returns is at least triple the expected number. Ancient authors often suggest that multiple births were unusually common in Egypt: T. G. Parkin, *Demography* (1992) 113, esp. notes 99 and 101; such reports should be treated with suspicion.

other cases (most notably the half-siblings aged 20 in 131-Ox-1) probably result from coarse age rounding. But many reported twins were probably in fact just close in age to one another; declarants only approximated their ages.

Other problems are minor and predictable. Declarants were evidently often permitted to file returns up to a year after the nominal census year had ended, but they normally do not declare persons who had died in the meantime.[43] This failure is statistically significant for ages when mortality is very high, above all for newborns aged 0 up to 1. For males, the census returns report only five persons aged 0, but 18 aged 1, as against an average of nine for those aged 2 to 5; if newborns survived their first year, they were apparently often registered as 1.[44]

Objective tests

The census returns do provide occasional grounds for concern about their accuracy, but the problems are neither broad nor deep. If the ages of Egyptians are at times only estimates, can they nonetheless be considered at least approximately accurate? As scholars have often observed,[45] most surviving demographic data for the Greco-Roman world, such as the ages at death on tombstones or mummy labels, are heavily contaminated by age exaggeration (overstatement of age, particularly among the elderly) and age rounding (reporting of age in exact multiples of 5). Further, these phenomena are linked, since age rounding apparently makes it easier to skip ahead from age to age prematurely, a problem especially among the elderly. Both phenomena are also frequent in modern censuses as well, particularly in those of less developed countries.

By contrast, the Egyptian returns display little obvious age exaggeration; for example, only one man is declared as 80 (215-He-1: a lodger), and only four persons as aged 75–79, in conformance with the characteristics of a high mortality population like that in Table 2.1. As for age rounding, the standard modern test, Whipple's Index,[46] examines the number of persons

---

[43] Only three declarants do so: 145-He-1 (deceased son, 9); 201-Ox-3 (deceased grandfather and father); 215-He-3 (deceased daughter).

[44] This tendency recurs in modern Egyptian censuses: G. T. Acsádi, "Age" (1976) 22–50, at 25–26; this whole essay is helpful.

[45] E.g., K. Hopkins, "Graveyards" (1987); R. Duncan-Jones, *Structure* (1990) 79–92. On Egypt, see also B. Boyaval, "Remarques à propos des indications d'âges des étiquettes de momies," *ZPE* 18 (1975) 49–74, and "Remarques sur les indications d'âges de l'épigraphie funéraire grecque d'Egypte," *ZPE* 21 (1976) 217–243; R. P. Duncan-Jones, "Age-Rounding" (1979).

[46] H. S. Shryock and J. S. Siegel, *Methods* (1980) 205–206; C. Newell, *Methods* (1988) 24–25. "Only the ages 23 to 62 are used because outside of this range shifting and other problems often tend to confuse the normal pattern of heaping." Newell, p. 24. The United Nations describes Whipple's Index as "a simple, yet highly sensitive, index" that is "relatively free from consideration of factors not connected with the accuracy of age reporting." United Nations, *Demographic Yearbook* 40 (1988) 9.

reported as having ages in the forty-year range from 23 to 62. Whipple's Index is based upon the proportion of persons in this age range who have reported ages exactly divisible by 5; the Index ranges from 100 (no tendency to age heaping) to 500 (all ages exactly divisible by 5). Modern populations in less developed countries often have a very high index; for example, Whipple's Index for the Bangladesh census of 1974 is 316, meaning that 316 persons out of every 500 have ages divisible by 5.[47]

For the Egyptian census returns, Whipple's Index can be calculated from the figures in Table A. For the 322 persons who have reported ages from 23 to 62, the Index is 124.2. The standard United Nations scale for estimating the reliability of age data yields a "score" for Roman Egypt that is near the borderline between "approximate" (110–125) and "rough" (125–175). This score, among the lowest ever recorded for a pre-modern population, indicates that we should place some trust in reported ages.[48]

Myers' Blended Index, another standard objective test, also yields results favorable to Roman Egypt. Myers' Blended Index measures the propensity among the adult population to prefer or avoid last digits from 0 to 9; the index ranges from 0 (no propensity to heap on digits) to 90 (heaping on just one digit).[49] For 519 reported ages from 10 to 69 in the returns, the overall index is 9.2, which is low in comparison with most pre-modern populations—and also lower, for instance, than the United States in 1880 and the Philippines in 1960. Beyond the digits 0 and 5, Egyptians display some preference for 9, and some avoidance of 1 and 7; but these biases are markedly stronger for women than for men, who, in fact, display no pronounced digit preferences at all except for 0.[50]

---

[47] C. Newell, *Methods* (1988) 24. In 1960 censuses, the Index was 156.0 for the Philippines, 100.9 for the United States; other modern statistics are collected in United Nations, *Demographic Yearbook* 40 (1988) 19–20. With the Egyptian returns, contrast the heavy age rounding and exaggeration in the Florentine Catasto: D. Herlihy and C. Klapisch-Zuber, *Tuscans* (1985) 169–182.

[48] See B. W. Frier, "Statistics and Roman Society," *JRA* 5 (1992) 287–288 (reviewing R. Duncan-Jones, *Structure*, 1990). The Egyptian score (which is close to that of York, England, in 1851, and of Peru in 1981) would improve substantially if we eliminated a few papyri, such as 131-Ox-1, in which age rounding is unusually pronounced. Age rounding is also low in lists of adult male taxpayers derived from the census returns: R. Duncan-Jones, "Age-Rounding" (1979) 175–176, on *P.Lond.* II 257–258, and T. G. Parkin, *Demography* (1992) 21–22, on *P.Princ.* I 8; see Chapter 5, Section 3. Ages reported in other, less official documents are much likelier to be rounded estimates.

[49] R. J. Myers, "Errors and Bias in the Reporting of Ages in Census Data," *Transactions of the Actuarial Society of America* 41 (1940) 411–415; H. S. Shryock and J. S. Siegel, *Methods* (1980) 206–208 (whence the modern statistics cited below).

[50] Of course, in the Greek numerical system, this is not literal preference for 0, but preference for a single-digit age.

Richard Duncan-Jones has recently argued that prevalence of age rounding is statistically correlated with the general level of illiteracy.[51] However, although high rates of age rounding are almost invariably associated with a high level of illiteracy, the converse is not always true; among some populations with high illiteracy, ages on census returns are nonetheless both approximately accurate and little affected by age rounding. As demographers have long recognized,[52] "rough knowledge of age on the part of most persons does not require a high level of literacy but merely a culture in which numerical age has importance." Since Roman Egypt may have had such a culture, the low level of age rounding in the returns does not of itself prove that Egyptians were generally literate.[53]

On the other hand, among some portions of the Egyptian population there are gradations conceivably linked to relative levels of literacy. For example, age rounding is almost absent for Egyptian males (Whipple's Index is 103.9 for 154 males), but more salient for females (150.9 for 159 females), perhaps indicating that female ages are more often estimates.[54] Similarly, Whipple's Index is 149.7 for 187 persons resident in villages, as against only 88.9 for 135 persons in the metropoleis of Egyptian nomes. Still, even these higher indices are low by pre-modern standards.

Finally, as is evident from Table A, age rounding on exact multiples of 5 increases sharply for the Egyptian elderly. From age 60 onward, nearly half the reported ages (23 of 47) are exact multiples of 5. There is also probably at least some age exaggeration among the elderly. For example, the number of persons aged 60 to 64 (14) and 65 to 69 (12) is less than the number aged 70 to 74 (16), which is suspicious in a high-mortality popula-

---

[51] R. Duncan-Jones, *Structure* (1990) 79–92.

[52] United Nations, *Manual IV: Methods of Estimating Basic Demographic Measures from Incomplete Data* (1967) 21, with examples from Central America. Compare also traditional rural China: G. W. Barclay et al., "Reassessment" (1976) 608–609. Chinese peasants knew their ages because they were important for astrology; could a similar explanation obtain also in Roman Egypt?

[53] On Egyptian illiteracy, see esp. H. C. Youtie, "*Agrammatos*: An Aspect of Greek Society in Egypt," *HSCPh* 75 (1971) 161–176, reprinted in *Scriptiunculae* II (1973) 611–651. More generally, W. V. Harris, *Ancient Literacy* (1989), with the responses in M. Beard et al., *Literacy in the Roman World (Journal of Roman Archaeology* Suppl. 3, 1991), esp. K. Hopkins at pp. 149–152 and A. E. Hanson at pp. 159–198 (both on Egypt). M. Hombert and C. Préaux, *Recherches* (1952) 128–129, estimated that about two-thirds of census declarants were illiterate in Greek; but many of those who could write their names may have been functionally illiterate.

[54] But K. Hopkins, "Brother-Sister" (1980) 318 n.43, is rightly uneasy "about separating male and female ages for this purpose, since a husband might record his wife's age inaccurately or imprecisely, but whom then do we count as innumerate?" On female illiteracy, see S. B. Pomeroy, "Women" (1988) 715–721, with further bibliography. Since women were not subject to the poll tax, accuracy may have been less important.

tion; doubtless some persons registered as in their early 70s were actually in their mid- or late 60s.[55]

Outside of ages exactly divisible by 5, the age statistics in Table A suggest heaping on a few particular ages: for example, ages 8, 29, 38, and 54 for females. Such heaping apparently results from chance, rather from latent numerology or from a cultural sense that, e.g., young girls are "likely" to be 8. At least, there is no obvious numerical pattern in the preferred ages. If reported ages in a census helped determine ages in subsequent censuses, then we might anticipate fourteen-year "cycles" of heaping; for instance, heaping on age 8 would also lead to heaping on ages 22, 36, 50, and so on. But this does not occur.

In general, objective statistical tests confirm autopsy: the information in the census returns is not perfect for demographic purposes, but should be at least approximately accurate. Above all, as to ages, we think it justified to trust the census returns except when clear grounds exist for suspecting them. In almost all instances, no systematic correction is called for; and in any case we had no desire to create new artifacts of that kind. So we have normally sought to work with the ages as they are preserved, but have also flagged possible distortions as seems warranted.

Social bias

Even modern censuses often fail to capture a significant number of persons; and these difficulties are far more acute in the censuses of less developed countries.[56] Among possible sources of error are inadvertent bureaucratic omission of whole areas, the use of incomplete or out-of-date lists of addresses or of villages as a basis for organizing the census, and the difficulty of catching hard-to-reach persons such as transients and isolated rural dwellers. The result can be not only undercount of population, but also bias in reproducing the population's social composition.

Although the Egyptian census was doubtless afflicted by similar problems,[57] there is no way to measure the resulting distortion. However, even

[55] This phenomenon is "age shoving": systematic displacement of age through under- or overstatement. See, e.g., H. S. Shryock and J. S. Siegel, *Methods* (1980) 212. Another probable instance in the census returns is the understatement of the age of metropolitan males approaching age 14. In addition, the female age distribution (in Table 4.1) may also betray some age shoving from the 20s into the 'teens. This pattern of female age shoving is common in pre-modern census returns: P. M. Visaria, *Sex Ratio* (1971) 18–19 (the "African-South Asian pattern"). On age exaggeration among the elderly, see also Chapter 5, Section 4.

[56] See, e.g., C. Newell, *Methods* (1988) 15–18; for a fuller discussion, H. S. Shryock and J. S. Seigel, *Methods* (1980) 102–111. "[T]he ability to carry out a census from inception to final publication stretches even the best administrative organisations." Newell, p. 17.

[57] Compare P. Brunt, *Italian Manpower 225 B.C.–A.D. 14* (2d ed., 1987), esp. 61–83, estimating a normal undercount of around 10 percent in late Republican censuses.

casual inspection of the returns indicates that declarants were often of humble origin, and certainly not predominantly of high status. For example, although declarants were evidently not always required to give the occupations of household members, some do so anyway, though only for adult males. Occupations survive for about 70 persons, around 15 percent of all adult males in the returns. In Chapter 3, Section 3, we consider these occupations in more depth; but it may help to summarize them here. The occupations include a sprinkling of professionals (two scribes, two doctors) and a pair of army veterans; but most occupations relate to farming (18), manufacture and processing of cloth (16), construction (7), and other crafts and commerce (12). Six persons are described simply as "workers" (*ergatai*), apparently unskilled laborers.

In returns from the Oxyrhynchite nome, persons are often characterized as *atechnos*, "without a craft," apparently indicating they lack an occupation and live from accumulated wealth; but only six *atechnoi* are males aged 14 or older, all from the metropolis. In the Arsinoite nome, the equivalent term is *idiotes*, usually applied only to free adult males; the census returns provide fourteen instances, all but one from Arsinoe.[58] No government officials (apart from priests) leave surviving returns for their households; and Roman citizens are scarce prior to the general grant of citizenship by Caracalla in AD 212.[59]

Since the returns do not declare household wealth, it is not possible to determine whether registered households are comparatively well-to-do.[60] One potential substitute is the number of slaves declared in various households (see Table D). Slightly under 11 percent of the persons in our data base are slaves (118 of 1084), a percentage that may seem unexpectedly high.[61] However, less than a sixth of households declare slaves (36 of

---

[58] *Atechnos*: 19-Ox-1 (probably); 33-Ox-1; 131-Ox-1 and 16; 201-Ox-1; 243-Ox-1. *Idiotes*: 103-Ar-1 (*bis*), 3, 5, and 12; 117-Ar-2 and 9; 145-Ar-5 (*bis*), 9, and 10; 173-Ar-5 and 13; 187-Ar-32. The Memphite equivalent is *argos*: 159-Me-1 and 3 (cf. 173-Me-3), all from Memphis. Against the prevailing scholarly view, we believe that all three terms, when applied to adult males, imply relatively high economic status, as is evident especially from the reports on their households; almost all persons so declared have Greek names.

[59] On Roman citizens, see Chapter 1, Section 2; before 215/216 census takers may not have insisted on obtaining returns from all Roman citizens, but that is by no means certain. Among declarants of unoccupied property are a member of the *hiera synodos* at Alexandria (243-Ox-2), a town councillor (243-Ox-3), a former gymnasiarch (131-Ar-6), and two or three former *exegetai* (187-Ox-5).

[60] House fractions are an unreliable guide to wealth. In 187-Ar-4 from Arsinoe (*BGU* I 115 i = *W.Chr.* 203), twenty-seven people reportedly occupy a tenth of a house; but it is impossible to determine the size of the house or whether the family owned additional property.

[61] So also M. Hombert and C. Préaux, *Recherches* (1952) 170. Slaves are less frequent in villages (8 percent) than in metropoleis (13). I. Biezunska-Malowist, *L'Esclavage* II (1977) 156–158, estimates slaves as about 7 to 11 percent of the non-Alexandrian population; also *eadem*, in *Egitto* (1989) 263–264.

233).[62] Of these, nearly three-fifths have only one or two slaves (22 of 36), a further ten have from three to six, and only four households have seven or more slaves. Slaves in the returns are evidently for the most part domestic servants (only one slave has a declared occupation: a 29-year-old male weaver in 117-Ar-3); the incidence of slavery may therefore express the actual wealth of households.[63] If so, census households generally appear to be of modest means. On the other hand, a couple in Antinoopolis has at least thirteen slaves (187-An-1); they were doubtless quite wealthy. So too the 60-year-old woman living alone in Tebtunis with nine female slaves, three of whom are currently fugitive (187-Ar-30).

In sum, although the persons declared in surviving census returns may well be a cut above the larger Egyptian population, the difference is not inherently likely to be great.[64] The census population is in any case probably less well socially and economically positioned than the Egyptians encountered in most Greek documentary papyri.

Other sources of bias
In one respect, however, the way in which returns survive creates considerable bias. Of returns containing usable information on household residents, 117 out of 233 (or 50.2 percent) are from the metropoleis of nomes; and of the personal entries, 537 of 1084 (or 49.5 percent) are metropolitan. This ratio, which results from underlying patterns of preservation, means that about half of both our data bases is metropolitan.

The surviving returns therefore significantly underrepresent villages, which are likely to have embraced a total population at least twice that of the metropoleis and other cities. We discuss this source of bias in Chapter 3, Section 1; but in the course of our study it became clear that major demographic distinctions divide metropoleis from villages, so that underrepresentation of villages is not inconsequential. For example, village families are larger and internally more complex than those in metropoleis; houses in villages are much likelier to be owner-occupied; and metropolitan households contain significantly higher numbers of both slaves and non-kin lodgers. Metropolitan women may also marry a few years later than village women, and they are much more likely to enter brother-sister marriages; and, perhaps most significant, the attested village sex ratio differs appreciably from that in metropoleis. These and other significant dissimilarities are explored in subsequent chapters; but the bias that underrepresentation of villages introduces is large and must be continually borne in mind.

---

[62] The proportion is virtually identical in households where the principal family is complete or nearly complete (26 of 167).
[63] See Chapter 3 at notes 69–74; also Chapter 7, Sections 2 and 4.
[64] So also, on somewhat different grounds, K. Hopkins, "Brother-Sister" (1980) 316.

Finally, it bears repeating that geographic and chronological limits on surviving census returns are of some importance. Thus, for example, as will emerge in Chapter 6, brother-sister marriage was apparently more frequent in the Arsinoite nome than in some other parts of Egypt. Since three-fifths of surviving returns come from the Arsinoite nome, they undoubtedly exaggerate the true incidence of this extremely interesting practice.[65] Nonetheless, in general the surviving census returns give the impression of considerable demographic homogeneity, such as would be anticipated in slow-moving ancient societies. The main source of chronological bias may be the Antonine plague (discussed in Chapter 9, Section 2).

4. Assessment of the census returns

It is not easy to arrive at a completely balanced verdict on the returns as demographic evidence. They are less than perfect records; vigilance is enjoined. Nonetheless, most problems apparently relate more to the paucity of their numbers than to their inherent lack of quality.[66] If twice as many returns survived, our present study would surely be much more than twice as reliable. But since discovery of a large number of new returns is unlikely in the foreseeable future, the only realistic question is whether it is worth risking premature analysis.

We obviously concluded that this risk is acceptable. Several considerations favor such a judgment. First, broad demographic issues underlie much recent scholarship on Roman social and family history. But these studies take little account of what is, on the most sober evaluation and despite cavils, not only by far the best and fullest demographic source for the Greco-Roman world, but also quite probably the best available source for any population prior to the Renaissance.[67] At minimum, the apparent demographic implications of the census returns deserve much wider attention.

Second, no doubt the major reason why the returns are not more widely considered is that they are published in scattered editions of markedly

---

[65] We thus do not necessarily share Keith Hopkins's confidence, "Brother-Sister" (1980) 314, that "deductions based on the surviving census returns are plausibly generalizable to a much wider population." Similarly, D. Barker, "Findings" (1985) 139: "there is no seriously damaging bias [in survival] that is observable."

[66] On problems of sampling and sample size in demography, see J. D. Willigan and K. A. Lynch, *Sources* (1982) 193–200. As T. G. Parkin, *Demography* (1992) 166 n. 57, observes, surviving census returns are only a tiny fraction of those ever filed; but this is not itself a source of weakness, provided that the surviving returns are reasonably representative, as they appear to be.

[67] A major exception is K. Hopkins, "Brother-Sister" (1980). The census returns are all but shunned by T. G. Parkin, *Demography* (1992), who nonetheless admits their value (pp. 21, 58–59); and wholly ignored by, e.g., R. Duncan-Jones, *Structure* (1990), and S. Treggiari, *Marriage* (1991).

divergent excellence and accessibility; further, misreadings of crucial demographic information are not rare. Our Catalogue makes available, in standard form, all demographically relevant data in the returns; it represents several years of work in examining, and in some instances publishing or republishing, all known census returns and some hitherto unknown or not fully published. The Catalogue is therefore worth having in its own right.

Third, in 1952, when Marcel Hombert and Claire Préaux published their renowned study, they knew "quelque 200" returns; four decades on, this number has increased by fifty percent.[68] The statistics that Hombert and Préaux produced are often cited, but need updating and, in a few instances, correction (although virtually all vital measurements have not changed or altered only slightly with the increase in data). Further, Hombert and Préaux wrote at a time when modern demographic analysis, with its heavy use of computer modelling for imperfectly known populations, was still in its infancy; the way in which they present statistics is often demographically naive and may mislead the unwary.[69] In this respect, therefore, a more modern discussion of the returns is also worthwhile, if only to indicate potentially fruitful lines of future research; for, as we shall see, the returns permit development of numerous demographic hypotheses that may well be verifiable through other evidence.

The present book seeks only to establish the demographic characteristics that surviving Egyptian census returns most probably support. Another way of stating our project is that we aim to reconstruct the demographic features of a larger hypothetical population, of which the surviving returns may be considered a fairly accurate sample.[70] This hypothetical population is likely to represent well the historical population of at least the Arsinoite and Oxyrhynchite nomes in the early Roman Empire; it should also have a broad "family resemblance" to the entire population of the province of Egypt, and perhaps a still broader one to the Roman Empire generally.[71]

---

[68] M. Hombert and C. Préaux, *Recherches* (1952) 40. By 1980, Keith Hopkins, "Brother-Sister" (1980) 315, knew about 270 returns listing 880 persons; our data base is both more accurate and, as to persons, almost 25 percent larger. The number of persons whose sex and age are both known has also risen strikingly: Hombert and Préaux had 503, and Hopkins has 553, as against 687 in our Catalogue.

[69] For example, they give figures for average parental age at childbirth without observing that younger parents are likelier to be attested because of their higher life expectancy: M. Hombert and C. Préaux, *Recherches* (1952) 163–167. In fairness, Hombert and Préaux concentrate more on the census process than on demography.

[70] Our approach is similar to that used by G.W. Barclay *et al.*, "Reassessment" (1976), for rural China in the 1930s (raw data originally gathered by the University of Nanking)—a seminal study of how to reconstruct historical populations.

[71] On the extent to which Roman Egypt can be considered a typical Mediterranean population, see Chapter 9, Section 1.

But the exact extent of resemblance is difficult if not impossible to establish on present evidence, so we make no wider claims. When we write in subsequent chapters of "Roman Egypt," the caveat in this paragraph should be kept in mind; our focus is always concentrated chiefly on the census population.

3

Households

Although the Egyptian census returns are often poorly preserved, they contain much valuable information on the form of ordinary households; in better-preserved returns, the kinship between household members can virtually always be reconstructed with considerable confidence. As will emerge in subsequent chapters, the form of Egyptian households is of considerable importance to Egyptian demography.

We begin with a brief discussion of Egypt's probable population during the early Roman Empire, then treat in more detail the composition of households, especially the large differences between the metropoleis and villages.

1. The population of Egypt

Roman Egypt's total population has long been the subject of dispute, mainly because the two principal literary sources contradict each other. The historian Diodorus Siculus, writing toward the end of the first century BC, places current Egyptian population at 3 million (1.31.6-9). By contrast, Josephus, in the latter half of the following century, gives a population of 7.5 million for Egypt exclusive of Alexandria, an estimate allegedly based on the amount collected from the poll tax (BJ 2.385, in a speech). This would imply a total Egyptian population on the order of eight to nine million.

Many historians accept Josephus' estimate as close to accurate; accordingly they denigrate or explain away Diodorus' figure.[1] However, not only is Josephus' estimate of doubtful provenance—avowedly not derived from an actual count, in any case—it also supposes a population level that Egypt would not reattain until the late nineteenth century, after the introduction of perennial irrigation and Egypt's partial integration into Euro-

---

[1] E.g., P. Salmon, *Population* (1974) 35-36; N. Lewis, *Life* (1983) 158-159; A. K. Bowman, *Egypt* (1986) 17-18.

pean industrial economies.[2] Dominic Rathbone has recently argued that Diodorus deserves more credence than Josephus, and that for various reasons, Roman Egypt's population must in any case have been far lower than Josephus' figure: around 3 to 5 million, though with appreciable oscillation over time.[3] Although the exact population of Roman Egypt is not of central moment for our present study, we consider Rathbone's conservative estimate far more realistic than the usually accepted figure.

More important for present purposes is the geographical disposition of this population within Egypt. The population of Egypt had three main components: Alexandria; the nome capitals (metropoleis) including the cities with Greek constitutions; and the countryside, where most of the population lived in small villages.

For the provincial capital Alexandria, after Rome one of the largest cities in the Empire, Diodorus (17.52.6) gives a figure of 300,000 free persons in 59 BC; he adduces local officials as his source, but it is uncertain which civic groups they included in their reckoning. Diana Delia's recent survey of the sources concludes that Alexandria's population was generally around 500,000 to 600,000 during the Roman period.[4] A half million would mean, for example, a built-up area of 1,250 hectares at a density of 400 persons per hectare. Given the probability of multistory buildings and a walled area of about 825 hectares, this estimate seems reasonable enough.[5] Delia characterizes her estimate as "a mere approximation," and in these terms 500,000 is probably close enough.

The nome metropoleis are harder to estimate. Rathbone offers a figure of 500,000 or more inhabitants for these cities as a whole.[6] The only one for which there is good evidence is Hermopolis, where a third-century papyrus shows that two of the four city quarters had 4,200 "houses" (*oikiai*).[7] Even

---

[2] See A. R. Omran, *Egypt* (1973) 9–15. The first modern census, in 1882, registered 6.8 million persons, usually corrected to about 7.5 million; prior censuses substantially undercounted. For speculation on earlier Egyptian population, see D. Panzac, "La population de l'empire Ottoman et de ses marches du XVe au XIXe siècle: bibliographie (1941–1980) et bilan provisoire," *Revue de l'Occident Musulman et de la Méditerranée* 31 (1981) 119–137.

[3] D. W. Rathbone, "Villages" (1990) 103–110, 122–124; Rathbone rightly streses the carrying capacity of the Nile valley, but may exaggerate the extent of fluctuations in the population. Demographers have also long been skeptical about higher estimates: e.g., J. C. Russell, "Population" (1958) 78–80; K. W. Butzer, *Early Hydraulic Civilisation in Egypt* (1976) 92; C. McEvedy and R. Jones, *Atlas* (1978) 226–229.

[4] D. Delia, "The Population of Roman Alexandria," *TAPhA* 118 (1989) 275–292. Still higher estimates are canvassed by D. Rathbone, "Villages" (1990) 119–120; but they seem unduly influenced by inflated total population counts for Roman Egypt.

[5] See A. Marcus, *The Middle East* (1989) 337–341. Cairo had 398 persons per hectare in 1798.

[6] D. W. Rathbone, "Villages" (1990) 120–121, 123. Rathbone rightly emphasizes the developed urbanism of Roman Egypt, which contrasts with nineteenth-century Egypt.

[7] *SPP* V 101; see U. Wilcken, *APF* 6 (1920) 429.

if we assume that the remaining quarters had fewer houses, a total of about 7,000 seems easily justifiable. But *oikia* may mean either a house in the sense of a building, or a household (of which more than one might live in a house); both meanings are found in the census returns in different contexts. Taking the latter sense and allowing a *minimum* average of 5.3 persons per urban household (a figure calculated below in Section 3), we come to a total population of nearly 37,000.[8] Hermopolis occupied an area of about 120 ha., and its density would therefore be about 300 persons/ha. This figure compares very closely with eighteenth-century Aleppo, where the best modern estimate suggests a population of around 110,000 to 120,000 in a 365-ha. area, or again about 300 persons/ha.[9] Both cities were predominantly of two-story houses, thus less dense than the great urban centers with multistory apartment houses. Although such estimates are far from foolproof, they are likely to be fairly close to the mark.

Hermopolis was doubtless larger than many metropoleis, but by no means the largest; Arsinoe, Athribis, Herakleopolis, and Tanis are all known to have been larger, and Memphis may still have been.[10] If we take a figure of 100 ha. as a modal size, and estimate a population of 25,000 as typical,[11] it remains to determine the number of such cities. But this is by no means a simple task. The traditional figure of forty nomes, used for example by Rathbone, is undoubtedly too low. The number in Upper Egypt did not vary much from the historical twenty (there were probably 22 in the fourth century); but the development of the Delta in Roman times led to subdivision of nome areas and the creation of new metropoleis, and the eventual number of metropoleis in Middle and Lower Egypt was not below thirty. A total of fifty cities with 25,000 residents each would make 1.25 million.[12]

For the rural population, a variety of cogent arguments lead to placing the total number of villages at somewhere between 2,000 and 3,000, with an average population ranging from 1,000 to 1,500, for a total rural population of about 3 million, in line with the probable rural population of Egypt before the nineteenth century.[13] However, villages varied enor-

---

[8] See R. S. Bagnall, *Egypt* (1993) 53. This is a minimum figure, on the most conservative assumptions.
[9] A. Marcus, *Middle East* (1989) 337–341.
[10] R. S. Bagnall, *Egypt* (1993) 52.
[11] D. Rathbone, "Villages" (1990) 121, argues that many metropoleis in Middle Egypt were comparable in size to Ostia (not over 27,000, he believes), but that all metropoleis had an average of only 15,000. However, we see no reason to suppose that metropoleis elsewhere were smaller than those in Middle Egypt.
[12] The number of nomes in the second century was not fewer than fifty; this figure is based on a forthcoming study of the "nome coins" of Roman Egypt by Jennifer A. Sheridan.
[13] D. Rathbone, "Villages" (1990) 124–137; R. S. Bagnall, *Egypt* (1993) 110–111.

mously in size, from about 4,000 (e.g., Karanis in the mid-second century AD)[14] down to a hundred or so.

For Egypt as a whole, these calculations yield a total population of about 4.75 million persons, of which 1.75 million (37 percent) would have been urban. Both figures seem high to us, but we lack means to test their accuracy; we therefore more prudently estimate that the population of early imperial Egypt fluctuated within a "normal" range from about 4 to 5 million. Of more significance, in any case, is that around a third of the Egyptian population is likely to have lived in cities—a degree of urbanization that resulted from the renowned density of Egypt's population, and that was high even by the standards of the Roman Empire, the most urbanized state of the Western world before modern times.[15] However, many Egyptian "cities" would count as towns by modern standards.

Overall population change in early imperial Egypt is impossible to measure precisely. Rathbone proposes a paradigm that accords with available evidence: slow rise during the first and early second centuries AD, followed by sharp decline with the onset of the Antonine plague in 166, but general recovery by the first half of the third century.[16] Apart from the Antonine plague, present evidence does not point to large population swings during the early Roman Empire; the normal growth rate was therefore probably very close to zero.

The Egyptian population and the census returns

Surviving census returns are very unevenly distributed among the geographic sectors of this population. There are no returns at all from Alexandria. Almost half the returns (149 of 300) come from metropoleis, with Arsinoe (86) and Oxyrhynchos (38) overwhelmingly predominant; returns survive from only five other metropoleis, namely Hermopolis (9), Memphis (8), Antinoopolis (4), Herakleopolis, and Lykopolis (2 each).

The villages are proportionately much less well represented, by only 151 returns.[17] Of these, nearly two-thirds (98) are from the Arsinoite nome,

---

[14] A. E. R. Boak, "Egypt" (1959); H. Geremek, *Karanis: communauté rurale de l'Egypte romaine au II–IIIe siècle de notre ère* (1969) 36–40.

[15] R. W. Goldsmith, "Estimate" (1984) 271–272, 283. The inhabited portion of Roman Egypt is usually estimated at about 28,000 square kilometers; density is therefore between 140 and 180 persons per square km, about ten times as dense as the rest of the Empire.

[16] D. Rathbone, "Villages" (1990) 123–124. Rathbone, relying on Diodorus' figure of 3 million for late Ptolemaic Egypt, supposes population growth from 3 to 5 million between 31 BC and AD 166, implying an actual annual long-term growth rate near 0.3 percent, which seems to us improbably high. Likelier is long-term growth on the order of 0.1 percent per annum (e.g., from 4 to 5 million), with growth slowing as the population neared the land's carrying capacity of about 5 million. Similarly, C. McEvedy and R. Jones, *Atlas* (1978) 226: "at about 5m [Egypt's] population reached a maximum that was not exceeded until modern times." On the Antonine plague: Chapter 9, Section 2 below.

[17] These returns include twenty-four that cannot be assigned to an exact locality; see Chapter 2, note 25.

with the villages of Karanis (22), Soknopaiou Nesos (17), Theadelphia, and Tebtunis (12 each) dominating; no other Arsinoite village is represented by more than four returns. Egyptian villages from other nomes are also scantily represented, with the exception of Thelbonthon Siphtha in the Prosopite nome (16) and Tanyaithis in the Apollonopolite (9), for each of which there survives a long fragment from a continuous census volume (*tomos*). As is usual with papyri, the vast majority are from Middle Egypt; the Delta is represented by only twenty returns (all from the Prosopite nome in the extreme southwest), and Upper Egypt by scarcely any.

The population figures given above indicate that village population probably outnumbered Egypt's total urban population (including Alexandria) by about two-to-one, a ratio we have regularly employed in subsequent chapters when "weighting" the rural returns against the metropolitan. This ratio is obviously imprecise,[18] but, with few exceptions, the differences produced by using a multiplier of 1.5, 2.5, or even 3 are not substantial enough to warrant concern about the exact ratio chosen.

2. Household forms

The Egyptian census was organized "by household" (*kat' oikian*). However, the returns suggest that, as is often the case in pre-modern censuses, a "household" was poorly conceptualized, probably by census takers and declarants alike.[19] The Egyptian census served diverse functions, not only to register complete households but also to assemble lists of taxpaying males and to inventory all habitable land. These functions often collide. In five cases, married couples register in different returns, apparently not because they are separated but because they or their extended families each own property (145-Ar-24; 201-Ar-8/9; 201-Ox-1; 215-An-1; 215-Hm-1/2). In 159-Me-1 from Memphis, a divorced renter registers himself and a son aged 5; his older son, aged 14, is co-resident but registers

---

[18]Further inexactitude is introduced by including Alexandria; there is no way to avoid this problem, though we presume that metropolitan demographic characteristics were only accentuated in Alexandria. Weighting is also complicated by the demographic interaction of cities and villages through migration, see Chapter 8.

[19]In modern historical demography, a household is defined as a "group of coresidents, people who live under the same roof and typically share in common consumption": D. I. Kertzer, "Household History" (1991) 156. Whether all Egyptian *oikiai* in the census returns meet this definition is uncertain; but in any case the definition itself presents difficulties, see R. Wall, in *Family Forms* (1983) 6–13. The United Nations uses a different (and preferable) typology based less on cohabitation than on common consumption: *Principles and Recommendations for Population and Housing Censuses* (1980) 72–74. J. D. Willigan and K. A. Lynch, *Sources* (1982) 81–83, discuss the problems in definition.

separately in 159-Me-2, obviously because he has just reached taxable age.[20]

On other occasions, declarants list, or at least mention, persons not resident in the household, but who had probably been resident in the previous census, or whose registration might otherwise have been anticipated: not only deceased relatives (145-He-1; 201-Ox-3; 215-He-3), but a former wife (173-Ar-2), children from prior marriages (187-Ar-32), a brother currently in tax flight (173-Ar-9), daughters now married and living with their husbands (145-He-2; 201-Ox-1), or fugitive slaves (187-Ar-30). Even ages are often given for these non-residents.

Finally, it is often uncertain whether non-kin lodgers who shared a dwelling with its owners, but lived physically apart from them, were invariably registered as distinct households, or rather as non-kin lodgers in the owner's household.[21] Return 103-Ar-1 from Arsinoe is a good example of the difficulty: there is no way to be certain whether one or several households are being registered. The ambiguity of the Greek word *oikia*, which can mean either a physical house (a discrete dwelling) or a household, doubtless contributes to the difficulty.

Vagaries of this sort are not always easily diagnosed, particularly granted the current state of preservation of many returns; and other difficulties arise when, as is sometimes the case, returns survive only in later documents excerpting them. Further, as emerged in Chapter 2 above, the returns may well be affected by deeper problems, above all as to young males nearing taxable age. In consequence, the census returns should be treated as giving at best an approximate picture of typical households.

The Cambridge typology of households
Of the 300 returns listed in our catalogue, 36 register habitable property with no current residents, while 31 are so fragmentarily preserved that nothing more can be said about them than that they were census returns. In the remaining 233 (about 78 percent of the total corpus), at least some information about residents is preserved. Of these, 63 are evidently so incomplete that we are unable to reconstruct even an approximately reliable stemma of the principal resident family. Three additional returns either declare only persons resident in other households (159-Me-2; 215-Hm-2) or register only the resident slaves (187-Ar-3).

We are thus left with a "sample" of 167 returns in which a stemma of the principal resident family can be reconstructed with complete or consi-

---

[20]This may be a Memphite peculiarity, see the Discussion on 159-Me-2.

[21]As D. W. Hobson, "House and Household" (1985), observes, often several Egyptian households shared a single house. With 103-Ar-1, contrast 187-Ar-33: the declarant files a separate return for a renter occupying one-third of his house.

derable confidence.[22] These stemmata may then be analyzed according to the well-known Cambridge typology developed by Peter Laslett and his colleagues for the comparative study of households in early modern Europe.[23] Their categories work sufficiently well if, in particular, allowance is made for the large differences between ancient marriage and that of early modern Europe.[24]

The Cambridge typology divides households into five formal categories: (1) solitary persons; (2) multiple persons with no conjugal family present (mainly co-resident siblings); (3) conjugal families in their various phases (from a married couple without children, through to a formerly married parent with unmarried children); (4) conjugal families "extended" through the presence of co-resident kin; and (5) multiple families linked usually by kinship. This fifth category, the most complex, includes both households in which children remain after they marry, and so-called *frérèches* consisting of co-resident brothers more than one of whom is married.

The results of this analysis are summarized in Table 3.1. As the table shows, Egyptian household structure resembles a pattern frequently found in the pre-modern Mediterranean: households with extended and multiple families are a very large proportion of all households.[25] For comparison, we give the household structure of Florence and its territory during the early fifteenth century.[26]

[22] We focus mainly on the principal family (kin group) in the household, regardless whether the family owns or rents its dwelling. "Family" refers either to this larger kin group or to a conjugal "nucleus" within it. Inclusion of 30 "nearly complete" households did not much alter the overall proportions between types, except to reduce the proportion of solitaries (whose returns are almost always complete). The families of lodgers are dealt with separately below; slave families are discussed in Chapter 7, Section 4.

[23] P. Laslett, in *Household and Family* (1972) 23–44; J.-L. Flandrin, *Families* (1979) 66–74. See also E. A. Hammel and P. Laslett, "Comparing Household Structure Over Time and Between Cultures," *Comparative Studies in Society and History* (1974) 73–103. Laslett includes many subcategories, only some of which we have adopted below; in particular, "stem families" have no relevance to Roman Egypt. D. I. Kertzer, "Household History" (1991), surveys modern research in this area.

[24] See Chapters 6 and 7 below. Particular problems arise from divorce (for which Laslett does not allow), from the informal spousal relationships that often produced "fatherless children" (*apatores*), and from brother-sister marriages.

[25] J.-L. Flandrin, *Families* (1979) 73–74; T. W. Gallant, *Risk and Survival* (1991) 21–27. On southern France, see A. Fauve-Chamoux, in *Population française* II (1988) 334–338. In Chapter 9, Section 1, we return to the vexed issue of whether there is, in fact, a distinctive "Mediterranean" household structure; but for our immediate purposes this issue makes little difference.

[26] D. Herlihy and C. Klapisch-Zuber, *Tuscans* (1985) 280–336 (figures at 292).

Table 3.1. *The household structure of Roman Egypt*

Types	% of households in Tuscany 1427	Egypt I–III	Roman Egypt, % of Family members	Household residents
1. Solitary	13.6	16.2	3.8	6.0
2. No family	2.3	4.8	2.5	3.1
3. Conjugal family	54.8	43.1	35.5	35.7
4. Extended family	10.6	15.0	15.4	14.9
5. Multiple families	18.7	21.0	42.8	40.4
Number:	59,770	167	715	840

Solitaries: In 27 Egyptian households, one person lives without kin.[27] The proportion of solitaries is exaggerated since short returns have a better chance of being well preserved. The average age of solitaries is 40.2 (19 ages); many solitaries are of advanced age (three are 70 or above),[28] though three are still in their teens (131-Ox-16; 173-Pr-1; 187-Ar-37). Males greatly predominate (twenty, as against seven females); but their number is swollen by a single papyrus containing, for an unknown administrative reason, only returns of solitary male taxpayers from Theadelphia (159-Ar-14 to 17).[29] Solitaries were probably most often the sole survivors of their families, living alone because they had been unable to marry or their marriages had ended. Three solitaries have taken in lodgers; five have slaves.

Co-resident siblings: Eight households contain co-resident unmarried siblings.[30] Most siblings are young, usually in their teens or twenties. Their

[27] 103-Ar-14; 117-Ar-8; 131-Ar-4; 131-He-1; 131-Ox-16; 145-Ar-4 (divorced woman) and 5 (probably); 145-Ox-3; 159-Ar-14, 15, 16, 17, 19, and 25; 159-Hm-1 (probably); 173-Ar-5; 173-Me-2; 173-Pr-1, 2, 8, and 12; 187-Ar-5, 6, 30, 33, and 37; 215-Hm-3.

[28] 173-Pr-8; 187-Ar-5; 215-Hm-3. It should be noted that two of these solitaries have slaves to care for them.

[29] Similar are 145-Ar-1 to 4 from Tebtunis, in which households headed by females are grouped together. Why Egyptian authorities wanted such groupings is mysterious, but they imply at least a limited measure of "demographic" research on the basis of the census returns (this against T.G. Parkin, *Demography*, 1992, 37).

[30] 103-Ar-6 (probably) and 12; 131-Ar-10; 145-Ar-10; 173-Pr-3; 187-Ar-7; 187-Ox-3; 243-Ox-1. Never more than three siblings. There is no case where several unrelated and unmarried individuals live together.

average age is 27.1 (18 ages), but this average is inflated by an exceptional household with three siblings in their 40s or 50s (173-Pr-3); the other fifteen persons have an average age of 22.7. Males slightly predominate (eleven, as against eight females; one person of uncertain sex), and with one exception there is an adult male in each household; the exception is 187-Ox-3 from Oxyrhynchos, where two sisters aged 25 and 22 live alone. Households of this type, which doubtless usually resulted from the death of both parents, would then break up or mutate into other forms as siblings married. None of these households has lodgers, but two have slaves.

Conjugal families: As in almost all pre-modern populations, a plurality of Egyptian households are conjugal families of "nuclear" form. They might seem to call for little comment; but in some respects Egyptian conjugal families are unusual by modern standards. Attention focuses especially on three households in which a married couple has no children,[31] and thirty-eight in which a married couple has children.[32] What is unusual about these families is that only rarely is the couple young; there are, in fact, only three probable cases.[33] Normally the spouses are of more advanced age; the average age of husbands is 45.9 (26 ages), and of wives, 37.3 (27 ages). This indicates that newly married Egyptian couples did not regularly leave their parents' homes and form new households, as was widely the case in pre-modern Europe. Instead, the Egyptian conjugal family more commonly resulted from attrition, through the death of parents and other kin.[34]

In twenty-eight conjugal families, only one parent remains after a marriage has broken up through divorce or a spouse's death: in eleven cases the father, in seventeen the mother.[35] As would be anticipated, the remain-

---

[31] 187-An-2; 201-Ar-6 (plus the former wife of one of the house's owners); 229-Hm-1 (probably).

[32] 33-Ox-1 and 2; 61-Ar-1 (probably); 75-Ar-2 (probably); 103-Ar-1, 3 (probably), 5, 7, and 11; 117-Ap-7; 131-Ar-3; 131-Me-1 (child from a former marriage); 145-Ar-12, 17, 23, and 24; 145-He-1; 145-Ox-1 (probably); 159-Ar-7, 9, 20, and 26; 159-Hm-3; 173-Ar-3 and 15; 173-Pr-7; 187-Ar-2, 11, 12, and 32; 187-Hm-1; 201-Ar-2 and 12 (probably); 215-An-1 (probably); 215-Ar-7; 215-He-1 (probably); 229-Ar-2; 243-Ar-2.

[33] 103-Ar-5 from Arsinoe (husband 21, wife 18); 187-An-2 from Antinoopolis (husband 24, wife 21); 187-Ar-12 from Arsinoe (husband 21; wife's age lost, but probably young). At least two are close-kin marriages. See also, perhaps, 173-Ar-15 and 201-Ar-2, in which the wife is young and the husband's age is unknown.

[34] For computer simulations demonstrating this point, see S. Ruggles, *Connections* (1987) 106–126; Ruggles' model DEV broadly resembles Roman Egypt.

[35] Father: 131-He-3; 131-Ox-14 (probably); 145-Pr-1 (not certain); 159-Ar-6; 159-Hm-2 (probably); 159-Me-1/2; 173-Ar-2 and 7 (probably); 173-Me-1; 201-Ox-1; ???-Me-1. Mother: 33-Ar-2; 103-Ar-9; 117-Ar-5; 145-Ar-1 and 2; 145-Ly-1; 173-Pr-4, 11, 14, and 17; 187-Ar-29 and 34; 187-Me-1; 187-Ox-4 (probably); 215-Ar-1; 243-Ar-4 (probably); 257-Ar-1. Also two cases in which mothers live alone with *apatores* children: 145-Ar-1 and 187-Me-1; on *apatores*, see Chapter 7, Section 3 below.

ing parent is usually of advanced age; the average age of fathers is 45.1 (eight ages), and of mothers, 43.0 (thirteen ages). However, in a few instances the remaining parent is in his or her twenties (173-Ar-2, male aged 22; 145-Ar-2, female 29).

Three other households are probably simple conjugal families, but cannot be exactly reconstructed (117-Ap-4 and 9; 131-Ox-7). Ten conjugal families own slaves; seven have lodgers.

Extended families: Extended households are conjugal families with co-resident kin, but no other conjugal family present. Families are extended upward when the kinsperson is from an older generation; the census returns have nine examples, invariably a spouse's parent.[36] The parent is usually elderly; the youngest is 50, and two are in their seventies. Such families provide evidence on how the elderly were cared for in Roman Egypt; but at least in some cases the parent was probably still the actual head of the household.[37]

Families are extended laterally when the kinsperson is a relative in the same generation; the returns have thirteen examples.[38] Most cases involve a husband's brothers, in households that were probably evolving toward *frérèches* (see below). Two other families are extended both upward and laterally; and one other is not exactly classifiable but probably extended.[39] Two extended families have slaves; two have lodgers.

Multiple families: Much the most complex households have more than one co-resident conjugal family. In Roman Egypt, households of this type have almost luxuriant variety, as the elements discussed above are combined and recombined. However, these households may be divided into two broad groups: those in which at least two conjugal families are in different generations, and those in which all families are in the same generation.

The census returns provide nineteen examples of two-generational multiple families.[40] The archetype of such a household is a married couple

---

[36] 11-Ar-1 (husband's mother); 117-Ar-6 (husband's mother); 131-He-2 (wife's mother) and 4 (husband's father); 159-Ar-1 (probably; husband's father); 201-Ar-8 (wife's mother) and 10 (both spouses' mothers); 201-Ox-3 (probably; husband's father); 215-Ar-5 (husband's mother). Husband's parents are more frequent.

[37] The parent files the census return in 131-He-4 (with his children, who are married half-siblings), 159-Ar-1, and 201-Ar-8.

[38] 33-Ar-1 (husband's brothers); 89-Ar-1 (husband's brothers); 103-Ar-8 (husband's brothers); 117-Ar-2 (husband's brother); 117-Ox-2 (wife's brother, plus possible cousin or apprentice); 145-Ar-18 (husband's half-brother); 159-Ar-13 (husband's first cousin?); 173-Ar-16 (probably; wife's brothers); 173-Pr-13 (probably; a cousin?); 187-Ar-10 (husband's brother) and 26 (three *apatores* females, probably kin); 215-He-2 (probably; husband's sister and half-sister); 215-Hm-1/2 (both spouses' brother).

[39] 145-Ar-20 (both spouses' mother 55, plus two cousins); 201-Ar-1 (husband's mother 59, plus probable female kin 54). Unclassifiable: 131-Ox-11.

[40] 89-Hm-1 (probably); 117-Ap-5 and 6 (probably); 117-Ar-1 and 11; 145-Ar-3 and 9; 145-He-2; 159-Ar-10 and 11; 173-Ar-9 and 11; 173-Pr-5 and 15; 187-Ar-4, 8, and 22; 201-Ar-9; 215-He-3.

whose children marry without leaving the household. 187-Ar-4 from Arsinoe, one of the most intricate households in the returns, illustrates the possible complexities. The declarant is Herodes, a weaver in his fifties; Eirene, his full sister and wife, is 54. The couple have eight surviving children, five sons and three daughters, ranging in age from 29 to 7. Their oldest son, aged 29, has married his sister; they have two 1-year-old boys. The next oldest son, aged 26, has married a non-kin woman aged 29;[41] they also have two sons, the elder of whom is 13.[42] In addition, the household contains four adult children of the declarant's deceased brother; two of these siblings are married with a 1-year-old daughter.

On the other hand, there are fifteen examples of same-generational multiple families.[43] Here the archetype is the *frérèche*, a household in which siblings (especially brothers) remain in the household after more than one of them has married.[44] A good example is 173-Pr-10 from Thelbonthon Siphtha. The joint declarants are four brothers ranging in age from 49 to 21; each is married with children, and the oldest has a son from a previous marriage probably to his sister. In most cases, a *frérèche* probably originates when the parents in a two-generational multiple family die. In any event, strong social bonds kept siblings together; for example, the four brothers in 173-Pr-10 also owned other potentially habitable but unoccupied property in Thelbonthon Siphtha, which they declare in 173-Pr-16.

In one additional household (131-Be-1 from Peptaucha), two apparently unrelated families are living together. Of 34 households with multiple families, eight have slaves and three contain lodgers.

This "sample" of 166 Egyptian households, although small, probably does not drastically misrepresent the household structure of the census population.[45] Among the sixty-seven households we classify as incomplete

---

[41] The wife's two unmarried brothers, aged 34 and 32, are also in this household as lodgers.

[42] In Chapter 2, Section 3, this age is doubted because the father would be so young at paternity. It may be that, as in 131-Pr-1 and 145-Pr-1, an *apator* child is being registered as legitimate.

[43] 75-Ox-1 (probably); 117-Ar-4 and 7 (probably); 131-Pr-1; 145-Ar-19; 159-Ar-4 and 21; 173-Me-3; 173-Pr-10; 215-Ar-4 and 6; 243-Ar-3; ???-Ar-3 (probably) and 5 (probably); ???-Ox-2 (probably).

[44] However, not all such multiple families are *frérèches*. E.g., 243-Ar-3 from Arsinoe: a woman and her three children, living with her deceased husband's brother and his son (described as lodgers). This is, presumably, a disintegrating *frérèche*. Similar, but much more complex, is ???-Ar-3 from Soknopaiou Nesos.

[45] K. Hopkins, "Brother-Sister" (1980) 330, derived a household structure almost identical to ours on the basis of 116 households; so also D. Barker, "Findings" (1985) 139–140, on the basis of 132 households. As Hopkins observes (pp. 331–333), lists of male taxpayers also point to a heavy concentration of complex households.

because of their inadequate preservation, many are simply so complex as to resist reconstruction; good examples are 131-Ox-1, 159-Ar-5, and 215-Ar-3.

The "life cycle" of households

The crisp formality of the Cambridge categories misleads if it is taken to imply orderly evolution of households from simple to complex. The census returns give only static cross-sections of households at a particular moment in time. However, as we tried to suggest above, actual households undoubtedly exhibited a much more intricate and irregular life cycle, alternating erratically over generations between simpler and more complex forms.[46] This inference is confirmed by seven households for which returns survive from two or even three successive censuses.[47]

In 89-Ar-1 from Arsinoe, three brothers aged 30, 20 and 7 live together; the oldest brother is married to a woman aged 25.[48] In the next census (103-Ar-8), the brothers are still together, but the oldest brother's marriage has ended in divorce or his wife's death; the youngest brother, now 21, is married to a woman aged 25, but there are still no children. Fourteen years later, in 117-Ar-4, the oldest brother has evidently died; the two remaining brothers are now both married with children. In this household, a laterally extended family has thus finally mutated into a full *frérèche*.

117-Ar-1, also from Arsinoe, is a multi-generational household of renters: a woman aged 53, her sons 33 and 32, the younger son's full sister and wife 28, and a woman 70 who is the sister of the mother's (presumably deceased) husband. Fourteen years later, in 131-Ar-3, the older generation is apparently dead, as is the older son; the younger son and his wife now live with their three sons and two daughters, all born since the last census.[49] Here the change is from a quite complex form to a simple conjugal family, by attrition; similar, but less elaborate, are the sequences from 131-He-2 to 145-He-1 (Ankyronpolis), and from 159-Ar-1 to 173-Ar-3 (Arsinoe).

---

[46] T. W. Gallant, *Risk and Survival* (1991) 27–30, theoretically reconstructs the life cycle of a typical Greek household; but the Egyptian census returns suggest that because of vagaries in mortality and fertility, the "typical" rarely occurs. Compare L. K. Berkner, "The Use and Misuse of Census Data for the Historical Analysis of Family Structure," *Journal of Interdisciplinary History* 4 (1975) 721–738; T. Hareven, "Family History at the Crossroads," in *Family History* (1987) vi–xx, and "The History of the Family and the Complexity of Social Change," *AHR* 96 (1991) 95–124. On Egypt, R. S. Bagnall, *Egypt* (1993) 199–207.

[47] Such returns usually survive by being excerpted in later documents.

[48] A good portion of this family's archive survives; for a complete stemma, see *P.Mich.* III p. 180.

[49] 145-Ar-8, which is incompletely preserved, may record the subsequent marriage of one of the daughters.

131-Pr-1, probably from a village in the Prosopite nome, is a *frérèche* of four brothers ranging in age from 47 to 38; each is married with children, and the entire household contains sixteen persons. The second brother, aged 45, has a wife (whose age is not entered), their daughter 10, and son 6.[50] In the next return (145-Pr-1), either the *frérèche* has broken up or, more probably, only this brother's family is excerpted from a larger return; in any case, his wife is now gone (probably dead), but the two children are still with him.[51]

187-Hm-1 is a conjugal family from Hermopolis: father, mother, three sons, and a daughter.[52] Twenty-eight years later, in 215-Hm-1/2, the older generation and the oldest son are gone, probably dead; the two younger sons still live together, and the youngest is married to his sister. By 229-Hm-1, only the couple are left, probably still living as husband and wife but with no declared children. Here a conjugal family has encountered difficulty reproducing itself into the next generation; so too, probably, in the sequence from 229-Ar-2 to 243-Ar-4 (Arsinoe).

Lodger families
About fifty-seven persons in the census returns are registered as *enoikoi*, "indwellers" or lodgers.[53] These are free, usually non-kin persons living with the principal family members in the household; in most cases they doubtless rented rooms. In households we reconstruct as containing lodgers, the majority (14 of 20) have only one to three; but two households have as many as nine (33-Ar-1; 103-Ar-1). On some occasions, at least distant kinship links lodgers to the principal family.[54]

Lodgers seem frequently to lack kin with whom they might live; for example, seven are freedpersons who, especially in villages, probably often remained within the households of their former masters when unable to

[50] In the petition excerpting this return, the daughter is described as *apator*, the mother's child before her marriage; but the return registers her as legitimate. See the Discussion.

[51] A likelier example of household fission is 201-Ox-1 from Oxyrhynchos, where the declarant registers two slaves belonging to him, his non-resident brothers, and others.

[52] This still unpublished return derives from the archive of Theognostos; P. J. Sijpesteijn, "Theognostos" (1989), reconstructs the family's history, but additional *P.Lond.* documents await examination. The sister in 215-Hm-1/2 and 229-Hm-1 may not be the same as the daughter in 187-Hm-1; see Chapter 2, Section 3 above.

[53] The number is not exact; lodger-status is often determined from position in the return and lack of kin relationship to the principal family. In the Catalogue, they are "free non-kin"; but the Cambridge typology characterizes them as "lodgers."

[54] So in 159-Ar-6 (possibly); 187-Ar-4 (free non-kin 4 and 5 are brothers of a wife in the principal family; 6 and 7 may be distant relations, to judge from their names); 243-Ar-3 (declarant's kin by marriage). The oddest case is 117-Ar-3, where a freeborn non-kin woman is the "wife" of one of the declarant's slaves, with several children; this family is discussed in Chapter 7, Section 4.

form families of their own.[55] Kinship among lodgers is poorly reported and hence difficult to reconstruct; but in about eleven cases families can be made out. As would be anticipated, lodger families are usually small and simple by Egyptian standards: either co-resident siblings or conjugal families.[56] The exception is 33-Ar-1 from Arsinoe, where eight lodgers appear to form a *frérèche*, though this may be an independent household.

3. Metropoleis and villages

The household structure of Roman Egypt, as derived from the census returns, is misleading if no account is taken of the large differences between metropoleis and villages. As Table 3.1 shows, in the census population about 58 percent of principal family members, and 55 percent of all persons, live in complex households with extended or multiple families. But these figures undoubtedly understate the true proportions.

Household structures

As Table 3.2 (p. 67) demonstrates, in metropoleis the preponderance of census households are of simple form: solitaries, co-resident siblings, or conjugal families; less than a quarter of households have extended or multiple families, although some, such as 187-Ar-4 discussed above, are extremely large. By contrast, better than two-fifths of village households have complex principal families. This difference in household structures between metropoleis and villages is statistically significant.[57]

Further, since complex households are usually larger than simple ones (see below), metropoleis and villages also differ sharply in the proportion of family members who reside in complex households. In metropoleis, considerably less than half do so; but in villages the proportion is nearly two-thirds.

---

[55] 117-Ap-8 (two); 145-Ox-3; 173-Ar-9; 187-An-2; 215-He-1 (freedwoman of a male lodger aged 80); 215-He-3; 243-Ox-1 ("slave" 3). See also 145-Ly-1, an 8-year-old girl who is probably an orphan; and 215-He-1, an 80-year-old male lodger (the oldest person in the returns, but his age is obviously rounded).

[56] Co-resident siblings: 145-Ar-5; 187-Ar-4 (*bis*). Conjugal families: 103-Ar-1 (*bis*); 117-Ar-3 and 8; 159-Hm-2; 187-Ar-4; 243-Ar-3.

[57] If simple households (types 1–3) are compared with complex ones (4–5) for metropoleis and villages, chi-square is 4.301 with one degree of freedom (using Yates's correction for continuity); there is less than one chance in twenty that metropolitan and village household structures were identical. As S. Ruggles, *Connections* (1987), shows, the incidence of multiple families in Egyptian villages approached the maximum possible under conditions of utmost extension.

Table 3.2. *Household structure in metropoleis and villages*

Types:	% of households: Metrop.	Villages	% of family members: Metrop.	Villages
1. Solitary	16.7	15.8	4.1	3.5
2. No family	5.6	4.2	2.7	2.4
3. Conjugal family	51.4	36.8	47.4	27.4
4. Extended family	11.1	17.9	13.1	17.0
5. Multiple families	15.3	25.3	32.6	49.8
Number:	72	95	291	424

Complex households obviously played a much larger role in the Egyptian countryside than in the more urbanized metropoleis.[58] But since villages are underrepresented in surviving returns (as was shown in Section 1 above), the impression left by the extant census returns needs correction. It is likely that, in Egypt as a whole, at least three-fifths of principal family members lived in complex households. Further, since smaller and simpler households are likelier to be well preserved in the returns, even this estimate is doubtless too conservative.

Size of families and households
The average size of principal resident families in the complete or nearly complete census returns is 4.3 persons (167 returns).[59] Because complex

[58] This point needs to be kept in mind when evaluating modern arguments in favor of "nuclear households" in Roman antiquity. Virtually all evidence invoked has a strong urban bias; see S. Dixon, *Family* (1992) 1–11, with bibliography, esp. R. P. Saller and B. D. Shaw, "Tombstones and Roman Family Relations in the Principate," *JRS* 74 (1984) 124–156 (who expressly note this urban bias: p. 145).

[59] Average size is still smaller, only 4.0, if just complete returns are used (136 families). This strange effect, which holds true uniformly in the statistics given below, results from the increasing likelihood that households will be incomplete when more persons are declared; for this reason, we use the nearly complete returns also, but recognize that the figures we give probably understate actual family size. Earlier estimates of Egyptian household size—e.g., M. Hombert and C. Préaux, *Recherches* (1952) 154–155 (5.8 persons); K. Hopkins, "Brother-Sister" (1980) 329 (5.1)—apparently include slaves and lodgers along with families, but are still a bit high (see below). Looking at complete houses (rather than households), D. W. Hobson, "House and Household" (1985), obtains an average of 7.3 persons in Egyptian villages.

households are so common in Roman Egypt, this figure may well seem smaller than anticipated, but it is in fact consistent with most data on populations that have large numbers of extended and multiple families.[60] Demographic simulations have repeatedly shown that in a high-mortality population, even if maximum extension is practiced, average family size is unlikely to exceed about five persons.[61] Since the survival rate for returns favors smaller families, a figure somewhere between 4.3 and 5.0 is not unlikely.

Again, however, a coarse average derived directly from surviving returns is misleading in that it conceals important differences between metropoleis and villages. The size of known families and households is summarized in Table 3.3, where "families" are only principal family members while "households" include lodgers and slaves as well. As this table shows, families are on average somewhat larger in villages than in metropoleis, although with considerable variance by household type; the overall village advantage derives chiefly from the larger proportion of complex households with extended or multiple families (Table 3.2). If village returns are accorded double weight, the average attested size of Egyptian families is about 4.4 persons.

Table 3.3. *Average size of families and households*

Types	Av. size of families		Av. size of households	
	Metrop.	Villages	Metrop.	Villages
1. Solitary	1.00	1.00	2.08	1.67
2. No family	2.00	2.50	3.50	3.00
3. Conjugal family	3.73	3.31	4.86	3.43
4. Extended family	4.75	4.24	6.13	4.47
5. Multiple families	8.64	8.79	10.36	9.38
All household types	4.04	4.46	5.31	4.82
Number of persons:	291	424	382	458

[60] Compare, e.g., D. Herlihy and C. Klapisch-Zuber, *Tuscans* (1985) 282–290: average size of Tuscan households in 1427 is 4.42 persons. The "myth" of large pre-modern families has often been demolished; e.g., M. Mitterauer and R. Sieder, *The European Family* (trans. K. Oosterveen and M. Hörzinger; 1982) 24–47.

[61] A. J. Coale, "Estimates of Average Size of Household," in *Aspects of the Analysis of Family Structure* (ed. M. Levy; 1965) 64–69; T. K. Burch, in *Household and Family* (1972) 91–102.

When lodgers and slaves are added in, however, it is the metropoleis that have the advantage, not only in the overall average but in each household type. Only the discrepancy in proportion of various household types prevents the difference in overall average household size from being larger.

Owners, renters, and lodgers

Census returns also regularly indicate ownership of the house in which the principal family resides; from this information it is possible to determine the relative incidence of house ownership against renting in the metropoleis and the villages.[62] Renting is common in the returns; just under a sixth of families reside in houses, or parts of houses, that they do not own (27 of 167). However, as would be anticipated, the incidence of renting is far higher in metropoleis than in villages.[63]

If house ownership is taken as at least a crude indicator of relative household wealth, it deserves note that as household size increases, the incidence of renting declines in both villages and metropoleis. In villages, 11 percent of households with four or fewer members are renters (6 of 56), but no household with five or more members (38 examples). In metropoleis, 34 percent of households with four or fewer members rent their dwelling (12 of 35), as against 24 percent of those with five or more members (9 of 37). The returns have only one certain case where a household with eight or more members is renting: 145-Ar-9 from Arsinoe, with fifteen members (including eight slaves).

This pattern is also striking when simple household forms are compared with complex forms. In the metropoleis, the incidence of renting is about the same for simple as for complex households (30 as against 27 percent). By contrast, in villages all renters live in simple households (11 percent), none in complex households.

Although house ownership is doubtless a reasonably good sign of relative wealth, it may function somewhat differently in metropoleis and villages. For villagers, large families usually signified wealth in direct fashion.[64] By contrast, in metropoleis, and particularly in fairly large cities like Arsinoe, the advantages of large families (typically, a broader and more reliable

---

[62] Doubtful cases have been called in favor of ownership, so the figures below are minimums. We have treated all non-owning families as renters, although, of course, some may be guests.

[63] Metropoleis: 21 of 72 (29.2 percent); villages: 6 of 95 (6.3 percent). The difference is significant at a 99.9 percent confidence level (chi-square test). O. Montevecchi, "Ricerche di sociologia nei documenti dell' Egitto greco-romano III. I contratti di compravendita," *Aegyptus* 21 (1941) 93–151, at 104–105, notes the low price of village houses in Egypt; see also D. W. Hobson, "House and Household" (1985) 224–225, on the infrequency of rental in villages.

[64] See J. Goody, in *Household and Family* (1972) 121–22. Compare D. Herlihy and C. Klapisch-Zuber, *Tuscans* (1985) 282–290, on late medieval Tuscany.

labor pool) appear to have been offset by higher costs of living, above all by the higher cost of housing. But it should not be inferred that metropolitans were on average less wealthy than villagers; the opposite is far likelier to have been true.[65]

Further indication of the disparity between metropoleis and villages comes from the presence in households of non-kin lodgers, who presumably often paid rent.[66] Our Catalogue lists twenty households that contain such lodgers, of which more than two-thirds are metropolitan (14 of 20). Likewise, the average number of lodgers in households that have them is much higher in metropoleis (3.6) than in villages (1.2).[67] Finally, although it is probable that lodgers were generally poor, a lodger family in 159-Hm-2 from Hermopolis has four slaves.[68]

Slaveholding

Slaves constitute about 11 percent of the census population (118 of 1084).[69] In census returns with complete or nearly complete principal families, slightly under a sixth of households register slaves (26 of 167, or 16 percent). This proportion is approximately the same in both simple households (17 of 107, or 16 percent) and complex households (9 of 60, or 15 percent).[70] To the extent that slaveholding reflects relative household wealth,[71] it initially appears uncorrelated with household complexity.

[65] As we observed in Chapter 2 (at note 58), adult males registered as lacking a profession (*atechnos* or *idiotes*), and hence probably living on accumulated wealth, are concentrated in metropoleis. Compare, e.g., D. Herlihy and C. Klapisch-Zuber, *Tuscans* (1985) 95: "Florence in 1427 included only 14 percent of the total lay population, but it claimed two-thirds of the region's wealth." Average household wealth was also immensely higher in Florence than elsewhere in Tuscany, though very maldistributed (pp. 97–105).

[66] Statistics on such lodgers are, however, not very reliable, since the returns often make their detection difficult.

[67] Half of the metropolitan households with lodgers have more than three; no village household has more than two, and the majority of village lodgers are freed slaves. See also Chapter 8.

[68] Compare, possibly, 145-Ar-9: at least four slaves belong to "family member" 7; his relation to the rest of the principal family is uncertain, and he may be a lodger.

[69] In villages, slaves are 8.5 percent (46 of 544); in metropoleis, 13.4 percent (72 of 537). The difference is significant at a 98 percent confidence level (chi-square = 6.473; Yates's correction). On slavery in Roman Egypt, see J. A. Straus, "L'Esclavage" (1988), and I. Biezunska-Malowist, in *Egitto* (1989) 261–270, both with further bibliography. Slaves are also uncommon on large rural estates (from which no census returns survive): D. Rathbone, *Rationalism* (1991) 89–91, 106–107.

[70] K. Hopkins, "Brother-Sister" (1980) 330–331, produced figures to show that the incidence of slaveholding drops as households become more complex. We were unable to duplicate this result, which relied on a sample about a third smaller than ours (116 households). Our figures on households with slaves are minimums; some lists break off before reaching slaves (e.g., 61-Ar-1).

[71] In Chapter 2 at notes 60–63, we suggest that slaveholding may be an accurate measure of household wealth.

However, once again villages differ from metropoleis. For complete or nearly complete households, the overall incidence of slaveholding is a good deal higher in metropoleis (15 of 72 households, or 21 percent) than in villages (11 of 95, or 12 percent); there are about four chances in five that this difference is significant.[72] But in villages, 15 percent of complex households register slaves (6 of 41), as against 11 percent of simple households (6 of 54); since complex village households were probably wealthier than simple ones, the difference may be important, although the numbers are far too small for confidence. By contrast, metropolitan complex households are slightly less likely to have slaves (3 of 19, or 16 percent) than simple households (11 of 53, or 21 percent): again, this result would cohere with the pattern of renting described above.

In sum, it is not unlikely that, at least in villages, household wealth, size, and complexity, and the incidence of slaveholding were all positively correlated with one another, as one would anticipate; but granted the paucity of surviving evidence, this inference is not certain. The metropolitan situation is less straightforward; there the dynamics of urban life may have favored smaller and simpler households, which accordingly become more common than in villages. In any case, most households in both metropoleis and villages have only one or two slaves, and few have more than six or seven.

As we noted in Chapter 2 (at notes 60–63), the slaves declared in returns were for the most part probably domestic servants rather than workers.[73] This is clear in a number of ways: only one male slave has a declared occupation (117-Ar-3, a weaver); the sex ratio among slaves is heavily unbalanced in favor of females; and male slaves are apparently often manumitted quite early, while still capable of productive labor. As Table D shows, the oldest male slave is 32, but females often remain slaves into their 40s, until they could no longer bear children. The youngest freed males are 0 (243-Ox-1) and 19 (145-Ox-3); the youngest freed female is aged 22 and married (159-Ar-1, see 173-Ar-3), but the next youngest are 35 and 36 (117-Ap-8).[74] All this implies that ownership of slaves was associated more with consumption than production.

---

[72] Chi-square is 2.011 with one degree of freedom (using Yates's correction). See also note 69 above.

[73] On employment of Egyptian slaves, I. Biezunska-Malowist, *L'Esclavage* II (1977) 73–108, esp. 107; J. A. Straus, "L'Esclavage" (1988) 867–868.

[74] See also 187-Me-1: a freedwoman bears an *apator* daughter at age 25. Female freedpersons only narrowly predominate over males (five to four), but information on freed status may often be lost. The only slave older than 50 is a female runaway, aged 68, in 187-Ar-30. On manumission, see J. A. Straus, "L'Esclavage" (1988) 897–898.

Occupations

Declarants were not required to estimate household wealth, and the census returns are also of no direct help in determining the possible origins of wealth.[75] However, in about seventy cases declarants state occupations for themselves and other household members.[76] Occupations are given only for adult males, never for females, doubtless indicating that adult males were the main source of wage income in most households; this accords with the presumption underlying the poll tax, exacted only from males aged 14 up to 62.[77] Males obviously began work early; eight with listed occupations are still in their 'teens, though none younger than 15.[78] Some may have continued working even beyond the age of tax liability.[79]

Surviving returns give occupations for only about 15 percent of adult males, so that inference about patterns of employment is perilous. Further, only twenty-one village occupations are preserved. As would be expected, most villagers are described as farmers; but the returns also produce a doctor, a scribe, a mason, a quarry worker, and a family of four *nekrotaphoi* (probably mummy-makers).[80]

Metropolitan occupations are more diverse, as would be expected.[81] Agriculture, though still found even at Arsinoe, is infrequent. Clothmaking is more salient as a source of employment; sixteen persons produce or process cloth.[82] Other occupations are attested more fitfully: the military (two

[75]On the economy of Roman Egypt, see A. Gara, "Aspetti di economia monetaria dell'Egitto romano," *ANRW* II.10.1 (1988) 912–951, with bibliography: still basically a "peasant economy," but (under Roman influence) with increasing importance of private property and the market; also A. K. Bowman, *Egypt* (1986) 90–120; D. W. Rathbone, "The Ancient Economy and Graeco-Roman Egypt," in *Egitto* (1989) 159–176.

[76]The returns also frequently give indicators of status, especially priesthoods. As is observed in Chapter 1, status or occupation often affected tax rates; but local census takers evidently varied in inquiring about occupations.

[77]Of course, some women may have worked outside the home; but presumably they did not do so as a rule.

[78]117-Ap-7 (doctor aged 17; see 89-Hm-1); 131-Ox-11 (weaver, 17); 187-Ar-4 (goldsmith, 19), 7 (workman, 17), 8 (scribe, 17), 22 (woolcarder, 18), and 37 (workman, 19); 243-Ar-3 (linenweaver, 16). Boys aged 9 and 12 in school: 215-He-1. On child labor, K. R. Bradley, *Family* (1991) 103–124, esp. 107–108.

[79]Four cases in the census returns: 117-Ap-7 (scribe aged 70); 117-Ox-2 (stonecutter, 74); 173-Me-3 (*nekrotaphos*, 75); 187-Ar-8 (farmer, 68). But these may be former occupations.

[80]Farmers: 117-Ap-4 and 6 (*bis*); 131-He-3; 145-Ar-19. Public farmers: 11-Ar-1; 89-Ar-1; 103-Ar-8; 117-Ar-4; 131-Ar-10 (*bis*); 159-Ar-21 and 22. Doctor and scribe: 117-Ap-7. Mason: 61-Ar-1. Quarry worker (*metallikos*): 131-Pr-1. *Nekrotaphoi*: 173-Me-3 (four). Compare the village occupations in *P.Lond.* II 257 (from Philadelphia): mostly farmers and weavers, but also, e.g., a barber.

[81]On the urban economy, R. S. Bagnall, *Egypt* (1993) 78–92.

[82]Farmers: 187-Ar-8 (three), 18, and 33. Weavers: 117-Ar-3 (slave); 131-Ox-7 (*bis*) and 11; 187-Ar-4 (*bis*?); 201-Ar-6. Linenweavers: 187-Ar-16; 243-Ar-2 and 3 (*bis*). Woolcarder: 187-Ar-22. Woolwasher: 187-Ar-11. Fullers (*rhabdistai*, "cloth-beaters"): 187-Ar-4 (*bis*). Tailor (?): 159-Ar-6.

veterans); professionals (a doctor, a scribe); light manufacture (two gold-smiths, a ropemaker, a locksmith); construction (four stonecutters and a *torneutes*, apparently a lathe operator); commerce and transport (a wine-seller; two donkey-drivers); service (a gardener); and six men described simply as "workers," *ergatai*, evidently unskilled laborers.[83]

Adult males in larger households often pursue the same occupation. Examples are 117-Ox-4 (four stonecutters), 131-Ox-7 (two weavers), 173-Me-3 (four *nekrotaphoi*), and 187-Ar-3 (two linenweavers). Such "inher-ited" professions are not uncommon in premodern societies; the household is conceived as a single economic unit, with sons succeeding to their fathers.[84] But some households pursue a more diversified strategy. The clearest case is the sprawling household in 187-Ar-4 from Arsinoe; it con-tains two weavers, two goldsmiths, two "cloth-beaters" (*rhabdistai*), two laborers, a donkey-driver, and a gardener. Here the household aims for diversity of occupation, which shields it to some extent from economic change. In any event, this and other census returns make clear that on occa-sion sons did pursue different occupations from their fathers.[85]

Whatever their strategy, such large households were better insulated against the threat of mortality than were, for instance, conjugal families with only one wage-earning male. An example of the latter is 61-Ar-1 from Kerkesis: a mason aged 52, his wife 30, their daughter 11, and sons 3 and 1. For this family, the risk was substantial that the householder would die before his sons reached majority and were able to support themselves.[86] Indeed, the returns report nine households in which previously married women live alone with minor children.[87]

---

[83] Veterans: 159-Ar-6 (*bis*; one apparently discharged before end of service). Doctor: 89-Hm-1. Scribe: 187-Ar-8. Goldsmiths: 187-Ar-4 (*bis*). Ropemaker: 187-Ar-10. Locksmith: 201-Ar-10. Stonecutters: 117-Ox-2 (four). *Torneutes*: 89-Hm-1. Wineseller: 201-Ar-5 (agent of the dwelling's owner). Donkey-drivers: 187-Ar-4 and 22. Gardener: 187-Ar-4. *Ergatai*: 103-Ar-11; 187-Ar-4 (*bis*), 6 (?), 7, and 37.

[84] This issue is discussed by many essays in *Family Forms* (1983). Since the sample is so small, we have not pursued the relationship between household size and occupational status.

[85] E.g., 187-Ar-8 from Arsinoe: a farmer aged 68 has three sons, of whom two are farmers and one is a scribe. Less difficult is change of profession: in 117-Ap-7, the father is a scribe, his son a doctor. In 89-Hm-1, one son is a doctor, another a lathe operator.

[86] Table 5.3 indicates at least one chance in three that the mason would die within ten years. This problem could also arise in complex households; e.g., 201-Ar-10, a locksmith aged 33 apparently supporting five other family members and two slaves.

[87] These households are listed in Chapter 6, note 55. Compare A. K. Bowman, *Egypt* (1986) 98: "In a society where life expectancy was short, the loss of the working capacity of the adult male might be catastrophic if it could not easily be compensated for by grown sons." Bowman gives as an example the Soterichos archive; see R. S. Bagnall, "Theadelphian Archives," *BASP* 17 (1980) 97–104.

In this and other respects, as we shall see, the economic vitality of Egyptian households was intricately bound up with many aspects of its demographic regime: prevailing mortality and fertility rates, patterns of nuptiality and family formation, and even migration.

4

Female life expectancy

The Egyptian census returns preserve reported ages for 337 women. These ages are collected in Table A, which lists females resident in villages and nome metropoleis, and the total for each age. Table 4.1, derived from Table A, groups the same females into five-year age groups.

Table 4.1. *Grouped ages for Egyptian females*

Age	Vill.	Met.	Total	Smoothed	Weighted
0–4	28	8	36	36.00	42.67
5–9	18	18	36	36.71	37.62
10–14	24	14	38	37.14	38.32
15–19	21	11	32	37.71	38.50
20–24	15	20	35	32.57	31.17
25–29	13	17	30	28.29	26.93
30–34	18	6	24	27.86	29.05
35–39	22	9	31	26.71	28.25
40–44	9	9	18	18.29	18.76
45–49	11	3	14	14.29	15.11
50–54	13	5	18	16.00	16.97
55–59	4	2	6	11.43	12.51
60–64	6	1	7	5.57	6.15
65–69	3	1	4	4.43	4.78
70–74	5	2	7	5.43	5.92
75–79	1	0	1	1.29	1.47
All ages	211	126	337	339.71	354.18

Even casual inspection of Table 4.1[1] indicates that Egyptian females were subject to heavy mortality. For ages 0 to 24, there are an average of more than 35 females in each five-year age group. By contrast, for ages 55 to 79, this average drops to only five females in each age group. Although the figures in Table 4.1 display many statistical inconsistencies, it appears that only a small proportion of Egyptian females—perhaps as little as a fifth—survived from their teens to their sixties.[2]

To what level of mortality do the figures in Table 4.1 correspond? This chapter attempts to determine this at least approximately. But we begin with a more theoretical introduction to our working methods.

1. Life tables and stable populations

Life tables were introduced above in Section 1 of Chapter 2, where we discussed the Coale-Demeny Model West, Level 2, for females. Table 4.2 (p. 77) reintroduces that model, but with three additional columns of interconnected figures.[3] As will be recalled, $q(x)$ is the probability that females of exact age x (that is, on their birthday x) will die before their next indicated birthday, usually within five years; $l(x)$ gives the number of survivors to exact age x from a theoretical "cohort" of 100,000 newborn females; and $e(x)$ represents the average life expectancy of females aged exactly x.

How is life expectancy calculated? The first step is to estimate the number of person-years that the cohort members are likely to live between exact age x and the next birthday indicated in Table 4.2 (usually, five years). This figure, $L(x)$, is calculated in the following way.[4] Take for example the interval from age 20 up to 25. As the figures for $l(x)$ indicate, at age 20 there are 41,899 survivors from the original cohort of 100,000; at age 25, only 38,386 survivors. All those surviving from age 20 to 25 obviously live 5 years each during this age interval; but those who die in the interval also live a certain number of years. During much of adult life, mortality rises so slowly as to remain almost constant; we may therefore initially assume that women dying between ages 20 and 25 live an average of 2.5 years in this interval. On this assumption, the value of $L(20)$ is approxi-

---

[1] The "smoothed" and the "weighted" figures in Table 4.1 are used below in Sections 2 and 3, where their purpose is explained. Despite a large increase in data, female age distribution is virtually unchanged since M. Hombert and C. Préaux, *Recherches* (1952) 159 (247 attested females); compare K. Hopkins, "Brother-Sister" (1980) 317 (270 females). However, some statistical anomalies have eased. The same is true also for male age distribution (see Chapter 5).

[2] In modern more developed countries, about 90 percent of women survive from 10 to 60.

[3] A. J. Coale and P. Demeny, *Model Life* (1983) 42. On life table functions, see, e.g., C. Newell, *Methods* (1988) 63–79.

[4] For calculation of $L(x)$ in the models, see A. J. Coale and P. Demeny, *Life Tables* (1983) 20, 22–24; also, more generally, C. Newell, *Methods* (1988) 74–77.

mated by adding $l(20)$ and $l(25)$, and then multiplying the result by 2.5. The result is 200,713 person-years lived by the cohort members.

The model life table, however, gives a slightly higher figure for $L(20)$: 201,066. This is because Coale and Demeny take into account that mortality will not in fact remain constant during this age interval: women aged 20 will have fractionally lower mortality than women aged 21, and so on. As a result, women who die in the age interval will actually live a bit more than an average of 2.5 years. Coale and Demeny use more complex formulas for periods of life when mortality rates are swiftly changing: both in the years immediately after birth when mortality rates fall sharply, and in old age when they rise swiftly.

Table 4.2. *Model West, Level 2, females*

Age	$q(x)$	$l(x)$	$m(x)$	$L(x)$	$T(x)$	$e(x)$
0	0.33399	100,000	0.42661	78,290	2,250,000	22.500
1	0.23760	66,601	0.07044	224,642	2,171,710	32.608
5	0.06657	50,776	0.01382	244,586	1,947,068	38.346
10	0.05205	47,396	0.01068	231,061	1,702,481	35.920
15	0.06744	44,930	0.01394	217,375	1,471,420	32.750
20	0.08385	41,899	0.01747	201,066	1,254,045	29.930
25	0.09369	38,386	0.01962	183,300	1,052,979	27.431
30	0.10558	34,790	0.02224	165,133	869,680	24.998
35	0.11511	31,117	0.02437	146,987	704,546	22.642
40	0.12227	27,535	0.02598	129,594	557,559	20.249
45	0.12967	24,168	0.02766	113,319	427,965	17.708
50	0.16518	21,034	0.03588	96,832	314,646	14.959
55	0.20571	17,560	0.04565	79,129	217,814	12.404
60	0.29144	13,947	0.06777	59,982	138,684	9.943
65	0.37188	9,833	0.09033	40,609	78,703	7.964
70	0.49858	6,214	0.13109	23,636	38,093	6.130
75	0.63720	3,116	0.18703	10,616	14,458	4.640
80	0.75601	1,130	0.26948	3,172	3,841	3.398
85	0.87919	276	0.39559	613	670	2.429
90	0.95785	33	0.57740	55	57	1.709
95	1.00000	1	0.84237	2	2	1.187

Calculating $L(x)$ is the crucial step in determining life expectancy. The column labelled $T(x)$ simply sums the $L(x)$ column from the bottom up; it thus represents the number of person-years that all cohort survivors aged exactly x will live until all of them are dead. Thus, in the model, the 41,899 cohort survivors to age 20 will live a total of 1,254,045 years between them before they all are dead.

The final column, $e(x)$, expresses average life expectancy at age x. It is obtained by dividing $l(x)$ into $T(x)$; that is, the number of cohort survivors to age x is divided into the total number of person-years that these survivors will live during the remainder of their lives. In Table 4.2, life expectancy for females on their twentieth birthday, $e(20)$, is 41,899 divided into 1,254,045, or 29.9 years.[5]

Life expectancy figures, and particularly life expectancy at birth, are of interest because each of them is dependent on mortality rates during the entire remainder of life. Life expectancy at birth, $e(0)$, thus expresses in highly compressed form the complete mortality experience of a population, from the birth of a representative cohort through to the death of its last surviving member.[6] For this reason, life expectancy at birth is a normal indicator of development and social welfare in populations.[7]

Stable populations
The preceding description of a life table rests on an essentially static view of a population: a cohort of 100,000 persons is born at the same instant and then gradually dies, at given mortality rates, until no one is left. On this view, $l(x)$ is the number of these newborns still alive at exact age x.

There is, however, a far more dynamic way to look at a life table.[8] In this alternative view, it is assumed that the 100,000 children are born at a constant rate during a given calendar year, and that this birth pattern continues for a long period of time; these newborn children subsequently die at a rate expressed by $q(x)$. On this dynamic interpretation of the life table, $l(x)$ has a different meaning: it represents the number of persons who cele-

---

[5] The remaining column of figures, $m(x)$, is the central death rate in the life table population (number of deaths per person-years lived) between age x and the next indicated birthday. It is obtained by subtracting $l(x)$ from $l(x+n)$, and dividing the result by $L(x)$.

[6] A life table is usually derived from current death rates; it indicates a population's mortality experience under current conditions of mortality. Hence it is not a prediction about particular individuals, and it does not take into account possible future changes in mortality. This is important mainly for populations that are undergoing rapid changes in death rates, as modern populations are.

[7] See, e.g., A. Sen, "The Standard of Living," in *The Tanner Lectures on Human Values* 7 (1986) 3–51, at 45–48; United Nations Development Programme, *Human Development Report* (1990) 9–16, and (1993) 100–114 (the Human Development Index).

[8] C. Newell, *Methods* (1988) 78–79.

brate their x birthday during any calendar year; and $L(x)$ is the number of persons whose current age is from x up to the next indicated age.

The total number of persons in this theoretical population is therefore expressed by $T(0)$.[9] The fraction of all living persons whose current age is between x and the next indicated age can be obtained by dividing $L(x)$ by $T(0)$; thus, for instance, in Table 4.2 the proportion of females aged 20 to 24 is 201,066 divided by 2.25 million, or 0.089. About 9 percent of all females are aged 20 to 24.

On this interpretation, what a life table portrays is a "stationary" population under particular conditions of mortality. The population is stationary because it has a given and unvarying birth rate, and a set of probabilities of death, $q(x)$, that result in an overall death rate identical to the birth rate; therefore the population neither grows nor falls, and its age structure also remains unchanging. Further, the stationary population's annual birth and death rates are easily calculated: they are the inverse of $e(0)$, or 44.4 births and deaths per thousand persons in Table 4.2.[10]

But it is also possible to go a step further, and to ask what the age structure of the population would be if it were not stationary, but instead growing or declining at a constant intrinsic annual rate r. Such a population is defined as "stable" because, like a stationary population, it has constant birth, death, and growth rates, and a constant age structure; a stationary population is in fact just a special case of a stable population, one in which the growth rate is zero. However, unlike a stationary population, a growing or declining stable population does not have equal birth and death rates. The difference between its birth and death rates is the pace at which the stable population is intrinsically growing or declining.[11]

Obviously, no historical population has ever been entirely stable, much less stationary. But in recent decades, stable populations have assumed increasing importance in studying the demography of less developed nations with imperfect records. The reason is that "the stable age distribution is often closely appproximated under the demographic conditions found in many underdeveloped areas."[12] Therefore stable age distributions

---

[9] $T(0)$ can be reset to any number. If $l(x)$, $L(T)$, and (x) are then appropriately rescaled so that the $q(x)$ and $e(x)$ values remain unchanged, the number of persons of a given age in a stationary population of any given size can then be estimated. See Chapter 5, Section 4.

[10] On this calculation, C. Newell, *Demography* (1988) 77, 120–121.

[11] C. Newell, *Methods* (1988) 123–126, describes how to calculate age distribution of a stable population from a life table. A stable population is not necessarily homogeneous: sectors of it may have higher or lower mortality than the population as a whole. Only the population as a whole is described as stable.

[12] A. J. Coale and P. Demeny, *Life Tables* (1983) 3–8, at 8. The theory, first formulated by A. J. Lotka in 1907, received its modern form through J. Bourgeois-Pichat, *The Concept of a Stable Population* (1966), and esp. A. J. Coale, *The Growth and Structure of Human Populations* (1972). See C. Newell, *Methods* (1988) 120–127; also United Nations, *Manual X* (1983) 21–22; N. Keyfitz, *Demography* (1985) 77–111. For a critique, see W. Brass, *Methods for Estimating Fertility and Mortality from Limited or Defective Data*

are often used to analyze and correct imperfect empirical statistics. Coale and Demeny give age distributions of stable populations associated with their model life tables at various growth rates and levels of fertility.[13]

Even under constant conditions of mortality, a population's intrinsic growth rate has a large impact on its age structure. This is illustrated in Figure 4.1, which plots the age structure of various stable populations associated with Model West, Level 2, Females. For instance, in a stable population with a 2 percent annual growth rate ($r = 2.0$), the total population doubles every 35 years.[14] Because of its high birth rate, young persons are proportionately much more numerous than in populations with lower growth rates. The average age is accordingly much lower: for Model West, Level 2, 20.0 in a rapidly growing stable population ($r = 2.0$), as against 26.4 in a stationary population ($r =$ zero). By contrast, in a stable population with negative growth rate ($r = -1.0$), females have an average age of 30.2 years.

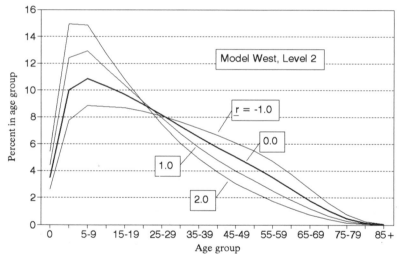

Figure 4.1. *Age distribution of females at various growth rates*

(1975) 85–87; also S. S. Halli and K. Vaninadha Rao, *Advanced Techniques of Population Analysis* (1992), esp. 30–36, with further bibliography.

[13]E.g., for Model West, Level 2, Females, at A. J. Coale and P. Demeny, *Life Tables* (1983) 56 and 81; these numbers are used for Figure 4.1. Coale and Demeny also give average ages in these stable populations.

[14]The doubling time for a stable population is 69.3 divided by the intrinsic growth rate expressed as a percent: C. Newell, *Methods* (1988) 126–127. Thus, a growth rate of 2.0 doubles the population in 34.7 years.

As Coale and Demeny showed for the Indian census of 1911,[15] even when census data are badly askew the age distributions in stable model populations can be used to reconstruct the probably prevailing mortality for historical populations, provided that two conditions are satisfied: first, the historical age distribution is at least approximately known; and second, the population's growth rate is also known. For Roman Egypt, the first condition is met in the case of females. The second condition is not met, though our remarks on population in Chapter 3, Section 1, imply that Egypt's long-term intrinsic growth rate was probably not far from zero.

2. The female age structure

What we seek to determine is the approximate level of female mortality in Roman Egypt during the early Empire.[16] During this long period of time, no evidence indicates that the Egyptian population (and more specifically the population in the areas from which the census returns chiefly derive) grew or declined by any very large amount.[17] We may thus start from a provisional hypothesis that the Egyptian population was close to stationary, with at most a tiny growth rate. In this respect it would resemble most premodern populations.[18]

In examining the female age structure of Roman Egypt, we have looked only at women aged 5 and above; the reason is that, as Table 4.1 shows, young girls are obviously underregistered particularly in the metropoleis.[19]

[15] A. J. Coale and P. Demeny, *Life Tables* (1983) 32–33. The Indian census statistics were marked by "extreme age heaping and other indications of faulty data," plus signs "that persons in some age intervals [were] subject to exceptional underenumeration"; these problems were much more severe than for the Egyptian census returns. United Nations, *Manual X* (1983) 156–177, describes in more detail the procedure whereby an age distribution is fitted to a stable population.

[16] Prior estimates of mortality in Roman Egypt have lacked a solid demographic foundation. E.g., on studies such as M. Hombert and C. Préaux, "Note sur la durée de la vie dans l'Egypte gréco-romaine," *Chronique d'Égypte* 31 (1945) 139–146 (using mummy labels), see T. G. Parkin, *Demography* (1992) 5–19; on A. E. Samuel *et al.*, *Death and Taxes: Ostraka in the Royal Ontario Museum* I (1971) 25–47 (using ostraka), see Parkin, pp. 22–27. M. Hombert and C. Préaux, *Recherches* (1952) 156–157, gave average ages but did not estimate life expectancy from the census returns (against Parkin, p. 20).

[17] See Chapter 3 at notes 15–16. We there conjecture a population of 4.5 million, plus or minus 10 percent; and a normal actual growth rate on the order of 0.1 per year.

[18] Mortality rates cannot be derived directly from the age distribution of a living population, as K. Hopkins, "Brother-Sister" (1980) 318–320, tries to do; even in a stationary population, this confuses $L(x)$ with $l(x)$, resulting in large error both for the very young and the elderly.

[19] "Undercutting" of the age pyramid is common in pre-modern census returns. A part of the underrepresentation results from the failure to register newborns who die in their first year; however, even when this is taken account of, the Egyptian figures are still unaccountably low. Why female infants should be especially underregistered particularly in metropoleis is unclear, but perhaps related to their "undervaluing": P. M. Visaria, *Sex Ratio* (1971) 26–27. As we argue in Chapter 8, metropolitan underregistration of females may continue,

Also, to bring out more clearly the central tendencies of the data, we have smoothed the census statistics for females aged 5 and over by employing both seven-year moving averages of ages (the "smoothed" figures in Table 4.1), and also figures that recalculate the "smoothed" figures on the assumption that the village population was twice that of the Egyptian cities (the "weighted" figures).[20]

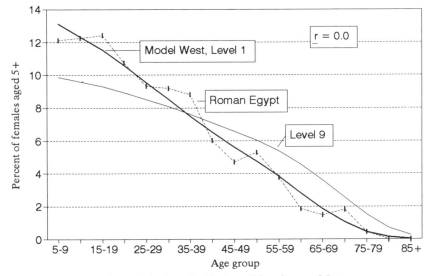

Figure 4.2. *Age distribution of females aged 5+*

Figure 4.2 shows the age distribution of stationary populations lying roughly at the outer limits of the possible for pre-modern populations: Model West, Level 1, Females, in which *e(0)* is 20.0 years; and Level 9,

---

though at a lower rate, for ages 5 to 14.

[20] For the argument supporting this assumption, see Chapter 3, Section 1. Moving averages, which reduce chance irregularity in data, are always centered on the target age; see R. Floud, *An Introduction to Quantitative Methods for Historians* (2d ed.; 1979) 117–121. D. P. Smith, *Formal Demography* (1992) 23–47, has a good discussion of data adjustment, especially for small samples. Moving averages also incidentally erase most effects of age rounding; see N. Keyfitz, *Demography* (1985) 43. For ages 0 to 4, moving averages are not used, and the figures shown are calculated directly from the data in Table A. United Nations, *Manual X* (1983) 241–247, describe some more aggressive methods for smoothing age distributions; these methods yield the same results described below.

Females, in which $e(0)$ is 40.0 years.[21] Against these, the "smoothed" but still much more jagged age distribution of Egyptian females is shown.[22] As Figure 4.2 reveals, the Egyptian age distribution lies much closer to the age distribution for a stationary population at mortality Level 1. If the Egyptian population was approximately stationary in the early Empire, then its female life expectancy at birth probably lay in the mid- to lower 20s. This is the general level within which further search is warranted.

Table 4.3. *Age distribution in stable populations*

Ratio of females aged 5–29 / 30–79 (Egypt = 1.31)

Model West Level	$e(0)$	Growth rate of stable populations					
		-1.0	-0.5	0.0	0.5	1.0	1.5
1	20.0	0.98	1.14	1.33	1.54	1.78	2.05
3	25.0	0.85	1.00	1.16	1.35	1.57	1.82
5	30.0	0.75	0.88	1.04	1.21	1.41	1.64
7	35.0	0.67	0.80	0.94	1.10	1.28	1.50
9	40.0	0.61	0.73	0.86	1.01	1.18	1.38

Dependency ratio of ages 5–14 and 60+ / 15–59 (Egypt = 0.425)

Model West Level	$e(0)$	Growth rate of stable populations					
		-1.0	-0.5	0.0	0.5	1.0	1.5
1	20.0	0.420	0.439	0.464	0.495	0.532	0.574
3	25.0	0.431	0.442	0.460	0.485	0.516	0.554
5	30.0	0.448	0.452	0.464	0.483	0.509	0.541
7	35.0	0.469	0.467	0.472	0.485	0.506	0.534
9	40.0	0.494	0.484	0.483	0.491	0.507	0.531

We may now relax our hypothesis of a stationary population, and examine, instead, stable populations at various growth rates. Table 4.3 gives

[21] A. J. Coale and P. Demeny, *Life Tables* (1983) 55, 63.
[22] The "weighted" distribution is still more erose, but does not vary significantly from the "smoothed."

two sets of figures for the age distributions of various Model West stable populations.[23] The first set is the ratio of females aged 5 to 29, to those aged 30 or more. As Table 4.3 shows, this ratio increases rapidly for each Coale-Demeny model as the intrinsic growth rate rises; but the ratio also falls from model to model at the same growth rate.

For the Egyptian "smoothed" figures, the same ratio is 1.31. To allow for possible error in this figure, in Table 4.3 all the model ratios that fall between 1.08 and 1.60 are underlined; these values are within the standard sampling error.[24] As one moves from model to model, the range of underlined values shifts gradually to the right. That is, a ratio such as the one from Egypt is consistent only with a stationary or near-stationary population in which the life expectancy of women at birth is 20.0 years, but only with an improbably rapidly rising population if female life expectancy at birth is 40.0 years.[25]

The second set of figures is the ratio of females aged 5 to 14 and 60 or more, to those aged 15 to 59.[26] Because this set of ratios compares the interrelationship of three age groups, it behaves more complexly than the first set. For the Egyptian "smoothed" figures, the same ratio is 0.425. In order to take account of possible error in this ratio, all the model ratios that fall within 0.035 of 0.425 (from 0.390 to 0.460) are underlined. The group of underlined ratios lies at or near the left and top of the stable population figures; it does not shift to the right, unlike the first set of figures.[27]

In Table 4.3, only two stable populations are common to both sets of figures: Level 1 ($e(0)$ = 20.0 years) with a growth rate of -0.5, and Level 3 ($e(0)$ = 25.0) with a growth rate of zero. This table therefore confirms the initial hypothesis that the Egyptian female population was probably near stationary, and it further indicates that Egyptian female life expectancy at birth probably lay in the lower to mid-20s. Such experiments can be repeated over and over, with various groups of ages. The results are always approximately the same.

3. The female life table

The female age structure strongly favors a female life expectancy in the lower twenties in a near stationary population. However, because "it is essential to recall that each stable age distribution is the consequence of a

---

[23]Both sets of figures derive from A. J. Coale and P. Demeny, *Life Tables* (1983) 55–63.

[24]The range of possible error is determined at a 90 percent confidence level (the z test).

[25]For the "weighted" figures, the same ratio is 1.25, a slightly lower figure that produces much the same result.

[26]The ratio here is a variant of the "Dependency Ratio," based on the likelihood that the very young and very old are probably dependent on adults.

[27]For the "weighted" figures, the same ratio is 0.434, with almost identical results.

mortality schedule and a growth rate,"[28] and the long-term growth rate in Roman Egypt is not precisely known, the most probable life expectancy for Egyptian females cannot be exactly determined. Nonetheless, some further progress is possible by using two complementary tests.

First, Kenneth Weiss has devised an "index of dissimilarity" whereby an empirical age distribution can be compared with the age distribution in a model.[29] This index sums the absolute value of the differences in percentage for each age group, in order to determine the overall closeness of fit; the lower the value, the better the fit, though anything less than 10 is considered a good match. Table 4.4 (p. 86) gives the Weiss index for the Egyptian female age distribution (for females aged 5 and over) in stable populations of Model West, Levels 1 to 3, with 0.1 increments in the intrinsic growth rate from zero to 0.5. Table 4.4 gives results for both the "smoothed" and "weighted" figures.[30] As this table shows, the "smoothed" figures have low indices throughout the entire range; but the closest fits are Level 1 ($e(0) = 20.0$ years) with an annual growth rate from zero to 0.1, and Level 2 ($e(0) = 22.5$ years) with growth from 0.1 to 0.2. The "weighted" figures, which accentuate village returns, produce similar but rougher results; they favor the same models but slightly higher intrinsic growth rates.

Second, Nathan Keyfitz describes an elegant method to calculate the likeliest growth rate for a known age distribution in relation to a possible life table; this method is particularly useful when dealing with age distributions that contain apparent statistical anomalies, as is true of the census returns.[31] Keyfitz's method compares the $L(x)$ figures in the life table with the attested proportion of the population in various age groups. We applied this method to both "smoothed" and "weighted" figures for females aged 5 and above, and tested the proportions of four groups: ages 5 to 19, 24, 29,

[28] A. J. Coale and P. Demeny, *Life Tables* (1983) 30. If the growth rate were more exactly known for Roman Egypt, a model could be interpolated between those in the Coale-Demeny tables; but under the circumstances, it is more reasonable to determine the likeliest printed table and allow it to stand for a range of probable mortality schedules.

[29] K. H. Weiss, *Models* (1973) 65.

[30] The empirical data were actually evaluated against stable populations of Model West, Levels 1 to 6, with 0.1 increments in the growth rate from 0 (stationary population) to 1.0; only the most relevant portion of the results are presented in Table 4.4. A. J. Coale and P. Demeny, *Life Tables* (1983) 55-60, provide age distributions at growth rates of 0.0, 0.5, and 1.0; they describe the procedure for calculating intermediate age distributions on p. 30. Prior to each evaluation, the empirical percentages were adjusted so that the total percentage of females aged 5 and over matched that in the stable population being tested. We also tested using linear regressions comparing the age distributions to the model stable populations; results were identical to the Weiss indices.

[31] N. Keyfitz, *Demography* (1985) 92-94. This method establishes the growth rate through iteration (progressively more exact approximation of *r*). Ten cycles of iteration produce values of *r* converging to six decimal points.

and 34, in relation to the first three Model West levels. Table 4.5 gives the resulting growth rates for the "smoothed" figures from the census returns. Keyfitz's method consistently yields an estimated annual growth rate *r* lying between about -0.10 and +0.05 for Model West, Level 1; between 0.15 and 0.30 for Level 2; and between 0.35 and 0.50 for Level 3. As with the Weiss test, higher Coale-Demeny models imply a higher growth rate; but for traditional populations an intrinsic growth rate as high as 0.4 is implausible, at least in the long term.

Table 4.4. *Comparison of female age structure with models, ages 5+*

"Smoothed" figures

Model		Intrinsic annual growth rate (%)				
West	0.0	0.1	0.2	0.3	0.4	0.5
Level 1	8.02	8.18	8.36	8.73	9.31	9.90
Level 2	7.94	8.08	8.22	8.36	8.51	8.77
Level 3	8.88	8.32	8.18	8.25	8.38	8.51

"Weighted" figures

Model		Intrinsic annual growth rate (%)				
West	0.0	0.1	0.2	0.3	0.4	0.5
Level 1	8.70	9.05	9.41	9.76	10.12	10.51
Level 2	8.93	8.81	8.77	9.06	9.42	9.78
Level 3	9.60	9.34	9.10	8.94	8.89	9.21

Table 4.5. *Growth rates estimated from proportion in age groups*

	Age groups of females ("smoothed" figures)				
Model West	5–19	5–24	5–29	5–34	Estimated growth
Level 1	-0.032	-0.008	-0.040	0.054	-0.04 to 0.05
Level 2	0.170	0.215	0.195	0.299	0.17 to 0.30
Level 3	0.347	0.415	0.405	0.514	0.35 to 0.51

These two tests establish a set of options from among which we think it reasonable to select. On the basis of them, we restore a female life expectancy at birth of 22.5 years (Model West, Level 2: Table 4.2) in a population with an estimated annual growth rate of 0.2 percent. These values should not be understood as exact; they are only the most plausible approximations for Egyptian females in the light of currently available evidence.[32]

There are four reasons why we choose the values we do. First, the analysis of age distributions presented above favors values such as these. In Figure 4.3 (p. 88), the age distribution of females in the Coale-Demeny stable model is compared with the "smoothed" Egyptian age distribution; however, in order to take account of the likely underrepresentation of females under age 5 in the census returns, the Egyptian age distributions are rescaled so that the percentage of Egyptian females aged 5 and over matches that in the Coale-Demeny stable population (85.87 percent). This makes comparison much sharper. As Figure 4.3 shows, the match is extremely close.[33] Results are rougher, but still well within the range of possibility, if the "weighted" figures are compared with the same stable population.[34]

Second, although the "smoothed" figures might also be interpreted to favor an even lower life expectancy (in a virtually stationary population), the "weighted" figures, which give more emphasis to village returns, support somewhat higher values. As we noted in Chapters 1 and 2, surviving returns drastically underrepresent Egyptian villages, which may even have had a slightly higher life expectancy than nome metropoleis. Although the "weighted" figures involve much guesswork, we think it justified to accord the village returns considerable importance in selecting a model stable population.

Third, the restored values also correspond well with the best available evidence for life expectancy and population growth rates in the early

---

[32] The main alternatives are to restore a life expectancy at birth of 20.0 (Level 1) and a stationary population, or a life expectancy of 25.0 (Level 3) and a growth rate of 0.4. Reasons for preferring intermediate values are discussed below. Our restored values are most exact in estimating female mortality and life expectancy from age 5 onward, in relation to the Coale-Demeny models; on the problem of determining infant mortality, see Chapter 2, note 10.

[33] For the "smoothed" values for fourteen age groups from 5 to 9 up to 70 and over, as measured against predicted values from the stable population, chi-square is 4.217 with 13 degrees of freedom; the odds are better than 50 to 1 that empirical variation could be due to chance. For females aged less than 5, moving averages are not used in Figure 4.3; values are calculated directly from the statistics in the returns.

[34] Chi-square is 4.171; again, the odds are better than 50 to 1 that empirical variation could be fortuitous. For sixteen five-year age groups of females aged 5 and over, average deviation from the model values is 0.49 percent for the "smoothed" figures, 0.55 for the "weighted" figures.

Roman Empire generally.[35] Further, they are also broadly similar to the mortality schedules and growth rates that probably prevailed in India and rural China during the early decades of this century; both then had life expectancies at birth near 22.5 years, but while rural China's population was nearly stationary, India's was already growing at a rate near 0.5.[36] A life expectancy only slightly higher than this obtained among French women as late as the mid-eighteenth century.[37] Our estimated values are therefore comfortably within the range of the possible.

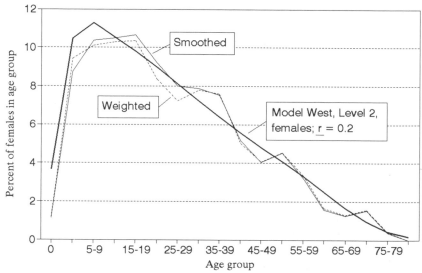

Figure 4.3. *Female age structure compared with model*

[35] See B. W. Frier, "The Demography of the Early Roman Empire," forthcoming in *Cambridge Ancient History* XI, estimating a general life expectancy at birth in the lower 20s and an actual growth rate near 0.15. M. Livi-Bacci, *History* (1992) 31, gives similar figures as the most probable estimates for the Roman Empire.

[36] On India, P. N. Mari Bhat, in *India* (1989) 73–118, along with the regional essays by A. W. Clark (pp. 119–149) and T. Dyson (pp. 150–196) in the same volume. On China, G. W. Barclay *et al.*, "Reassessment" (1976) 617–621; also several papers in *East Asian History* (1985). On historical growth rates, see N. Keyfitz, *Demography* (1985) 6–7. As late as 1940, life expectancy in Egypt was still in the low 30s: V. G. Valaoras, *Population Analysis of Egypt, 1935–1970* (1972) 53; *Estimation* (1982) 12; compare P. Fargues, "Un siècle de transition démographique en Afrique méditerranéenne, 1885–1985," *Population* 41 (1986) 205–232, at 218 (for 1927 to 1937).

[37] French life expectancy at birth in the late Middle Ages was about 25 years: J. N. Biraben, in *Population française* I (1988) 424–425; female life expectancy at birth is reliably estimated as low as 25.7 in 1740–1750, in large part because of extremely high infant mortality: A. Bideau, J. Dupâquier, and H. Gutierrez, in *ibid.* II (1988) 222–238, with bibliography. Spain and Italy probably had similar life expectancy at this date: M. Livi-Bacci, *Population* (1991) 69 and 133 n.29.

Finally, for more pragmatic reasons, it is desirable to envisage a small but numerically significant annual growth rate for Roman Egypt, so that its population has a "cushion" on which to fall back during intermittent mortality crises.[38] An annual growth rate of 0.2 percent doubles the population every 3.5 centuries, and thus provides exactly the sort of "cushion" that is required. On the other hand, restoring a higher female life expectancy at birth (say, Model West, Level 3, with $e(0) = 25$ years) would mean also restoring a higher intrinsic growth rate (around 0.4), which on present evidence appears implausibly elevated.[39]

With an illustrative stable model for Egyptian females now in place, it is possible to calculate a number of other statistics that illustrate the plausible mortality experience of Egypt.[40] In the stable model, the annual birth rate of females is approximately 46.9 per thousand females, and the annual death rate of females is 44.9 per thousand; the difference between these two figures is the annual growth rate r.[41] The death rate of females over age 1 is about 30.3 per thousand; of females over age 5, 25.4 per thousand; of females over 65, 125.1 per thousand. The average age of females at death is about 21.2 years; and of females over age 5, 42.4 years. About 35 percent of female deaths would be of girls less than one year old; more than fifty percent, of girls less than 5.

The average age of females in the stable model is 25.7 years; the average of the 337 ages in the census returns is 26.1, a slightly higher figure that results almost entirely from the undercount of female infants.[42] About 46 percent of the stable female population is aged 15 to 44; the ratio of

[38] The long-term intrinsic growth rate may well have been partially offset by periodic mortality crises (see Chapter 9, Section 2); we are not arguing that Egypt's population actually grew at this rate during the early Empire (see the following note). The intrinsic growth rate is distinct from the actual long-term growth rate: C. Newell, *Methods* (1988) 122–123. Normal age distribution is much more heavily influenced by the former.

[39] See note 32 above. In Chapter 3 at note 16, we suggest an *actual* long-term growth rate (before AD 166) on the order of 0.1 percent per annum, about half our restored intrinsic growth rate, with the difference ascribable mainly to mortality crises. Our population model for Roman Egypt virtually duplicates that in C. McEvedy and R. Jones, *Atlas* (1978) 226–229.

[40] These statistics are calculated from the ones given in A. J. Coale and P. Demeny, *Life Tables* (1983) 56, using the method for interpolation described at p. 30. Note that the figures below are relative to the female population only.

[41] In our chosen model, a similar birth rate also consistently emerges from the unsmoothed Egyptian age distribution of females aged 5 and over, confirming the closeness of fit between the raw data and Model West; for the technique, see United Nations, *Manual X* (1983) 158–166. Mortality and fertility rates this high or higher prevailed in early nineteenth-century Egypt: A. R. Omran, *Egypt* (1973) 9–10; even higher birth rates are still common in less developed countries. T. G. Parkin, *Demography* (1992) 84, is mistaken in describing a birth rate this high as difficult to attain; see Chapter 7, Section 1.

[42] M. Hombert and C. Préaux, *Recherches* (1952) 157, calculated an average age of 26.4 for 247 women.

females aged 4 or less to those aged 15 to 44 (the "Daughter to Mother" ratio) is 0.31; and the Dependency Ratio of females aged 0 to 14 and 60 or over to those aged 15 to 59 is 0.72.[43] As will emerge below in Chapters 6 and 7, the model also has implications for the fertility rate that probably prevailed in Roman Egypt.

Despite obvious uncertainties, we think it warranted to reconstruct for Roman Egypt female life expectancy at birth of from 20 to 25 years, life expectancy at age 10 of from 34.5 to 37.5 years, an annual female birth rate of about 42 to 54 per thousand, and an annual female death rate of 42 to 49 per thousand.[44] The intrinsic annual female growth rate probably lay between zero and 0.5 percent. In each case, values toward the middle of these ranges are more likely than values at their extremes.

[43] In the census returns, the respective figures are 51.5, 0.20, and 0.62; in each case the difference results mainly from undercount of female infants.

[44] Values for female birth and death rates are taken from A. J. Coale and P. Demeny, *Life Tables* (1983) 55–57. These are long-term values; short-term rates undoubtedly varied considerably. In the late 1980s, Africa's estimated average birth rate (for both sexes) was about 45 per thousand; eight countries still had birth rates higher than 50. United Nations, *Demographic Yearbook* 42 (1990) 141, 304.

5

Male life expectancy and the sex ratio

The female age distribution in Roman Egypt is easily interpreted through the Coale-Demeny model life tables. By contrast, the male age distribution presents greater difficulties, and reconstruction of male mortality is much more uncertain. The census returns preserve the ages of 350 males. The raw data are in Table A, from which derives the summary in Table 5.1.

Table 5.1. *Grouped ages for Egyptian males*

Age	Vill.	Met.	Total	Smoothed	Weighted
0–4	24	26	50	50.00	49.33
5–9	16	26	42	40.00	37.34
10–14	7	16	23	26.57	23.57
15–19	13	23	36	36.29	33.54
20–24	13	18	31	30.43	28.74
25–29	14	12	26	25.86	25.10
30–34	16	19	35	33.14	32.29
35–39	10	6	16	19.29	19.39
40–44	12	6	18	16.43	16.79
45–49	13	11	24	22.29	22.28
50–54	4	6	10	13.14	12.99
55–59	11	3	14	12.00	12.82
60–64	3	3	6	7.71	8.02
65–69	5	2	7	7.29	7.63
70–74	6	3	9	7.14	7.59
75–79	2	0	2	2.71	2.80
80–84	0	1	1	0.57	0.43
All ages	169	181	350	350.86	340.65

Although the male figures also clearly point to a population with very high mortality, they are apparently somewhat disturbed, as will emerge below, by external influences on the reporting of male ages. The resulting distortion, although not great, suffices to impede an accurate estimate of male mortality. The results in this chapter are therefore more tentative than those in Chapter 4.

This chapter proceeds circuitously to explore the male age distribution and to bring out the problems with it. We begin by examining the overall sex ratio in the returns, then the age-specific sex ratio, and then a possible male life table. We conclude with broader observations on mortality in Roman Egypt.

1. The sex ratio

The sex ratio expresses the relative numbers of males and females in a population.[1] By convention, it is stated as the number of males per hundred females. In populations of contemporary more developed countries, females outnumber males because female life expectancy is much higher than male; for example, in 1985 the United States had a sex ratio of 94.8 males per hundred females. But in India, where female life expectancy has historically lagged behind that of males, the sex ratio is reversed; in 1971, for instance, India had 107.5 males per hundred females.

Our data base contains a total of 1022 persons whose sex is identifiable: 540 males and 482 females, for a sex ratio of 112.0. But this initial figure needs correcting because of twelve returns in which only a portion containing the name of a resident declarant is preserved, but the return breaks off without reaching the list of household members. As it happens, ten of twelve declarants are male.[2] Since this chance preservation favors males, the bias is best eliminated by ignoring all twelve returns. The resulting corrected sex ratio for 1010 persons is 530 males to 480 females, or 110.4, a sex ratio fairly close to the Indian sex ratio for 1971.[3]

---

[1] C. Newell, *Methods* (1988) 27–31; the figures below come from his Table 3.2 on p. 30. "The overall Sex Ratio is entirely determined by 1. The Sex Ratio at Birth. 2. Sex differences in mortality. 3. Differential migration" (p. 27). The first two factors are examined in this chapter; migration, in Chapter 8.

[2] 131-Ar-2; 131-Ox-3, 5, 8, 9, and 12; 159-Ar-23; 159-Me-3; 173-Ar-13; 187-Ar-14 and 24; ???-Ar-1. Three of these returns are from villages, nine from metropoleis. They are ignored for all subsequent calculations in Sections 1 and 2.

[3] *Caveat lector!* Even in a sample this large (and even assuming it to be random), the standard sampling error is high, and the effect of standard error is compounded by converting proportions into a sex ratio. At 95 percent confidence, the total attested numbers of males and females are consistent with a population sex ratio ranging from 96 to 124 (the *z* test). Such inexactitude increases in the calculations below, where still smaller "samples" are employed. In short, the various sex ratios discussed below are closer together than they seem to be; inferences based on small differences in the sex ratio are therefore suspect. See P. M. Visaria, *Sex Ratio* (1971) 26–27.

The sex ratio in villages and metropoleis

However, the picture is more enigmatic if village returns are examined separately from metropolitan returns.[4] The village returns have 242 males and 281 females, for a sex ratio of only 86.1. By contrast, the metropolitan returns have 288 males as against 199 females, for a sex ratio of 144.7. This enormous difference strongly militates against using raw data in reconstructing the sex ratio for Roman Egypt.[5] If village returns are assigned two-for-one weight, the resulting sex ratio is 772 males to 761 females, or 101.4. In other words, the village returns, when weighted, bring into near parity the sex ratio computed from raw data.

The sex ratio changes slightly, though always in favor of males, if we look only at returns in which the principal family is complete or nearly complete. The overall sex ratio is 111.0 (424 males, 382 females). For villages, the sex ratio is 88.2 (209 males, 237 females); for metropoleis, 148.3 (215 males, 145 females). The weighted sex ratio is therefore 102.3 (633 males, 619 females). However, this ratio is probably too low, since many fewer metropolitan than village returns have complete households;[6] if the weighted sex ratio is corrected to account for this difference, it rises to about 104.

Calculating the sex ratio is thus problematic; much depends upon whether, and how and how much, we "weight" raw data from the returns. Earlier scholars, in calculating the sex ratio directly from raw data, overlooked the discrepancy between villages and metropoleis.[7] As will emerge in Section 2 below, part of the problem involves the representativeness of surviving returns, but part also almost certainly involves their completeness.

Free persons and slaves

Among free persons in all returns, the sex ratio is considerably more favorable to males. The overall sex ratio is 120.4 (496 males, 412 females). For

---

[4] As noted in Chapter 2 (note 25), a few returns that are not assignable to an exact location are treated as village.

[5] The difference is significant at a 99 percent confidence level (chi-square test).

[6] About 80 percent of attested males and females are in complete or nearly complete households (806 of 1010). However, for village returns the percentage is 85 (446 of 523); for metropolitan returns, only 74 (360 of 487). This statistically significant difference, which is similar for both sexes, is probably caused by a higher publication rate for fragmentary documents from Arsinoe and (esp.) Oxyrhynchus. Note that more males than females appear to be lost from incomplete returns.

[7] E.g., M. Hombert and C. Préaux, *Recherches* (1952) 155–156 (sex ratio of 105.5 for 715 persons); K. Hopkins, "Brother-Sister" (1980) 316 (sex ratio of 107.2 for 802 persons). The sex ratio has edged upward with the increase in data. But in any case, sex ratios this low do not in themselves imply a significant incidence of female infanticide; against S. B. Pomeroy, *Women* (1984) 137, see J. M. Riddle, *Contraception* (1992) 10–14.

the villages, the sex ratio is 96.3 (236 males, 245 females); for the metro-poleis, 155.7 (260 males, 167 females). The weighted sex ratio is thus 111.4 (732 males, 657 females). What this weighted sex ratio indicates is that males were almost certainly a majority of the free population, although the exact extent of their predominance is not precisely ascertainable.[8]

Among slaves, however, the sex ratio is reversed. The overall sex ratio is 50.0 (34 males, 68 females). But for the villages, the sex ratio is an astonishingly low 16.7 (6 males, 36 females); while for the metropoleis, it is 87.5 (28 males, 32 females). The weighted sex ratio is thus 38.5 (40 males, 104 females). The village sex ratio for slaves should not, however, be taken too seriously; it results, in large measure, from the chance preser-vation of several village households that contain only female slaves.[9] Female slaves were perhaps in fact more numerous than male slaves in Egypt; but raw data also exaggerate the sex ratio since it appears that male slaves were typically manumitted earlier than females.[10]

The sex ratio over time
Finally, the sex ratio in the census returns also varies capriciously with the passage of time. The scattered first-century returns are heavily unbalanced toward males (44 males, 15 females, for a sex ratio of 293.3). This sex ratio is obviously implausible; the likeliest explanation is that, during the first few censuses, declarants omitted to declare many females, perhaps because tax collectors were initially less careful about securing complete returns. So too, conceivably, for the returns of the last three censuses, from 229/230 to 257/258 (23 males, 11 females, for a sex ratio of 209.1).

The bulk of datable returns are from the second and early third centuries. During this period there is an erratic but still fairly steady downward drift in the sex ratio. In the four censuses from 103/104 to 145/146, the sex ratio is 120.9 (191 males, 158 females); by contrast, in the five censuses from 159/160 to 215/216, the sex ratio is only 93.1 (257 males, 276 females).[11] This change can hardly be real. The explanation is complex.

---

[8] Males also outnumber females in the modern Egyptian censuses of 1897 and 1907: A. R. Omran, *Egypt* (1973) 22. Neither census is especially reliable, but the current sex ratio still hovers around 105: United Nations, *Demographic Yearbook* 42 (1990) 190.

[9] 117-Ar-7 (three female slaves); 187-Ar-3 (three female slaves, one of unknown sex); 187-Ar-30 (Tebtunis; nine female slaves, three of whom are fugitive); 215-Ar-3 (Soknopaiou Nesos; three female slaves, two of unknown sex). Determining sex is often more difficult for slaves than for free persons.

[10] Thus, among slaves with attested ages who are less than 30, the sex ratio is 71.0 (22 males, 31 females); the oldest male slave is 32. See Chapter 3 (at notes 73–74) for discus-sion. The reasons for the sex imbalance among slaves are examined below in Chapter 7, Section 4. Because of manumission practices, it is not possible to calculate separate life tables for slaves and free persons.

[11] The difference is significant at about a 92 percent confidence level (chi-square test). The sex ratio in undatable returns is 75.0 (15 males, 20 females); the sample is too small to be meaningful.

The metropolitan sex ratio remains virtually constant over this period (125.7 as against 132.1), but the village sex ratio drops drastically and most improbably (117.0 as against 68.8). In addition, among returns with information on residents, village returns are slightly outnumbered by metropolitan returns in the earlier period (42 to 44), but are much more numerous in the later (65 to 52); this shift in provenance exacerbates the swing in the overall sex ratio between the two periods. The problem with the village returns may result from the intersection of two long-term tendencies: a more thorough inclusion of females as time passes, coupled with increasing effort by declarants to conceal males. In any case, the shift in provenance appears to have little effect on figures for age distribution.[12]

The returns from the second and early third centuries may be the best indicator of the normal metropolitan sex ratio: around 125 to 130. The village sex ratio is not recoverable from present evidence, but is inherently unlikely to have lain outside a range from 90 to 115. The overall Egyptian sex ratio was thus probably between 100 and 120. If we tentatively assume a village sex ratio of about 100 (see Chapter 8), the overall sex ratio would be around 108, similar to that of present-day India.

2. The age-specific sex ratio

The vagaries in the Egyptian sex ratio are perplexing, but the explanation for them is somewhat clearer if we examine the age-specific sex ratio. In most human populations, male newborns outnumber females by a ratio that fluctuates, but usually lies around 105 males per hundred females.[13] In populations of more developed countries, females now have much lower mortality than males, and thus the initial imbalance in the sex ratio gradually shifts in favor of females, usually at least by their early 30s. However, in present-day less developed countries with high mortality levels, the imbalance often does not shift to favor females until their early 50s.[14] The reason is that mortality differences between males and females are much less pronounced in less developed countries, so that the sexual imbalance at birth takes longer to reverse; in general, as overall mortality has declined in recent decades, females have benefited much more than males.[15]

---

[12] See Chapter 9, Section 2, discussing the changing age distribution. But small samples are notoriously susceptible to vagaries of this kind.

[13] C. Newell, *Methods* (1988) 27, 30; also H. S. Shryock and J. S. Siegel, *Methods* (1980) 195–196. The sex ratio of newborns fluctuates between 104 and 107.

[14] D. Yaukey, *Demography* (1985) 86–87 (statistics are for 1975), 130–135; see also H. S. Shryock and J. S. Siegel, *Methods* (1980) 190–199, 219–223. This tendency weakens in more recent statistics, but many low-income countries still have sex ratios above 100.

[15] G. J. Stolnitz, "Mortality: Post-World War II Trends," in *International Encyclopedia of Population* (ed. J. A. Ross; 1982) 461–469; C. A. Nathanson, "Sex Differences" (1984).

However, in some less developed countries (mainly in the Indian sub-continent), the number of females never passes that of males because female mortality is higher than male through most of life; the initial unbalanced sex ratio at birth is thus preserved and even accentuated in the adult population.[16] There is reason to suspect that this situation was once much more widespread.[17]

The age-specific sex ratio in Roman Egypt is summarized in Table 5.2 (p. 97) for attested ages, "smoothed" ages, and "weighted" ages.[18] One complication, however, is that, for reasons we cannot fully explain, male ages are less frequently preserved in the census returns than female ages. About 66 percent of known males have preserved ages (350 of 530), as against 70 percent of known females (337 of 480).[19] As a result, the overall Egyptian sex ratio cannot be calculated solely on the basis of persons with preserved ages;[20] a corrective of approximately 1.05, in favor of males, must be applied to the male statistics.

The age-specific sex ratios in Table 5.2 are plotted in Figure 5.1 (p. 98), *after* applying the 1.05 corrective in favor of the male figures. Because the age-specific ratios depend upon underlying figures that are subject to statistical fluctuations, they seem at first chaotic; and fluctuations grow wilder

[16] C. Newell, *Methods* (1988) 30, who explains the difference as "probably due to worse malnutrition among young females and the risks of maternity." Indian statistics are for 1971. See also P. M. Visaria, *Sex Ratio* (1971), with a good discussion of the historical evidence and of causes (pp. 53–63); B. D. Miller, *The Endangered Sex: Neglect of Female Children in Rural North India* (1981); L. C. Chen, E. Qua, and S. D'Souza, "Sex Bias in the Family Allocation of Food and Health Care in Rural Bangladesh," *Population and Development Review* 7 (1981) 55–70.

[17] E.g., United Nations, *The Determinants and Consequences of Population Trends: New Summary of Findings on Interaction of Demographic, Economic and Social Factors* I (*Population Studies* no. 50; 1973) 115; S. H. Preston, *Mortality Patterns in National Populations with Special Reference to Recorded Causes of Death* (1976) 120–159, 172–173. Compare rural China in the 1930s: G. W. Barclay *et al.*, "Reassessment" (1976) 617–621, 623 (sex ratio *ca* 110).

[18] As in Chapter 4, the "smoothed" figures reflect seven-year moving averages of ages; the "weighted" figures are an adjustment of the "smoothed figures" on the assumption that villagers are two-thirds of the entire population. Also as in Chapter 4, moving averages are not used for persons aged less than 5; instead, figures are calculated directly from the data in Table A.

[19] The chi-square test indicates that this discrepancy is probably not due to chance (chi-square = 1.827, using Yates's correction; three chances in four that the distribution is not fortuitous); the bias may lie in the way that census returns are preserved. The bias does not ease, nor do age-specific sex ratios much alter, if persons with estimated approximate ages are added in. (In this calculation, we omit the returns discussed above at notes 2–3.)

[20] T. G. Parkin, *Demography* (1992) 98 and 141 (Table 1), failed to realize this; his explanation of the Egyptian sex ratio (p. 104) also lacks substance. Rationally, the sex ratio for persons with preserved ages cannot differ from that for all persons regardless of age, and the latter figure has obvious priority.

in older ages as the data base shrinks because of high mortality. However, upon closer inspection significant patterns begin to emerge.

Table 5.2. *Age-specific sex distribution*

Age	Attested figures			"Smoothed" figures			"Weighted" figures		
	M	F	Ratio	M	F	Ratio	M	F	Ratio
0–4	50	36	138.9	50.00	36.00	138.9	48.28	39.46	122.3
5–9	42	35	120.0	40.00	36.71	108.9	37.34	37.62	99.3
10–14	23	38	60.5	26.57	37.14	71.5	23.57	38.32	61.5
15–19	36	32	112.5	36.29	37.71	96.2	33.54	38.50	87.1
20–24	31	35	88.6	30.43	32.57	93.4	28.74	31.17	92.2
25–29	26	31	83.9	25.86	28.29	91.4	25.10	26.93	93.2
30–34	35	24	145.8	33.14	27.86	119.0	32.29	29.05	111.2
35–39	16	31	51.6	19.29	26.71	72.2	19.39	28.25	68.6
40–44	18	18	100.0	16.43	18.29	89.8	16.79	18.76	89.5
45–49	24	14	171.4	22.29	14.29	156.0	22.28	15.11	147.4
50–54	10	18	55.6	13.14	16.00	82.1	12.99	16.97	76.6
55–59	14	6	233.3	12.00	11.43	105.0	12.82	12.51	102.4
60–64	6	7	85.7	7.71	5.57	138.5	8.02	6.15	130.4
65–69	7	4	175.0	7.29	4.43	164.5	7.63	4.78	159.5
70–74	9	7	128.6	7.14	5.43	131.6	7.59	5.92	128.2
75–79	2	1	200.0	2.71	1.29	211.1	2.80	1.47	190.3
80–84	1	0	--	0.57	0.00	--	0.43	0.00	--
Total	350	337	103.9	350.86	339.71	103.3	339.59	350.98	96.8

First, the largest gap between the attested and "smoothed" sex ratios, on the one hand, and the "weighted" sex ratios, on the other, is from ages 0 to 19. The likeliest explanation for this large discrepancy is that, in reporting their male children, declarants were often driven by a desire to evade the poll tax levelled on adult males aged 14 up to 62.[21] Declarants chose between two strategies: either to conceal young males altogether, or to underdeclare the true ages of young males.[22] Concealment of males was

---

[21] See Chapter 1; use of the census returns for the poll tax undoubtedly undermined the accuracy of the Egyptian census. On the phenomenon, which is common, see P. R. Cox, *Demography* (1975) 32–33.

[22] At least in the first century AD, subsequent bureaucratic investigation attempted to locate "missing" young males: *P. Corn.* 23a + *P.Gen.inv.* 221 recto, lines 210 ff. (AD 53/54); *P.Mich.* XII 640.75–76 (55–57; corrected text). We owe this information to Ann Hanson, who adds that she knows of no similar evidence after the first century.

probably more common in villages, which explains why the "weighted" sex ratio is so much lower than the "smoothed."[23] Metropolitan declarants, by contrast, may underreport the age of many younger males.[24] Concealment and underdeclaration of age converge for the male age group from 11 to 13, just before entry onto the tax rolls; as Table A shows, village declarants report no males at all, and the metropoleis only eight.

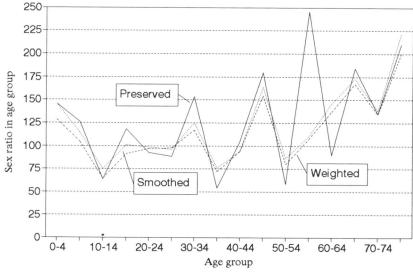

Figure 5.1. *Age-specific sex ratio*

Second, at least from age 15 onward, attempted concealment of males abates, although it may not entirely disappear. "Smoothed" and "weighted" sex ratios are now usually quite close together, though the "weighted" figures lag slightly behind as a result of the consistently lower sex ratio in villages.[25] By age 20, the two sexes are reported as in approximate parity. But from then on, despite increasing fluctuations as the data decline in number, both "smoothed" and "weighted" sex ratios move in

[23] Because of the "sweep" methods used by census takers in recording villages, concealment of boys may have been easier in villages than in metropoleis. We return to this subject in Chapter 7 below (at notes 59–64). See also Chapter 8 and Table 8.1.

[24] This explains why, in Figure 5.3 below, the attested numbers of males aged 1 to 9 are higher than the model would predict; the "surplus" comes entirely from metropoleis. Metropolitan declarants also apparently fail altogether to report many girls, especially very young girls; see Chapter 8 at notes 4–9.

[25] We return to this issue in Chapter 8, but a main cause of the higher sex ratio in metropoleis may be migration of young males from Egyptian villages. Some readers may wish to examine that argument before reading on.

favor of males, at first gradually and then rapidly. This movement is much clearer in Figure 5.2, which uses three-figure moving averages of the sex ratios in order to bring out central tendencies of the data. The resulting pattern is coherent, but no easy explanation for it can be given.

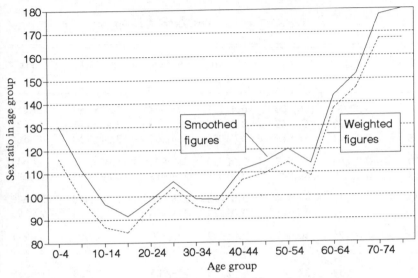

Figure 5.2. *Age-specific sex ratio with moving averages*

The movement of the sex ratio in favor of older males exactly reverses the normal tendency in modern populations where females have a higher life expectancy than males. As it might seem, the most plausible cause of the sex ratio's movement is that Egyptian males had a higher life expectancy than females, and therefore predominated in older ages. However, as will emerge below, this explanation is not without major difficulties; above all, because of the normal distribution of male and female mortality across their lifetimes, the sex ratios in the returns do not correspond to predictable patterns even in populations with higher male than female life expectancy.

3. A provisional male life table

Under the circumstances, restoring a male life table is hazardous. Only the figures from about age 15 or 20 onward can be regarded as reasonably credible, and even here doubt arises because of possible undercount of males. Nonetheless, we have attempted to restore, *on a provisional basis,*[26] what we believe is approximately the *lowest* male life table consistent with the

---

[26]Doubts about the male model are discussed in the following section.

census returns. In Chapter 4, we argued that female life expectancy at birth was probably in the vicinity of 22.5 years, and that the intrinsic rate of female population growth was around 0.2 percent per year. We adopt the same intrinsic growth rate for the male population, and restore a male life expectancy at birth of *at least* 25.0 years.[27]

Table 5.3. *Model West, Level 4, males*

Age	q(x)	l(x)	m(x)	L(x)	T(x)	e(x)
0	0.32257	100,000	0.41151	78,388	2,525,991	25.260
1	0.19523	67,743	0.05605	235,950	2,447,603	36.131
5	0.05141	54,517	0.01058	264,878	2,211,654	40.568
10	0.03697	51,517	0.00753	253,984	1,946,775	37.645
15	0.05017	49,803	0.01028	243,018	1,692,791	33.990
20	0.07110	47,304	0.01472	228,450	1,449,773	30.648
25	0.07951	43,941	0.01653	211,320	1,221,323	27.795
30	0.09175	40,447	0.01919	193,330	1,010,003	24.971
35	0.10709	36,736	0.02258	174,420	816,673	22.231
40	0.12838	32,802	0.02736	153,905	642,433	19.585
45	0.14754	28,591	0.03176	132,832	488,528	17.087
50	0.18383	24,373	0.04032	111,111	355,696	14.594
55	0.22059	19,892	0.04925	88,947	244,585	12.295
60	0.29059	15,511	0.06754	66,739	155,638	10.034
65	0.37125	11,004	0.09035	45,215	·88,900	8.079
70	0.48085	6,919	0.12503	26,609	43,685	6.314
75	0.62398	3,592	0.18139	12,356	17,076	4.754
80	0.74408	1,351	0.26084	3,853	4,720	3.495
85	0.86924	346	0.38184	787	867	2.508
90	0.95201	43	0.55581	77	80	1.772
95	1.00000	2	0.80890	3	3	1.236

[27] As will emerge in Section 4, little depends upon the exact figure that is chosen. An even closer fit is with Level 5 (male *e(0)* = 27.7); higher models fit much less well and are inherently unlikely in any case. As to the intrinsic growth rate, see N. Keyfitz, *Demography* (1985) 115: "... always in the long run, the males and females of any population increase at nearly the same rate."

Table 5.3 gives the life table for Model West, Level 4, males, in which male life expectancy at birth is 25.3 years.[28] We consider this the *minimum* life expectancy consistent with the attested age distribution of Egyptian males from age 20 onward. Table 5.3 should be closely compared with Table 4.1, our proposed life table for Egyptian females. At almost every age, the male mortality functions are slightly but significantly more favorable; the predictable result would be a marked imbalance in the sex ratio in favor of males. Figure 5.3 shows the resulting stable age distribution (*r* = 0.2) plotted against the "smoothed" and "weighted" male age distribution in the census returns.[29] The fit is reasonably close, though rougher than in Figure 4.3 for females. For reasons discussed below, however, there is little point in attempting to make the match more perfect.

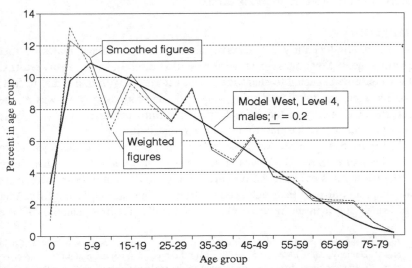

Figure 5.3. *Male age structure compared with model*

[28] A. J. Coale and P. Demeny, *Life Tables* (1983) 43. It is in fact easy to calculate a Coale-Demeny life table in which male life expectancy at birth is exactly 25.0 years, by using MORTPAK, an extremely useful computerized demographic program available from the United Nations (Population Division, Sales No. E.88.XIII.2); the MATCH option (based on the first edition of the Coale-Demeny tables) does this in seconds. The STABLE option can then be used to calculate the stable age distribution at various rates of intrinsic growth. However, the results are virtually identical to those in Table 5.3, so we have preferred to give the more accessible Coale-Demeny life table.

[29] This graph was calculated in a way similar to Figure 4.3 for females, but on the assumption that males aged 15 and older are 65.69 percent of all males, as in the stable model. This percentage is in fact close to accurate for both the "smoothed" figures (66.95) and the "weighted" figures (67.60). Age 15 is used as a cut-off because percentages for younger males are clearly affected by omission or age misreporting. For fourteen age groups from age 15, average variance is 0.73 percent for "smoothed" figures, 0.79 for "weighted."

In the stable model,[30] the annual birthrate of males is 41.8 per thousand males; the annual death rate, 39.8 per thousand males. The annual death rate for males over age 1 is 27.2 per thousand males; for males over age 5, 24.0; for males over age 65, 123.3. The average age of males at death is 23.9; and of males aged 5 and over, 44.7. (For females, the comparable statistics were 21.2 and 42.4 years, respectively.) Male life expectancy at age 5 is about 40.6 years, compared with 38.3 years in our female model.

The average age of males in the stable model is 26.3; in the census returns it is 26.5, a close match.[31] In the model, some 47.5 percent of males are aged 15 to 44; in the returns, it is 46.3. The ratio of males aged less than 5 to those aged 15 to 44 (the "Son to Father" ratio) is 0.275 in the model; the Dependency Ratio of males aged aged 0 to 14 and 60 or more, to those aged 15 to 59, is 0.667.

The tax lists

From the first century AD survive several lists of village males of tax-paying age.[32] Since these lists were compiled directly from census returns, they could be expected to share many characteristics with them; and in fact, for instance, the tax lists display very little age-rounding.[33] However, the returns date mainly to the second and early third centuries AD, so the tax lists provide an earlier picture of male age distribution.

In Figure 5.4 (p. 103), we give the age distribution for males aged 15 to 59; the returns have 209 males in this age group, while the tax lists have 462 males. As is evident, the two are closely similar not only in their over-all shape but also in their age-specific trends. This similarity confirms that the surviving census returns give a generally credible sample of the

---

[30] As in Chapter 4, the figures that follow are calculated from the ones given in A. J. Coale and P. Demeny, *Life Tables* (1983) 108, using the method for interpolation they describe at p. 30. Figures given below are in relation to the male population only, not the population as a whole.

[31] M. Hombert and C. Préaux, *Recherches* (1952) 157, gave an average age of 27.2 for 256 males.

[32] We are grateful to Ann Hanson for supplying us with the data. (1) Name list for AD 38/39: *P.Harris* 72; *P.Mich.inv.* 890 and *P.Princ.* III 123; *P.Mich.inv.* 791; *P.Mich.inv.* 811: 232 taxpayers, with ages for 129 (the rest are lost). (2) Year ledger for 42/43: *P.Mich.inv.* 619 recto: 33 taxpayers, all with ages. (3) Name list for 46/47: *P.Brit.Lib.* 2253 and *P.Mich.inv.* 881 and *P.Mich.inv.* 877: 169 taxpayers with ages for 101 (60 are lost, 8 left blank). (4) Year ledger for 46/47: *P.Princ.* I 8: 152 taxpayers with ages for 120 (32 left blank; considerable overlap with previous list). (5) House-by-house register of males for 94: *P.Lond.* II 257–259: 317 taxpayers with ages for 264 (the rest are lost). Because of the overlap, we have not used the fourth list in our calculations. These lists are all from Arsinoite villages.

[33] As was observed already by R. Duncan-Jones, "Age-Rounding" (1979) 175–176. Whipple's Index for the tax documents of 94 is about 104, identical to that in the census returns. On the United Nations scale, this figure scores as "highly accurate."

reported male ages, and it also suggests the homogeneity of census reports in Egypt during the early Empire. However, the overall slope of the male age distribution in the tax lists is slightly less oblique than that in the returns, possibly indicating that male life expectancy was a bit higher in the first century AD than in the second and early third.[34]

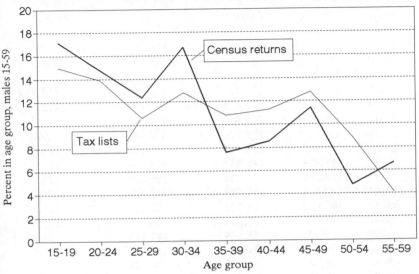

Figure 5.4. *Male age structure compared with tax lists*

4. The total Egyptian age distribution

With the two stable models now in place (the male model, let us again stress, adopted only *provisionally*), it is possible to reconstruct a model of the entire Egyptian population, both females and males. For purposes of this reconstruction, we assume a total Egyptian population of 4.5 million persons, the sex-specific mortality schedules in Tables 4.1 and 5.3, an intrinsic growth rate of 0.2 percent per year, and a sex ratio at birth of 105 males per hundred females. The results are given in Table 5.4, the purpose of which is only to illustrate what the Egyptian population *might* have looked like during the early Roman Empire.[35] The reconstructed Egyptian

---

[34]In Chapter 9, Section 2, we suggest that normal Egyptian mortality may have been lower before the outbreak of the Antonine plague in AD 165/166.

[35]Numbers include fractions (not given), so they do not always appear to add correctly. Table 5.4 does not take account of the possibility of additional, non-natural infant mortality as a result of infanticide or exposure; on this problem, see Chapter 7, Section 2. The ratio of males aged 14 to 62 (poll tax payers) to the total population is 1 to 2.909; this figure is often used in calculating local populations from tax statistics. But in villages it would be somewhat lower, in metropoleis much higher.

population would have a life expectancy at birth of slightly over 23.9 years, and a sex ratio of about 118.

Table 5.4. *A restored population for Roman Egypt*

Age	Males	Females	Total	Sex ratio
0	79,666	75,679	155,345	105.3
1–4	238,609	216,049	454,658	110.4
5–9	265,343	233,027	498,370	113.9
10–14	251,611	217,825	469,436	115.5
15–19	238,414	202,830	441,244	117.5
20–24	221,760	185,728	407,488	119.4
25–29	203,207	167,675	370,883	121.2
30–34	183,924	149,541	333,464	123.0
35–39	164,299	131,736	296,035	124.7
40–44	143,604	115,088	258,692	124.8
45–49	122,908	99,721	222,629	123.3
50–54	101,871	84,354	186,226	120.8
55–59	80,737	68,409	149,146	118.0
60–64	59,993	51,430	111,423	116.6
65–69	40,369	34,370	74,738	117.5
70–74	23,520	19,870	43,390	118.4
75–79	10,859	8,799	19,658	123.4
80+	3,993	3,181	7,174	125.5
Total	2,434,688	2,065,312	4,500,000	117.9

How well does this reconstructed total population match the age figures in the census returns? Quite well indeed.[36] The model population has an average age of 26.0 years; the returns give an average of 26.2 years (710 persons). This is a very young population; persons aged 65 and older are only about 3 percent of the total population, while persons less than 15 are about 35 percent.[37]

The percentage of the model population aged 15 to 44 is 46.8; for the returns, the figure is 48.4 (344 of 711). In the model, the ratio of persons aged less than 5 to those aged 15 to 44 (the "Child to Parent" ratio) is

---

[36]Figures below include the 23 persons whose age is known but whose sex is indeterminate.
[37]H. S. Shryock and J. S. Siegel, *Methods* (1980) 234; the percentage of elderly is almost identical to that in India, 1961.

0.289; the returns have a ratio of 0.262 (90 to 344). The Age Dependency Ratio is the ratio of persons aged 0 to 14 and 60 or more, to those aged 15 to 59; for the model this ratio is 0.692, while for the returns it is 0.650.[38] The slight shortfall in the last three statistics is apparently owing mainly to the undercount of female infants. The census statistics do not change substantially if "weighted" figures are instead used as a basis for comparison.

The model population presupposes an annual birth rate of about 44.1 per thousand persons, and an annual death rate of 42.1 per thousand; the difference between these two figures produces the population's slow intrinsic growth rate. The death rate for persons over age 1 is about 28.6 per thousand; for those above age 5, 24.6 per thousand; for those above age 65, 124.2 per thousand. The average age at death is 22.7; for persons over age 5, the average age of death is 43.7. These figures should be understood as, at best, merely exemplifying values that may have obtained in Roman Egypt.

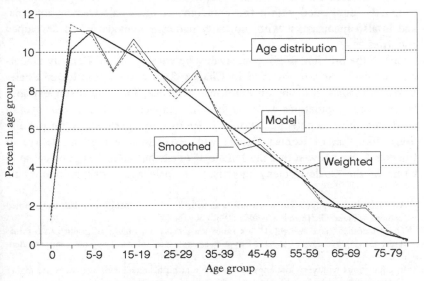

Figure 5.5. *Total Egyptian population compared with model*

Figure 5.5 plots the age distribution in the model population against the attested age distribution in Roman Egypt;[39] both the "smoothed" and

---

[38] On the Age Dependency Ratio, see H. S. Shryock and J. S. Siegel, *Methods* (1980) 235 (with a slightly different measure).

[39] Because the total Egyptian figures include 23 persons of unknown sex, the correction to the male figures discussed above at note 19 has not been made. For 19 five-year age groups, average variance from the model is 0.50 percent for "smoothed" figures, 0.57 for "weighted."

"weighted" figures are given, but the two are generally near to one another. The model is obviously a very close fit for either set of figures.

Doubts

Unfortunately, although a model broadly similar to this one *may* have obtained in early imperial Egypt, one strong reason argues against adopting it with any fervor, namely the age-specific sex ratios that it implies. As Table 5.4 shows, the sex ratio during the first year of life ought to be close to 105, the natural sex ratio obtaining at birth. But thereafter, if males have in fact an appreciably higher life expectancy at birth than females, the sex ratio should rise rapidly into a range between 115 and 125, where it remains until the end of life; or so at least the Coale-Demeny models would predict.[40] But the attested Egyptian sex ratio is irreconcilable with this pattern, as Figure 5.6 shows.[41] The sex ratio in the census returns is substantially below the projected sex ratio for most age groups until the mid-fifties, but then shoots above it at an accelerating rate. This phenomenon cannot be duplicated within the paradigm of the Coale-Demeny models, and is also inconsistent with mortality patterns of modern less developed countries.[42]

Part of the problem might conceivably lie with the Coale-Demeny models themselves.[43] As we observed in Chapter 2, Section 1, the lower Coale-Demeny models rest not on empirical evidence, but instead on extrapolation from populations with higher life expectancy and lower overall mortality; this is a potential source of serious error, particularly for populations (like that of Roman Egypt) with exceptionally high mortality. In Chapter 4, we showed that the female age distribution makes good sense in terms of the Coale-Demeny models. The male age distribution presents

---

[40] An example of a population where this rise actually occurs (though in a less exaggerated fashion) is India: C. Newell, *Methods* (1988) 30, for 1971.

[41] The "smoothed" and "weighted" sex ratios are taken from Figure 5.2, which uses three-figure moving averages of attested Egyptian sex ratios in order to bring out central tendencies.

[42] In populations with very low expectation of life at birth, female mortality rates are higher than male from ages 1 to 30, but lower thereafter, so that the sex ratio tends downward in later life; the female disadvantage is highest not during childbearing years, but in early childhood prior to puberty, presumably as a result of differential child-rearing. C. A. Nathanson, "Sex Differences" (1984) 195, summarizes modern research. However, in the Indian subcontinent sex-specific mortality rates are least favorable to women during their childbearing years. P. M. Visaria, *Sex Ratio* (1971) 41–47.

[43] As A. J. Coale and P. Demeny concede, *Life Tables* (1983) 25, "there is no strong reason for supposing that the age patterns in these four [Models] cover anything like the full range of variability in age patterns in populations under different circumstances." For example, mortality in rural China during the 1930s was "different from the structure of any [Coale-Demeny] model life tables," apparently because of a high incidence of tuberculosis among adolescents. G. W. Barclay *et al.*, "Reassessment" (1976) 621–624.

more problems. Ideally, we would seek to derive life tables directly from the census data, without using models at all, but surviving data are insufficiently robust for this purpose.[44]

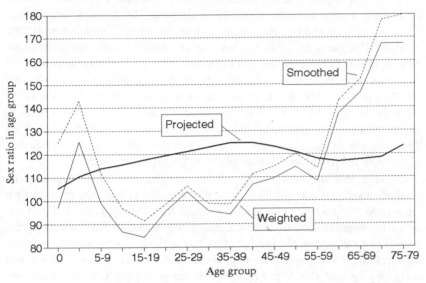

Figure 5.6. *The Egyptian sex ratio compared with model*

More probably, the source of the difficulty lies with the returns. The exact problem is hard to diagnose; there are several possibilities, among them that, particularly in villages, adult males of taxable age continue to be underreported in the returns,[45] or (less probably) the female age statistics are somehow systematically distorted.[46] But the likeliest explanation is that, especially from about age 60 onward, male ages are exaggerated to a larger extent than female; this exaggeration produces the misleading impression that elderly males outnumber females at an accelerating rate.[47]

---

[44] See, with a good discussion of methodology, E. A. Wrigley and R. S. Schofield, *England* (1989) 708–714. For Egypt in this century, good results are obtained by "splicing" Model West values for mortality up to age 5 with Model South values thereafter: *Estimation* (1982) 34–36. This method produces life tables for Roman Egypt that are not wholly implausible (esp. for males), but also not substantially different from those using Model West alone; but in any case, fit with raw data is actually worsened.

[45] The main evidence that this may have been a factor is that the sex ratio jumps just at age 60, as males pass taxable age. Since citizens of metropoleis paid a reduced poll tax, they had less reason than villagers to conceal adult males.

[46] As P. R. Cox, *Demography* (1976) 33, observes, "a suspected consistency of understatement of ages over a wide range by women is not readily proved or allowed for" in evaluating census returns; see Chapter 2, Section 3, on possible "age shoving" among younger women.

[47] This explanation was suggested to us by Prof. Coale, who points out that male age exaggeration may have been "triggered" by efforts to escape the poll tax. Testing the expla-

The "weighted" age-specific sex ratios in Figure 5.2 can be construed to support this explanation. From about age 20 to age 59, the "weighted" sex ratio remains close to a broad band between 95 and 115; this is consistent with the supposition that the adult sex ratio in Roman Egypt altered little from the sex ratio at birth, about 105 males per 100 females, presumably because male mortality rates were similar to female rates. Overall, the "weighted" figures in Table 5.2 for persons aged 20 and over yield a sex ratio of 104.0 (after applying the corrective of 1.05 to the male figures);[48] this ratio also is wholly consistent with the proposition that male and female mortality differed very little at least up to age 60. The sex ratios after age 60 may therefore be dismissed as a statistical aberration. In sum, we are permitted to speculate that male and female life expectancy did not differ widely in Roman Egypt.[49] It is probably safe to restore male life expectancy at birth at somewhere between 22.5 and 25 years.

Although this solution seems likely enough, it obviously cannot be pressed; above all, the problems surrounding the village sex ratio remain intractable on present evidence. The most that can now be said is that, under the general conditions of mortality prevailing in Roman Egypt, the overall sex ratio probably lay between 100 and 110, as in most less developed countries until quite recently; the census returns certainly do not tell decisively against this likelihood.[50] It is unrewarding to carry discussion further; the question of the Egyptian sex ratio seems destined to remain *sub judice* for the foreseeable future, until the discovery of major new evi-

---

nation is difficult because the number of those aged 60 and over is so small; but much the same phenomenon apparently occurs also in the Egyptian censuses of 1897 and 1907, at a time when Egyptian life expectancy at birth may have been still in the twenties: A. R. Omran, *Egypt* (1973) 22. Age exaggeration is a constant problem in the censuses of less developed countries: United Nations, *Manual III: Methods for Population Projections by Sex and Age* (1956) 14; K. Hopkins, "On the Probable Age Structure of the Roman Population," *Population Studies* 20 (1966) 245–264, at 246. Age exaggeration among elderly males (especially if coupled with an undercount of younger males) tends, of course, to drive upward the estimate of male life expectancy; at ages when mortality is very high and rapidly increasing, even small exaggeration has large effects on age distribution among the elderly.

[48] Because the number of persons aged 60 and older is so small, it has slight effect on this overall sex ratio.

[49] If this speculation is correct, then for males Model West, Level 3, may be preferable to Level 4; in Level 3, males have a life expectancy at birth of 22.9 years, and at age 5, 39.0 years. A. J. Coale and P. Demeny, *Life Tables* (1983) 43. Granted that the census returns are also likely to underreport the number of males under age 15, the relatively high attested number of young males may also favor Level 3.

[50] It should be noted that a sex ratio in this range can be attained without supposing an appreciable incidence of female infanticide or death through exposure. See also Chapter 7, Section 2 below.

dence. It is a pity, in any case, that sex is unknown for the three elderly residents in 131-Ox-6 from Oxyrhynchos (ages 62, 68, and 78).

The upshot of this discussion is that, on the whole, the census returns report females more comprehensively and accurately than they do males,[51] and that the female age distribution is therefore probably more credible than the male. Our restored female life table can be regarded as relatively secure. We are much less confident about our restored male life table, although we believe it may not be far off in approximating the true level of male mortality, particularly among adults. From a demographic standpoint, this result is in one respect fortunate, since demographers regard it as especially important to follow females through their life cycle of marriage and fertility.

5. Egyptian mortality: a general assessment

Despite many uncertainties, the census returns make it likely that overall Egyptian life expectancy at birth was in the lower twenties, probably between 22 and 25 years. In 1973, the anthropologist Kenneth Weiss estimated, on the basis of virtually no empirical evidence, that life expectancy at birth in the classical and medieval periods probably fell in a range from 22 to 29 years, closely comparable to that of present-day primitive societies.[52] Subsequent demographic research on the limited statistical evidence available for the Roman world has tended to confirm Weiss's estimate, but has also suggested that Roman life expectancy at birth more typically lay at the lower end of his estimated range; indeed, Roman life expectancy does not appear to have been appreciably higher than that believed to have obtained in agricultural communities of the late Neolithic period.[53] Although obstacles to research on Roman demography remain formidable, and some scholars are therefore skeptical about the usefulness of any empirical evidence for the Roman Empire,[54] convergence of the best available statistics still demands a measure of respect.

[51] The likeliest reason for accurate female reporting is that females were not subject to the poll tax; declarants thus had no reason to conceal them or misreport their ages.

[52] K. M. Weiss, *Models* (1973) 48–51. This view is now generally accepted: e.g., M. Livi-Bacci, *History* (1992) 31.

[53] B. W. Frier, "Roman Life Expectancy: Ulpian's Evidence," *HSCPh* 86 (1982) 213–251, and "Roman Life Expectancy: The Pannonian Evidence," *Phoenix* 37 (1983) 328–344; accepted by F. Jacques, "L'ethique et la statistique: à propos du renouvellement de sénat romain (Ier–IIIe siècles de l'empire)," *Annales ESC* 42 (1987) 1287–1303, at 1296–1297. See also R. Duncan-Jones, *Structure* (1990) 93–104. Compare G. Acsádi and J. Nemeskéri, *History of Human Life Span and Mortality* (1970) 216–217: Roman "mortality characteristics do not differ substantially from those of the Eneolithic or Bronze Age. It would seem therefore that the increase in [life expectancy] slowed down at the beginning of historical times, then came to a halt to turn into stagnation in ancient empires."

[54] E.g., K. Hopkins, "Graveyards" (1987); and, less judiciously, T. G. Parkin, *Demography* (1992), e.g., 58 (all our sources "are in fact so plagued with biases and produce such

The Egyptian census returns are usually conceded to be the most credible demographic evidence that survives from the Greco-Roman world.[55] They too yield values for life expectancy at birth in a range from the mid- to lower 20s. But like all other ancient evidence, they too have their problems, and these problems will inevitably provide a wedge for continued skepticism. Nonetheless, we are convinced that the returns provide solid support for the emerging picture of life expectancy in the early Roman Empire. To be sure, this picture raises many additional questions, both as to the explanation for low Roman life expectancy and as to its broader social implications. But since the returns provide no direct help in answering such questions, we leave them for other scholars to explore.[56]

---

potentially misleading or improbable information that they cannot be considered as usable"). Although this might be true, Parkin falls far short of proving it as "fact"; see the review by B. W. Frier, *BMCR* 3 (1992) 383–385. In any case, it seems more sensible to determine the demographic import of ancient sources before dismissing them out of hand. At p. 173 n.164, Parkin quotes with approval A. H. M. Jones' *obiter dictum* "that there are no ancient statistics"; this suggests the aprioristic origin of Parkin's hyperskepticism.

[55] So even T. G. Parkin, *Demography* (1992) 19–21, 58–59.

[56] See, however, Chapter 9, Section 2, for one demographic scenario that may explain high mortality rates. The central issue here is whether high Egyptian mortality was ultimately caused mainly by factors exogenous to the demographic regime (such as the chronic maldistribution of social and economic goods, and resulting poor nutrition), or rather by endogenous factors such as high fertility.

6

Marriage

Marriage in Roman Egypt differed arrestingly from its modern equivalent. Although marriage was a legal state with consequences especially for the legitimacy of children, the government regulated it lightly. For the most part, among native Egyptians, Greeks, and Roman citizens alike, marriage was a private matter between the spouses (as well as, in many cases, their families); both formation of marriage and its termination through divorce or otherwise usually occurred without the government intervening or even being notified.[1] In discussing the census returns, it is important to bear in mind the relative informality of marriage institutions in Roman Egypt.[2]

For demographers, the sequence of marriage, separation or widowhood, and remarriage (collectively referred to as nuptiality) is important less in itself than for its relationship to the age at which regular sexual relations normally begin and end for women, as well as to the forming and dissolution of families and households.[3]

1. Age at first marriage

The census returns do not declare the ages at which spouses were married. However, this question can be approached indirectly.[4] Table B summarizes

---

[1] On the law in Roman Egypt, see esp. R. Taubenschlag, *Law* (1955) 101–130; also generally R.S. Bagnall, *Egypt* (1993) 188–199. The legislation of Augustus on marriage and childbirth applied to Egyptians only if they were Roman citizens; e.g., women acting without tutors on the basis of the *ius liberorum*: 173-Ar-10, 243-Ar-3, and ???-Ar-2.

[2] In particular, the beginning and ending of marriage are often temporally indistinct (marriage is a process, not an event); thus, e.g., couples in the Greco-Roman world did not celebrate anniversaries. Present-day Egypt is similar: G. T. Acsádi, "Age" (1976).

[3] C. Newell, *Methods* (1988) 90, see 90–102. In traditional populations, nuptiality has large effects on fertility: P.C. Smith, "The Impact of Age at Marriage and Proportions Marrying on Fertility," in *Determinants* II (1983) 473–531.

[4] The method used here is based on J. Hajnal, "Age at Marriage" (1953).

111

the current marital status of 206 free females and 218 free males whose reported age is 10 or older; data are taken only from returns in which the principal resident family is complete or nearly complete, so that marital status is likely to be determinable. Persons are counted as married if the census return attests a current spouse, regardless whether that spouse is known to be co-resident;[5] and as formerly married if described as such, or if there are other signs of prior marriage, especially the presence in the household of apparently legitimate children. All others we classify as not married, although many probably had been married and a few may still be married (when the return is unclear).

A special problem arises in categorizing two women with children declared as *apatores*, without legitimate father.[6] Most such women probably either were or had been in stable consensual relations broadly similar to Roman concubinage; only barriers of legal capacity stood in the way of their entering formal marriage. However, since no male partner is declared in their households, it is uncertain whether this relationship continues at the time of the census. We count both women as not married.

Figure 6.1 (p. 113) plots the percentage of women who are married, and who are known ever to have been married, from age 12 to age 50; the curve is smoothed by four-year moving averages (six-year moving averages from age 40). The earliest marriages in Table B are at age 13, when three of nine women are already married (145-Ar-9; 159-Ar-13; 173-Pr-5). However, one census return attests a birth to a woman aged 13; the reasonable inference is that she was married by age 12.[7] In antiquity, age 12 was commonly associated with the onset of female puberty, and hence considered the earliest appropriate time for female marriage.[8] It appears, then, that Egyptian women began to marry at or soon after age 12.

---

[5] E.g., 145-Ar-24 (wife apparently declared in a separate return); 201-Ar-8 and 9 (a couple with one child are, for some reason, registered in different households); 215-An-1, and 215-Hm-1 and 2 (husband and wife register separately).

[6] 173-Ar-9: Taos aged 38, with a daughter aged 12; 187-Me-1: a freedwoman Herakleia aged 45, with daughters aged 20 and 12. On such illegitimate children, see H. C. Youtie, *"Apatores"* (1975). See further below, Chapter 7, Section 3.

[7] 201-Ar-12: the mother is 16, her child 3, but the relationship is not certain; we assume *at least* one year of marriage prior to the birth of the first attested child. The birth to a woman aged 9 in 131-Pr-1 (the mother is 29, her son 20) is probably due to scribal error, see Chapter 2, note 37. Except for Roman citizens, there was apparently no legal minimum age for marriage in Roman Egypt: R. Taubenschlag, *Law* (1955) 112. Roman law permitted women to marry at 12, see S. Treggiari, *Marriage* (1991) 39–43.

[8] D. W. Amundsen and C. J. Diers, "The Age of Menarche in Classical Greece and Rome," *Human Biology* 41 (1969) 125–132. Regular ovulation, the last stage of female puberty, can be substantially delayed by low female body weight resulting from poor nutrition, especially during childhood: J. Menken, J. Trussell, and S. Watkins, "The Nutrition and Fertility Link: An Evaluation of the Evidence," *Journal of Interdisciplinary History* 11 (1981) 425–441; T. G. Parkin, *Demography* (1992) 123. The census returns suggest that few if any Egyptian women bore children before age 15, when seven births are reported.

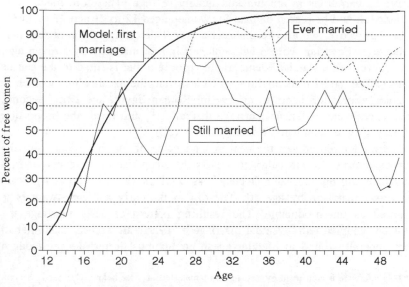

Figure 6.1. *Age at marriage: females*

As Figure 6.1 shows, the percentage of women who are married climbs steeply during their later teens, until by age 20 three-fifths or more of women have married. By their late twenties, virtually all free women appear to have married at least once.[9] These two figures are consistent with each other and display a pattern of early female marriage and eventual marriage by almost all women. Historically, early marriage and universal marriage have regularly gone together.

However, for women during their early and mid-twenties, the curve for the percentage of married women dips curiously and most improbably, from around 60 percent down to below 50 percent.[10] But this dip is plainly a statistical fluke. As it happens, in Table B the number of attested women aged 12 to 21 averages 6.5 per year (65 women); but from ages 22 to 28, the average unaccountably drops to just three (21 women), only to rise again to five for ages 29 to 35 (36 women). The curve in Figure 6.1 is sen-

---

[9] From ages 26 to 32, 96 percent of women are reported as either married or previously married (25 of 26); for ages 26 to 36, 93 percent (41 of 44).

[10] No known population displays this kind of dip over a long term. A curve representing the percent of women married is always approximately monotonic: a smooth S-curve rising from the earliest age at marriage to the point where all women who will marry have done so. A. J. Coale, "Age Patterns" (1971). Prof. Coale suggests to us that the dip may result from slight understatement of the age of young women; see Chapter 2, note 55, on age shoving.

sitive to variations in amount and quality of data. Therefore much more reliance should be placed on data for women aged 12 to 21 and 29 to 35.[11]

In Figure 6.1, we also reconstruct a model describing the probable percentage of Egyptian women who enter their first marriage by a given age; this curve uses a standard demographic program that is fitted to the census data.[12] The model rests on three variables: first, the age at which women in a given population begin to marry (for Roman Egypt, age 12);[13] second, the general rate of female marriage thereafter;[14] and third, the proportion of surviving women who eventually marry (all).

The model reproduces the central tendencies of our best data from the census returns. In particular, it depicts the steep rise in incidence of first marriage during the later 'teens,[15] as well as the likelihood of near-universal marriage by age 30. The dip in the early and mid-twenties is ignored as unreproducible. The resulting pattern of early marriage for women, coupled with eventual marriage by nearly all women, is similar to that generally found in Mediterranean populations during the pre-modern

[11] This inference is confirmed by statistics on female fertility, see below, Chapter 7, Section 1. Variation in the quantity of data was not considered by K. Hopkins, "Brother-Sister" (1980) 333–334, who argued for "a median age of marriage for both sexes in the mid-twenties." It is probably fortuitous that no women are attested as previously married before age 29 (145-Ar-2 and 159-Ar-4; contrast 89-Hm-1 and 173-Ar-2 for previously married men in their early 20s); doubtless some unmarried women in their mid-20s were divorced or widowed. Although it is possible to restore a Coale-McNeil model that gives more weight to the "dip," the model could not then represent near-universal female marriage by the late twenties.

[12] A. J. Coale, "Age Patterns" (1971); A. J. Coale and D. R. McNeil, "The Distribution by Age of the Frequency of First Marriage in a Female Cohort," *Journal of the American Statistical Association* 67 (1972) 743–749. See also United Nations, *Manual X* (1983) 22–23 (whose formula we use); N. Keyfitz, *Demography* (1985) 178–180; C. Newell, *Methods* (1988) 167–170. On sociological determinants of rates and patterns of first marriage: G. Hernes, "The Process of Entry into First Marriage," *American Sociological Review* 27 (1972) 173–182; United Nations, *First Marriage: Patterns and Determinants* (1988); L. L. Cornell, "Age at Marriage, Female Labor Force Participation, and Parental Interests," *Annales de Démographie Historique* (1989) 223–231.

[13] This variable is $a(0)$. On Prof. Coale's suggestion, in implementing the program we use a first age at marriage of 9 in order to reproduce the steep rise in percentages of married women at ages 12 to 14; this does not mean, of course, that women actually married before 12. United Nations, *Manual X* (1983) 23: "The exact value of a_0 is generally not crucial."

[14] This rate is expressed through the Singulate Mean Age of Marriage; on the concept, see J. Hajnal, "Age at Marriage" (1953); United Nations, *Manual X* (1983) 225–235; C. Newell, *Methods* (1988) 97–101. We estimate SMAM at 19.5, visually fitted to Egyptian data for ages 12 to 20 and 28 to 32. This age is typical of most traditional populations.

[15] This corresponds to the normal marriage pattern in the Western Empire as reconstructed by B. D. Shaw, "The Age of Roman Girls at Marriage: Some Reconsiderations," *JRS* 77 (1987) 30–46. In the Egyptian model, the median age of female first marriage is about 17.5. Compare *P.Austin Troph.* (unpublished; summaries of marriage contracts, 2nd cent. BC), showing heavy incidence of marriage in late teens and early twenties.

period: early marriage for women is the norm, and permanent female celibacy is rare.[16] The pattern is important especially because delay in female age at marriage can serve as a social means for limiting fertility; but in Roman Egypt this means is evidently not utilized.

The proportion of women still married reaches an apex of over eighty percent around age 30. Thereafter, the percentage declines more or less steadily, to less than 40 percent in the later forties. The reasonable inference is that many women whose marriages ended prematurely through divorce or their husband's death did not remarry;[17] we return to this issue below. Among older unmarried women, it is increasingly difficult to determine, from the census returns alone, whether they had been previously married.[18] However, evidence for women up to age 35 shows that virtually all older unmarried women had in fact been previously married.

The extent to which a pre-modern society has mustered its reproductive capacity is indicated in part by the percentage of fertile women who are married at any given time. In complete or nearly complete returns, 55 percent of free women with attested ages from 15 up to 50 are registered as currently married (76 of 139), but this percentage is clearly a bit too low. In Figure 6.1, a reconstructed curve of free women who are *still* married indicates that, of all free women aged 15 to 50, somewhat over 60 percent are married at any one time.[19] Of *all* Egyptian women aged 15 to 50 *regardless of legal status*, about 55 percent are married at any given time.

The index of the proportion of women married (I_m) is calculated from the proportion of all women (regardless of legal status) who are married in five-year age groups from 15 up to 50; for Roman Egypt, I_m is near 0.600,

[16] See esp. J. Hajnal, "European Marriage Pattern in Perspective," in *Population in History: Essays in Historical Demography* (ed. D. V. Glass and D. E. C. Eversley; 1965) 101–143, and in *Family Forms* (1983) 65–104, esp. 66–67; also A. J. Coale, "Age of Entry into Marriage," *Demography* 29 (1992) 333–341. T. W. Gallant, *Risk and Survival* (1991) 17–19, summarizes empirical evidence; compare also D. Herlihy and C. Klapisch-Zuber, *Tuscans* (1985) 203–215. On Rome, S. Treggiari, *Marriage* (1991) 83: "lifelong celibate women are . . . . practically unexampled." Present-day rural Egypt is similar: A. F. Hasan, "Age" (1989); see also A. J. Coale, in *Egypt: Demographic Responses to Modernization* (ed. A. H. Hallouda, S. Farid, and S. H. Cochrane; 1988) 31–32 (median age of women at marriage is 18; 98 percent of women marry).

[17] This too is common in the Mediterranean: see Chapter 7, note 67. In the complete or nearly complete returns, of women aged 50 and over (twenty-six cases), 35.1 percent are still married at the census, while 83.8 percent are attested as married or previously married.

[18] Unlike in modern censuses, indication of current marital state (single, married, widowed, or divorced) was not required by census takers and is given only as incidental information; women are not described as "never married."

[19] On any plausible reconstruction of the curve, between 60 and 63 percent of free women aged 15 to 50 were married; this range is also compatible with the attested percentage at 95 percent confidence (the z test).

comparable to most indices obtaining in Mediterranean Europe in 1870.[20] We use this index below in Chapter 7, at notes 32–35, when discussing marital fertility.

Male marriage

The first-marriage pattern of males is knottier. Figure 6.2 (p. 117) was calculated on much the same basis as Figure 6.1, from data for 218 free males aged 10 and over in households with complete or nearly complete principal resident families. Results are given for males aged 16 to 52, with six-year moving averages. The earliest attested married male is 19, and another man is formerly married by age 20.[21] The earliest age of paternity is 13, raising the possibility of marriage much earlier; but there are no further instances until age 17.[22] Male marriage before the later teens was therefore probably rare. Many males seem to marry in their early twenties; by age 25, about half of males are married, implying that males were not adverse to fairly early marriage if it was possible. This pattern may be distinct from that prevailing in the Western Empire, where males seem generally to delay marriage until their mid- or late twenties.[23] However, young adult males may be underrepresented in the returns (see Chapter 5); and since the census takers were perhaps likelier to "catch" married males, the curve in Figure 6.2 may exaggerate youthful male marriages. Therefore the median male age at first marriage may in fact be slightly later than 25.

In any case, the rate of male marriage slows substantially after age 25. However, unlike for women (Figure 6.1), the percentage of men who are married continues to rise as they age, until around 70 percent are married in their mid-forties. By their early 50s, all surviving males are reported as married or previously married.[24] In Section 2 below, we advance an explanation for this pronounced difference between males and females.

[20] On the calculating I_m, see C. Newell, *Methods* (1988) 47–48. I_m is not a true proportion, but a proportion weighted to reflect potential female fertility at various ages; it facilitates comparing fertility rates among populations with different marital patterns. Crudely smoothing the curve of women still married in Figure 6.1, we estimate this index at about 0.584. Mediterranean indices: A. J. Coale and R. Treadway, in *Decline of Fertility* (1986) 48–52, with their Map 2.6 (Spain, Southern France, Italy, Dalmatia, and Greece), and pp. 157–159 on the index itself.

[21] Married at 19: 173-Pr-15 (not certain). Formerly married at 20: 89-Hm-1 (with son aged 1, implying marriage by 18). The couple in 173-Pr-13 are apparently not married.

[22] Paternity at age 13: 187-Ar-4 (father aged 26, son aged 13; queried in Chapter 2 at note 38). At age 17: 131-He-4 and 145-Oa-1 (uncertain); at age 18: 117-Ar-2 (*bis*?) and 173-Pr-15; at age 19: 89-Hm-1 and 173-Pr-10. The reconstructed paternity curve (Figure 7.3) also indicates a low incidence of male marriage before age 20.

[23] R. P. Saller, "Men's Age at Marriage and Its Consequences in the Roman Family," *CPh* 82 (1987) 21–34; also T. W. Gallant, *Risk and Survival* (1991) 18, on classical Greece. But in rural modern Egypt, men usually marry in their early 20s: S. A. Huzayyin, in *Marriage and Remarriage* (1981) 100.

[24] For ages 50 to 55, all males in the returns are reported as married or previously married (only 10 cases, however). So also for ages 63 to 69 and 71 to 76 (10 cases). In complete

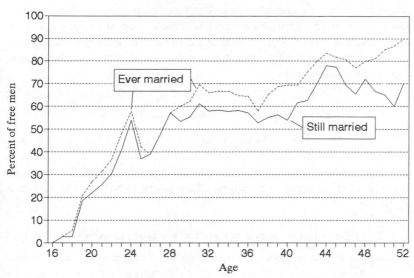

Figure 6.2. *Age at marriage: males*

Marriage in metropoleis and villages

Because the data base is so small, we have not made detailed comparisons of marriage rates in the villages and the metropoleis. However, for households with complete or nearly complete principal families, about 54 percent of free village women aged 15 to 25 are married (19 of 35), as against only about 39 percent of metropolitan women (9 of 23).[25] But in the next decade of life, the statistics are virtually identical: of women aged 26 to 35, 93 percent of village women are married or previously married (25 of 27), as against 93 percent of metropolitans (13 of 14). In both villages and metropoleis, women begin marrying at about the same age; but village women appear to marry at a somewhat faster rate during their mid- and late teens, while metropolitan women may delay marriage by about two or three years, into their later teens or early twenties.[26]

---

or nearly complete returns, of males aged 50 and older (40 cases), 57.5 percent are still married, while 85.0 percent are attested as married or previously married; the percentage still married is much higher than for women (see note 17).

[25] However, this difference is not significant even at a 90 percent confidence interval (the z test).

[26] For a possible explanation of delayed female marriage in metropoleis, see Chapter 7 at note 66. Such a pattern, though by no means invariable, is at least not unusual in premodern populations; complex village households presumably assisted early family formation, see P.C. Smith, in *Determinants* II (1983) 492–499, 508. In late medieval Tuscany,

Marriage

For men aged 15 to 25, about 31 percent of village men have been married (8 of 26), as against about 20 percent of metropolitans (6 of 31). From age 26 to 35, about 65 percent of village men are married or previously married (20 of 31), as against 52 percent of metropolitans (12 of 23). The adverse sex ratio may account for the slight lag in marriages among metropolitan males.

2. The age difference between husbands and wives

In 78 cases, the census returns preserve the ages of both husband and wife.[27] The mean gap in age between husband and wife is 7.5 years, a fairly high figure that also accords with the age gap commonly found in traditional Mediterranean populations where women marry young and men only later.[28]

Table 6.1. *Age-specific age gap between husband and wife*

| Females | | | Males | | |
Age	Cases	Age gap	Age	Cases	Age gap
13–19	14	8.9			
20–29	23	7.3	19–29	18	4.1
30–39	21	8.2	30–39	24	6.2
40+	20	6.0	40–49	19	8.2
			50+	17	12.4
Total	78	7.5		78	7.5

rural and urban ages at marriage are very similar: D. Herlihy and C. Klapisch-Zuber, *Tuscans* (1985) 86–88, 203–211.

[27] To eke out the surviving evidence, we include two prior marriages. In 159-Ar-4, the declarant aged 31 is divorced from his full sister aged 29, but she still resides in the household. In 173-Ar-2, the declarant aged 22 notes his divorced wife and half-sister aged 26, although she no longer resides in the household. We also include the slave-freewoman "marriage" in 117-Ar-3, and three probable marriages (173-Me-3; 173-Pr-15; 229-Hm-1).

[28] E.g., D. Herlihy and C. Klapisch-Zuber, *Tuscans* (1985) 87, 204–207, 211; so also in modern Egypt: A. F. Hasan, "Age" (1989) 295–296 (especially for very young brides). Gap in age is defined as husband's age minus wife's. Median age gap for Roman Egypt is 6 years. Average gap in villages is 7.4 years (52 cases); in metropoleis, 7.9 (26 cases). The difference is not significant.

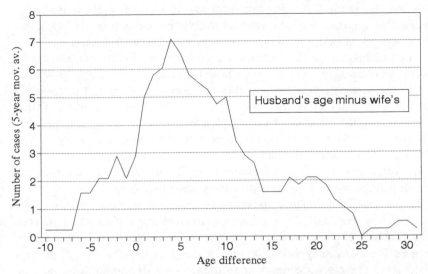

Figure 6.3. *Gap in age between husband and wife*

However, as Figure 6.3 shows, there is considerable dispersion in the gap in age. The standard deviation around the mean is approximately 7.8 years, meaning that the age gap in about two-thirds of marriages would be from 0 to 15 years—a large range indeed. Egyptian husbands are normally as old as or older than their wives, by from 0 to 13 years (54 of the 78 cases, or 69 percent), with the apex at about 2 to 6 years. However, in 9 cases (12 percent of the sample), the wife is older than her husband, in one instance by as much as 8 years.[29] At the other extreme, there are 15 cases (19 percent) in which a husband is 15 years or more older than his wife; the largest gap is 31 years.[30] Though Egyptians evidently expected a husband to be older than his wife, no clear structural pattern is present, exactly as would be predicted from the male marriage curve in Figure 6.2.

However, patterns do emerge if we examine the age gap across successive decades of female and male adulthood. Table 6.1 (p. 118) gives average age-specific age gaps for 78 females aged 13 and above, and for 78 males aged 19 and above. For each sex, the evidence is divided into four age groups with about an equal number in each group. As Table 6.1 shows, the age gap between husbands and wives drifts erratically *downward* as women

[29] 187-Ar-4, from Arsinoe: a lodger is 52, her brother and husband (a donkey-driver) is 44. The next lowest age gap is -4 years (five cases).
[30] 117-Ap-7, from Tanyaithis: a scribe aged 70 registers his wife aged 39. His age may be rounded upward. The next largest gap is 28 years: 173-Pr-10; then 22 years (three cases). If Chares' age in 145-Ar-9 is 73 (and not 63), he was 32 years older than his wife.

grow older, but moves strongly *upward* as men age. For women aged 13 to
19, the age gap is 8.9 years; but from age 40 onward, the age gap is 6.0
years. By contrast, for men aged 19 to 29, the age gap is 4.1 years; but
from age 50 onward, the gap rises to an extraordinary 12.4 years.

The explanation for this phenomenon becomes clear if we examine the 25
wives who are aged 13 to 25, and whose husbands' ages are also preserved.
In 19 instances, the age gap is within the usual range, from 2 to 13 years;
in one additional case, the wife is four years older than her husband.
However, in the other five cases, the husband is much older than the wife,
by from 17 to 28 years.[31] That is, in a fifth of the sample a young woman
has married a much older man; the average age gap among these women is
19.8 years. It is this large admixture of marriages between older men and
much younger women that produces the pattern in Table 6.1.

In the case of women, a hypothetical example may clarify this explanation. A woman aged 15 could anticipate an average of about 33 years of
life (Table 4.2); by contrast, if she married a husband aged 35, her husband's life expectancy would be only about 22 years (Table 5.3, perhaps
too high). Therefore she had a good chance of outliving her husband. But
since, as Figure 6.1 shows, many widowed or divorced women did not
remarry, the age gap in surviving marriages tends to decline as women age,
and particularly from age 30 on.

When the age gap was large, women often married while still very
young. In four of the five cases where a woman aged 25 or younger is married to a man at least seventeen years her senior, the census returns point to
her marriage by age 16 at latest; in the fifth case, marriage is by age 18.[32]
Other returns for older women exhibit the same pattern.[33]

In four of these five cases, there is no evidence that the husband had
previously married. In the fifth case, however, the husband had previously
married. In this completely preserved return (173-Pr-10, from Thelbonthon
Siphtha), four brothers declare a *frérèche* with seventeen family members.
The oldest brother is Pantbeus, son of Petos and Thaeies, aged 49. Pantbeus has a son Petos aged 10, whose mother is described as Thapsathis,
daughter of Petos; she was probably, though not certainly, Pantbeus' sister.

---

[31] The cases are listed in the following footnote.

[32] 103-Ar-11: wife aged 25 has son 6, implying her marriage by age 18. 131-Pr-1: wife aged
21 has son 4. 173-Pr-5: wife is aged 16, no issue. 173-Pr-10: wife aged 21 has son 5.
187-Ar-4: wife aged 17 has daughter 1. We allow at least one year of marriage before
birth of the first attested child; this interval is fairly typical, see H. S. Shryock and J. S.
Siegel, *Methods* (1980) 519, but of course it yields only approximate maximums.

[33] 187-Ar-11: wife aged 34 has son aged 15 (marriage by 18). 145-Ar-9: wife aged 41 has
son 21 (marriage by 19). Of the fifteen marriages in which the husband is at least fifteen
years older than his wife, six are metropolitan and nine are village; the data base is too
small to indicate that such marriages were more frequent in villages.

The declaration does not say so, but Thapsathis is now probably deceased. Pantbeus' present wife is Theros, daughter of Ammonios and Taphibichis, evidently no kin to her husband; she is aged 21, thus twenty-eight years younger than her husband. Pantbeus and Theros have a son aged 5, and two daughters aged 4 and 2. In other words, soon after the end of his first marriage Pantbeus remarried a much younger woman who was probably no more than 15 at the time of her marriage.[34]

This admixture of marriages between young women and much older men may have had considerable effect on the "marriage market" in Roman Egypt. As Figure 6.2 suggests, many males did seek to marry during their early twenties; Table 6.1 shows that they usually married women just a few years younger than themselves. From the model population in Table 5.4 (which may overstate the number of males), it emerges that males aged 20 to 24 could have outnumbered females aged 15 to 19 by a ratio of almost eleven to ten. However, if as much as a fifth of women aged 15 to 19 married much older males, the ratio rises to nearly fourteen younger males for every ten females.

In short, young males in search of a wife probably encountered serious obstacles stemming not just from any imbalance in the Egyptian sex ratio,[35] but also from the competition of older males who were either marrying for the first time or remarrying, often to women much younger than themselves. The result, we argue, was an appreciable "surplusage" of younger males unable to marry and begin a family of their own. The male "surplusage" may have formed a somewhat transient group within Roman Egypt: many younger males, unable to begin a family, may have left the countryside and migrated to the nome metropoleis or to the great city of Alexandria, thus unbalancing the urban sex ratio still further.[36] This reconstruction, although obviously hypothetical, seems to account for much of the data in the census returns.

3. Marriage patterns

In Roman Egypt as represented in the census returns, marriage is monogamous.[37] Virtually always, marriage is also "virilocal": the wife resides in

---

[34]Other cases of remarriage to a much younger woman in 173-Pr-5 and 187-Ar-22. The latter case is exceptionally complex; see below at note 60.

[35]As was shown in Chapter 5 at note 8, the sex ratio was probably unbalanced at least for free persons. A similar effect has been observed in present-day India, which also has a sex ratio unbalanced toward males: P. M. Visaria, *Sex Ratio* (1971) 64–65.

[36]We return to this subject in Chapter 8, on migration.

[37]M. Hombert and C. Préaux, *Recherches* (1952) 169; cf. P. W. Pestman, *Marriage* (1961) 3, 62–63. We deal here only with what is designated marriage in the returns. Free births outside of marriage, and possible concubinage, are discussed in Chapter 7, Section 3; slave "marriages," in Section 4.

her husband's household, often with his extended family. In at least one instance, however, the wife is the owner of the house.[38] On occasion, a wife's close relatives (her parents, siblings, or children from a former marriage) may reside with her in her husband's house.[39] But what seems not to occur is a husband moving into the house of his wife's relatives; in the one case where this may have happened (201-Ar-8/9), the couple's current residence is unfortunately left open to conjecture.

Long-term stable marriages are ubiquitous in the returns.[40] One of the more interesting is 159-Hm-3, a household from Alabanthis in the Hermopolite nome: the declarant aged 72, his wife 57, their daughter 40 and son 8. The mother was therefore married by at least age 16 to a man 15 years her senior; their marriage has lasted more than four decades. Her two attested children (there may well have been others) were born when she was 17 and 49, respectively, virtually at the outer limits of her fertility. The daughter had probably been previously married; her marriage having ended, she has returned to her parents' household.[41]

On the other hand, the returns also record numerous broken marriages. The cause is seldom mentioned.[42] When it is omitted, speculation is usually idle. For example, in 89-Hm-1 from Hermopolis, a doctor aged 20 has a son aged 1, but no wife; it seems not unlikely that his wife died in or soon after childbirth, but the couple might also have divorced. The returns mention only death of a spouse and divorce as possible causes for a marriage's dissolution.

---

[38] Wife is owner: 159-Ar-7, from Karanis. See also 131-Me-1, 173-Pr-7, and 215-Hm-2 (wives are declarants). In 159-Ar-9, a nuclear family lives in a house owned by a daughter aged 16; it is not clear why she is the owner, but the house might have been a "bride price" gift to the family in anticipation of her imminent marriage.

[39] Parent (invariably a mother): 131-He-2; 201-Ar-8 and 10; see also 145-Ar-3. Siblings: 117-Ox-2 (an adult brother); 173-Ar-16 (three brothers, all probably adults; their sister is probably married to the declarant); 187-Ar-4 (two adult brothers). Children from former marriage: see below.

[40] In addition to 159-Hm-3, seven marriages are attested as lasting more than 25 years. 46 years: 117-Ox-2. 41 years: 131-Be-1; 159-Ar-11. 34 years: 145-Ar-12. 30 years: 117-Ap-6. 29 years: 173-Pr-10. 27 years: 215-Ar-3. In addition, twenty marriages have lasted 15 to 25 years. Length of marriage is reconstructed either from the difference in age between parent and child, or from the difference in ages between full siblings (in which case the parents may no longer be alive); the figures above are therefore minimums. Possible misreporting of age is ignored.

[41] In ???-Ar-3, a household that appears to be a disintegrating *frérèche*, a widow aged 60 remains with her three children in her former husband's household; in 145-Ar-12, a divorced woman aged 33 has returned to her parents. In 159-Ar-5 and 6, divorced full siblings both remain in the same household; the woman presumably has no other place to live. But there are other cases where previously married women live alone with their children although they have surviving kin: e.g., 145-Ar-1 and 2 (kinsmen are *kyrioi*); 187-Ar-29 (father is *kyrios*). No clear pattern is discernible.

[42] Despite difficulties in enumeration, we count nearly eighty probable broken marriages in which the cause of dissolution is not specified.

Death of a spouse
Granted the very high mortality levels in Roman Egypt, dissolution of marriage by the death of a spouse was always a real possibility. For example, if a man aged 25 married a woman aged 15, the figures in Tables 4.2 and 5.3 indicate better than one chance in four that one or both spouses will die within ten years. For this reason, a large proportion of "causeless" broken marriages were probably terminated in fact by a spouse's death.

In only eight instances do the census returns expressly indicate death of a spouse as the reason for a marriage's dissolution; in each case there are surviving children from the marriage, who provide the occasion for noting the death.[43] The current age of the surviving spouses is often young: widowers aged 26, 31 (*bis*), and 33; widows aged 36 and 60. Three widowers have remarried; none of the widows has.

Divorce
Although divorce on demand of either spouse was legally available in Roman Egypt as elsewhere in the Roman Empire, scholars have debated its commonness in the lower classes.[44] The returns show that divorce was not rare among the general population of Egypt. There are at least seventeen instances in which a marriage has ended in divorce.[45] Further, in each case the reason for the divorce was not the former wife's infertility since the marriage has surviving children, who, in fact, always provide the occasion for mentioning divorce. A wife's failure to produce a male heir is also unlikely to have been a common cause of divorce; in eight of the thirteen cases where the sex of the children is known, at least one is a son.[46] Since

---

[43] Five widowers: 131-Ox-14; 201-Ar-2 and 9; 215-Ar-4; 243-Ar-3. Three widows: 243-Ar-3 and 4 (see 229-Ar-2); ???-Ar-3. See also, probably, 117-Ar-5, 145-Ar-20, and 173-Pr-4 and 11, in all of which a child has apparently inherited from a deceased father; the presumed widows are 30, 55, 47, and 48, respectively, and none has remarried. The husband of the 60-year-old declarant in 173-Pr-14 may be deceased (see the Discussion). An ex-spouse is perhaps normally mentioned in order to confirm a child's legitimacy. If P_h is the probability that a husband aged 25 will die within ten years, and P_w is the probability that a wife aged 15 will die within ten years, then the probability that one or both will die is $P_h + P_w - (P_h)(P_w)$, $= 0.1456 + 0.1640 - (0.1456 \times 0.1640)$, $= 0.2857$; values of P derive from Tables 4.2 and 5.3, the probability formula is from R.E. Kirk, *Statistics: An Introduction* (3d ed.; 1990) 241–243.

[44] Availability of divorce in Roman Egypt: R. Taubenschlag, *Law* (1955) 121–125; cf. P. W. Pestman, *Marriage* (1961) 64–79. Commonness among lower classes: S. Treggiari, *Marriage* (1991) 482 n. 222, with bibliography, esp. S. Treggiari, "Divorce Roman Style: How Easy and How Frequent Was It?" in *Marriage, Divorce and Children in Ancient Rome* (ed. B. Rawson; 1991) 31–46; also T. G. Parkin, *Demography* (1992) 132–133.

[45] 131-Ar-11; 145-Ar-2, 3, 4 (see Discussion), and 12 (probably; see Discussion); 159-Ar-4, 5, 6, and 8 (*bis*); 159-Me-1/2; 173-Ar-2; 187-Ar-10 and 32 (the declarant is twice divorced, and mentions that one of his former wives had divorced before marrying him); 201-Ar-6. Seven instances are from villages, ten from metropoleis.

[46] On sex preference in Egypt, see below, Chapter 7, at notes 59–66.

the returns mention divorce only when there are surviving children, it may well have been appreciably more frequent than the attested cases suggest.

The current age of divorced spouses is often young: males are attested as aged 22, 31, 32, and 37 (two others, whose ages are uncertain, are probably at least in their forties); females, as aged 29 (*bis*), 33, 40, 49, and 57. Two divorced males (out of nine) have since remarried, and one has remarried after two divorces; none of the divorced females (out of eight) has remarried.[47]

In the few instances where we can judge from the ages of surviving children, divorce seems to have occurred in the couple's twenties or early thirties, suggesting that incompatibility was the usual reason for divorce. In 145-Ar-3 from Tebtunis, a divorced woman aged 40 has children aged 21, 19, and 15; her marriage may well have ended in her late twenties. In 159-Ar-4 from Arsinoe, full siblings have divorced; he is aged 31, she is 29, and their son is 8. In 159-Me-1/2 from Memphis, the declarant is a man aged 37; his younger son is 5. The Arsinoite declarant in 159-Ar-6 is a Roman veteran who must be at least in his early forties; his son is 6. Though the sample is tiny, the large number of minor children[48] implies that parents had little impulse to preserve a failed marriage "for the sake of the children."

Marriages between close kin may have been more likely to end in divorce. At any rate, the sample contains two divorces between full siblings (159-Ar-4 and 5), one between half-siblings (173-Ar-2).[49] Usually the kinship, if any, between former spouses cannot be determined.

Children of broken marriages

The fragility of Egyptian marriage[50] meant that children were often raised, for at least part of their youth, by one parent or by other persons. When marriage is attested as ending because of one spouse's death, children are invariably with the surviving parent (eight sure cases, five probable; five fathers, eight mothers).

When divorce is the attested cause, children usually remain with their father (eleven cases), less often they reside with their mother (three cases);[51] but it is seldom possible to determine whether the other ex-spouse

[47] But in 187-Ar-32 from Arsinoe, the declarant is divorced from a woman whom he married after she had been divorced from her first husband.

[48] See also 159-Ar-5 (younger daughter aged 10); 187-Ar-10 (daughter 10); 187-Ar-32 (son 10).

[49] The divorce in 145-Ar-12 may also be between full siblings. *P.Mil.Vogl.* 85 = *P.Kron.* 52 (Tebtunis, AD 138) is a divorce agreement between a man aged 54 and his full sister 50; see K. Hopkins, "Brother-Sister" (1980) 322–323.

[50] Lest the picture be unrelievedly gloomy, we should report nearly eighty families in which children aged 14 or less live with two married parents. Happy families have no history.

[51] Father: 131-Ar-11; 145-Ar-4 (see Discussion) and 12 (probably); 159-Ar-6 and 8 (*bis*); 159-Me-1/2; 173-Ar-2; 187-Ar-32 (*bis*, see Discussion); 201-Ar-6. Mother: 145-Ar-2 and

is still alive.[52] The most complex return, in this respect, is 187-Ar-22 from Arsinoe. The male declarant has twice divorced and remarried; both his former wives are alive. Each of his prior marriages had resulted in a son; one son now resides with the declarant, the other with his mother. Further, his second ex-wife had married and divorced before marrying the declarant; her children from *that* marriage, who had doubtless lived in the declarant's household during her marriage to him, now reside with their father (her first husband). This return vividly illustrates the intricacy of family life when divorce is common.[53]

In the many cases when the cause of a marriage's dissolution is unknown but at least one parent survives, attention focuses particularly on nineteen instances where one or more surviving children are currently aged 14 or less. In nine cases, the children are with their mother; in ten, with their father.[54] The age of mothers is usually young (one in her twenties, seven in their thirties, one in her forties); none has remarried. The census returns report about nine instances where a previously married woman lives alone with her minor children.[55]

As to fathers, most are older (one in his twenties, three in their thirties, one in his forties, four in their fifties); three have remarried, and most reside with relatives who presumably assisted in raising children. But in two instances, a father lives alone with young children. In ???-Me-1 from Memphis, the father is aged 33, his son 3; in 229-Hm-2 from Alabastrine, a father is aged 57 and his son 8.[56]

3; 187-Ar-32 (see Discussion).

[52] In 173-Ar-2, the divorced husband aged 22 has the three sons; his former wife, a half-sister aged 26, is still living and resides elsewhere. Similarly in 145-Ar-4 and 12 (see Discussion), and 201-Ar-6. Former husbands remained responsible for the maintenance of young children, even when they resided with their mothers. If children were ever split between former spouses, the census returns provide no evidence. In two cases of brother-sister marriage that end in divorce (159-Ar-4 and 5), the divorced sister remains in the household; these cases are discussed at the end of this chapter.

[53] On "dislocation" in the Roman family, see K. R. Bradley, *Family* (1991) 125–155.

[54] Children reside with mothers: 33-Ar-2; 103-Ar-9; 173-Ar-11; 187-Ar-29; 187-Ox-4 (probably); 243-Ar-1 (possibly); 257-Ar-1; ???-Ar-3 (*bis*). With fathers: 11-Ar-1; 75-Ox-1 (possibly); 89-Hm-1; 173-Me-1; 173-Pr-10 (*bis*; both remarried); 187-Ar-26; 215-Ar-4 (remarried); 229-Hm-2; ???-Me-1.

[55] 33-Ar-2; 103-Ar-9; 117-Ar-5 (husband probably dead); 145-Ar-2 (divorce); 173-Pr-4; 187-Ar-29; 187-Ox-4 (possible); 243-Ar-1 (possible); 257-Ar-1. In 243-Ar-3, a woman aged 36 with sons aged 16, 11, and 7 has as lodgers the brother of her late husband and his wife. See also 187-Me-1, where a freedwoman aged 45 lives with her daughters 20 and 12 (both *apatores*) and a slave; but the father may still be living and resident elsewhere.

[56] The reconstruction of this poorly preserved return is speculative; another boy, age 6, is also part of the household but apparently not the declarant's son. Compare 159-Me-1 and 2: a father aged 37 with sons 14 and 5; also 173-Ar-2: father 22 with three young sons.

When neither parent survived, children were apparently often raised by relatives.[57] More unusual is 145-Ly-1 from Lykopolis, where a female "lodger" aged 8 is described (if the text is correctly restored) as an orphan evidently taken in by strangers. In 103-Ar-12 from an Arsinoite village, a declarant aged 20 is evidently raising his sisters 14 and 8; they are presumably orphans.

Remarriage

After a marriage was broken, the former spouses not infrequently remarried. The census returns give thirty likely cases; ten are women, twenty are men, again indicating that men were considerably more likely than women to remarry.[58] Since surviving issue of prior marriages provide the invariable occasion for mentioning remarriage, its incidence was certainly higher than the returns indicate.[59]

When they remarried, spouses often brought with them children from prior marriages.[60] The most remarkable ménage is 187-Ar-22, a family of renters from Arsinoe. The husband, aged 61, and his probable third wife, aged 40, may well have been married for some time; they have a daughter aged 5. In addition, the husband has a son aged 30 from his first marriage, and a daughter aged 18 from his second; these half-siblings have married. His wife also has a daughter 22 and a son 18 from *her* prior marriage. Husband and wife thus have co-resident children from four distinct marriages.

As Figures 6.1 and 6.2 show, the percentage of women still married drops from a peak around 80 percent in the late twenties, to between 30 and 40 percent by age 50; by contrast, the percent of men still married climbs to about 70 percent in their forties. To a large extent, this results from men aggressively continuing to marry or remarry into their forties,

---

[57] 145-Ar-20 (brothers aged 8 and 1 living with a cousin); 159-Ar-13 (girl aged 12, probably with her first cousin); 173-Ar-11 (boy, with his aunt and cousin); 173-Pr-13 (girl 13, apparently living with cousins); 215-Ar-3 (girls 10 and 8, with their uncle). See also 187-Ar-8 (girl 8) and 26 (females aged 25, 15, and 4): all are *apatores*, apparently taken in by relatives after their mother's death. More doubtful are 131-Ox-1, 201-Ar-5, and 229-Hm-2. The domestic situtation in 131-Ox-13 is unclear.

[58] Women: 117-Ar-7; 131-Me-1; 145-He-2; 173-Ar-2 (declarant's mother) and 11 (*bis*); 187-Ar-22, 29, and 32 (declarant's former wife, see Discussion); 229-Hm-2 (possible). Men: 33-Ar-1 (lodger's father; probable); 131-Ar-11 (declarant's father); 131-He-4; 131-Ox-1; 145-Ar-9 (the couple's father); 159-Ar-5; 173-Me-1; 173-Pr-5 and 10 (*bis*); 187-Ar-8, 22 (twice remarried), 32 (twice remarried); 187-Ox-3 (declarants' father); 201-Ar-2 (to the full sister of his deceased wife) and 5; 215-Ar-4; 215-He-2 (declarant's father). In 187-Ar-32, one of the declarant's former wives had also remarried.

[59] On remarriage, M. Humbert, *Le remariage à Rome: étude d'histoire juridique et sociale* (1972); but his argument for its frequency (pp. 76–112) does not adequately distinguish by sex and class. See also K. R. Bradley, *Family* (1991) 156–176.

[60] These children often remain into their adulthood: 131-He-4; 131-Ox-1; 145-Ar-9; 145-He-2; 173-Ar-11; 173-Pr-5; 187-Ar-8 and 22; 187-Ox-3.

while, for one reason or another, women do not consistently remarry after age 35.[61] In Chapter 7 (at notes 67-70), we argue that the tendency of fer tile adult women not to remarry acted as, in effect, a control on population growth.

4. Brother-sister marriage

Endogamous marriage between extremely close kin is very frequent in the census returns until the general grant to Egypt of Roman citizenship by the Constitutio Antoniniana of AD 212.[62] Roman law then suppressed the practice at least as a public phenomenon.[63] Returns before this date are the best surviving evidence for close-kin marriage in the broader Egyptian population.

Since declarants are usually careful to indicate the lineage of household members, the kinship, if any, between husband and wife is usually determinable. As Table 6.2 shows, out of 121 marriages in which the degree of kinship between the spouses is ascertainable with some certainty,[64] more than a fifth of spouses are either full siblings, half-siblings, or first cousins. Full brother-sister marriages are much the most frequent of these close-kin

[61] In six cases female age at remarriage is roughly ascertainable: 131-Me-1 (after age 22); 145-He-2 (shortly after 28); 173-Ar-11 (between 16 and 33; between 29 and 30); 187-Ar-22 (between 18 and 34); 187-Ar-29 (between 23 and 31). Seven cases where male age at remarriage can be estimated: 131-He-4 (age 31); 173-Me-1 (between 34 and 49); 173-Pr-5 (between 34 and 47); 173-Pr-10 (between 39 and 43); 187-Ar-22 (between 31 and 42, and again between 43 and 55); 215-Ar-4 (30?). The male ages are substantially older, and there is no secure case of female remarriage after 35.

[62] The literature is extensive. See esp. M. Hombert and C. Préaux, *Recherches* (1952) 149–153; J. Modrzejewski, "Geschwisterehe" (1964); N. Sidler, *Inzesttabu* (1971) 64–85; K. Hopkins, "Brother-Sister" (1980), on which J. Goody, *The Oriental* (1990) 319–341, is largely based; B. Shaw, "Brother-Sister," partially refuting Hopkins and Goody. All have further citations. We take no position on the broader "Goody thesis"; for a recent discussion, see M. Mitterauer, "Christianity and Endogamy," *Continuity and Change* 6 (1991) 295–333, esp. 301–303. For Roman law, see Gaius, *Inst.* 1.60–64; also the *Gnomon* 23, applying the law to Roman citizens in Egypt.

[63] Roman authorities encountered resistance: Diocletian, in *Coll.* 6.4 (AD 295), 5 (AD 291). In 215-Hm-1 and 2, full siblings state they are married, but register in separate returns and nominally live apart; the couple are in their thirties and may have married well before 212. They live together in 229-Hm-1, but no longer state they are married. The question would have arisen more acutely for them had there been surviving issue from their marriage, as there apparently was not in 229/230; but the couple apparently had a son at some point during the reign of Alexander Severus, see *P.Lond.* III 947 I k and II c, with P. J. Sijpesteijn, "Theognostos" (1989) 217–218. So few census returns survive from after 212 that we are unable to study the demographic effects of the Roman ban.

[64] Save as indicated, we use in this Section only datable and complete or nearly complete census returns from 215/216 and earlier; but we omit as too uncertain marriages in 33-Ar-1, 201-Ox-1, and 215-An-1. Doubtful cases were called against kinship, so the figures below are minimums.

unions, amounting to nearly a sixth of all marriages.[65] The incidence of full brother-sister marriage is remarkable since, in a near-stationary population, only about 40 percent of families will have both sons and daughters who survive to marriageable age.[66]

Table 6.2. *Incidence of close-kin marriage*

	Urban/rural			Nome distrib.	
	All	Metr.	Vill.	Arsin.	Other
Brother/sister	20	13	7	17	3
Half-sibling	4	3	1	3	1
First cousin	2	1	1	1	1
Non-kin	95	26	69	59	36
Total	121	43	78	80	41

The four pairs of married half-siblings all have a common father; but in 173-Ar-2 from Soknopaiou Nesos, the declarant aged 22 has recently divorced his half-sister on his mother's side, aged 26. Of the two marriages between cousins, kinship is agnatic in one, enatic in the other.[67] Since, as we saw above, half-siblings and cousins not infrequently grew up in the same households, these marriages may be deemed functionally equivalent to full brother-sister marriages—perhaps contracted in cases where no full sibling was present or where potential spouses were incompatible.

Brother-sister marriages are not formalities, but real marriages. The great majority result in issue, in one case eight children (187-Ar-4) and in another, six or seven (103-Ar-3); since such marriages were usually entered when spouses were young (see below), they could be very prolific if they endured. In four returns, brother-sister or half-sibling marriages continue through two generations.[68]

[65] There are twenty certain or very likely cases of full brother-sister marriage before 215: 103-Ar-1, 3, 5; 117-Ar-1; 131-Ar-3 (same couple as in 117-Ar-1); 145-Ar-9, 19, and 20; 159-Ar-11 (*bis*) and 26; 173-Ar-9; 173-Pr-5 and 10; 187-Ar-4 (four cases) and 12; 215-Hm-1/2 (with 229-Hm-1). Among incomplete returns, see also 187-Ar-16 (possibly) and 23. Assuming that the 121 marriages are a random sample (as will emerge, there are good reasons to doubt this), at 95 percent confidence the incidence of full brother-sister marriage lay between 10 and 24 percent of all marriages (the z test).

[66] K. Hopkins, "Brother-Sister" (1980) 304; we independently verified this estimate. If the sister is ordinarily younger than her husband, the percentage is lower still.

[67] Half-siblings: 131-He-4; 145-Ar-9; 187-Ar-8 and 22. First cousins: 187-An-2 (agnatic; uncertain, see Discussion); 201-Ar-10 (enatic).

[68] 145-Ar-9; 159-Ar-4 (the deceased parents were siblings) and 11; 187-Ar-4. K. Hopkins, "Brother-Sister" (1980) 321–322, notes two other papyri (*P.Tebt.* II 320 and *P.Amh.* II 75; not census returns) in which full brother-sister marriages continue across three gener-

Origins

In the census returns, the earliest examples of brother-sister marriage are from 103/104, at just the point when the papyrological record becomes abundant; but three full brother-sister marriages are attested in that census, and the practice was obviously common by then. Surviving evidence does not provide a sound basis for determining whether close-kin marriage became more or less frequent during the second century AD.

Granted the notorious onomastic complexity of Roman Egypt, it is also impossible to be sure whether brother-sister marriage was more frequent among those of Greek or of Egyptian ancestry; but both ethnicities probably practiced it fairly widely, whatever the actual origin of brother-sister marriage may have been. To be sure, most names of surviving spouses look to be Greek;[69] but there is a fair admixture of Egyptian names, and brother-sister marriage occurs in small villages with, as it appears, a predominantly Egyptian population.

However, as Table 6.2 also shows, in at least two respects the data do display significant patterns. First, there is a marked difference in the incidence of close-kin marriages if the metropoleis are compared with villages. Of the 121 well-attested marriages, 43 couples reside in metropoleis and 78 in villages. Among the metropolitan marriages, some forty percent (17 of 43) are between close kin—more than one marriage in every three; by contrast, only twelve percent of the village marriages are between close kin (9 of 78). A statistical test suggests small likelihood that close-kin marriage was as common in villages as in the metropoleis.[70] As to full brother-sister marriage, its incidence is thirty percent in metropoleis (13 of 43), as against only nine percent in villages (7 of 78).

Second, brother-sister marriages are heavily concentrated in the Arsinoite nome, which embraces the Fayyum area. There, of 80 well attested marriages, 21 (or 26 percent) are close-kin. By contrast, of 41 marriages in other nomes, only five (or 12 percent) are close-kin. At issue here is not

---

ations. On genetic effects of inbreeding, see Hopkins, pp. 325–327 ("statistically significant but small"; "probably not . . . visible . . . not remarked in any surviving source"). More negative views in, e.g., J. Shepher, *Incest: A Biosocial View* (1983) 87–93.

[69] This has mainly to do with the heavy weight of Arsinoe in surviving evidence; see below. Demotic texts also suggest that close-kin marriage was rare among native Egyptians; consanguinity is no closer than half-sibling, cf. P. W. Pestman, *Marriage* (1961) 3–4.

[70] Chi-square is 11.272 (using Yates's correction for continuity); higher than 99 percent likelihood that the variance is significant. However, both here and in the next paragraph readers should be warned that surviving census returns are not a true sample, and that the samples are in any case small. S. B. Pomeroy, "Women" (1988) 722, rightly doubts that brother-sister marriage was more common in metropoleis because of a desire to retain metropolitan civic status by making it easier to prove paternal and maternal citizenship, an idea canvassed by M. Hombert and C. Préaux, *Recherches* (1952) 152.

the occurrence of brother-sister marriage outside the Arsinoite nome (clearly it was not unknown[71]), but rather its normal frequency. There is a high, though less than conclusive, probability that brother-sister marriage was more common in the Arsinoite nome than in other attested nomes.[72]

These two patterns are consistent with the hypothesis that, in the early Roman Empire, the practice of brother-sister marriage was spreading from north to south through Egypt, and likewise from the metropoleis outward to the countryside. That is, brother-sister marriage may have had fairly recent origins (probably in the Hellenistic period), rather than being an aboriginal Egyptian usage.[73] Unfortunately, nomes to the north of the Arsinoite, in the Nile Delta, are poorly represented in surviving returns; but the well-preserved returns from the largely Egyptian village of Thelbonthon Siphtha in the southwestern Delta (173/174) show that brother-sister marriage was common there.[74] By contrast, it seems less frequent in the better-attested upper Nile valley, although it does occur.[75]

Spread

Whatever the exact origin of brother-sister marriage (and the census returns shed limited light on this question), the more important issue is this: granted the initial legal acceptability and social tolerance of the practice, why did it then become so common in areas like the Fayyum?[76] A standard

---

[71] For example, among the seven well-attested marriages from the Oxyrhynchite nome, none is close-kin; but a prior brother-sister marriage is probably reported in 75-Ox-1 from Oxyrhynchos. Compare, e.g., *P. Oxy.* I 111, III 524, XXXVIII 2858, XLVIII 3096.

[72] Chi-square equals 2.396 (using Yates's correction); about eight chances in ten that the variance is significant. Usual statistical practice would demand a chi-square higher than 3.841 in order to be certain of the inference.

[73] The census returns thus tend to confirm the most common modern scholarly view. Of the scholars cited in note 62, see J. Modrzejewski, N. Sidler, and B. Shaw, against K. Hopkins and J. Goody. But a proclivity to (or at least a tolerance of) endogamous marriage is fairly widespread in the Eastern Mediterranean; what distinguishes Roman Egypt is the extension of endogamy to the full brother-sister relationship. *P. Tebt.* III (1) 766, lines 4–9 (from 136 BC), probably shows that full brother-sister marriage was at least Hellenistic; the Ptolemies may have set the example. But Greek authors uniformly consider it indigenous: Diodorus Sic. 1.27.1; Philo, *Spec. Leg.* 3.23–24; cf. Seneca, *Apoc.* 8.3.

[74] Two current brother-sister marriages: 173-Pr-5 and 10. Former brother-sister marriages: 173-Pr-10 (probable), 13 (possible; Pantbeus' parents), and 17. The villagers are mostly illiterate in Greek and have predominantly Egyptian names. But other returns from the Prosopite nome attest eight non-kin marriages: 131-Pr-1 (three cases); 173-Pr-5 (two), 7, 10 (three), 13 and 15. The four attested marriages from the Memphite nome are also non-kin: 131-Me-1; 173-Me-3 (three).

[75] 131-He-4, from Machor (half-siblings); 215-Hm-1/2, from Hermopolis (full siblings).

[76] As B. Shaw, "Brother-Sister" (1992) 270–272, notes, forms of close-kin marriage (although not full brother-sister marriage) were commonly permitted in Greek city-states, but were evidently rare and often subject to popular derision. Social acceptability of close-kin marriage must be somehow linked to its incidence; but for Egypt the exact link seems likely to remain murky. In any case, we do not argue that avoidance of dowry provides in itself a sufficient cause for the origin of close-kin marriage.

theory holds that endogamous marriage is advantageous because it avoids the immediate necessity of providing brides with dowries, thereby temporarily staving off partition of a family's property.[77]

In somewhat roundabout fashion, the returns support this view.[78] Not surprisingly, the difference in age between husbands and wives is less for close-kin than for exogamous marriages. In the fifty-eight cases of exogamous marriage where the age of both spouses is preserved, the average age difference is 8.3 years. By contrast, in the nineteen cases of close-kin marriage, the average gap is only 5.4 years; and virtually the same gap obtains for the fourteen cases of full brother-sister marriage.[79] The obvious explanation is that siblings are normally near in age to one another, so that wide disparity in the age of husband and wife is less likely to occur, although there are exceptions.[80]

However, when this pattern is juxtaposed with the more general marriage patterns prevailing in Egypt, oddities emerge; they are illustrated in Table 6.3. These statistics are generated for cases where the age of one spouse is preserved and where the kin relationship (if any) between the spouses can be determined with some confidence. Among women still in their 'teens, there is a fairly high incidence of brother-sister or other close-kin marriage, suggesting that women, if they married early (as many women did), often

---

[77] This is true in two senses: families that can afford dowry may prefer not to have to provide it, and families that cannot may still feel pressured to marry off daughters. See S. Treggiari, *Marriage* (1991) 108–119, with bibliography. For Egypt: M. Hombert and C. Préaux, *Recherches* (1952) 140; also N. Sidler, *Inzesttabu* (1971) 79–80, and J. Goody, *The Oriental* (1990) 332–339. (Plato, *Laws* 7, 773a–e, already recognizes the point.) The counterargument in K. Hopkins, "Brother-Sister" (1980) 322–323, accepted by B. Shaw, "Brother-Sister" (1992) 276–277, seems to miss the short-term calculation that is involved; compare S. Atran, "Managing Arab Kinship and Marriage," *Social Science Information* 24 (1985) 659–696 (on cross-cousin marriage among the Druze of Isfiya), and L. L. Cornell, in *Family History* (1987) 146–152, on the "ideology" of joint households. (This issue is, however, complex; for another view, T. W. Gallant, *Risk and Survival*, 1991, 41–45.) Shaw, who probably exaggerates ethnic tensions between Greeks and Egyptians, seeks a deeper explanation in cross-cultural conflicts during the Hellenistic period; so already S. B. Pomeroy, *Women* (1985) 85.

[78] What follows is inspired by K. Hopkins, "Brother-Sister" (1980) 351–353, and J. Goody, *The Oriental* (1990) 335–339; but Hopkins rejects his own argument, for unconvincing reasons (see note 82 below). In the following calculation, all census returns are used for exogamous marriages; for close-kin marriages, only those before 229/230.

[79] This difference is probably significant. In any event, husbands are normally older than their wives in close-kin marriages, just as in exogamous marriages. In only three cases are wives older: 187-Ar-4 (-8 years), 173-Ar-2 (-4; half-siblings), and 201-Ar-10 (-2; first cousins).

[80] The largest are 187-Ar-4 (17 years) and 145-Ar-9 (22 or possibly 32 years; half-siblings). As a rule, the gap in age is more concentrated for brother-sister marriage than for Egyptian marriage in general; 14 of 19 are in a range from 2 to 12 years. If this was by preference, marriage options with siblings would often be limited.

married within their families. The figures for young married males, aged
16 to 29, display a similar pattern; a third of their marriages are close-kin,
predominantly brother-sister.

Table 6.3. *Age-specific incidence of close-kin marriage*

	Females				Males		
Age	All marr.	Close-kin	%	Age	All marr.	Close-kin	%
13–19	18	6	33.3				
20–29	24	3	12.5	19–29	20	7	35.0
30–39	26	4	15.4	30–39	26	7	26.9
40+	23	6	26.1	40–49	22	6	27.3
				50+	20	2	10.0
Total	91	19	20.9		88	22	25.0

Therefore, for both males and females, a very large proportion of first
marriages were close-kin between spouses near in age to one another. This
seems confirmed by remarriage patterns: there is no probable instance of
close-kin remarriage, but several instances where a previous spouse had
been close-kin.[81] The *maximum* age of a spouse at marriage can often be
calculated either from the person's current age or by comparing the current
age of parents and children. Most females in close-kin marriages were
clearly married in their teens (10 of 17 cases); most males, in their teens,
twenties, or early thirties (17 of 21 cases), following the usual pattern of
delayed male marriage.[82]

[81] 159-Ar-5; 173-Pr-10; 201-Ar-2; see also 159-Ar-4 and 173-Ar-2. Three of these marriages
ended in divorce, one through death, one probably through death. Despite the coincidence
of fathers' names, the wife of the declarant in 117-Ar-4 is probably not his sister, since she
is not mentioned in the family's previous census returns (89-Ar-1, when she was 17; and
103-Ar-8).
[82] For close-kin marriages, *maximum* female age at first marriage: 13 (145-Ar-9; 173-Pr-5);
14 (131-He-4; 145-Ar-19); 15 (187-Ar-4); 16 (187-Ar-4); 17 (103-Ar-1 and 5); 18 (187-
Ar-22); 19 (145-Ar-9); 21 (187-An-2); 22 (103-Ar-3); 24 (187-Ar-4); 29 (131-Ar-3); 20s
(145-Ar-20); 30 (215-Hm-1/2); 34 (201-Ar-10). *Maximum* male age at first marriage: 12
(?) (187-Ar-4); 16 (131-He-4); 20 (103-Ar-5; 187-Ar-12); 21 (145-Ar-9; 173-Pr-5); 22
(145-Ar-19); 24 (187-An-2); 25 (103-Ar-3); 28 (187-Ar-4); 30 (187-Ar-22); 32 (117-Ar-1;
145-Ar-20; 159-Ar-11; 201-Ar-10); 33 (131-Ar-3; 187-Ar-4); 36 (215-Hm-1/2); 38 (159-
Ar-11; 173-Pr-10); 42 (145-Ar-9). One year of marriage is allowed prior to birth of oldest
attested child. As to women, K. Hopkins's counterargument, "Brother-Sister" (1980) 353,
incorrectly assumes late female age at marriage.

For women during their next two decades of life, from ages 20 to 39, the incidence of close-kin marriage drops off sharply, only to pick up again from age 40 onward, a period when increasingly few women are still married (Figure 6.1). By contrast, among males, who tend progressively to be married as they age (Figure 6.2), the incidence of brother-sister marriage falls off steadily; of still married males aged 50 and older, only a tenth are married to close kinswomen, a decline that is statistically significant.

What this pattern suggests is that many young males who sought to marry in a highly competitive "marriage market" found it attractive, for one reason or another, to marry a full sister or other close kinswoman, if one was available; but males became increasingly averse to close-kin marriage as they aged. The reasons for the initial attractiveness of close-kin marriage perhaps lay in the dynamics of household life, particularly among the intricate complex households that typified Roman Egypt; sisters, or other close kinswomen, were more to hand than other potential brides. Further, it is reasonable to believe that many first marriages were arranged within the household, to suit the convenience of a senior generation.[83] But as that generation's influence waned and as men matured, they looked increasingly outward for their brides.

Relaxation of incest taboos against close-kin marriage has the unexpected demographic effect of raising the population's intrinsic growth rate, all else being equal.[84] The reason is that early marriage is facilitated for both sexes: choice is widened, and the need for personal initiative in finding a spouse is reduced; marriage thus tends to be earlier for both sexes.[85] As we have seen, this seems in fact to happen in Roman Egypt. But an accelerated growth rate could make control of population growth more difficult; we return to this issue in Chapter 7, Section 2.

---

[83] Parents may also be responsible for many marriages between young women and much older men; compare P. C. Smith, in *Determinants* II (1983) 508: "wherever marriage decisions are controlled by parents, [early] marriage will be more prevalent." In the census returns, chances are better than one in two that if a 15-year-old woman marries, her spouse will be either her sibling or a much older man. On love in brother-sister marriages, see K. Hopkins, "Brother-Sister" (1980) 343–353; J. Goody, *The Oriental* (1990) 339–341. There are certainly families in which brother-sister marriage could occur but did not (e.g., 103-Ar-3, 187-Ar-22). In other families, brother-sister marriage seems to occur without an older generation present (e.g., 103-Ar-5).

[84] E. A. Hammel, C. K. McDaniel, and K. W. Wachter, "Demographic Consequences of Incest Tabus: A Microsimulation Analysis," *Science* 205 (Sept. 1979) 972–977; also N. Keyfitz, *Demography* (1985) 300–301. The theoretical effect on the growth rate is not large: about 0.17 percent additional growth per year if all taboos are removed; but, as Hammel *et al.* show, this difference could be crucial to the survival of small communities such as Thelbonthon Siphtha.

[85] These consequences are usually regarded as negative from a sociological standpoint. R. Fox, *Kinship and Marriage: An Anthropological Perspective* (1967).

Families and households

The census returns provide only a "snapshot" of households at various phases in their development; more dynamic aspects of ordinary Egyptian family life remain largely a matter of conjecture. It may be helpful, therefore, to conclude by describing two households, both from Arsinoe during the census of 159/160, that at least suggest the intricacy of Egyptian family life. The first (and much the better preserved) is 159-Ar-4, a fairly typical *frérèche* of twelve family members and two slaves. The declarant is Herodes aged 31; he is the guardian of two boys who own the house in which Herodes' family lives as renters. Herodes' two older brothers, aged 45 and 33, are each married with children.

Also co-resident in this household are Herodes' two full sisters. The older, aged 47, has a son aged 19; her marriage having ended probably through her husband's death, she has returned to live with her brothers. Attention focuses, however, on the declarant's younger sister, Zoidous aged 29; she is Herodes' divorced wife, but continues to live in the household, presumably because she has nowhere else to go. Herodes and Zoidous have one child, a son aged 8, so they had married fairly young.

That this undoubtedly awkward situation may not have been unusual is indicated by a second return, 159-Ar-5, where the household is far more difficult to reconstruct. The declarant, whose name is lost, resides in what appears to be a sprawling *frérèche* of twenty-two family members and five slaves. Co-resident is his full sister and divorced wife, along with their two daughters (the younger aged 10). But since his divorce the declarant has remarried, with two additional daughters by his second wife. The emotional intricacy of this household can only be imagined.

7

Fertility

High mortality placed a heavy burden on Egyptian women; this population's survival depended upon sustaining relatively high overall fertility. As E. A. Wrigley has observed, in societies with very high mortality, "a population could hardly allow private choice since it must mobilize maximum fertility if it is to survive at all."[1] Roman Egypt typifies such populations. However, as we shall see below, Wrigley's observation must be qualified. Mobilizing "maximum fertility" was certainly not a demographic goal in Roman Egypt; and restraints on fertility, though different in kind and operation from those used after the modern fertility transition, played a major part in the general social survival of Egypt's population.

1. Overall female fertility

In 211 instances, census returns preserve the age both of a mother and of her child.[2] In these instances, the age of the mother at childbirth can be reconstructed by subtracting the child's from the mother's age, as we have done in Table C. The results for ages 12 to 49 are plotted in Figure 7.1 (p. 137), with four-year moving averages used to smooth the figures.[3] As the

[1] E. A. Wrigley, *People* (1987) 209 (of Model West, Level 1; but also stressing that premodern fertility controls were mainly "social," not "private").

[2] Women with more than one such child are counted more than once. Statistics include births to slaves and unmarried women; these births do not substantially alter the curve's shape, see note 17. In what follows, we reconstruct not actual Egyptian fertility rates (this is impossible because the age of a mother or child is so often lost), but rather the age distribution of fertility. The level of fertility is largely inferred from the general age distribution of females (discussed in Chapter 4); see note 18 below.

[3] We have not corrected these reconstructed ages of maternity for possible error in reporting the age of the mother, the child, or both; thus we include attested female childbirths at age 9 (131-Pr-1), 13 (201-Ar-12) and 51 (187-Ar-4), although all three are treated skeptically in Chapter 2 at notes 37–38. On the normal fertility curve, A. J. Coale and P. Demeny, *Life Tables* (1983) 27: "In all populations where reliable records have been kept, fertility is

graph shows, the peak period of an Egyptian woman's fertility lies between ages 17 and 30; thereafter the number of known births drops off. This graph strikingly confirms the argument in Chapter 6 (at notes 7–9) that Egyptian women married at an early age, usually by their later 'teens.

However, the curve in Figure 7.1 needs adjustment. We want to know the probability that a woman will bear a child at a given age. But statistics derived directly from census returns are affected by a second consideration: the probability that a woman who gave birth at a given age will then be attested as having done so. The probability of attestation is mainly determined by both the likelihood of a mother surviving to her attested age, and the likelihood of her child surviving to its attested age.[4] Census statistics are corrected for this probability by the "Own Children" method of fertility estimation, a complex procedure that back-projects fertility rates from census reports of the number of women aged x who have surviving children aged y.[5]

In Figure 7.1, fertility figures are shown after adjustment and rescaling in order to give the same number of total births as in the raw data. The adjustment reconfigures the fertility curve by shifting it somewhat to the right. In the unadjusted census data, the average age of mothers at childbirth (the average age of maternity) is 26.7 years;[6] in the adjusted rates, it is 27.1 years, which is the likeliest estimate for average age of maternity. The latter figure is almost identical to the average age in Bangladesh, 1974.[7] In the adjusted rates, the *median* age of Egyptian maternity is approximately

---

zero until about age 15, rises smoothly to a single peak, and falls smoothly to zero by age 45–50. The mean age of the fertility schedule is usually between about 26 and 32 years."

[4] Thus, for example, in determining actual fertility rates from census returns, a woman aged 30 with a newborn child should receive less weight than a woman 40 with a child 10; similarly, a woman aged 30 with a child 10 should receive less weight than a woman 40 with a child 10.

[5] L.-J. Cho, R. D. Retherford, and M. K. Choe, *The Own Children Method of Fertility Estimation* (1986); see also United Nations, *Manual X* (1983) 182–195. Cho *et al.* discuss strengths and limits of this technique at pp. 4–7; one strength is that it corrects for the effects of intrinsic growth rates. We use a highly simplified form of the "Own Children" method, as described on pp. 8–9, for children aged 30 and less (186 cases); because our interest is mainly in the shape of the fertility curve, we assume a stable population and have not tried to correct the census returns for age misrepresentation or for missing children. Six-year moving averages smooth fertility rates. The data base is too small to permit separate calculation of metropolitan and village fertility rates, but they appear to be similar.

[6] Compare M. Hombert and C. Préaux, *Recherches* (1952) 163: 26.5 years on the basis of 143 cases. This illustrates the homogeneity of the data.

[7] C. Newell, *Methods* (1988) 110–111; the figure is also about normal for present-day less developed countries with early female age at marriage. (We ignore some subtle differences in measurement, which Newell explains, pp. 111–112.) In populations with late age at marriage, average age at childbirth can reach about 31 to 33 years; e.g., E. A. Wrigley and R. S. Schofield, *England* (1989) 232–234.

25.7, within the almost universally prevailing range of medians.[8] In Figure 7.2 below, we use fertility rates adjusted through the "Own Children" method.

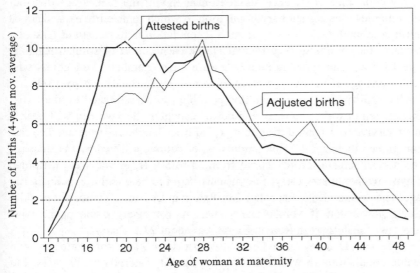

Figure 7.1. *Attested age of maternity and adjusted fertility rates*

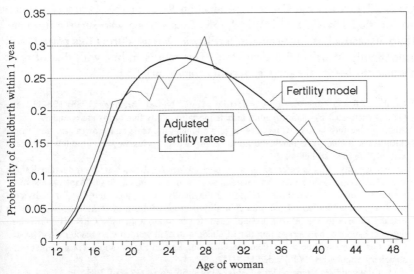

Figure 7.2. *Model fertility curve and adjusted fertility rates for Egypt*

---

[8] H. S. Shryock and J. S. Siegel, *Methods* (1980) 473–474; the normal range is about 25.4 to 29.1, with "early marriage" populations usually at the lower end of the range.

The Gross Reproduction Rate

It is also possible to approach female fertility more theoretically, by estimating the Gross Reproduction Rate.[9] We may start from what we already know with some confidence about Roman Egypt: the female age distribution implies a near-stationary population in which female life expectancy at birth is around 22.5 years.[10] If such a population is to remain at least stationary, the minimum requirement is that each cohort of women reaching age 15 bears enough daughters to ensure a like number of daughters who also reach age 15; each generation of women must exactly replace itself.[11]

The fertility needed to make this possible can be estimated by the Gross Reproduction Rate, the total number of daughters that women will bear if they survive to 50 and during this period bear daughters at the average rate for women their age.[12] This number is, of course, affected by the shape of the normal female fertility curve from 15 to 50. If, as was true in Roman Egypt, women marry early, they usually begin to bear children at an earlier age, and so the Gross Reproduction Rate required for a stationary population is lower than if women marry later. As has emerged above, the average age of maternity in Roman Egypt was about 27.1 years.

Coale and Demeny give Gross Reproduction Rates for stationary and stable populations in which the average age of maternity is 29 years, but also provide a formula for recalculating the Gross Reproduction Rate when the average age of maternity is lower.[13] If, as in Roman Egypt, the average age is 27.1 years, the Gross Reproduction Rate for the stationary population of Model West, Level 2, is 2.758. Thus women who survive from age 15 to 50, and whose age-specific fertility is average during this period, will bear slightly less than 2.8 daughters. This rate is in line with that of most populations before the modern fertility transition.[14]

---

[9] On the GRR and other measures of fertility, see C. Newell, *Methods* (1988) 106–112; the GRR is calculated by ignoring adult female mortality. Only live births are counted.

[10] Although we rely here on Chapter 4 as to the female life table and growth rate, the procedure below would yield much the same results if other plausible stable models were used instead. See note 18 below.

[11] In demography, this is referred to as cohort replacement; the Net Reproduction Rate is 1.0. That at least such a rate was obtained is the primary conclusion in Chapter 4 above.

[12] However, since women bear children differentially, and since fertility for individual women is somewhat correlated with mortality because of death in childbirth, women who actually survive to age 50 will probably bear fewer children than the GRR. The GRR also does not estimate the average number of children that all women who reach menarche will bear; this figure will be lower than the GRR (for Roman Egypt, about 2.2 daughters in a stationary population: $l(0)$ divided by $l(15)$).

[13] A. J. Coale and P. Demeny, *Life Tables* (1983) 56, for a GRR of 2.815 in Model West, Level 2, if $r = 0.0$ (stationary population); and p. 27 for the formula used to calculate GRR when mean age at childbirth is other than 29 years. The mean age at maternity accounts for almost all variation in maternity schedules.

[14] See L. Henry, "Data" (1961) 84. E.g., mid-eighteenth-century France had a GRR of 2.53, despite a late age at first marriage for women: L. Henry and Y. Blayo, "La population de la France de 1740 à 1860," *Population* 30 (num. spéc.; 1975) 71–122, at 109; also E. A.

For Egypt, this Gross Reproduction Rate should be understood as in one respect inexorable. For instance, under the estimated constant conditions of mortality, had the rate declined from about 2.8 to 2.3, the Egyptian population, when it stabilized, would have halved every century. Since such a decline is inconceivable, the long-term Gross Reproduction Rate in Roman Egypt was certainly not much below the reconstructed rate.

However, as we argued earlier, the Egyptian population was in fact probably increasing at a slow intrinsic rate; therefore allowance must be made for stable population growth similar to that estimated in Chapter 4, around 0.2 percent per year.[15] This small correction raises the Gross Reproduction Rate by about six percent, from 2.758 to 2.917, meaning that women who survived to age 50, and who bore children at an age-specific rate average for women their age, would bear about 2.9 daughters.

Finally, the Total Fertility Rate for children of both sexes can be estimated at 2.05 times the Gross Reproduction Rate of 2.917, or 5.979.[16]

Reconstructed fertility
We can now use a standard demographic model to reconstruct the likeliest fertility curve for Roman Egypt, on the assumption that the population was slowly growing.[17] This model has five determinants (three variables and

---

Wrigley and R. S. Schofield, *England* (1989) 230, 246–247. Modern Egypt's GRR remained above 2.7 into the mid-twentieth century: A.R. Omran, *Egypt* (1973) 81–82.

[15] The procedure for making this adjustment is described by A. J. Coale and P. Demeny, *Life Tables* (1983) 27. Revised GRRs are calculated for stable Level 2 populations that have growth rates of 0.0 and 0.5, and a mean female age at childbirth of 27.1; then a GRR is interpolated for a growth rate of 0.2.

[16] We assume a sex ratio at birth of 105 males per 100 females (Chapter 5, note 13); and we take no account of possible female infanticide, on which see Section 2 below. E. Vielrose, "Fertility of Families in Egypt in the Greco-Roman Epoch," *Studia Demograficzne* 43 (1976) 51–57 (in Polish, with English abstract), also estimated a TFR approximately this high for Roman Egypt, but by dubious methods. In the 1930s, Egypt's TFR was 6.5, and it remains near 5.5 today: *Estimation* (1982) 17. Contemporary less developed countries often have even higher TFRs. "In 1982 the total fertility rate was between 6.2 and 8.3 for 36 of the 45 lowest income countries of the globe where income per capita in 1982 dollars ranged from $80 to $660." L. Donaldson, *Fertility Transition: The Social Dynamics of Population Change* (1991) 9. This situation is largely unchanged in 1991: United Nations Development Programme, *Human Development Report* (1993) 181.

[17] A. J. Coale and T. J. Trussell, "Model Fertility" (1974), and "Technical Note: Finding the Two Parameters That Specify a Model Schedule of Marital Fertility," *Population Index* 44 (1978) 203–213. See also A. J. Coale and P. Demeny, *Life Tables* (1983) 27–28; United Nations, *Manual X* (1983) 23–25; C. Newell, *Methods* (1988) 170–175. The Coale-Trussell model is designed for marital fertility (estimated below as about 85 percent of all Egyptian fertility); but inclusion of *apatores* and slave children does not signficantly affect the shape of the reconstructed fertility curve, chiefly because Egyptian marriage is early and contraception is rare.

two schedules): first, the proportion of women ever married by a given age (calculated in Chapter 6 at notes 12–14, and graphed in Figure 6.1); second, the Total Fertility Rate for children of both sexes (estimated above at 5.979);[18] third, an empirical schedule of typical "natural" fertility rates among women of a given age;[19] fourth, a schedule of the systematic deviation from "natural" fertility, particularly among women older than 30, if couples successfully limit family size; and fifth, a variable quantifying the extent to which couples do in fact succeed in limiting family size.

Pivotal is the model's fifth determinant, called m. Prior to the modern fertility transition, the age distribution of marital fertility, *although not its overall level,* is in the main a direct function of female fecundity as women age (their potential fertility), since married couples do not effectively regulate or limit family size. Age-specific marital fertility curves in pretransition populations therefore always have a characteristic, emphatically convex shape from ages 20 to 44; by convention, demographers describe this age distribution as "natural" fertility.[20] In the model, m alters the shape of this curve for older women if, as apparently first occurred during the modern fertility transition, married couples widely use contraception or induced abortion in order to limit births once they reach a desired family

---

[18] As C. Newell, *Methods* (1988) 171, notes, this independent variable simply scales the curve, but does not change its shape (our primary interest). Use of 5.979 results from previous adoption of Model West, Level 2, as the most probable life table for females in Roman Egypt, and 0.2 as the likeliest intrinsic growth rate. Selection of different values would only rescale the resulting curve. The discussion in Chapter 4 above favors a TFR between 5.550 (Level 3, growth rate of 0.3) and 6.540 (Level 1, growth rate of 0.1); our TFR is roughly intermediate. See Chapter 2, Section 1, on the relationship between mortality and fertility.

[19] This schedule is the average of ten "natural" fertility schedules collected by Louis Henry, "Data" (1961); the schedule is taken from A. J. Coale and T. J. Trussell, "Model Fertility" (1974) 202. The concept of "natural" fertility is defined below. The following schedule also derives from the Coale-Trussell model.

[20] This pattern recurs, with small variation resulting chiefly from differences in fecundity, in all pre-transition populations; "natural" is awkward, but there is no accepted substitute. C. Wilson, J. Oeppen, and M. Pardoe, "What Is Natural Fertility? The Modelling of a Concept," *Population Index* 54 (1988) 4–20; J. W. Wood, "Fecundity and Natural Fertility in Humans," *Oxford Reviews of Reproductive Biology* 11 (1989) 61–109. Louis Henry first noticed that this "natural" age distribution is independent of overall fertility levels (TFRs) in such populations. "Natural fertility is . . . quite compatible with a relatively low absolute level of fertility." E. A. Wrigley, *People* (1987) 198 n. 4. For examples, see note 51 (China in 1930), and also H. Hyrenius, "Fertility and Reproduction in a Swedish Population Without Family Limitation," *Population Studies* 12 (1958) 121–130 (Swedes in Estonia). On the close connection between physiological sterility and the "natural" fertility pattern, see J. Bongaarts, in *Determinants* vol. I (1983) 124 (age-specific table of sterility at p. 129), and T. J. Trussell and C. Wilson, "Sterility in a Population with Natural Fertility," *Population Studies* 39 (1985) 269–286.

size; the result is sharply reduced fertility as women age, and hence a pronouncedly concave fertility curve that peaks early in life but then declines swiftly by the late 20s.[21] The variable m thus objectively measures the extent of actual family limitation in a given population.

For Roman Egypt, we estimate m at 0.3 on a scale from zero (no use of contraception and abortion) to 2.5 (very heavy use), since no higher value of m is consistent with the fertility curve attested in the census returns.[22] Before the modern fertility transition, populations always have values of m close to zero, approximating "natural" fertility and thus indicating that couples were not effectively limiting family size.[23] Roman Egypt shares the universal pre-transition pattern. As will emerge in Section 2 below, this fact has major implications for our understanding of the character and effectiveness of fertility control in Egypt.

The reconstructed model fertility schedule is plotted in Figure 7.2. As the model shows, the peak of female fertility occurs between ages 20 and 30, but fertility continues at fairly high levels into the thirties and even the forties, as is normal for populations in which women marry early under conditions of "natural" fertility.[24] This model should be understood, of course, only as approximating what Egyptian fertility would have been if it followed predictable patterns.

For comparison, in Figure 7.2 the adjusted fertility rates calculated by the "Own Children" method are rescaled to match the model fertility sche-

---

[21] C. Newell, *Methods* (1988) 171. This concave pattern (m higher than 2.0) is found in all populations that have completed the fertility transition (e.g., Newell, p. 43, for the United States in 1984). It is referred to as "controlled" fertility: L. Henry, "Data" (1961) 81 ("Control can be said to exist when the behavior of the couple is bound to the number of children already born and is modified when this number reaches the maximum that the couple does not wish to exceed"). See also the essays in *Decline of Fertility* (1986), esp. J. Knodel, pp. 337–389, who allows a limited role for family limitation in some pre-transition populations. A. Bideau and J.-P. Bardet, in *Population française* II (1988) 359, discuss the connection between potential and actual fertility; M. Livi-Bacci, *History* (1992) 113–123, summarizes what is known about the fertility transition.

[22] Our estimate of m is the only "fitted" value in Figure 7.2; a value of 0.25 is even closer. In the census returns, about 20 percent of births occur after age 35; this also points to a low value of m, see B. A. Anderson and B. D. Silver, "A Simple Measure of Fertility Control," *Demography* 29 (1992) 343–356.

[23] See J. Knodel, "Family Limitation and the Fertility Transition: Evidence from Age Patterns of Fertility in Europe and Asia," *Population Studies* 31 (1977) 219–249, and "Natural Fertility: Age Patterns, Levels, Trends," in *Determinants* I (1983) 61–102. Contemporary rural Egypt, like many less developed countries, still has a value of m close to zero; fertility surveys also show very limited use of contraception. *Estimation* (1982) 21–23.

[24] The model replicates the age distribution in L. Henry, "Data" (1961) 84 (14 populations). Similar is Bangladesh, 1974: C. Newell, *Methods* (1988) 106. So too, late Medieval Florence: C. Klapisch-Zuber, "La fécondité des Florentines (XIVe–XVe Siècles)," *Annales de Démographie Historique* (1988) 41–57; and pre-transition Europe generally, see the various reconstructed national rates in M. W. Flinn, *System* (1981) 31.

dule in total number of births from ages 12 to 44.[25] Although the two curves were calculated largely independently, their fit is close, indicating that the census returns probably give an accurate picture of typical female fertility in Roman Egypt.[26] Female fertility reaches its apex when women are in their twenties but continues at high rates into their thirties and forties, as in the model. However, Egyptian women appear to bear slightly more children in their teens, and fewer in their early twenties, than the model predicts; whether this difference is real, or instead results from flaws in the census data, is hard to determine, although in any case the data base is small. The unlikely burst of births to women aged 45 and older undoubtedly results from modest age exaggeration among older women. We believe that the model is likely to better represent actual fertility rates in Roman Egypt.[27]

The fertility schedules in Figure 7.2 call for comment. Table 7.1 (p. 143) summarizes both the five-year fertility rates in the model and the adjusted and rescaled fertility rates derived from the returns; in each case, the figure given is the probability that a woman, during one year of her life in this age group, will give birth. The most salient, and perhaps surprising, feature of this table is that fertility rates during the peak period of female fertility, from ages 20 to 29, may well seem lower than would have been anticipated.[28] In the model, women this age give birth at an average rate of about one child every 45 months (3.7 years), a rate by no means excep-

---

[25] On Prof. Coale's suggestion, we ignore births from 45 on, since the census returns give a figure that is improbably though not impossibly high (see below); in any case, births after 45 are usually ignored in fitting a Coale-Trussell model. The rescaled fertility rates are not, of course, actual fertility rates; our main interest is in the shape (the age distribution) of the fertility curve.

[26] The same conclusion emerges from computing a more complex Brass-Gompertz relational fertility model (described by C. Newell, *Methods*, 1988, 175–178) for the attested Egyptian age-specific fertility rates in Table 7.1, ages 12 to 44; this model fits extremely closely ($r^2 = 0.997$). As with the Coale-Trussell model, the parameters of the Gompertz model describe a population in which women marry early under conditions of "natural" fertility (*alpha* $= 0.027$, *beta* $= 0.833$; cf. Newell on interpreting these parameters).

[27] In general, the adjusted fertility rates seem "squashed" in relation to the model: slightly lower in the middle, higher at both ends. The likeliest cause of the discrepancy is that the attested ages are pulled in two directions: slight understatement of age for younger women (see, e.g., Zosime in 159-Ar-1 and 173-Ar-3), and somewhat larger overstatement for elderly women. On age shoving, see Chapter 2, note 55. A Coale-Trussell model with closer fit is easily calculated, but only on unreasonable assumptions about marriage rates; however, since the likely value of *m* is unaffected by closer fitting models, we prefer to leave the model unchanged.

[28] Compare A. J. Coale, in *Decline of Fertility* (1986) 1–30, at 5: "The most surprising feature ... is the moderate level of fertility—TFR from about 4.1 to 6.2—in ... pre-industrial populations." This entire essay is very helpful. Ancient authors often describe native Egyptians as exceptionally prolific, see T. G. Parkin, *Demography* (1992) 113; such observations should be dismissed as racial stereotypes.

tionally high in pre-modern populations. The age-specific annual birth rate for women aged 20 to 29 is about 270 births per thousand.[29]

Table 7.1. *Probability of woman giving birth in one year of her life*

Age	Reconstructed fertility rates		Maximum Hutterite fertility	% of maximum fertility	
	Model	Egypt		Model	Egypt
12–14	0.0229	0.0259			
15–19	0.1397	0.1596	0.3000	46.6	53.2
20–24	0.2609	0.2311	0.5500	47.4	47.4
25–29	0.2751	0.2776	0.5020	54.8	55.3
30–34	0.2384	0.2129	0.4470	53.3	47.6
35–39	0.1779	0.1633	0.4060	43.8	40.2
40–44	0.0851	0.1300	0.2220	38.3	58.6
45–49	0.0120	0.0631	0.0610	19.7	103.5

In a population where women marry early, the challenge posed by high mortality is met through a demographic strategy in which the heavy burden of childbirth is distributed as widely as possible among fertile women; not only do women marry early, but all or virtually all women marry. Early socialization into marriage and childbirth is thus an all but invariable part of a woman's experience as she becomes an adult.[30] Although such a stra-

---

[29] This figure remains below 300 even if the TFR is as high as 6.5. The comparable age-specific annual birth rate in Bangladesh, 1974, was about 325 births per thousand women (in a rapidly growing population with substantially higher life expectancy; now about 250). The presumed maximum fertility rate (for married Hutterite women) is about 525 births per thousand women aged 20 to 29, double the Egyptian rate. C. Newell, *Methods* (1988) 40, 46. Pre-transition populations can attain very high fertility when new resources become available; e.g., in 1800 the United States had a TFR above 7, but even higher near the frontier. R. A. Easterlin, "Population Change and Farm Settlement in the Northern United States," *Journal of Economic History* 36 (1976) 45–75. French settlers in Quebec had similar rates: H. Charbonneau *et al.*, *Naissance d'une population: les Français établis au Canada au XVIIe siècle* (1987) 86–91.

[30] See S. Treggiari, *Marriage* (1991) 135–138, 170–180, 400–401. In pre-modern populations, "marriage for women ... was almost universally a life-cycle stage in a physiological as well as a social sense in that it occurred at or close to menarche. Few women failed to marry and those who married moved into their new state because of physical maturation." E. A. Wrigley, *People* (1987) 7 (contrasting early modern Western Europe and citing classic studies by John Hajnal).

tegy has self-evident social and cultural costs, it at least spreads the risk of childbearing as a burden placed specifically on women.

Finally, some correction in the calculated fertility rates may be needed to account for the sex ratio discussed in Chapter 5. This is a difficult subject since, as we argued, the degree of imbalance between the sexes (if any) cannot be securely established from the census returns. We return to this question in Section 2. However, any imbalance in the sex ratio is probably better explained, in our opinion, by positing that Egyptian male life expectancy was roughly the same as that of females; therefore the naturally occurring sexual imbalance at birth was preserved or perhaps slightly widened in later life.[31] There is thus no reason to suppose that the sex ratio was much affected by female death through infanticide or exposure.

Marital and non-marital fertility

Demographers stress the division of overall fertility between marital and non-marital fertility. Total fertility among women aged 15 up to 50 is today usually standardized by measuring it as a proportion of the highest fertility known to be socially sustainable. These maximum rates were attained earlier in this century by the Hutterites, a prolific Anabaptist sect settled in the upper Great Plains of North America.[32] For Roman Egypt, the fertility model reconstructed above implies an overall fertility index (I_f) of about 0.485, meaning that Egyptian fertility, as reconstructed, is slightly less than half of Hutterite fertility for women aged 15 to 50. In the census returns, around 15 percent of these births are non-marital, either to unmarried free women or to slaves (below, Sections 3 and 4); marital fertility is thus about 85 percent of all fertility.[33] The index of the proportion of women married (I_m), based on all women aged 15 to 50 irrespective of legal status, was estimated at about 0.600 in Chapter 6, Section 1.

From these three statistics, the index of marital fertility (I_g) can be reconstructed at approximately 0.700, indicating that fertility among mar-

---

[31] See Chapter 5 (at notes 45–50) for more detailed argument; also Chapter 8 below.

[32] Table 7.1 gives the age-specific Hutterite marital fertility rates for women married in the 1920s; see J. Eaton and A. J. Mayer, "The Social Biology of Very High Fertility among the Hutterites," *Human Biology* 25 (1953) 206–264, and C. Tietze, "Reproductive Span and Rate of Reproduction among Hutterite Women," *Fertility and Sterility* 8 (1957) 89–97. The four "Coale indices" are described by A. J. Coale and R. Treadway, in *Decline of Fertility* (1986) 31–35, 153–162; see also C. Newell, *Methods* (1988) 44–49. The equation for calculating these indices is $I_f = (I_m)(I_g) + (1 - I_m)(I_h)$. Calculations use the female age distribution in Table 5.4 and the Coale-Trussell model (including the TFR) reconstructed above; other possible TFRs would alter the indices somewhat.

[33] This figure is speculative, of course; it is based on the likelihood that slave births were about 10 to 12 percent of all births in the census population, and that about 3 to 5 percent of the remainder were *apatores*. The probable range is therefore 84 to 87 percent.

ried Egyptian women was around 70 percent of Hutterite fertility. By contrast, the index of non-marital fertility (I_h) is only about 0.175, concentrated mainly among slave women. These calculations are necessarily crude, but they suggest the degree to which Egyptian marriage was intrinsically associated with procreation; the Total *Marital* Fertility Rate in Roman Egypt will have been near nine children.[34] Although fertility among unmarried women was not low, the burden of reproduction fell emphatically on married women of fertile age, with important implications for population control in Roman Egypt (see Section 2 below).

Reconstructed Egyptian indices of overall and marital fertility lie at the high end of the normal Mediterranean ranges before the modern fertility transition; but because of slave births, non-marital fertility exceeds any attested European value. By way of comparison, in 1900 Greece had a slightly higher proportion married (0.632) and similar marital fertility (0.688), but lower overall fertility (0.440) because non-marital fertility was minute (0.015). In the mid-1930s, Egypt had a much higher proportion married (0.766), resulting in higher overall fertility than Roman Egypt (0.520) despite similar marital fertility (0.679); non-marital fertility was negligible.[35]

Paternity rates
The age of fathers at paternity is of less demographic interest;[36] we treat it briefly for completeness. Figure 7.3 (p. 146) is constructed on the same basis as Figure 7.1, for 155 cases in which the age of both a father and his child are known.[37] As Figure 7.3 shows, paternity is rare before age 20[38]

[34]The TMFR is the number of children born to a woman who from age 15 to 50 gives birth at the average rate for *married* women her age: C. Newell, *Methods* (1988) 43–44 (with a strong caution against misinterpreting this statistic). The Hutterite TMFR is about 12.5 children. For Roman Egypt, the annual marital fertility rate for ages 20 to 29 (when nearly 80 percent of free women were married) was probably near 375 per thousand married women, in line with rates often found under conditions of "natural" fertility: L. Henry, "Data" (1961) 84. A fitted Coale-Trussell model for marital fertility implies no significant family limitation among married couples ($m = 0.3$). The Brass-Gompertz model (see note 26) closely resembles that for all fertility ($alpha = 0.024$, $beta = 0.794$; $r^2 = 0.998$).

[35]Greece: A. J. Coale and R. Treadway, in *Decline of Fertility* (1986) 115. Egypt: *Estimation* (1982) 17. Because both populations then had lower mortality than Roman Egypt, they were growing rapidly. Greece underwent the fertility transition *ca* 1910–1920; Egypt, where the transition has not yet fully occurred, still had an I_g of 0.671 in 1975/1976.

[36]For the reasons, see N. Keyfitz, *Demography* (1985) 114–115. Age of paternity is important mainly in determining the probability that a father will survive to see children reach majority.

[37]The number of attested cases is smaller than for mothers because fathers are usually much older than mothers (hence have lower life expectancy) and no father is attested for slaves and *apatores* children; hence all attested paternity is marital. In Figure 7.3, ages of paternity are corrected only for male life expectancy.

[38]This confirms late male age at marriage, see Chapter 6 at notes 21–24.

and does not reach its apex until the early thirties, but continues, although at a declining rate, into the sixties; this pattern results both from late male marriage and from the increasing tendency of males to be married as they age (Figure 6.2). In the census returns, the average age of paternity is 35.4; however, if the raw data are crudely adjusted to take account of declining life expectancy as males age, this figure rises to about 39, though obviously with extremely wide variation. The *median* age of paternity is lower, between 37 and 38 years. This median is probably more trustworthy since older male ages may be affected by age exaggeration.

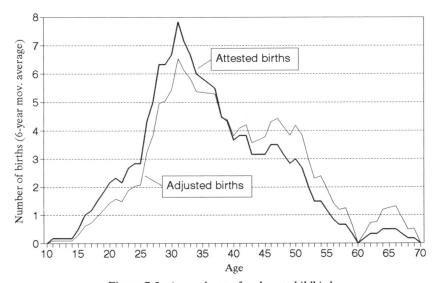

Figure 7.3. *Attested age of males at childbirth*

Fertility and household structure

Although high mortality rates might seem to make it unlikely that many households would have more than two generations,[39] the vagaries in age at marriage and maternity were great enough that three-generation families are not uncommon in Roman Egypt. The census returns provide at least 24 examples, in eleven of which the surviving grandparent is a grandmother;

[39]R. P. Saller, "*Patria Potestas* and the Stereotype of the Roman Family," *Continuity and Change* 1 (1986) 7–22, and "Men's Age at Marriage and Its Consequences in the Roman Family," *CPh* 82 (1987) 20–35. For an elegant theoretical discussion, see H. Le Bras and K. W. Wachter, "Living Forebears in Stable Populations," in *Statistical Studies of Historical Social Structure* (ed. Wachter; 1978) 163–188. The results are counterintuitive: "Even in the most severe situation, 90% of individuals still have a living parent or forebear at the age of 21" (p. 187).

in seven (or possibly eight), the grandfather; and in six, two grandparents.[40] These cases amount to more than one in seven of all well-attested households. The youngest grandmother is aged 42 (173-Pr-15), and ten others are in their late forties or fifties; the other four are in their sixties or seventies. By contrast, most grandfathers are in their sixties or seventies (six cases), though two are in their fifties (117-Ap-6, 187-Ar-4).

However, only one household (201-Ar-9 from Karanis) has four generations of the same family living together. In that household, as it was declared, the great-grandmother is 74; she has two surviving sons aged 56 and 46, and a daughter 56. The elder son is a grandparent; his son is 26, his granddaughter 6.[41] The average age gap between generations in this household is less than 20 years.

2. Controls on population growth

For the population of Roman Egypt to remain at least stationary, high mortality had to be offset by high fertility; but the burden of fertility should not be overstated. If a population with Roman Egypt's general level of mortality remains close to stationary, the reasons will have at least as much to do with personal and social restraints on maximum fertility, as with limitations stemming from high mortality.[42]

Families with as many as eight children are attested in the census returns,[43] but large numbers of surviving children are infrequent.[44] To a

[40] Grandmother: 11-Ar-1; 117-Ar-6 and 7; 131-He-2; 145-Ar-3; 159-Ar-10; 173-Ar-9 and 11; 173-Pr-15; 201-Ar-1 and 8. Grandfather: 89-Hm-1; 131-He-4; 131-Ox-1; 159-Ar-1; 173-Me-3; 201-Ox-3 (now deceased); 215-He-3; ???-Ar-4 (possibly). Two grandparents: 117-Ap-6; 117-Ar-11; 159-Ar-11; 187-Ar-4 and 8; 201-Ar-10 (both grandmothers). ???-Ar-3 has three generations of a disintegrating *frérèche*. In 173-Ar-9, three generations of slaves (linked enatically) are living together; the grandmother is aged 40.

[41] This son's first wife is deceased, and he has since remarried a woman declared in 201-Ar-8; they have a daughter aged 1. But the couple's current domestic arrangements are not certain; see the Discussion on these returns. The returns do not say that the couple have separated, and the husband is *kyrios* to his wife's mother in 201-Ar-8.

[42] K. M. Weiss, *Models* (1973) 52–57. On maximum fertility, see above, note 32; as Table 7.1 shows, our restored fertility rates for Egypt are well below maximum rates. For a survey of the factors affecting fertility rates: D. M. Heer, *Society and Population* (2d ed.; 1975) 68–79. J. W. Wood, "Fertility in Anthropological Populations," *Annual Review of Anthropology* 10 (1990) 211–242, is a good introduction to fertility control in pre-transition societies. Family limitation is a particular form of fertility control; we argue below that Egyptians practiced fertility control but not family limitation.

[43] Eight: 187-Ar-4. Seven (?): 103-Ar-3. Six: 159-Ar-1 with 173-Ar-3; 187-Ar-8 (one half-sibling). Five: 33-Ox-2; 117-Ap-5; 117-Ar-11; 131-Ar-3; 173-Pr-5 (one half-sibling). Five or more co-resident siblings in, e.g., 33-Ar-1 (*bis*); 145-Ar-19; 159-Ar-4 and 5 (possibly).

[44] This is almost always true in pre-modern populations: e.g., J.-L. Flandrin, *Families* (1979) 53–65.

large extent this is the obvious outcome of high infant mortality, but a
degree of more or less conscious fertility limitation is also likely. In pre-
modern societies, overpopulation was as great a threat as underpopulation,
and families often directly perceived the risks of both.[45] As Ansley Coale
observes,[46] "[T]raditional societies developed customs that kept fertility at
moderate levels, avoiding both fertility so low that negative growth would
make the population shrink to zero, or so high that positive growth would
lead to an overcrowded habitat, and hence to higher mortality, and greater
vulnerability to catastrophe or rival groups." What were these "customs"?
How did Roman Egypt avoid a population explosion? Present evidence
seems to permit no sure answer to this question; but in fact that is untrue,
thanks largely to recent developments in historical demography that permit
reliable inference from the age distribution of fertility.

Prenatal restraint of fertility
Demographers distinguish two broad forms of prenatal fertility checks, particularly within marriage: direct methods such as contraception and induced
abortion; and indirect methods, like breastfeeding, that act to delay postpartum pregnancy.[47] Indirect methods tend to have more or less uniform
impact across the whole duration of female fertility, and so usually reduce
the overall level of fertility without much modifying its "natural" pattern.
By contrast, direct methods, effectively used, facilitate far more conscious

[45]The reasons are well explained in E. A. Wrigley and R. S. Schofield, *England* (1989)
454–484. Pre-modern societies could achieve remarkable "homeostasis"; on one
reconstruction, from 1550 to 1750 the population of France (within current borders) varied
by no more than 7 percent from 22.3 million. J. Dupâquier, in *Population française* II
(1988) 52–68 and 413–436. On "unconscious rationality" in pre-modern populations, see
E. A. Wrigley, *People* (1987) 197–199; also pp. 270–321 on France.

[46]A. J. Coale, in *Decline of Fertility* (1986) 7 (Coale's emphasis); in fact, in most pre-
transition populations the birth rate only slightly exceeded the death rate irrespective of life
expectancy (pp. 5–6). This is a major modification of earlier transition theory, which
wrongly presumed that pre-transition societies had levels of both nuptiality and fertility
determined by inflexible social custom and therefore constant. Compare, e.g., R. S.
Schofield, in *Population and History from the Traditional to the Modern World* (ed. R. I.
Rotberg and T. K. Rabb; 1986) 17–18. The entire subject needs reexamination for the
ancient world; T. G. Parkin, *Demography* (1992), is still influenced by the older view,
with bizarre results (e.g., p. 84: "a birth ... rate of 47.38 per 1,000 ... would have been
very difficult to achieve in the social and economic context of the ancient world"; in fact,
it is easy).

[47]A. J. Coale, in *Decline of Fertility* (1986) 9–10. Good introductions to the fertility transition: D. Yaukey, *Demography* (1985) 188–196; G. Alter, "Theories of Fertility Decline:
A Non-Specialist's Guide to the Current Debate," in *European Experience* (1992) 13–27.
See also the reviews of *Decline* by C. Tilly, R. Andorka, and D. Levine, *Population and
Development Review* 12 (1986) 323–340. Use of contraception, in particular, is historically
linked to the rise of family planning by couples; but the exact sequence of this development remains controversial.

and immediate control of reproduction, a control that can and does bring about large alterations in the "natural" age distribution of fertility. The move from indirect to direct forms of fertility control is now considered much the single most important event in the modern fertility transition.

Ancient medical writings, in particular, describe various methods of contraception and abortion, showing that at least some Romans were interested in limiting fertility by direct methods. Of the suggested methods, some could have been effective for their purpose, some worked only by endangering the mother's life, but most partook of folk magic, and we know next to nothing about their actual use in the general population.[48]

Although little is also known about maternal breastfeeding of infants in ancient societies, its effect in delaying postpartum pregnancy may well have been substantial.[49] Contemporary wet-nursing contracts from Egypt regularly last from two to three years; further, these contracts also enjoin the nurse from sexual intercourse, indicating that abstinence during lactation was considered desirable or even mandatory—a belief common in many traditional societies.[50] As it appears, only wealthy families usually

[48] See esp. K. Hopkins, "Contraception in the Roman Empire," *Comparative Studies in Society and History* 8 (1964/1965) 124–151; T. G. Parkin, *Demography* (1992) 126–129, with further bibliography, to which add: A. McLaren, *A History of Contraception from Antiquity to the Present Day* (1990) 42–72, and J. M. Riddle, *Contraception* (1992) (pp. 66–73 on papyri), who argues that the Romans did have effective folk means of contraception and abortion. On withdrawal: Parkin, 193 n. 159 (a "woman's procedure," hence doubtless associated mostly with non-marital intercourse). On the theory of contraception and abortion, see N. Keyfitz, *Demography* (1985) 303–315; both have small effect on fertility rates unless either contraception is very effective or abortion is extremely frequent.

[49] T. G. Parkin, *Demography* (1992) 129–132, with bibliography; add K. R. Bradley, *Family* (1991) 13–36, on wet-nurses (used only by the well-to-do). Contraceptive effects of lactation (in delaying resumption of ovulation) were perhaps only dimly perceived: W. Suder, "Allaitement et contraception dans les textes médicaux latins et grecs antiques," in *Le Latin Médical* (1991) 135–141. This subject remains controversial today; the effects of nursing are substantial, but vary depending on the method used and other circumstances. D. Guz and J. Hobcraft, "Breastfeeding and Fertility: A Comparative Analysis," *Population Studies* 45 (1991) 91–108, with further bibliography.

[50] Surviving contracts in M. Manca Masciadri and O. Montevecchi, *I Contratti di baliatico* (1984); on their duration, pp. 25–27. (Compare Soranus, *Gyn.* 2.47: weaning normal after 18 to 24 months.) On prohibition of intercourse, K. R. Bradley, "Sexual Regulations in Wet-Nursing Contracts from Roman Egypt," *Klio* 62 (1980) 321–325. For reasons, see Soranus, *Gyn.* 2.19 (with the Budé edition's comment citing parallel texts), and Galen, *De sanitate tuenda* 1.9.4–6 (*CMG* 5.4.2, p. 49), who requires abstinence from all nursing women; both doctors report as fact some familiar (and uniformly erroneous) folk beliefs justifying abstinence during lactation, on which see A. Rouselle, *Porneia: de la maîtrise du corps à la privation sensorielle, IIe—IVe siècles de l'ère chrétienne* (1983) 37–63, esp. 57–59. Both pagan and Christian moralists take up the theme of intramarital abstinence; see esp. Clement Alex., *Paedagogus* 2.92.3–93.2, and *Strom.* 2.144.1 and 3.72.1, with D. Elliott, *Spiritual Marriage* (1993) 16–50. Postpartum abstinence from sex for up to three years is found in many pre-modern populations: M. Nag, "How Modernization Can Also Increase Fertility," *Current Anthropology* 21 (1980) 571–580; compare I. O. Orubuloye, *Abstinence as a Method of Birth Control* (1981).

arranged for wet-nurses, either for their own children or their slaves; however, the nursing practices detailed in these contracts are found so widely in other traditional societies that it is safe to assume the contracts simply reflect the prevalent maternal nursing practices in the general population. But fertility rates are also influenced by other less obvious community practices, such as health-related factors (e.g., reduced sexual activity in populations subject to chronic fevers) or separation of spouses during seasonal migration.[51] Characteristic of all these indirect methods of fertility control is that, unlike contraception and abortion, they largely tend to depress overall fertility rates without regard to "parity," the number of children a woman has previously borne. That is, they are consistent with a regime of fertility control in which individual family planning plays little or no part.[52]

Comparative evidence establishes beyond reasonable doubt that Egyptians restrained fertility chiefly through breastfeeding practices and other indirect methods, rather than through contraception and abortion.[53] The key indicator of this is fertility rates among older married women: if contraception and abortion are widely and effectively used, older couples regularly curtail childbirth after reaching a desired family size, and fertility rates therefore decline sharply as women age. But the fertility data in Table C, together

[51] See esp. J. Bongaarts, "A Framework for Analyzing the Proximate Determinants of Fertility," *Population and Development Review* 4 (1978) 105–132. Such indirect means can be very effective; rural China in the 1930s had a marital fertility index (I_g) of only 0.510, resulting in a near-stationary population despite almost universal marriage $(I_m = 0.874)$ and no use of contraception $(m = 0.05)$. G. W. Barclay *et al.*, "Reassessment" (1976) 611–617. Roman Egypt had much higher marital fertility, but a much lower incidence of marriage—a very different demographic strategy.

[52] Unfortunately, because of high infant mortality, normal birth intervals cannot be ascertained from the census returns. But some larger families, lucky with regard to infant mortality, indicate a two- to three-year interval between births (e.g., 103-Ar-3; 131-Ar-3; 145-Ar-19), though one has an even shorter interval (159-Ar-1 with 173-Ar-3); these intervals are common in pre-transition populations, cf. M. Livi-Bacci, *History* (1992) 12–15. In any case, only with the modern fertility transition "did the deliberate spacing of children within marriage become important" to family planning. S. C. Watkins, in *Decline of Fertility* (1986) 434. Before then, such spacing as occurred was mainly to protect the health of the mother and earlier children; see J. Knodel, in *Determinants* I (1983) 94.

[53] For marital fertility in pre-transition populations, this is a principal finding of the Princeton European Fertility Project: A. J. Coale, in *Decline of Fertility* (1986) 8–22; it is generalizable to all known populations, with only scattered deviations. J. M. Riddle, *Contraception* (1992), is unaware of the Princeton study, which tells decisively against his view that abortion and contraception were used to limit families in antiquity. As to the evidence for pre-transition fertility control, J. Knodel and E. van de Walle, in *Decline of Fertility* (1986) 400–408, observe (p. 403): "References to birth control ... are far more numerous [in pre-transition societies] than references to family limitation; that is, extra-marital relations are the privileged locus of contraception." This observation needs more study for the ancient world; see, e.g., Lucretius, *Rer. Nat.* 4.1263–1277.

with the reconstructed fertility curves in Figure 7.2, show that married women in Roman Egypt continued to bear children at quite high rates well into their 40s; this is an unequivocal sign that married couples were not making general and effective use of contraception and abortion.[54]

Thus, although Egyptian couples evidently accepted and implemented the widespread ancient belief that procreation was the main purpose of marriage,[55] they also regarded their acceptance as consistent with social practices that, although not overtly linked to family limitation, nonetheless served to reduce fertility. In this respect, Roman Egypt resembles all other traditional populations, and does not anticipate the fertility transition.[56]

Infanticide and exposure
In the Greco-Roman world before the advent of Christianity, no significant legal barriers prevented the killing or exposure of one's newborn children, nor was either practice generally viewed with much more than social distaste.[57] Exposure differs from infanticide in that an exposed child may be

[54]See A. J. Coale, in *Decline of Fertility* (1986) 12–13: "If the fitted value of *m* is close to zero, indicating that the decline of marital fertility is no steeper than in a typical schedule not affected by parity-related limitation [i.e., contraception and abortion], the presumption that such limitation is virtually absent is a strong one, even though the level of marital fertility may be low because of nonparity-related limitation." In Section 1 above, the estimated value of *m* was 0.3; any higher value very adversely affects the fit. The census returns record nineteen births to women reportedly aged 40 and over at maternity; all but one are to married women.

[55]S. Treggiari, *Marriage* (1991) 205–228, and S. Dixon, *Family* (1992) 61–71, with bibliography; compare the high index of marital fertility calculated above. However, as M. Livi-Bacci observes in *Decline of Fertility* (1986) 183–189, European aristocracies led the way in adopting family limitation as a deliberate goal; the same may be true for the Roman status elite, see S. Dixon, *The Roman Mother* (1988) 93–95, with further bibliography.

[56]A. J. Coale, "The Demographic Transition Reconsidered," in *International Population Conference, Liège, 1973* I (1973) 53–72, notes three preconditions for decline of marital fertility within marriage: fertility must be "within the calculus of conscious choice," parents must want smaller families, and means to limit fertility must be available. For pre-transition societies, vigorous debate continues about which preconditions were met, but scholars usually believe that at least the first was not: e.g., P. Ariès, "Interprétation pour une histoire des mentalités," in *La prévention des naissances dans la famille* (ed. H. Bergues *et al.*; 1960) 311–327. J. M. Riddle's argument in *Contraception* (1992) goes only to the third precondition.

[57]See, with bibliography, T. G. Parkin, *Demography* (1992) 95–105, esp. R. Oldenziel, "The Historiography of Infanticide in Antiquity: A Literature Stillborn," in *Sexual Asymmetry: Studies in Ancient Society* (ed. J. Blok and P. Mason; 1987) 87–107; also J. M. Riddle, *Contraception* (1992) 10–14, rightly doubting that infanticide was frequent. Egypt's high index of marital fertility leaves little room for an appreciable rate of infanticide among married couples; in any event, "historical cases of infanticide can almost always be traced to unwed mothers." G. Alter, in *European Experience* (1992) 15. Deliberate infanticide is distinct from negligent child-rearing, which can also be used as an indirect means to limit family size; high infant mortality ("concealed infanticide") may thus result from parental reaction to unwanted births. J. Knodel and E. van de Walle, in *Decline of Fertility* (1986) 405–407. Roman attitudes toward children are canvassed by S. Dixon, *Family* (1992) 98–119, with further bibliography; add P. Garnsey, in *Family*

taken in by strangers and then raised either as a fosterchild or (more frequently) as a slave.[58] Literary sources and papyri indicate that both practices were at least not extremely rare, although their incidence, especially in the general population, is the subject of on-going scholarly debate. In any case, ancient evidence also suggests that both practices were probably applied more commonly to newborn females than to males.

As to this last point, the census returns are of some help. In about fifty cases, the returns declare parents one or both of whom are aged 35 or less, together with their surviving children of identifiable sex and age.[59] From these cases, it is possible to infer whether parents display any pronounced preference as to the sex of their children. Obviously this method is not foolproof, particularly since there is no way to correct against, for example, the results of infant mortality or the nonreporting or misreporting of sons and daughters. But at least a coarse impression is possible.

The evidence is best understood if the twenty metropolitan returns are compared with the thirty village returns. In the metropoleis, sons are markedly more frequent than daughters (23 as against 11); in villages, this pattern is reversed (19 sons, 34 daughters). Similarly, about twice as many metropolitan families have more sons than daughters (13 to 5); in the villages the ratio is reversed (7 to 20). Where families have only one child, it is usually a son in the metropoleis (6 of 9), but a daughter in the villages (10 of 16). The son is the oldest child in 12 of 18 metropolitan families, but in only 14 of 30 village families.

These patterns, which are statistically significant,[60] doubtless result in very large measure from differences in reporting practices: failure to report young girls in metropoleis, concealment of boys in the villages.[61] But it cannot be entirely excluded that infanticide or exposure, especially of females, was more common in metropoleis than in the villages.[62] Overall

---

(1991) 48–65. Also M. Golden, *Children and Childhood in Classical Athens* (1990) 80–114, with comparative evidence.

[58] J. Boswell, *The Kindness of Strangers: The Abandonment of Children in Western Europe from Late Antiquity to the Renaissance* (1982) 51–137; M. Memmer, "*Ad Servitutem aut ad Lupanar* . . .," *ZRG* 108 (1991) 21–93. On exposure in Egypt, see J. A. Straus, "L'Esclavage" (1988) 854–856, with further bibliography. Exposure is mentioned much more frequently than infanticide; it is important to recognize that exposure did not necessarily, or perhaps even normally, result in death.

[59] The age of parents is restricted so that only fairly young families are considered. The results below do not differ significantly if a lower age is used.

[60] E.g., for sons as compared to daughters, significance is above a 95 percent confidence level (chi-square test).

[61] See Chapter 2, and the discussion of the sex ratio in Chapters 5 (Sections 2 to 4) and 8.

[62] N. Lewis, *Life* (1983) 54–55, argues that the more heavily Greek-influenced population of metropoleis accepted the practice, while Egyptian peasants found it abhorrent (e.g., Diodorus, 1.80.3; Strabo, 17.2.5; Tacitus, *Hist.* 5.5.6); see also S. B. Pomeroy, *Women* (1985) 135–138. More questionable is Lewis' linkage of female exposure to the desire to

in the free population, females under age 15 outnumber males in villages (57 to 42), but are greatly outnumbered by males in metropoleis (33 to 62).

The lopsided juvenile sex ratio in villages is probably not significant, since it is implausible that village parents practiced active postnatal sexual discrimination in favor of daughters; concealment of sons is the more obvious explanation. By contrast, the metropolitan sex ratio for juveniles cannot be brought into balance even if large allowance is made for underreporting of very young girls.[63] What this may point to is a small but nonnegligible rate of female infant death through infanticide and exposure in metropoleis, although the exact rate is impossible to ascertain.[64]

Patterns of family sex preference in children are demographically important because they can have large effects on fertility rates, particularly if sex preference is effectively enforceable through practices such as infanticide or exposure.[65] The consequence of enforceable sex preference is that couples can rationally aim for much reduced fertility. We suggest that the later age of metropolitan females at marriage may be linked to efforts by metropolitans to lower overall fertility.[66]

Tendency of women not to remarry
The pre- and postnatal forms of fertility limitation that are discussed above may have had appreciable effects in restraining population growth. But Egyptians also tacitly relied on another means: the tendency of women not to remarry, especially after age 30 or 35 (see Figure 6.1); this tendency is especially important because, as we saw above, marital fertility was so

---

avoid dowries; comparative evidence suggests that avoiding the costs of child raising is a more plausible explanation. The practice may thus have been more sex-neutral in its effects.

[63] For instance, if only children aged 5 to 14 are considered, boys still greatly outnumber girls (42 to 31); but continued metropolitan underreporting of girls is likely, see Chapter 8.

[64] So also K. Hopkins, "Brother-Sister" (1980) 316–317. The failure of metropolitans to register very young girls also suggests that they were "undervalued": P. M. Visaria, *Sex Ratio* (1971) 26–27, on India. On the fate of exposed children, see Section 4 below; it is not impossible that in metropoleis as many as three to five percent of metropolitan infants (almost all of them girls) were exposed and then enslaved.

[65] N. Keyfitz, *Demography* (1985) 332–344, esp. 344; the analogue in the modern world is sexually selective abortion (said to be widely practiced in present-day China). Parental preference for sons can dramatically raise fertility rates in the absence of pre- or postnatal enforcement of sexual preference; but if enforcement is possible, fertility rates can be much lower than replacement levels.

[66] See Chapter 6 at notes 25–26. This proposition is advanced hesitantly, since later female age of marriage in metropoleis is not certain. However, it should also be noted that the concentration of brother-sister marriage in metropoleis could have led to higher fertility in the absence of other restraints; see Chapter 6 at notes 84–85.

high. As we showed in Chapter 6, the social causes of the phenomenon were complex: high adult mortality and the relatively free accessibility of divorce resulted in numerous prematurely broken marriages; on the other hand, older males often married (or remarried) much younger women, rather than women closer in age to themselves. Nor is it in any way precluded that many older women, faced with the risks of childbearing, preferred not to remarry.

But the demographic consequences of this marriage pattern, which is common in the pre-modern Mediterranean,[67] should also be kept in mind. As Table 7.1 illustrates, Hutterite female fertility rates begin to decline especially from age 30 onward. Fertility declines also in Roman Egypt, but more steeply. From ages 25 to 29, Egyptian fertility in the model peaks at nearly 55 percent of Hutterite fertility; but from age 30 onward fertility drops below this level at a rapidly accelerating rate.

In pre-modern northwestern Europe, populations display some ability to control population growth by raising or lowering female age at first marriage, thereby in effect simultaneously raising or lowering the Total Fertility Rate for females.[68] By contrast, in the Mediterranean, where women more commonly married at an early age, a different demographic strategy evolved, though with much the same effect: through early marriage, relatively high female fertility was achieved as soon as possible (usually by the late 'teens), but overall fertility was limited in part through constraints on female remarriage.[69] This is the demographic equivalent of modest birth control among older but still fertile women.[70]

In sum, ordinary Egyptians apparently restrained population growth mainly through indirect methods, such as maternal breastfeeding or abstinence, that delayed postpartum pregnancy irrespective of parity. The rela-

---

[67] T. W. Gallant, *Risk and Survival* (1991) 26-27, with bibliography, especially M. Livi-Bacci, in *Marriage and Remarriage* (1981) 347-361, on nineteenth-century Italy. So too in fifteenth-century Tuscany: D. Herlihy and C. Klapisch-Zuber, *Tuscans* (1985) 214-221, who also link female failure to remarry with population control (p. 250).

[68] See, e.g., E. A. Wrigley and R. S. Schofield, *England* (1989) 255-256, 422-424, for England; J.-L. Flandrin, *Families* (1979) 184-187, for France. These and other north European populations pursued a Malthusian strategy in which fertility is limited by starting families later. In the fertility transition, the "starting" strategy was supplanted by a neo-Malthusian "stopping" strategy: women ceased having children at an earlier age.

[69] Restraint on remarriage is effective in limiting fertility only if mortality is very high and women marry early: A. J. Coale, H. Le Bras, and H. Leridon, in *Marriage and Remarriage* (1981) 151-156, 199-211, and 605-615, respectively. Both conditions obtained in Roman Egypt. Contrast T. G. Parkin, *Demography* (1992) 132: "For demographic purposes it was important that widows remarry"; in fact, the opposite is more likely.

[70] A. J. Coale, in *Marriage and Remarriage* (1981) 151-156, and in *Decline of Fertility* (1986) 8 n.4. See also P. N. Mari Bhat, in *India* (1989) 110-111, who notes this effect on Indian fertility from 1891 to 1911; in India, higher-caste widows were prevented from remarriage by taboo. (Compare in the same volume T. Dyson, p. 185, on Bihar.)

tively high divorce rate and the tendency of women not to remarry after age 30 or 35 also contributed substantially. By contrast, contraception and abortion, as prenatal forms of birth control, apparently had little conse- quence at least within marriage. The effects of deliberate or reckless infan- ticide, as postnatal forms of birth control, are harder to assess, but in any case were probably small and confined largely to metropoleis. Delay in female age of marriage was apparently not used as a method of population control, except perhaps to a very small degree in metropoleis.

How this combination of restraints operated in practice, and also its resilience in the face of varying demographic challenges, cannot be determined on present evidence; but Egyptian modes of fertility control, if regarded as Malthusian preventive checks on population growth, were probably less responsive to short- and perhaps even long-term changes than those used in early modern Europe. Nonetheless, the age distribution in the census returns does imply (and this point is fundamental) that Egyptians successfully avoided excessive population growth at least in the long term, although only under conditions of extremely elevated mortality.[71]

3. Births outside of marriage

Twenty-one persons are described in the census returns as *apatores*, free- born but "without a father" because they were not born in legitimate mar- riage.[72] Today it is believed that such persons were not "bastards" in the modern sense, but rather usually children of informal but enduring relation- ships that were not legitimate marriages solely because of legal barriers on capacity to marry. Little social stigma attached to illegitimacy, although it did affect inheritance.[73] The census returns and other sources suggest that the incidence of illegitimacy was low, perhaps around 3 to 5 percent of free births, though higher locally; in particular, illegitimate birth was much more common in villages than in metropoleis (18 of 21 cases).[74]

---

[71] See Chapter 9, Section 2, for the possible implications of high mortality.

[72] 131-Pr-1 (see Discussion; also reported in 145-Pr-1); 145-Ar-1, 3, and 19 (six persons); 159-Ar-13 and 16; 173-Ar-9; 187-Ar-8 (two) and 26 (three); 187-Me-1 (two); 201-Ar-1; 229-Ar-2 (also reported in 243-Ar-4). Five males, 16 females. Also 19-Ox-1, probably *apator*. Two owners of apparently unoccupied property are also *apatores*: 215-Ar-8 and 215-Ox-1; so too, probably, the declarant's father in 173-Pr-2.

[73] Thus, for example, the mother of Thaumistis in 131-Pr-1 and 145-Pr-1 married after bear- ing a child out of wedlock; her husband apparently raised the child as his own. This is the nearest the census returns come to reporting an adoption. In only four instances can the mother's age at childbirth be determined for an *apator*; in these cases the mother gives birth in her mid-twenties or early thirties (145-Ar-1, 174-Ar-9, and 187-Me-1).

[74] See esp. H. C. Youtie, *"Apatores"* (1975); also A. Calderini, *"Apatores,"* Aegyptus 33 (1953) 358–369. Compare B. Rawson, *"Spurii* and the Roman View of Illegitimacy," Antichthon 23 (1989) 10–41. On the incidence of illegitimacy: Calderini, 363–364; Youtie, 731–732. Presumably legal barriers to marriage had disproportionate impact on native Egyptians, who predominated in villages. But 131-Pr-1 and 145-Pr-1 suggest that

In 173-Ar-9 from Karanis, the declarant registers, in addition to his family, two co-resident kinswomen: twin sisters aged 38, one of whom has a 12-year-old daughter described as *apator*. Lodging in the same household is a freedwoman of the sisters' brother Valerius Aphrodisios; Valerius is currently serving in the Roman cavalry and therefore could not legitimately marry until after his term of service. It is not unlikely that Valerius had informally married his sister and fathered a daughter by her.[75] However, also declared in the same household are six slaves belonging to Sempronius Herminos, another soldier currently in service; the presence of these slaves is unexplained, but Sempronius, presumably another of the declarant's relatives, could also be the girl's father.

As this return illustrates, such irregular families are almost impossible to reconstruct. In 187-Me-1 from Moithymis, a freedwoman aged 45 declares her two daughters aged 20 and 12, both *apatores*, and a female slave aged 15. Her former master is a woman, so she is clearly not a concubine, but no male is mentioned in her return; her daughters might even have been born while she was still a slave and then freed with her.[76] Similarly, in 145-Ar-1 from Tebtunis, a woman aged 38 lives alone with her daughter 13, registered as *apator*; there is no sign of a spouse.

In any case, *apatores* children of the same mother (and often probably also of the same father) tend to remain together in adulthood, like children from legitimate marriages. The most remarkable case is 145-Ar-19 from Philagris: five or possibly six *apatores* siblings from the same mother, living together in a *frérèche*. They range in age from 30 to 14, a seventeen-year spread in age. The two oldest brothers are married, one to his sister.[77]

4. Births to slave women

Slaves present even greater problems than freeborn *apatores*. Like *apatores*, slaves do not have legal fathers; but declarants rarely name even the mothers of slaves unless the mother happens also to be a slave resident in

---

[75] some illegitimate births were reported as legitimate (see Discussion). See the Discussion on this return; also J. B. Campbell, "The Marriage of Soldiers under the Empire," *JRS* 68 (1978) 153–166. The sisters were perhaps the declarant's second cousins.

[76] On concubines, see S. Treggiari, "Concubinae," *PBSR* 49 (1981) 57–81. Concubinage is impossible to discern in the census returns. A possible case is 173-Pr-15, where the female declarant registers her son aged 19, and then immediately after him (and before her other children) a freedman's daughter aged 16 and her son 1; the declarant does not indicate that her son was legally married, but he is presumably the father.

[77] Compare 187-Ar-26 from Karanis: females aged 25, 15, and 4 probably from the same mother (a twenty-one-year gap in age), taken in apparently by relatives.

the household.[78] Further, though Egyptian slaves may have entered unofficial "marriages" and established informal families, declarants pay such families scant heed beyond (in many cases) listing slave children after their mother. As a result, slave families are virtually impossible to discern even by way of speculation; certainly the census returns reveal no sign of a deliberate policy by masters to encourage them.

The likeliest case of a slave family[79] is 243-Ox-1 from Oxyrhynchos. The declarants, the only freeborn residents, are two unmarried brothers aged 27 and 26; the younger brother owns the slaves. They are listed with males before females: a male Silbanos aged 19; then three boys aged 3, 0, and probably 0; a female Sinthonis aged 24; and a girl aged 5. Sinthonis is described as the mother of the first two boys and the girl. Their father could be Silbanos, or possibly one of the free brothers.[80] Somewhat favoring the latter possibility is an additional oddity. The second male child is Markos, aged 0; the third is Markos "the younger," listed with the slaves but in fact manumitted. Curiously, his mother and age are not given. The most plausible explanation is that he is a younger twin who has been freed as part of a scheme to encourage Sinthonis to bear children.[81] But this must remain conjecture.

Other returns are still more difficult. In 173-Ar-9 from Karanis, the oldest slave is Kopr[eia] aged 40; she has a daughter aged 20 and two sons 6 and 4. The daughter, in turn, has a daughter 4 and a son 0. This is the only group of slaves that can be traced through three (extremely short) generations; but there is no potential father among the slaves, and we must instead look, perhaps, to the declarant aged 48, his brother aged 44 (currently absent in tax flight, *anachoresis*), or the owner of the slaves (a Roman soldier not resident in the household).[82] In 187-Ar-30 also from Karanis, a solitary woman aged 60 declares nine female slaves, at least two of whom are women each with two young daughters; but there is no potential father in sight.

---

[78] When the mother is not a slave in the household, mothers are given only in 173-Pr-3, and 201-Ar-1 and 6. In 215-Hm-3, the mothers are evidently slaves in another household owned by the declarant. The difficulty of discerning slave families in Egypt is remarked also by K. R. Bradley, *Slaves and Masters in the Roman Empire: A Study in Social Control* (1984) 47–80 (esp. 52–69), and J.A. Straus, "L'Esclavage" (1988) 896–897.

[79] Also possible is 159-Hm-2: a male slave, followed by a female and her three daughters. But their ages are all lost, and the male belongs to the declarant while the females belong to lodgers.

[80] Silbanos would be very young as father of a 5-year-old, but see 187-Ar-4 for a father at age 13. Of course, the children may not all be from the same father.

[81] Such schemes are occasionally described in the *Digest*; e.g., Tryphoninus/Ulpian, D. 1.5.15–16. It is also unclear why the younger Markos is listed with the slaves. Compare 215-He-3, where a son of a slavewoman has also been manumitted.

[82] Similar problems in 215-Ar-2 from Soknopaiou Nesos.

Despite obstacles to reconstruction, it is reasonably clear that masters expected their adult female slaves to bear children, and that female slaves often did so; and this must also explain why females were not commonly manumitted while still of childbearing age.[83] In twenty cases a slave mother's age at childbirth can be reconstructed;[84] there are six births to women in their teens (the earliest at age 15: 187-Ar-30, 215-Ar-3), nine to women in their twenties, four in their thirties, and the latest at age 41 (187-Ar-30)—a pattern perhaps slightly more accelerated than that of Egyptian women generally (Figure 7.1). Although some large slave households remain wholly impervious to reconstruction (e.g., 187-An-1: at least thirteen slaves; 187-Ar-32: seven slaves), these twenty cases are nearly a tenth of the total 211 cases in which both mother's and child's age are known; the proportion is close to that of the slave population in the census statistics as a whole (119 of 1084, or 11 percent), indicating that slave fertility was probably about the same as that of all free women, though well below that of free married women.[85]

In twenty-eight cases, the sex of a child with a known slave mother can be ascertained; in twelve cases it is a son, in sixteen cases a daughter. The difference here could easily result from chance,[86] so no conclusions can be drawn about sex preference among slave children. There remains, however, the oddity of the sex ratio among slaves. As Table D shows, in metropoleis the sex ratio is nearly equal (32 females, 28 males), though metropolitan declarants register no female slaves younger than 5. By contrast, in villages males are heavily outnumbered (36 females, 6 males). Earlier we argued that the wildly unbalanced village sex ratio is probably caused chiefly by the chance survival of several village households with large numbers of female slaves, as well as by sexual differentiation in age of manumission.[87]

---

[83] Apart from Zosime (aged 22) in 159-Ar-1, all freedwomen are 35 or older; see Chapter 3 at notes 73–74. It is pointless to speculate on whether adult female slaves were valued more for their children, as K. R. Bradley contends, "The Age at Time of Sale of Female Slaves," *Arethusa* 11 (1978) 243–252; or for their labor, as A. Dalby argues, "On Female Slaves in Roman Egypt," *Arethusa* 12 (1979) 255–259.

[84] 145-Ar-9; 159-Ar-4; 173-Ar-9 (five); 187-An-2; 187-Ar-30 (four); 201-Ox-1; 215-Ar-3 (three); 243-Ox-1 (four).

[85] See I. Biezunska-Malowist, *L'Esclavage* II (1977) 19–21; J. A. Straus, "L'Esclavage" (1988) 853. The offspring of female slaves were frequently sold: Biezunska-Malowist, 27–28; this makes it more difficult to identify slave families. But slave women are about 13 percent of all women aged 15 up to 50 (24 of 185), nearly identical to the percentage of slaves among children less than 15 (32 of 232); this is strong evidence that slave women experienced approximately normal female fertility.

[86] Chi-square is 0.072 with one degree of freedom, using Yates's correction for continuity; significant only at about 0.25.

[87] See Chapter 5 at notes 9–10. It is also possible that villagers deliberately concealed their male slaves in order to avoid paying the poll tax on them.

However, it is worth noting a few village households that register a single female slave of young age, without reporting her mother.[88] Of course, the mother may have died or otherwise passed from the household;[89] but it is at least possible that these slaves are exposed children who were taken in and raised as slaves by villagers. Since exposure of female infants was, as it seems, primarily a metropolitan phenomenon (Section 2 above), the practice may have effected a slight migration from metropoleis into the villages; but the evidence is too feeble for certainty.[90] On the whole, it is likely that birth, and not exposure, was the principal origin of slaves in Roman Egypt.[91]

One household requiring special comment is 117-Ar-3 from Arsinoe. In this return, a freeborn woman lodger aged 26 is described as the wife of a slave Dioskoros aged 29, a weaver owned by the declarant's wife and her sister; the lodger is evidently unrelated to the declarant and his family. The couple have two daughters aged 8 and 6 and a son aged 1, all of whom, following normal rules, inherit their mother's civil status. The juridical nature of their marriage is problematic;[92] but the marriage, which obviously arose while the woman was still very young, has lasted nearly a decade. This household also contains two female slaves aged 49 and 23, and a male aged 1, all of whom also belong to the declarant's wife and her sister. The declarant omits the relationship, if any, between these slaves; but judging from the boy's name (Dioskoros "the second," *allos*), his father could well be Dioskoros and his mother the female slave aged 23. However, since the apparent mother's name is Dioskorous, the boy may have taken his name from her.

[88] 117-Ap-3 from Tanyaithis (aged 3); 145-Ar-3 from Tebtunis (aged 5); 187-Me-1 from Moithymis (aged 15). See also, perhaps, 103-Ar-1 (one female) and 117-Ar-3 from Soknopaiou Nesos (three belonging to different owners), where the ages are lost.

[89] In 117-Ap-8, the household includes two freedwomen lodgers aged 36 and 35; either could be the mother of the slave aged 3.

[90] On exposure as a source of slaves, I. Biezunska-Malowist, *L'Esclavage* II (1977) 21–27.

[91] So also I. Biezunska-Malowist, *L'Esclavage* (1977) 42.

[92] I. Biezunska-Malowist, *L'Esclavage* (1977) 132–133, comparing *P.Ryl.* II 103 from Arsinoe. The older Dioskoros is also the only male slave in the census returns whose occupation is given; possibly not a coincidence.

8

Migration

Migration is the third major demographic function, along with mortality and fertility.[1] In pre-modern populations, migration over very long distances (between countries, or, in historical empires, between provinces) usually had slight impact since populations were largely sedentary.[2] But internal migration over shorter distances, for instance between an urban center and the surrounding countryside, could play a major role in shaping the demographic characteristics of a population.[3]

It may help to have some advance idea of what we might expect regarding internal migration. Late medieval Tuscany exhibits a fairly typical pattern:[4]

Migration into the towns reduced the number of young adult males in rural areas, enlarged their numbers in the cities, and worked overall to even out the rural sex ratios . . . [T]he towns were lacking in girls and young women, but claimed

---

[1] D. Yaukey, *Demography* (1985) 254–330; C. Newell, *Methods* (1988) 82–89. On migration patterns in early modern Europe, see M. W. Flinn, *System* (1981) 65–75. On the demographic theory of migration, see W. Zelinsky, "The Hypothesis of the Mobility Transition," *Geographical Review* 61 (1971) 219–249, and "The Demographic Transition: Changing Patterns of Migration," in Int. Union for the Sci. Study of Pop., *La science de la population au service de l'homme* (1979) 165–189. Internal migration is an exceptionally complex subject, and the census returns are inadequate for studying it; below we do no more than raise some issues relevant to the returns. On technique, see United Nations, *Manual VI: Methods of Measuring Internal Migration* (1970). *International Handbook on Internal Migration* (ed. C. B. Nam, W. J. Serow, and D. F. Sly; 1990) surveys twenty-one countries, including Egypt (pp. 103–124) and India (pp. 189–206).

[2] The census returns indicate some travel outside Egypt: 131-He-2 from Oxyrhynchos (declarant's 3-year-old son was born abroad, *epi xenes*); 145-Ox-3 from Ankyronpolis (declarant of property only is currently abroad).

[3] The classic work on Egyptian internal migration is H. Braunert, *Binnenwanderung* (1964).

[4] D. Herlihy and C. Klapisch-Zuber, *Tuscans* (1985) 156–157 (footnote omitted and a typographical error corrected). Closely similar is late medieval France: A. Higounet-Nadal, in *Population française* I (1988) 270–297; so also contemporary India: P. M. Visaria, *Sex Ratio* (1971) 11–13.

numerous young males, many of them immigrants. The pattern changes in later life. The influx of males into towns slackened, but that of females increased. Old, often widowed, women from the countryside sought out the amenities and services which towns provided more readily than villages . . . The attractiveness of cities to older women is a near constant of social history.

As will emerge below, this pattern is at least partly found in Roman Egypt as well.

The sex ratio revisited
In Chapter 5, we considered the difficult problem of the age-specific sex ratio as it emerges from the census returns. There our concern was primarily with the likeliest male mortality rates; but the sex ratio is also germane to migration.

Table 8.1 (p. 162) gives the age-specific sex ratios in returns from villages and metropoleis. Except for ages 0 to 4, seven-age moving averages are used to smooth the data from Table A, as in Chapters 4 and 5. Some now familiar problems in the returns are evident in the resulting sex ratios, especially for juveniles. First, since metropolitan returns often do not declare young girls (especially those aged less than 5), the metropolitan sex ratios for ages 0 to 9 are hugely unbalanced toward males; but the reverse happens in villages especially for ages 10 to 14, owing to concealment of young males approaching taxable age. This problem makes the juvenile sex ratios unreliable for both metropoleis and villages.

Second, as was observed in Chapter 5 (at notes 18–20), male ages are less frequently preserved in the returns than are female ages; this occurs in both village and metropolitan returns. Thus the sex ratio for all ages is appreciably higher for both villages and metropoleis if persons of known sex but unknown age are figured in, as Table 8.1 shows. A corrective of approximately 1.05 to the age-specific sex ratios therefore seems in order.

In Figure 8.1 (p. 163) the age-specific sex ratios in Table 8.1 are plotted for ages 5 to 74, *after* applying the corrective of 1.05. Although the sex ratios bounce around wildly because of the sparseness of data, the metropoleis have a higher sex ratio than the villages in almost all age groups. The central tendencies of the data are much clearer in Figure 8.2 (p. 163), which uses three-figure moving averages of the sex ratios in order to bring out their central tendencies.[5] This figure shows only the apparently most reliable portion of the data, from ages 20 to 74.

---

[5] The sex ratios for ages 75–79 were not used in calculating Figure 8.2.

Table 8.1. *Sex ratio in villages and metropoleis*

Age	Villages			Metropoleis		
	Males	Females	Ratio	Males	Females	Ratio
0–4	24.00	28.00	85.7	26.00	8.00	325.0
5–9	16.29	22.57	72.2	23.71	14.14	167.7
10–14	8.00	23.43	34.1	18.57	13.71	135.4
15–19	14.00	22.86	61.3	22.29	14.86	150.0
20–24	13.14	15.00	87.6	17.29	17.57	98.4
25–29	12.71	12.71	100.0	13.14	15.57	84.4
30–34	16.57	18.29	90.6	16.57	9.57	173.1
35–39	11.00	18.43	59.7	8.29	8.29	100.0
40–44	10.00	11.29	88.6	6.43	7.00	91.8
45–49	12.43	9.86	126.1	9.86	4.43	222.6
50–54	7.00	11.14	62.8	6.14	4.86	126.5
55–59	8.57	8.86	96.8	3.43	2.57	133.3
60–64	5.00	4.43	112.9	2.71	1.14	237.5
65–69	4.86	3.29	147.8	2.43	1.14	212.5
70–74	5.00	4.14	120.7	2.14	1.29	166.7
75–79	1.71	1.14	150.0	1.00	0.14	700.0
80+				0.57		
All ages	170.29	215.43	79.0	180.57	124.29	145.3
Unc. age	76	70		114	75	
Total	246.29	285.43	86.3	294.57	199.29	147.8

In villages, the sexes remain in near-equilibrium from about ages 20 to 59; but from age 60 on the sex ratio moves unmistakably upward, in favor of males.[6] In the metropoleis, by contrast, males strongly predominate in all age groups.[7] A degree of stability obtains from ages 20 to 39, when there are approximately 130 males for every 100 females. But from age 40 onward, the sex ratio swings sharply upward, in favor of males; it reaches a peak in later life of around 200 males for every 100 females. The upward turn begins about fifteen years later in the villages than in the metropoleis, so that the gap between their respective sex ratios widens; but from age 60

[6] Applying the 1.05 corrective, the sex ratio for villagers aged 20 and above is 95.4 (109 males, 120 females). This sex ratio is depressed by the large number of female slaves in villages (for free persons, the sex ratio is 104.0: 108 males, 109 females), and also, perhaps, by some village concealment of adult males; see Chapter 5, Section 2.
[7] Applying the 1.05 corrective, the metropolitan sex ratio for persons aged 20 and over is 124.3 (90 males, 76 females). For free persons, the sex ratio is 136.7 (82 males, 63 females).

on, the upward movement of the village sex ratio is roughly parallel to that
of the metropolitan sex ratio.[8]

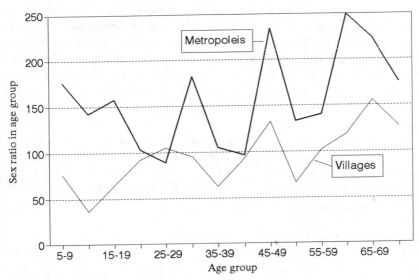

Figure 8.1. *Sex ratio in villages and metropoleis*

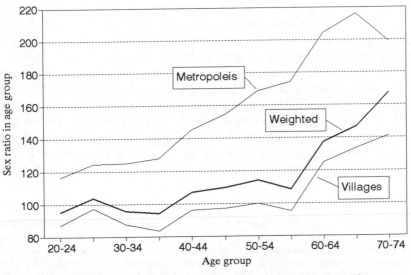

Figure 8.2. *Sex ratio (moving average) in villages and metropoleis*

[8] This difference is even clearer if the numbers in Figure 8.2 are replotted with a vertical
semi-log scale.

As we observed in Chapter 5, Sections 3 and 4, this upward movement of the sex ratio, in favor of elderly males, is impossible to duplicate or explain within the parameters of the Coale-Demeny model life tables; there we argue, albeit with hesitation, that the phenomenon is not "real," but instead probably produced by a higher rate of age exaggeration for elderly males than for females. In Figure 8.2, we also include sex ratios calculated from "weighted" age-group figures for females and males aged 20 to 74.[9] Since the "weighted" sex ratios depend more heavily on village than metropolitan statistics, they lie close to the village sex ratios, but are pulled higher by the metropolitan sex ratios. The "weighted" sex ratios approximate the "true" age-specific sex ratio as it is represented in the returns.

Whatever the correct explanation of the apparent upward rise in the sex ratio during later life, the gap between village and metropolitan sex ratios probably does not result from markedly different mortality schedules. The census data indicate, in fact, that both male and female adult mortality were more or less uniform from villages to metropoleis.[10]

The effect of internal migration: a hypothesis

The strongly unbalanced metropolitan sex ratio for adults (about 130 for ages 20 to 39) may result from a combination of factors: the initial imbalance in the sex ratio at birth (about 105 males per 100 females); sex-differentiated use of infanticide, exposure, or child care that exacerbated the sex ratio at birth still further; subsequent mortality patterns during youth (male mortality approximately equal to, or perhaps less than, female mortality);[11] and in-migration of young males from the countryside. The first and the third of these factors can be considered reasonably likely on the evidence of the census returns (see Chapter 5). The second is more problematic, as we showed in Chapter 7 (at notes 57–66); although female infanticide or death through exposure may have been associated especially with the metropoleis, the returns provide no clear evidence that its rate was appreciable. We may thus start from the conjecture that the general sex ratio at birth (105) remained approximately constant until age 15 in villages, but somewhat increased in metropoleis.

[9] These sex ratios come from Figure 5.2, which also uses three-figure moving averages to smooth out the ratios. The "weighted" figures were calculated on the assumption that villages outnumbered urban residents by approximately two to one; see Chapter 3, Section 1.
[10] See esp. the similarity between "smoothed" and "weighted" age distributions for both females (Figure 4.3) and males (Figure 5.3) aged 20 and over. Insofar as can now be determined, metropolitan and village fertility rates also appear to be similar.
[11] See Chapter 5, Section 4; also esp. C. A. Nathanson, "Sex Differences" (1984) 195, summarizing modern research on less developed countries.

The remaining discrepancy in the village and metropolitan sex ratios could be explained by supposing that, from each cohort of 15-year-old village males, approximately 9 percent migrated to metropoleis between ages 15 and 24;[12] this is equivalent to an annual out-migration of less than 1 percent of village males aged 15 to 24. As in late medieval Tuscany, the result of this migration was to reduce the sex ratio in villages to near or below parity, while raising that of metropoleis to about 130, as in Table 8.2. Most migrating males would be "marginal" villagers: perhaps most often young men unable to find brides and form families, or unable to find work.[13] This pattern is not unusual in pre-modern populations: migrants are very frequently young males aged 15 to 25, and their decision to migrate usually stems from the inability to marry or from lack of available land because of the size of rural families.[14] Such migrants normally maintain contact with their families, for instance by sending home remittances; but patterns of return vary extremely widely, with little or no return in some populations.[15] On our hypothesis, return was rare also in Roman Egypt.

After age 25, migration of males apparently slowed, as it does in most pre-modern populations; but the sex ratios in Figure 8.2 may suggest a small level of continuing male migration into metropoleis, thereby preserving near-parity of the sexes in villages while further swelling the metropolitan sex ratio. By about age 60, male migration from villages ceases, and the village and metropolitan sex ratios begin a parallel rise.

By contrast, the census returns do not clearly signal any migration of elderly women from villages into the metropoleis. On the whole, Egyptian females of all ages appear to be considerably less mobile than males.

---

[12] In a very rough manner, this result is obtained by solving for x and y in two equations: $x + 2y = 130$ (for metropoleis), and $x - y = 100$ (for villages); $x = 110$ (the hypothetical overall sex ratio at age 15), and $y = 10$ (the presumed change in the village sex ratio as a result of migration). The net male migration from villages is therefore y divided by x, or 9.1 percent of each cohort.

[13] On the relationship between migration and the sex ratio, see H. S. Shryock and J. S. Siegel, *Methods* (1980) 193–194, 197–198. In modern populations of developed countries, the same rationale has tended to attract women into cities, which thus often have a lower sex ratio than rural areas.

[14] See J. Connell *et al.*, *Migration* (1976) 18–24, 39–52, 179–181 (with data from India). The authors describe inability to marry as "the most general (or at least the most constant) cause of migration from villages" (p. 49). Compare A. S. Oberai and H. K Manmohan Singh, *Causes and Consequences of Internal Migration: A Study in the Indian Punjab* (1983) 52–64; K. N. S. Yadava, *Rural-Urban Migration in India* (1989) 51–57. The Indian case is pertinent because the Indian sex ratio is also heavily favorable to males.

[15] J. Connell *et al.*, *Migration* (1976) 90–120 (remittances), 121–139 (return).

Evidence for migration in the census returns

Self-evidently, the hypothesis presented above is oversimplified; it gives, at best, a general impression of net migration patterns. The returns themselves are poor records for the study of internal migration, but nonetheless do provide at least some clues.

In 145-Ar-24, Sambathion, the owner of a house in Theadelphia, records as resident there her brother Ptolemaios aged 35, his wife Anoubiana (actually registered elsewhere), and their minor son Dioskoros alias Heron aged 3 or 13. As it happens, fifteen years later Ptolemaios filed a petition in which he complains about the behavior of poll tax collectors; Dioskoros, so Ptolemaios alleges, had left home in AD 155/156 (thus at age 13 or 23), but the tax collectors are still seeking to collect the poll tax for him.[16] If Ptolemaios is to be believed, his son has lost contact with family and village; he did not register for the Theadelphia census of 159/160.

The fate of such migrants is uncertain; but many may have ended up among the lodgers in metropoleis. Village lodgers are few in number and usually freed slaves.[17] By contrast, metropolitan lodgers are much more numerous, rarely freed slaves, and overwhelmingly male.[18] Of particular interest are several metropolitan lodgers who are freeborn males living either alone or with one or more siblings.[19] Many of these males may well be migrants, although of course this is speculative.

The Roman army served as one vehicle for migration, by recruiting young males and then, after their long period of service had ended, discharging them as Roman citizens.[20] In 173-Ar-9 from Karanis, the declarant registers, along with his family, two sisters both aged 38, apparently his kinswomen. Their brother currently serves in the Roman

---

[16] H. C. Youtie, "P.Mich.Inv. 160 + P.Oslo II 18: *Medena Hyperalla Apaiteisthai*," *ZPE* 23 (1976) 131–138, reprinted in *Scriptiunculae Posteriores* I (1981) 375–382, with a discussion of the government's response to such problems. The two grandsons in 159-Ar-1 (from Arsinoe) are no longer in the household in 173-Ar-3; they may have left home upon reaching adulthood.

[17] A total of seven village lodgers: three males, four females. Ex-slaves: 117-Ap-8 (two freedwomen); 145-Ox-3 (freedman); 173-Ar-9 (freedman); 215-He-3 (freedman).

[18] A total of 51 lodgers: 27 males, 15 females, 9 uncertain. Freed slaves: 187-An-2 (male) and 215-He-1 (female).

[19] 33-Ar-1: five or six brothers, the oldest aged 25, two of whom may be married. 103-Ar-1: male solitary aged 18. 117-Ar-3: male solitary aged 57 (possible). 159-Ar-6: male solitary aged 29. 187-Ar-4: brothers aged 34 and 32, and a brother 26 with his sister 23. 187-Ar-9: male solitary aged 54 (possible). 187-Ar-34: male solitary aged 14(?) (possible). Compare also four young male renters living alone in metropoleis: 173-Me-2 (aged 28); 187-Ar-6 (worker, 18 or 28?), 33 (farmer, 33), and 37 (worker, 19).

[20] During the early Empire, when two legions plus auxiliaries were stationed in Egypt, the Roman army may have recruited as much as 2.5 percent of all young males in Egypt. (These figures can be calculated using the data in Tables 5.3 and 5.4.) On the Roman army in Egypt, see H. Devijver, in *Egitto* (1989) 37–54, with bibliography.

army; his freedwoman also resides as a lodger in the Karanis household.[21] The declarant registers, as well, several slaves belonging to another man, perhaps kin, currently in the cavalry. In three other returns, discharged veterans are declarants. The only one with useful information about residents is 159-Ar-6 from Arsinoe: a veteran is living with his son aged 6 (from a divorced wife) and a lodger aged 29 who had probably been invalided out of military service before completing his term.[22] As these returns suggest, military service may often have run in families.

Despite Ptolemaios' protestations regarding his son, many migrants from villages probably did often remain in contact with their families. At any rate, there are a fairly large number of returns filed by metropolitans for now usually unoccupied village property.[23] In one case (159-Ox-1), an Oxyrhynchite indicates that his property in the village of Mouchinor had come to him from his mother, presumably by inheritance.

A certain amount of continuing migration from villages by older males is suggested by 173-Ar-9 from Karanis: the declarant registers his 44-year-old brother, who is currently in tax flight (*anachoresis*). Tax flight became a significant problem in the second century AD, particularly in the Nile Delta where a host of social problems caused individuals and at times whole villages to desert the land.[24]

Beyond the limited evidence that the returns provide of more or less permanent male migration out from villages, there are also signs of continual, for the most part probably short-term movement of people among Egyptian villages.[25] Although the census required villagers to return to their "hearths" (Chapter 1, Section 2), the returns sometimes indirectly witness this migration. The most interesting case is 145-Ar-24 from Theadelphia, where the declarant Sambathion gives Theadelphia as her "fiscal domicile" (*idia*), but notes that she was also registered in Apias, a village some 30 to 40 kilometers distant. Sambathion registers her brother

[21] This brother may be unofficially married to one of the sisters; see Chapter 7, Section 3, on *apatores*.

[22] The other two returns are 61-Ox-1 from Oxyrhynchos and 229-He-1 of uncertain provenance, but probably Herakleopolis. It is not unlikely that veterans tended to congregate in metropoleis.

[23] 131-Ar-6; 145-Ar-15; 159-Ar-2; 159-Ox-1; 187-Ar-3 (four slaves in residence) and 27 (registered by a *phrontistes*); 187-Ox-6 (the owner is an Antinoite); 201-Ar-3.

[24] H. Braunert, *Binnenwanderung* (1964) 164–186; see also, for a summary especially of information from newly published sections of the Thmouis papyrus, D. W. Rathbone, "Villages" (1990) 114–119 (who cautions against overestimating its effects). On the tax surcharge for those in tax flight, see S. L. Wallace, *Taxation* (1937) 137–140, and N. Lewis, "*Merismos Anakechorekoton,*" *JEA* 23 (1937) 63–75; it may indicate considerable tax evasion.

[25] See A. E. Hanson, "Philadelphia" (1988) 261–277 (esp. 263–265). Compare H. Braunert, *Binnenwanderung* (1964) 149–164; and D. Herlihy and C. Klapisch-Zuber, *Tuscans* (1985) 155–158, for comparable phenomena in late medieval Tuscany.

Ptolemaios and his son as resident in the Theadelphia property, but omits Ptolemaios' wife Anoubiana, whose *idia* may be in yet another village. Ptolemaios is known to have had widespread business interests in the Fayyum.

Such short-term movement doubtless became even more intense among metropolitans; several returns suggest close contacts between families in metropoleis and even in Alexandria, presumably brought about, in most cases, through commerce.[26] In 187-Ar-32 from Arsinoe, the declarant notes that his divorced wife, an Antinoite, is now living in Antinoopolis with their son; she has evidently returned home. Similarly, in 201-Ar-6 also from Arsinoe, the declarant owners of a house are five men apparently all resident in Antinoopolis; the house is occupied by the parents-in-law of one owner, and by the divorced wife of another.[27] *Astoi*, citizens of Greek cities (most commonly of Alexandria), appear in four returns: the mother of a male infant in Theadelphia (145-Ar-24), absentee female declarants of property in Arsinoe (173-Ar-12, the daughter of a Roman citizen; 173-Ar-16) and Oxyrhynchos (243-Ox-2).

Migration of slaves

Although, in general, slaves are a particularly mobile form of capital, the census returns provide little precise information on their movement. The existence of a market in slaves[28] is confirmed by two returns mentioning sale of slaves: a female slave purchased by the declarant's wife (117-Ox-2 from Oxyrhynchos), and a 33-year-old woman and her 5-year-old son bought by the declarant's sister and former wife (159-Ar-4 from Arsinoe). These returns imply, what surviving sales contracts confirm, that most slaves were bought and sold in metropoleis. In Chapter 7 (at notes 89–92), we tentatively suggested that villagers may have taken in and raised as slaves some female infants exposed in metropoleis, presumably at least occasionally with the intent of later selling them.

In most instances, slaves appear to be owned by the declarant as head of the household, and so form part of the household's wealth. But it is not unusual for individual household members to own their own slaves.[29] Such

---

[26] See, e.g., 117-Ox-2 from Oxyrhynchos: the declarant's brother-in-law, a 57-year-old stonecutter, is "currently absent." On migration of metropolitans, see H. Braunert, *Binnenwanderung* (1964) 131–142; on Alexandrians and other residents of Greek cities in the rest of Egypt, 113–126.

[27] Compare 173-Ar-14: property in Arsinoe belonging to the freedman of an Antinoite.

[28] J. A. Straus, "L'Esclavage" (1988) 857–862 and 903–911 (listing known sales contracts and prices), with bibliography.

[29] 117-Ar-3 and 7; 117-Ox-2; 145-Ar-9 and 12; 159-Ar-4 and 5; 159-Hm-2 (lodger); 201-Ar-6 and 10; 201-Ox-1; 215-Ar-2; 243-Ox-1. In 173-Ar-9, slaves belong to a person not resident in the household.

slaves would normally accompany their owner if he or she left the household. Thus, for example, the declarant's daughter in 201-Ox-1 from Oxyrhynchos took with her a 13-year-old female slave when she married; the slave may have been part of her dowry. Correspondingly, in 145-Ar-12 from Karanis, the declarant's daughter brought with her a female slave when she returned to her parents' home after her divorce; so too did an owner's ex-wife in 201-Ar-6 from Arsinoe.

Inheritance patterns, in particular, often resulted in co-ownership of slaves, who then lived with one owner if the co-owners did not remain in the same household. A clear case is 201-Ox-1 from Oxyrhynchos, where two slaves are jointly owned by the declarant, his brothers, and others; only the declarant is in the household.[30] Conversely, the declarant in 187-Ar-32 from Arsinoe notes that he is half-owner of two slaves resident elsewhere.

Effect of migration

It is usually, and probably rightly, believed that internal migration acted to the general benefit of metropoleis at the expense of villages, especially during the second century AD.[31] The census returns provide no means to test this hypothesis, but do suggest appreciable levels of in-migration to metropoleis during the early Roman Empire, especially by marginal village males. If overall metropolitan population was in fact growing during this period, while village population remained more or less static or even declined, this effect must surely be explained through gradually increasing rationalization of Egyptian agriculture, which resulted in a larger carrying capacity for the limited agricultural land within the Nile valley.[32]

But such urbanization was arguably constructed upon increasingly slender foundations. Although the Fayyum region, and Middle Egypt in general, weathered fairly well the demographic and economic crisis in the later second century AD, rural conditions in at least portions of the Nile Delta deteriorated rapidly, for complex reasons related only in part to the onset of the Antonine plague.[33]

---

[30] Probably similar is 117-Ar-3 from Arsinoe, where the declarant's wife and her sister co-own four slaves; the sister evidently resides elsewhere.

[31] H. Braunert, *Binnenwanderung* (1964) 227–274, 281–292; D. Rathbone, "Villages" (1990) 119–122. Compare, on Tokugawa Japan, A. Hayami and Y. Sasaki, in *East Asian History* (1985) 110–132 and 133–153 (resp.), who also note that migration had a considerable depressing effect on fertility rates.

[32] D. Rathbone, "Villages" (1990) 121–122; and see generally D. Rathbone, *Rationalism* (1991).

[33] D. Rathbone, "Villages" (1990) 114–119 and 134–137, on the Mendesian nome, known mainly from the Thmouis papyrus; see S. Kambitsis, *Le Papyrus Thmouis 1 Colonnes 68–180* (1985), plus *BGU* III 902–903, *PSI* I 102–103, and *SB* I 8. See also below, Chapter 9, Section 2.

9

Conclusion

In this book, we have tried to reconstruct the most probable demographic characteristics that surviving census returns support for Roman Egypt. As we have repeatedly stressed, some aspects of the demography of Roman Egypt are baffling, and probably destined to remain so, particularly because of the paucity of our evidence. Unless major new discoveries are forthcoming, the difficulties that surround, for instance, infant mortality, male life expectancy, and the Egyptian sex ratio may well remain insoluble except by way of reasonable conjecture.[1]

By contrast, many important aspects of Egyptian demography are, on present evidence, at least relatively clear. These include especially household structure, the female life table, patterns of female and male first marriage, female fertility rates, the usual means of fertility control, and the way in which these features combined to preserve the delicate balance between mortality and fertility.[2] What is perhaps most surprising about these clearer aspects is this: despite persistent inexactitude in the measurement of detail, there is very little about Egyptian demography that would not have been anticipated, very little that lies outside the boundaries of the normal for pre-modern Mediterranean populations. To be sure, local peculiarities obtrude, of which brother-sister marriage is the most conspicuous example;[3] and allowance must also be made for the usual Greco-Roman social and institutional framework with respect to, especially, slavery, marriage, and infanticide and exposure. But what stands out about Roman Egypt is, in the end, not its oddness but its conformity. The very mundaneness of Egypt gives rise to an expectation that less certain aspects of its demographic regime lie also within the normal range.

---

[1] See esp. Chapters 5 and 8 above; on infant mortality, Chapter 2, note 10.
[2] See Chapters 3, 4, 6, and 7. On consistency as a reason for assuming the validity of results, see G. W. Barclay *et al.*, "Reassessment" (1976) 624, on rural China in the 1930s.
[3] See Chapter 6, Section 4.

1. A typical Mediterranean population?

From time to time throughout our book, we have observed the demographic similarity between Roman Egypt and late medieval Tuscany.[4] Although this resemblance is presumably not coincidental, its exact historical explanation is not only highly problematic, but in any case far beyond the compass of our present study. Still, the question deserves some closer scrutiny.

In 1983, Peter Laslett noted a large number of distinctive features of the Mediterranean "domestic group organization" in pre-modern Europe.[5] Whatever objections can be raised against Laslett's schematic typology (and, as we shall see, these objections are weighty), it comes astonishingly close to describing the Roman Egypt of the census returns.

Laslett divided his typology into four broad categories.[6] The resemblances with Roman Egypt are strongest for "procreational and demographic criteria": as emerged in Chapters 6 and 7 above, Roman Egypt had a relatively low female age at first marriage, a high (median) male age at first marriage, very high proportions of eventual marriage for both women and men, a wide average age gap between spouses at first marriage, a low proportion of wives who are older than their husbands, and a low (perhaps even very low) proportion of widows or divorced women who remarry.

Laslett's "criteria of kin composition of [household] groups" are more difficult to apply, mainly because of irregular patterns in the preservation of census returns. But Roman Egypt clearly had very high proportions of complex households extended by the presence of kin or with multiple families, although simple conjugal families are not uncommon especially in metropoleis. The proportion of multigenerational households is also very high. In general, Egyptian households attain a degree of internal complexity rarely matched in the historical record.

For Laslett, particular importance attaches to the "occasion and method of domestic group formation."[7] Here the returns are less adequate, since they only rarely allow a glimpse of households over a long period of time (Chapter 3 at notes 46–52); but it appears that new Egyptian households were infrequently formed at the marriage of a household head, and that marriage was also seldom important to household formation. Much more

---

[4] D. Herlihy and C. Klapisch-Zuber, *Tuscans* (1985).

[5] P. Laslett, in *Family Forms* (1983) 513–563, esp. 525–531. Laslett's paper extends his earlier article, "Characteristics of the Western Family Considered over Time," *Journal of Family History* 2.2 (1977) 89–115.

[6] We follow here the typology of P. Laslett, in *Family Forms* (1983) 576–577.

[7] P. Laslett, in *Family Forms* (1983) 531–533. See also L. L. Cornell, "Hajnal and the Household in Asia," in *Family History* (1987) 143–162, esp. 146–152.

frequently, a new head (often a son or a brother) just took over an existing household when an existing head died. How often new households were formed by the fission of existing households is difficult to determine.[8]

The "criteria of organization of work and welfare" are the most uncertain for Roman Egypt, since analysis of the census returns is complicated by the institution of slavery. But this is an area about which little is known for Roman Egypt, although it is believed that especially village households often served as units of production as well as units of consumption.[9] The returns confirm this, to some extent, by providing a few examples of households where adult males pursue the same occupation (Chapter 3 at notes 84–85). The addition to the household of working kin also appears to be common.

Although Roman Egypt is thus comfortably located within the broader context of Laslett's Mediterranean "domestic group organization," it must also be conceded that recent historical research has undermined his confidence in the uniformly identifiable household structure of traditional Mediterranean populations.[10] What has gradually emerged from modern research is a more diverse and intricate picture, in which local household structure can be complexly affected by culture, demographic forces, the labor demands of the prevailing economy, and political and legal frameworks such as the impartibility of inheritance.[11] As should perhaps have been anticipated, the "Mediterranean" has proven an elusive concept. Whether there has ever been, in the Roman world or later, a wholly typical Mediterranean population, is now a matter of debate.

The progress of research on this subject has been rapid during the past decade, as local records have opened for examination. The results suggest that we should be duly cautious in extrapolating from Roman Egypt to the remainder of the Roman world, particularly as concerns characteristics, such as nuptiality and household structure, where regional culture may well

---

[8] One possible case is the transition from 131-Pr-1 to 145-Pr-1, where, however, the second return may be excerpted from a longer return. Another is 201-Ox-1 from Oxyrhynchos: two slaves are co-owned by the declarant and his non-resident brothers, implying division of their household. See also K. Hopkins, "Brother-Sister" (1980) 331–333.

[9] D. W. Hobson, "House and Household" (1985) 211–219.

[10] Research summarized in D. I. Kertzer, "Household History" (1991) 155–179, esp. 160–162. See also many of the essays in *Family in Italy* (1991), esp. M. Barbagli, "Three Household Formation Systems in Eighteenth- and Nineteenth-Century Italy," pp. 250–270.

[11] In principle, the Egyptian law of succession permitted free testation, but in various informal ways encouraged partibility: R. Taubenschlag, *Law* (1955) 181–212; K. Hopkins, "Brother-Sister" (1980) 322, 338–339. On the connection between the law of succession and household forms: D. I. Kertzer, "Household History" (1991) 165–166; but "partible inheritance does not create a characteristic form of the family," cf. A. P. Wolf and S. B. Hanley, in *East Asian History* (1985) 2, with evidence. On the consequences of partibility in Egypt: D. W. Hobson, "House and Household" (1985).

have had large and even decisive impact.[12] Nonetheless, the basic demographic attributes of Roman Egypt are, at the least, thoroughly at home in the Mediterranean; they tend to recur in historical Mediterranean populations with considerable regularity. Nor is there any strong *a priori* reason why most of these attributes should be regarded as unique to Egypt among Roman provinces.[13] In this weaker sense, the Egypt of the census returns may fairly be described as "typical."

2. A stable population?

In this book, we have generally looked at the census returns from early imperial Egypt as a whole, and have attempted to reconstruct the long-term demographic characteristics of the population that these returns describe. However, as we have repeatedly emphasized, these characteristics were subject to considerable oscillation in the short term.[14] For example, it is well known that Egyptian grain prices fluctuated widely by region, season, and date;[15] such fluctuations are likely to have effected hefty swings not only in death rates, but perhaps also in nuptiality and fertility.[16]

During the long period that the returns cover, one event had more than usual impact, namely the outbreak of the great plague under Marcus Aurelius in AD 165/166. This epidemic, today usually identified as smallpox,[17]

[12]E.g., on regional patterns of nuptiality, see S. C. Watkins, in *Decline of Fertility* (1986) 314–336. On the need for caution in such matters: M. Golden, "The Uses of Cross-Cultural Comparison in Ancient Social History," *EMC/CV* 11 (1992) 309–331.

[13]Little supports the assertions of T. G. Parkin, *Demography* (1992), that "in any case Egypt cannot be regarded as typical of the empire as a whole" in its demography (p. 129), or that "a quite different marriage pattern appears to have operated in Egypt" (p. 113, cf. p. 193 n.153); compare p. 59 (demographic results from census returns are "only . . . valid for this particular province," where "valid" has an indeterminate meaning). On the propensity of ancient historians to marginalize Roman Egypt, see G. Geraci, in *Egitto* (1989) 55–88.

[14]Modern historical demography has increasingly emphasized the short-term variability of vital rates as well as their long-term "secular" trends: N. Crook in *India* (1989) 285–296.

[15]R. Duncan-Jones, *Structure* (1990) 143–155; note esp. the famine in AD 99 (p. 146; cf. Pliny, *Paneg.* 30–32). The issue is important because food probably constituted at least 60 percent of normal consumer expenditures in the early Roman Empire: R. W. Goldsmith, "Estimate" (1984). The Roman government took a large portion of Egypt's grain production as tribute; this placed a further strain on carrying capacity, cf. D. W. Rathbone, in *Egitto* (1989) 171–176.

[16]On this (basically Malthusian) theory, see E. A. Wrigley and R. S. Schofield, *England* (1989) 457–466. Compare, on modern Egypt, D. Panzac, "Endémies, épidémies et population en Egypte au XIXe siècle," in *L'Egypte au XIXe siècle: colloque international d'Aix-en-Provence* (1981) 83–100. On "mortality crises," see the excellent theoretical discussion by G. Cabourdin, in *Population française* II (1988) 175–192. The relation between mortality and nutrition is, however, controversial: M. Livi-Bacci, *Population* (1991); see also P.R. Galloway, "Basic Patterns in Fertility, Nuptiality, Mortality, and Prices in Pre-Industrial Europe," *Population Studies* 42 (1988) 275–303.

[17]R. J. and M. L. Littman, "Galen" (1973); D. R. Hopkins, *Princes and Peasants: Smallpox in History* (1983) 22–23.

"behaved as infections are wont to do when they break in upon virgin populations that entirely lack inherited or acquired resistances. Mortality, in other words, was heavy."[18] The consequences of the Antonine plague should not be exaggerated,[19] but were undoubtedly severe. Literary sources, among them eyewitnesses such as Galen and Dio, attest the plague across the whole breadth of the Empire; they also stress its heavy toll on human life both in cities and on the land, its persistence and recurrence, and the widespread famines that broke out in its wake.[20] As much as ten percent of the Roman Empire's total population may have perished in this plague; and in large cities and military camps, the percentage could well have been twice this high.[21]

Dominic Rathbone has recently surveyed the evidence for the Antonine plague in Egypt. On the basis of contemporary documentary papyri alluding to the plague, he concludes: "The Antonine plague thus does seem to have affected at least Lower and Middle Egypt from about AD 166 into the late 170s, and to have been characterised by sporadic, brief but devastating outbreaks in individual localities."[22] Rathbone estimates that the population of densely settled Egypt dropped by 20 percent or more, but also notes "a considerable if not a complete recovery" by the early third century, at least in localities not assailed by other social and economic difficulties.

Fortuitously, surviving census returns fall almost exactly astride the outbreak of the Antonine plague. Of datable returns, 155 are prior to AD 166, 135 after, in a proportion of approximately 7 to 6. About the same proportion obtains for registered persons: 567 before AD 166, 473 after. Although the small number of surviving returns provides no indication of movement in gross population, it is tempting to ask whether they betray other signs of the plague's consequences.

Table 9.1 (p. 175) gives the age distribution of females and males from returns before and after 166; "smoothed" figures are used for ages 5 and

[18]W. H. McNeill, *Plagues and Peoples* (1983) 116, who suggests (109–115) that the outbreak resulted from Roman contact with the hitherto isolated "disease pool" in China.

[19]J. F. Gilliam, "The Plague under Marcus Aurelius," *AJPh* 82 (1961) 225–251, repr. in *Roman Army Papers* (1986) 227–253; P. Salmon, *Population* (1974) 133–139.

[20]Evidence for the economic impact of the plague is discussed by R. Duncan-Jones, *Structure* (1990) 59–76. See also 146–147 and 150–152, raising the possibility of much higher Egyptian grain prices in the aftermath of the plague.

[21]This is the estimate of R. J. and M. L. Littman, "Galen" (1973) 252–255.

[22]D. W. Rathbone, "Villages" (1990) 119, cf. 114–119, with much additional bibliography. The most striking example is Soknopaiou Nesos, where nearly a third of the adult male taxpayers died in January and February, AD 179. D. W. Hobson, "P.Vindob.Gr. 24951 + 24556: New Evidence for Tax-Exempt Status in Roman Egypt," in *Atti XVII Congr. Int. Pap.* III (1984) 847–864, at 848–850. The "crash" at Karanis may have been similar: A. E. R. Boak, "Egypt" (1959) 248–250, whose figures, however, are not wholly trustworthy. See also Rathbone, 116–117, on Terenouthis in the Prosopite nome.

up.[23] This table also indicates the number of males and females in each age group as a percent of each sex aged 5 and over. The percentages are also plotted in Figures 9.1 and 9.2 (p. 176), but here three-figure moving averages are used to smooth the exiguous data still further.

Table 9.1. *Age distribution before and after AD 166*

Age	Females Before	Females After	% 5+ Bef.	% 5+ Aft.	Males Before	Males After	% 5+ Bef.	% 5+ Aft.
0–4	14.00	22.00			28.00	21.00		
5–9	18.14	18.29	12.5	12.1	21.57	17.86	13.7	12.9
10–14	18.86	16.86	13.0	11.1	12.43	13.29	7.9	9.6
15–19	20.57	16.86	14.2	11.1	21.29	14.29	13.5	10.3
20–24	15.43	17.14	10.6	11.3	18.14	12.14	11.5	8.8
25–29	14.43	13.57	9.9	9.0	12.57	13.29	8.0	9.6
30–34	14.57	12.71	10.0	8.4	17.14	15.29	10.9	11.1
35–39	11.86	10.29	8.2	8.4	9.29	9.29	5.9	6.7
40–44	7.00	10.29	4.8	6.8	9.00	6.86	5.7	5.0
45–49	4.14	10.14	2.9	6.7	9.71	12.57	6.2	9.1
50–54	6.43	9.57	4.4	6.3	5.29	7.71	3.4	5.6
55–59	4.86	6.14	3.3	4.1	6.00	5.29	3.8	3.8
60–64	2.71	2.29	1.9	1.5	5.00	2.57	3.2	1.9
65–69	2.86	1.57	2.0	1.0	4.29	3.00	2.7	2.2
70–74	2.71	2.71	1.9	1.8	4.14	3.00	2.6	2.2
75–79	0.57	0.71	0.4	0.5	1.57	1.14	1.0	0.8
80–84						0.57		0.4
Total:	159.14	173.57			185.43	159.14		

The male and female percentages are broadly consistent. In both cases, the percentages for the pre-166 age distribution are generally higher for ages 5 to 24, closely similar for ages 25 to 34, and then significantly lower for ages 35 to 59.[24] This suggests an underlying pattern. In reconstructing this pattern, it is helpful to think first in terms of two limiting alternatives: assuming stable populations both before and after 166, either Egyptians had the same life expectancy in both periods, but a lower intrinsic growth rate after 166; or they had higher life expectancy after 166, but the same growth rate in both periods.[25] Of these two explanations, the first is preferable, since only it accounts for the effects of the Antonine plague.

[23] As in Chapters 4 and 5, "smoothed" figures are based on seven-age moving averages.
[24] Accordingly, the average age of both males and females is lower before 166 than after: for males, 26.0 as against 27.1; for females, 25.5 as against 26.5.
[25] The reason for advancing these two possible explanations is explained in Chapter 4, Sec-

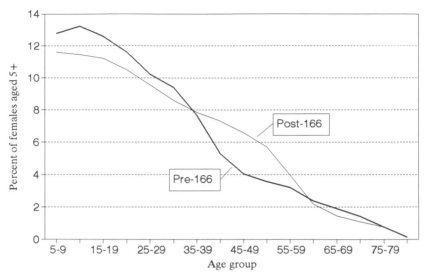

Figure 9.1. *Female age distribution, ages 5+, moving averages*

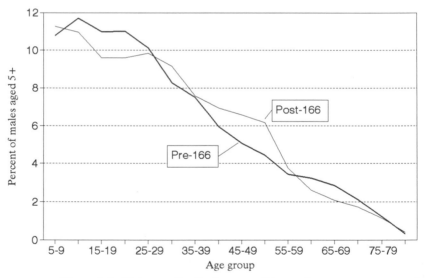

Figure 9.2. *Male age distribution, ages 5+, moving averages*

---

tion 1. See esp. the stable populations in Figures 4.1 (same life expectancy, different growth rates) and 4.2 (different life expectancies, same growth rate). Note that the relevant lines tend to cross at about age 25 to 35, as in Figures 9.1 and 9.2.

Still more plausible, however, is a more complex explanation: life expectancy was somewhat lower after 166 as the epidemic and then endemic effects of the plague set in, but the intrinsic growth rate was substantially higher as Egyptians tried to avoid population decline through increased fertility.[26] Because the data base is so parsimonious, we will not attempt to place numbers on the changes; but they can be completely and easily accounted for within the mortality parameters described in Chapters 4 and 5 above.

As this discussion should illustrate, the Egyptian population was not entirely stable over the long period covered by the census returns. Indeed, any other result would be not only counterintuitive, but also contrary to widespread demographic experience.[27] However, the exact causes and mechanisms of this instability remain, on available evidence, exceedingly obscure. Beyond doubt, Roman Egypt had a "high pressure" demographic regime, in which both mortality and fertility rates were, by modern standards, elevated. But what was the driving force of this regime?

On one plausible scenario, Roman Egypt could be held to resemble "the 'Chinese' situation," in which "the disease environment was less deadly but social conventions made early and universal marriage mandatory. As a result, fertility was high and, because rapid growth had to be short-lived, mortality was high too."[28] On such a scenario, fertility was more fundamental than mortality in constituting the Egyptian demographic regime; high mortality rates were not, as ancient historians have usually understood them to be, exogenous givens, but instead the direct consequence of overpopulation. Therefore the fertility controls discussed in Chapter 7, Section

[26]This possibility was suggested by J. C. Russell, "Population," (1958) 37–43; it is also advanced by D. W. Rathbone, "Villages" (1990) 119. On characteristic patterns of fertility after plagues and other mortality crises, see E. A. Wrigley and R. S. Schofield, *England* (1989) 363–366.

[27]See, for instance, E. A. Wrigley and R. S. Schofield, *England* (1989) 285–355, on short-term variations in England. As their table on 333 shows, mortality reached crisis level (higher than 10 percent above normal) in one out of of seven years from 1541 to 1871, and severe crisis level (25 percent or more above normal) in one year of every eighteen. "The decline in the intensity and frequency of mortality crises . . . constitutes the first aspect of the mortality transition." M. Livi-Bacci, *History* (1992) 107, cf. 106–113.

[28]E. A. Wrigley and R. S. Schofield, *England* (1989) xxiv (one of three limiting cases for populations before the demographic transition). Whether historical China actually experienced this Malthusian scenario is unclear, see T.-J. Liu, in *East Asian History* (1985) 13–61. For Roman Egypt, the scenario is rendered plausible by D. W. Rathbone's argument, in "Villages" (1990), that its population probably neared the limits of the carrying capacity of its land under ancient technological and economic conditions; compare R. Duncan-Jones, *Structure* (1990) 146–147, on rising Egyptian grain prices in the early Empire—possibly a Malthusian reaction. See also C. McEvedy and R. Jones, *Atlas* (1978) 226. But the issues here are very complex; see, e.g., E. Boserup, *Economic and Demographic Relationships in Development* (1990).

2, were effective in maintaining population equilibrium only after mortality had reached relatively elevated levels. By that point, Egyptian population was so dense as to be particularly vulnerable to external "positive" Malthusian checks such as the Antonine plague.

At present, we lack a remotely adequate statistical basis for testing whether this scenario, or any other, is correct. We must therefore remain content with a drastically simplified understanding of the demography of Roman Egypt. But despite the limits of such an understanding, it is, we believe, not without its value. Put succinctly, the value is this. Historical demography has long had, as the focus of its vision, the intricate, pressing, and today still unresolved problems associated with transition from traditional demographic regimes to modern "low pressure" regimes in which both mortality and fertility rates are much reduced.[29] By contrast, although Roman Egypt, like the Roman world more generally, undoubtedly fell into the former category, problems of transition were not even on its furthest horizon. Here the interest of historical demography is less in change and transition, than in the secular characteristics of a society that survived and prospered under the harsh conditions of a "high pressure" demographic regime.[30] Through the medium of the Egyptian census returns, we hope to have introduced an important aspect of the Roman world that is, in general, little noticed and even less observed.

[29]C. Newell, *Methods* (1988) 10–12 (e.g., 11: "Demographic Transition Theory remains at the heart of demography as an academic discipline, perhaps partly because of the lack of anything better to replace it."). See generally T. H. Hollingsworth, *Demography* (1969); M. W. Flinn, *System* (1981). On the demographic transition, J.-C. Chesnais, *The Demographic Transition: Stages, Patterns, and Economic Implications* (trans. E. and P. Kreager; 1992).

[30]Compare G. W. Barclay *et al.*, "Reassessment" (1976) 624: "we have in the Chinese Farmers data the nearest thing to a backward look into the demography of Imperial China that we are ever likely to have."

Catalogue of census declarations

The attached list of census declarations from Roman Egypt, brought up to date as of 1 November 1993,[1] has been produced according to a fixed scheme. Households are given numbers consisting of the digits of the first julian year of the regnal year of the census, two letters designating the nome, and a (largely arbitrary) serial number within the group; they are organized in order of these household numbers, i.e. first by census, then by nome, then by household. Persons are given by status groups, and within these in the order in which they are given in the papyrus. Cross-reference numbers operate within the status group unless indicated otherwise, except that the declarant is always referred to as such except when ambiguity would result.

All returns that were used in generating the data base are marked in this Catalogue with an asterisk (*) at the beginning of the entry. We provide stemmata for households in which there is a kin relationship between two or more members, or in which a relationship can plausibly be restored. In the stemmata, a triangle denotes a male; a circle denotes a female; and a diamond means that the person's sex is unknown. We give the person's age where it is known or likely. Between persons, a solid line indicates that the relationship is considered secure; a broken line means that the relationship is reconstructed or uncertain.

All available texts have been examined on the original or a good reproduction, and the readings are—to the best of my ability to determine—correct or at least not capable of improvement by me. Those not seen are indicated. This examination has generated a substantial body of corrections, the more important of which are published in *BASP* in a series of articles called "Notes on Egyptian Census Declarations."[2] Smaller corrections needing no explanation are grouped in Appendix 1, organized by papyrus citation rather than household number (a # sign is placed after papyrus citations for which this is applicable). Appendix 2 gives a concordance of

---

[1] The data analysis takes into account only additions and changes up to 15 September 1993.

[2] I: *BASP* 27 (1990) 1-14; II: *BASP* 28 (1991) 13-32; III: *BASP* 28 (1991) 121-33; IV: *BASP* 29 (1992) 101-15; V: *BASP* 30 (1993) 35-56.

papyrus citations and household numbers. A vast number of minor changes, the result mainly of changes in the way papyrologists used brackets in the infancy of the field and the way they are used now, are not included; none of these has any material effect on the data. As the annotation of the entries in the catalogue shows, my attempts to improve these texts rest upon a very large base of such improvements by others. The ungrateful task of correcting my betters has been a sufficient demonstration for me of editorial fallibility, as well as of the value of assembling parallels. I am under no illusion that the texts as corrected are perfect.

The weary labor of checking all these texts has been made possible and even, in many cases, pleasant by the help of those who made collections they are in charge of readily availale to me and who restored and photographed the papyri I needed; those whose hospitality made my peregrinations to Berkeley, Chicago, Ann Arbor, Princeton, London, Oxford, Florence, Strasbourg, Milan, Berlin, Vienna, Paris, and Minneapolis in search of census declarations a string of happy memories; those who helped me track down wandering papyri; those who made unpublished material available or waived rights to texts; those who supplied photographs of the more scattered items for which I have not seen the original papyrus. Some of these debts are acknowledged piecemeal in articles, but it will not be amiss to record them here: Zaki Aly, Guido Bastianini, Alain Blanchard, Anthony S. Bliss, William Brashear, Revel Coles, Johannes Diethart, Andrea Donau, I. F. Fikhman, Daniele Foraboschi, Inger Louise Forselv, Traianos Gagos, Alessandra Gara, Jean Gascou, Giovanni Geraci, Dieter Hagedorn, Hermann Harrauer, Armin Hetzer, Eva Horváth, Janet Johnson, William Joyce, Ludwig Koenen, Sigrid Kohlmann, Nita Krevans, Manfredo Manfredi, Alain Martin, Joseph Mélèze-Modrzejewski, Paul Mertens, Béatrice Meyer, Georges Nachtergael, Sayed Omar, Bernhard Palme, Peter Parsons, Thomas Pattie, Rosario Pintaudi, Günter Poethke, Virginia Pratt, John Rea, Jacques Schwartz, Jean Straus, William Voelkle, and Klaas Worp. I hope I have not forgotten many. There are others too, who unknown to me have worked behind the scenes in many places. My thanks to all. [RSB]

HOUSEHOLD NO.: 11-Ar-1
*Source: *P.Mil.* I 3 (cf. *BL* 6.75, 7.101) + P.Col.inv. 8: *GRBS* 32 (1991) 255–65
Prov., Date: Theadelphia (Arsinoite), 22/1/12
Stemma:

Declarant: Harthotes s. Marres, public farmer and priest of Tothoes
Family members: (1) Harthotes [declarant] s. Marres and Esersythis,
                            public farmer and priest of Tothoes, 55
                        (2) Harpatothoes s. Harthotes [declarant] and
                            Taanchoriphis, 9
                        (3) Esersythis d. Pasion, mother of Harthotes
                            [declarant], 70
Free non-kin, slaves: None
Verif./photo: *P.Mil.* I 3: Pl. IV; P.Col.inv. 8: original; plate of both in *GRBS*.
Discussion: Complete. Cf. above, p. 4.

HOUSEHOLD NO.: 19?-Ox-1
*Source: *P.Oxy.* II 254 (cf. *P.Mich.* X 578 introd.)
Prov., Date: Oxyrhynchos, 19/20?
Declarant: Horion s. Petosiris, priest of Isis
Family members: (1) NN s. Sintheos, ἄτεχνος
Free non-kin, slaves: None preserved
Verif./photo: Union Theological Seminary, New York; seen 10/12/1990.
Discussion: Complete at top, left, and right; broken at the bottom, with loss of
    most of list of persons, date, and subscription. On the date, see above, p. 3.
    The first person listed has a name ending in -ων, followed by μη(τρός) and
    the mother's name: an ἀπάτωρ, apparently, age not preserved. He is not the
    declarant, who lived in another house (so Wilcken, *Chr.* 201 introd.). Not
    enough of lines 12–13 is readable to determine if they concern the first per-
    son listed or, as seems more likely, a second person.

HOUSEHOLD NO.: 33-Ar-1
*Source: *SB* X 10759 (*ZPE* 5 [1970] 18) (cf. *BASP* 28 [1991] 31–32)
Prov., Date: Arsinoe, 33/4
Stemma:

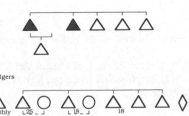

Declarants: Zosimos and Alexandros sons of Alexandros
Family members: (1) Zosimos [declarant] s. Alexandros and
                    Aphrod[, age lost
                (2) Alexandros [declarant] s. Alexandros and
                    Aphrod[, age lost
                (3) Alexandros s. Zosimos [declarant], age lost
                (4) Isidoros s. Alexandros and Aphrod[, brother of
                    nos. 1 and 2, age lost
                (5) Mystharion s. Alexandros and Aphrod[, brother
                    of nos. 1 and 2, age lost
                (6) Philoumenos s. Alexandros, brother of nos. 1
                    and 2, age lost
Free non-kin: (1) B[ ] s. Aphrodisios and Sarapias, age lost
                (2) NN (Aphrodisios?) s. Aphrodisios and Thermion, 25
                (3) NN (Sarapion the elder?) s. Aphrodisios and
                    Thermion, age lost
                (4) Sarapion the younger s. Aphrodisios and
                    Thermion, 18
                (5) NN s. (or d.?) of Aphrodisios and Thermion, 18
                (6) Herakl[, s. (or d.?) of Aphrodisios and Thermion,
                    age lost
                (7) NN wife (?) of Aphrodisios [no.2?], age lost
                (8) NN wife (?) of Sarapion [no.3 or no.4?], age lost
                (9) NN, no information preserved
Slaves: None
Verif./photo: P.Mich.inv. 124 recto; seen 9/11/1990.
Discussion: Broken at right and below; perhaps some additional renters lost along
    with subscription and date.

HOUSEHOLD NO.: 33-Ar-2
*Source: *SB* I 5661 (cf. *BL* 2.2.119–20; *BASP* 27 [1990] 13–14)
Prov., Date: Philadelphia (Arsinoite), 13/6/34
Stemma:

Declarant: Tatybynchis d. Mares, with *kyrios* her kinsman Patouamtis s. Ptollis
    (age 36)
Family members: (1) Panetbeueis s. Kephalon and Tatybynchis [declarant], 5
                (2) Tatybynchis [declarant], d. Mares, 35
Free non-kin, slaves: None

Verif./photo: Oslo, formerly Eitrem collection; now P.Oslo inv. 421; photograph.
Discussion: Complete

HOUSEHOLD NO.: 33-Ox-1
*Source: *P.Oxy.* II 256#
Prov., Date: Oxyrhynchos, *ca* 34
Stemma:

Declarants: NN d. Thoonis, with *kyrios* —ros s. Apollophanes; Taos d. Thoonis,
with *kyrios* NN s. —kos; and Tamenneus d. NN, with *kyrios* her husband
NN
Family members: 1) Kronios s. NN and —this, ἄτεχνος, age omitted
(2) NN s. Kronios [no.1], minor, age lost
(3) NN d. NN and NN alias Taseus, wife of Kronios
[no.1], ἄτεχνος, age lost
(4) NN d. Kronios [no.1] and NN [no.3?], minor,
ἄτεχνος, 5
Free non-kin, slaves: None
Verif./photo: Union Theological Seminary, New York; seen 10/12/1990.
Discussion: Broken at left with substantial loss (about two-thirds), and damaged at
bottom; complete at top and most of the right side. Assignment to census of
33 is uncertain, but it is probably not later. The declarants own but do not
live in the house; they declare the family occupying it. The reconstruction of
the latter is probable but not certain. Probably no persons are lost, but that
too is not certain.

HOUSEHOLD NO.: 33-Ox-2
*Source: *P.Oxy.Hels.* 10# (cf. *BL* 8.272)
Prov., Date: Sinary (Oxyrhynchite), 2–3/34
Stemma:

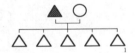

Declarant: Pausas s. Hephaistion
Family members: (1) Pausas [declarant] s. Hephaistion and Herakleia,
age lost
(2) Hephaistas s. Pausas [declarant] and Soerous
[no.7], age lost
(3) Hermogenes, s. Pausas [declarant] and Soerous
[no.7], age lost
(4) Amois s. Pausas [declarant] and Soerous [no.7],
age lost

(5) Ar... s. Pausas [declarant] and Soerous [no.7], age
    lost
(6) Hermogenes surnamed Horos, s. Pausas [declarant]
    and Soerous [no.7], 1
(7) Soerous d. Hermogenes and Ploutarche, wife of
    Pausas [declarant], age lost

Free non-kin, slaves: None

Verif./photo: Oxford, Ashmolean, inv. 21 3B.23/E(4–5)b; Pl. 7; seen 4/4/1991.

Discussion: Virtually complete except for some loss at right; surface badly
damaged throughout; minor loss at bottom. The ed. supposes a possible
daughter listed in a damaged passage/lacuna in line 14, but the space seems
insufficient for a full entry. It is not certain that the ages were all actually
filled in; except for no.6, there are no surviving traces of numerals.

HOUSEHOLD NO.: 47-Ox-1

*Source: *P.Oxy.* II 255 = *W.Chr.* 201 (cf. *BL* 1.319, 3.130, 8.234; *P.Oxy.Hels.*
10.22n.; *JJurPap* 21 [1991] 7–8)#

Prov., Date: Oxyrhynchos, 9–10/48

Stemma:

Declarant: Thermoutharion d. Thoonis, with her *kyrios* Apollonios s. Sotades

Family members: (1) Entry lost
                       (2) Thermoutharion freedwoman of Sotades, 65

Free non-kin, slaves: None

Verif./photo: Union Theological Seminary, New York; seen 10/12/1990.

Discussion: Minor losses except for a discontinuity between lines 7 and 8 and the
consequent loss of an entry (total of 2 women given in line 11, cf. *PSI* I 53
introd.). No. 2's status of freedwoman is restored from *P.Oxy.* II 305 (see
Aegyptus 46 [1966] 87–89; in AD 20 she was married to Herakleios s.
Soterichos). Wilcken showed that she was not identical to the homonymous
declarant, as Grenfell and Hunt had thought.

HOUSEHOLD NO.: 61-Ar-1

*Source: *JEA* 52 (1966) 135–37 (improved version of *SB* VI 9572)#

Prov., Date: Kerkesis (Arsinoite), 61/62

Stemma:

Declarant: Kronion s. Haryotes, mason

Family members: (1) Kronion [declarant] s. Haryotes and Thasos,
                       mason, 52
                       (2) Kronion s. Kronion [declarant] and Taorseus, 3
                       (3) Patron s. Kronion [declarant] and Taorseus, 1

(4) Thensokeus d. Kronion [declarant] and
Taorseus, 11
(5) Taorseus d. Patron and Tetaros, wife of Kronion
[declarant], 30

Free non-kin: None
Slaves: More than one (δουλικὰ); entries lost
Verif./photo: London, British Library, inv. 2196; seen 2/4/1991.
Discussion: Broken at bottom in the middle of the list of persons. Coles' reedition corrects the text substantially.

HOUSEHOLD NO.: 61-Ox-1
Source: *SB* XII 10788B (*BASP* 7 [1970] 87–98)
Prov., Date: Oxyrhynchos, 28/4/62
Declarant: Lucius Pompeius L.f. tribu Pollia Niger, discharged solder
Family members, free non-kin, slaves: None
Verif./photo: P.Yale inv. 1545B; pl. in *BASP*, p. 89.
Discussion: Complete. Declaration of a quarter of a house in which no one is registered.

HOUSEHOLD NO.: 75-Ar-1
***Source:** *BGU* XI 2088#
Prov., Date: Arsinoe, 75/6 or 76/7
Stemma:

Declarant: NN s. NN and Helene
Family members: (1) NN [declarant] s. NN and Helene, 48
(2) NN d. NN, 30 (possibly not kin)
Free non-kin, slaves: None certain
Verif./photo: W. Berlin, P. 21662; seen 11/4/1991.
Discussion: Complete at top and right, but large loss at left and broken at bottom perhaps still in the middle of the list of persons. There were at least three other persons declared, but nothing useful can be said about them.

HOUSEHOLD NO.: 75-Ar-2
***Source:** *P.Harr.* I 70 = *SB* XVIII 13324 (cf. *Cd'E* 23 [1948] 123 [*BL* 3.78]; *BL* 4.38, 6.49, 8.147; *BASP* 27 [1990] 5–6)
Prov., Date: Arsinoe, 75/6 or 76/7
Stemma:

Declarant: Aphrodous d. Chairas, with *kyrios* kinsman Herakleides s. Herakleides
Family members: (1) Hermas s. NN (s. Hermas) and Hero (d. NN),
age lost

(2) NN. s. Hermas [no.1] and Heraklous [no.5], 17
(3) Hera— s. Hermas [no.1] and Heraklous [no.5], 15
(4) NN, s. Hermas [no.1] and Heraklous [no.5], 11
(5) Heraklous wife of Hermas [no.1], age lost

Free non-kin, slaves: None preserved

Verif./photo: Birmingham, Selly Oak, inv. 27; plate in *Cd'E* 23 (1948) fig. 10 (opp. p. 122); photograph.

Discussion: Broken at right and bottom with loss of much information about persons declared. Copy of a supplementary return covering a house occupied by renters; she had registered separately her own residence. See *BASP* 28 (1991) 5–6 for a detailed attempt to unravel the identities of the persons mentioned. There could have been another son between nos. 3 and 4 (thus between 11 and 15 in age), and daughters may be lost after the mother [no.5].

HOUSEHOLD NO.: 75-Ar-3
Source: *P.Minnesota* inv. 1381982
Prov., Date: Arsinoe, 75/6 or 76/7
Declarant: Chairemon s. M[(?)
Family members: (1) ?Aphrodisios s. Aphrodisios and Thermoutharion, age lost

Free non-kin, slaves: None

Verif./photo: Minneapolis/St. Paul, University of Minnesota Library; photograph; seen 29/9/1993.

Discussion: Preserved in two fragments broken on all sides with a gap between them. There is much uncertainty in the reconstruction, but it appears that this was a declaration of a household containing only lodgers; only of the first of these is any of the name preserved.

HOUSEHOLD NO.: 75-Ox-1
*Source: *P.Oxy.* II 361 descr.
Prov., Date: Oxyrhynchos, 76/7
Stemma:

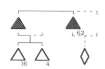

Declarants: NN and NN, sons (?) of Sirion
Family members: (1) NN [declarant] s. (?) of Sirion, age lost
(2) NN [declarant] s. (?) of Sirion, 62
(3) Sirion the elder s. NN (no.1?) and S—eus, 16
(4) Sirion the younger s. NN (no.1?) and S—eus, 4
(5) NN s./d. NN and Sarallion (d. Sirion), age lost

Free non-kin, slaves: None

Verif./photo: Oxford, Bodleian Library; photo in Ashmolean, seen 5/4/1991.

Discussion: The top of the document is lost, with opening statements. The household is probably complete, but the loss of the right side makes the information about the males incomplete. The relationships as shown are thus somewhat uncertain.

HOUSEHOLD NO.: 89-At-1
Source: *SB* XIV 12110 = *ZPE* 25 (1977) 137
Prov., Date: Antaiopolite, 90/91
Declarant: Psais s. Herakles
Family members, free non-kin, slaves: None preserved
Verif./photo: P.Mich. inv. 4315; seen 9/11/1990.
Discussion: Complete on all sides except at bottom, where the entire listing of persons has been lost.

HOUSEHOLD NO.: 89-Ar-1
*Source: *P.Mich.* III 176 (cf. *BL* 7.108)
Prov., Date: Bacchias (Arsinoite), 10/5/91
Stemma:

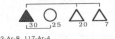

cf. 103-Ar-8, 117-Ar-4

Declarant: Peteuris s. Horos (s. Horos) and Herieus (d. Menches), public farmer
Family members: (1) Peteuris [declarant] s. Horos (s. Horos) and Herieus
        (d. Menches), public farmer, 30
        (2) Tapeine d. Apkois, wife of Peteuris [declarant], 25
        (3) Horos s. Horos (s. Horos) and Herieus (d. Menches),
        brother of Peteuris [declarant], 20
        (4) Horion s. Horos (s. Horos) and Herieus
        (d. Menches), brother of Peteuris [declarant], 7
Free non-kin, slaves: None
Verif./photo: P.Mich. inv. 104; seen 9/11/1990.
Discussion: Complete with a few small breaks and some abrasion. The family is known from several other documents; an extensive stemma on *P.Mich.* III, p. 180. For the following declarations of this household, see 103-Ar-8 and 117-Ar-4.

HOUSEHOLD NO.: 89-Hm-1
*Source: *P.Hamb.* I 60 (= *CPJud.* III 485)
Prov., Date: Hermopolis, 7 or 10/12/90
Stemma:

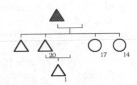

Declarant: Pascheis s. Kapais (s. Sambathios) and Chenanoupis (d. Pascheis)
Family members: (1) Pascheis [declarant] s. Kapais (s. Sambathios) and
        Chenanoupis (d. Pascheis), age lost

(2) Harpaesis s. Pascheis [declarant] and Taurous (d. Tithoes), lathe turner, age lost

(3) Inarous s. Pascheis [declarant] and Taurous (d. Tithoes), doctor, 20

(4) Tothes s. Inarous [no.3] and Tapsotis (d. Diskas), 1

(5) Taseus, d. Pascheis [declarant] and Taurous (d. Tithoes), 17

(6) Tanarous, d. Pascheis [declarant] and Taurous (d. Tithoes), 14

Free non-kin, slaves: None
Verif./photo: Hamburg, inv. 318; photograph.
Discussion: Damaged at both sides. The edition in *CPJud.* contributes no improvements. There is a lacuna of 5 letters before the two women's names, but no compounds of these names are known, and we cannot tell what stood there (if anything). The uncompounded names are attested. The sequence and phrasing of nos. 5–6 would lead one to think that they were daughters of no. 3, but this clearly cannot be the case.

HOUSEHOLD NO.: 103-Ar-1
*Source: *PSI* IX 1062 (cf. *BL* 3.227, 8.405)
Prov., Date: Arsinoe, 104/5
Stemma:

Declarant: NN s. NN (s. —on) and Megiste (d. Horigenes)
Family members: (1) NN [declarant] s. NN (s. —on) and Megiste (d. Horigenes), age lost

(2) Eudaimonis d. NN and NN, wife of declarant, *idiotis*, 26

(3) NN [prob. male], s. NN [declarant] and Eudaimonis [no. 2], age lost

(4) Didymos, s. NN [declarant] and Eudaimonis [no. 2], 1

(5) Tasoucharion, d. NN [declarant] and Eudaimonis [no. 2], 8

Free non-kin: (1) Ptolemaios s. Petheus, *idiotes*, age lost

(2) Samb[ ], wife of Ptolemaios [no.1], age lost

(3) Horos, son of Ptolemaios [no.1] and Samb[ ] [no.2], age lost

(4) — s.? of Onnophris, *idiotes*, 18

(5) NN s.? Ptolemaios and Helene (d. Kastor), age lost

(6) —arion, full sister and wife of NN [no.5], 35 (45 poss., but 35 better)

(7) NN, child of NN [no.5] and —arion [no.6], age lost

(8) NN, child of NN [no.5] and —arion [no.6], age lost
(9) NN, identity unknown, ?34 (1st digit probable, 2nd
    certain)
Slaves: (1) Isidora, age lost
Verif./photo: Florence, Biblioteca Laurenziana; seen 25/5/1989.
Discussion: Broken at left and below; probably no names lost at bottom, but massive damage at left makes reconstruction uncertain. Above omits lines 30–35 because too fragmentary. It is not clear if all of these lived in the same house; the fragmentary remains suggest possibly more than one household.

HOUSEHOLD NO.: 103-Ar-2
*Source: *PSI* X 1136 (cf. *BL* 8.407)
Prov., Date: Tebtunis (Arsinoite), 104/5
Declarant: Vestinus s. Herakleides (s. Orseus) and Taapis
Family members: None preserved
Free non-kin, slaves: None preserved
Verif./photo: Florence, Biblioteca Laurenziana; seen 25/5/1989.
Discussion: Broken at the bottom before reaching the list of persons declared; many holes in what survives. It is not certain that anybody was declared. The suggestion in *BL* for the date is wrong.

HOUSEHOLD NO.: 103-Ar-3
*Source: *P.Corn.* 16.1–13 (see *BASP* 28 [1991] 19–27)
Prov., Date: Arsinoe, 104/5
Stemma:

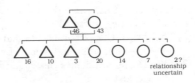

Declarant: Name lost
Family members:
    (1) NN s. NN and Leontous, *idiotes*, 46
    (2) NN s. NN [no.1] and NN [no.5], 16
    (3) NN s. NN [no.1] and NN [no.5], 10
    (4) NN s. NN [no.1] and NN [no.5], 3
    (5) NN d. NN and Leontous, wife and full sister of NN
        [no.1], 43
    (6) NN d. NN [no.1] and NN [no.5], 20
    (7) NN d. NN [no.1] and NN [no.5], 14
    (8) NN d. NN [no.1] and NN [no.5], 7
    (9) NN d. NN [no.1] and NN [no.5], [.]2
Free non-kin, slaves: None
Verif./photo: Michigan, P.Corn. inv. II, 16; seen 9/11/1990.
Discussion: Mentioned in the introduction to the first edition but not published. The relationships (and for the most part the sex) of the children are deduced from their position. This is an extract, most of which is lost at left; it is uncertain if it began on a preceding column. If a digit is in fact lost in no.9, this could be a slave rather than another child.

HOUSEHOLD NO.: 103-Ar-4
***Source:** SB* VI 9639 (cf. *BL* 5.118)
Prov., Date: Arsinoe, 104/5
Declarant: NN s. Demetrios
Family members: (1) NN s. Onesimos, age lost
Free non-kin, slaves: None preserved
Verif./photo: St. Petersburg, Hermitage, inv. 8431; photograph.
Discussion: Broken at top, at both sides, and at bottom, where almost all of the listing of persons is lost; there was at least one additional person. The declarant is registering a house and its renters, not his own residence (for which he submitted another declaration).

HOUSEHOLD NO.: 103-Ar-5
***Source:** P.Lond.* II 476a (p. 61) (cf. *BL* 3.94, *BASP* 28 [1991] 124–25)
Prov., Date: Arsinoe, 105 (?)
Stemma:

Declarant: Name lost
Family members: (1) Leontas s. Chairemon (s. —on) and Thermoutharion
                   (d. —on), *idiotes*, 21
               (2) Thaisas, d. Chairemon (s. —on) and Thermoutharion
                   (d. —on), sister and wife of Leontas [no.1], 18
               (3) Theogeiton, s. Leontas [no.1] and Thaisas [no.2],
                   age lost
Free non-kin, slaves: None preserved
Verif./photo: London, BL inv. 476a; microfilm; original seen, 2/4/1991.
Discussion: Broken at top, with loss of declarant's name; broken at bottom, but since υἱόν is singular and Theogeiton is μὴ ἀναγεγραμμένον ἐν ἐπιγεγενημένοις, probably no names are lost. This is evidently a family of renters. The second digit of Leontas' age is uncertain.

HOUSEHOLD NO.: 103-Ar-6
***Source:** P.Lond.* III 1119a (p. 25) = *CPJud.* II 430 (cf. *BL* 1.274, 3.96, 4.44)#
Prov., Date: Theadelphia (Arsinoite), 105
Stemma:

Declarant: NN d. Iesous and Ta—, with *kyrios* her husband Agathonikos
Family members: (1) NN s. —archos and Marous, 35
               (2) NN, 29
Free non-kin, slaves: None
Verif./photo: London, BL inv. 1119a; microfilm; original seen 2/4/1991.

Discussion: Damaged at left and broken below, with considerable loss. Declarant is registering renters in property owned by her. It is not certain that there was not a third person mentioned (in line 12); the papyrus is very damaged at this point. If the editor's μητ(ρὸς) τῆς] αὐτ(ῆς) with the second person is correct, he or she was a sibling of no.1.

HOUSEHOLD NO.: 103-Ar-7
*Source: *P.Oxf.* 8
Prov., Date: Arsinoe, 104/5
Stemma:

Declarant: Athenais d. Isidoros (s. Asklepiades) and Ptolema alias Athenarion (d. NN alias Sarapion), daughter of a *katoikos* of the 6475, with as *kyrios* her husband NN s. Heliodoros (s. Euboulos) and Herakleia (d. He—)
Family members: (1) Athenarion *(sic)* [declarant], d. Isidoros (s. Asklepiades) and Ptolema alias Athenarion (d. NN alias Sarapion), age lost
(2) NN s. Heliodoros (s. Euboulos) and Herakleia (d. He—), husband of Athenarion [declarant], *katoikos*, [56]
(3) Heliodoros s. NN [no.2] and Athenarion [declarant, no.1], 8
(4) Isidoros s. NN [no.2] and Athenarion [declarant, no.1], 1
Free non-kin, slaves: None
Verif./photo: P.Ashm.inv. 8; Pl. VIII; seen 4/4/1991.
Discussion: Complete at top and bottom, partially complete at left, substantial loss at right in most lines. The husband's age is restored from the date given for his *epikrisis* in year 9 of Nero, 62/3, presumably at age 14. The readings of the children's ages are secure, and confirmed by the dates of their registration at birth (also partially preserved).

HOUSEHOLD NO.: 103-Ar-8
*Source: *P.Mich.* III 177 (cf. *BL* 7.108)#
Prov., Date: Bacchias (Arsinoite), 1/12/104
Stemma:

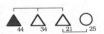

Declarant: Peteuris s. Horos (s. Horos) and Herieus (d. Menches), public farmer
Family members: (1) Peteuris [declarant] s. Horos (s. Horos) and Herieus (d. Menches), public farmer, 44
(2) Horos s. Horos (s. Horos) and Herieus (d. Menches), brother of Peteuris [declarant], 34

(3) Horion s. Horos (s. Horos) and Herieus
(d. Menches), brother of Peteuris [declarant], 21
(4) Thenatymis d. Chariton and Tapetosiris, wife of
Horion [no.3], 25

Free non-kin, slaves: None
Verif./photo: P.Mich. inv. 105; seen 9/11/1990.
Discussion: Complete except for a narrow center strip where the two halves have separated. For previous declaration of this household, see 89-Ar-1; for the following, see 117-Ar-4.

HOUSEHOLD NO.: 103-Ar-9
*Source: *SB* XIV 11577 (*ZPE* 21 [1976] 209) = *P.Mich.* IX 537 (cf. *BL* 8.372)#
Prov., Date: Karanis (Arsinoite), 20/10/104
Stemma:

Declarant: Terpos d. Mines (s. Harpagathos) and Tapetheus
Family members: (1) Onnophris s. Phanomgeus (s. Onnophris) and
Terpos [declarant], 5
(2) Petesouchos s. Phanomgeus (s. Onnophris) and
Terpos [declarant], 4
(3) Phanomgeus s. Phanomgeus (s. Onnophris) and
Terpos [declarant], 1
(4) Terpos [declarant] d. Mines (s. Harpagathos)
and Tapetheus [declarant], 35
Free non-kin, slaves: None
Verif./photo: P.Mich. inv. 5869; checked by Traianos Gagos, Ludwig Koenen, and Peter van Minnen, who read the age of no.1.
Discussion: Small losses at both sides in the upper part, minor damage at the end. No loss of entries. The age of no.3 is uncertain.

HOUSEHOLD NO.: 103-Ar-10
Source: *SPP* XXII 32 (cf. *BL* 8.480; *BASP* 28 [1991] 132–33)
Prov., Date: Soknopaiou Nesos (Arsinoite), 105
Declarant: Ptollous with *kyrios* NN s. Akousilaos
Family members, free non-kin, slaves: None
Verif./photo: Vienna, inv. G 24886; seen 22/4/1991.
Discussion: Broken at top with loss of introductory formulas; broken at left. This is evidently a registration of property in which no one is declared.

HOUSEHOLD NO.: 103-Ar-11
*Source: *P.Lond.* III 1221 (p. 24) (cf. *BL* 1.274, 8.187)#
Prov., Date: Arsinoe, 105

Stemma:

Declarant: Anchorimphis s. Anchorimphis (s. Areios) and Tamarkis (d. Panes-
neus), workman
Family members: (1) Anchorimphis [declarant] s. Anchorimphis (s. Areios)
                            and Tamarkis (d. Panesneus), workman, 43
                         (2) Heraklous d. Peneus, wife of Anchorimphis
                            [declarant], 25
                         (3) Anchorimphis s. Anchorimphis [declarant] and
                            Heraklous [no.2], 6
Free non-kin, slaves: None
Verif./photo: London, BL inv. 1221; microfilm; original seen 3/4/1991.
Discussion: Minor damage throughout; broken at bottom, just after end of names
   of persons.

HOUSEHOLD NO.: 103-Ar-12
*Source: *Pap.Lugd.Bat.* XIII 12 (cf. *BL* 7.97)#
Prov., Date: Polemon Division (Arsinoite), ?2–3/105
Stemma:

Declarant: Orsenouphis s. Harphaesis (s. Harphaesis) and Tapontos, *idiotes*
Family members: (1) Orsenouphis [declarant] s. Harphaesis (s. Harphaesis)
                            and Tapontos, *idiotes*, 20
                         (2) Tapontos d. Harphaesis (s. Harphaesis) and Tapontos,
                            sister of Orsenouphis [declarant], 14
                         (3) Soumenis d. Harphaesis (s. Harphaesis) and
                            Tapontos, sister of Orsenouphis [declarant], 8
Free non-kin, slaves: None
Verif./photo: Vienna, inv. G 27705; seen 22/4/1991.
Discussion: Minor losses only.

HOUSEHOLD NO.: 103-Ar-13
Source: *P.Mich.* XV 693 (cf. *BL* 8.219)
Prov., Date: Tebtunis (Arsinoite), 104/5
Declarant: Didymos s. Herakleides alias Lourios, *katoikos* of the 6475
Family members, free non-kin, slaves: None
Verif./photo: P.Mich. inv.5582; Pl. V.
Discussion: Complete except at bottom, where nothing essential is lost. This is a
   declaration of property, in which no one is registered.

HOUSEHOLD NO.: 103-Ar-14
*Source: *P.Heid.* IV 298

Prov., Date: Theadelphia (Arsinoite), 104/5
Declarant: Heron alias Theogiton s. Herod( ) (s. Philadelphos)
Family members: (1) Chonsis s. Horos, age not given
Free non-kin, slaves: None
Verif./photo: Heidelberg, inv. G 1696; Tafel VI.
Discussion: Left side partly damaged; broken at bottom. Heron, a metropolite, declares a house in Theadelphia belonging to the children of C. Petronius Abaskantos, whose names are not given and whose *phrontistes* he is, in which a renter lives.

HOUSEHOLD NO.: 117-Ap-1
*Source: *P.Alex.Giss.* 16 = *SB* X 10632
Prov., Date: Tanyaithis (Apoll.), 15/5/119
Stemma:

Declarant: Hartbos s. Pachoumis
Family members: (1) Hartbos [declarant] s. Pachoumis, age lost
                          (2) NN s./d. Tazbes, age lost
                          (3) NN, 29
Free non-kin, slaves: No name survive
Verif./photo: Giessen inv. 236.
Discussion: Small upper fragment broken except at right has names of persons declared, number of lost persons unknown; lower part has date and name of declarant.

HOUSEHOLD NO.: 117-Ap-2
Source: *P.Alex.Giss.* 18 = *SB* X 10634
Prov., Date: Tanyaithis (Apoll.), 16/5/119
Declarant: —oeris, s. Psais
Family members, free non-kin, slaves: No names survive
Verif./photo: Giessen inv. 228; photograph.
Discussion: Only oath, date, and subscription preserved. Name of declarant preserved only in Demotic.

HOUSEHOLD NO.: 117-Ap-3
*Source: *P.Alex.Giss.* 20 = *SB* X 10636 (cf. *BASP* 30 [1993] 35)
Prov., Date: Tanyaithis (Apoll.), 118/9
Stemma:

Declarant: Orsenouphis s. NN and Senmersis
Family members: (1) Orsenouphis [declarant] s. NN and Senmersis, age lost
                          (2) NN d. NN and Tazbes, wife of Orsenouphis [declarant], 29
Free non-kin, slaves: No names survive

Verif./photo: Giessen inv. 234; photograph.
Discussion: Broken after second (incomplete) entry; amount lost unknown.

HOUSEHOLD NO.: 117-Ap-4
***Source:** P.Alex.Giss.* 21 = *SB* X 10637
Prov., Date: Tanyaithis (Apoll.), 118/9
Stemma:

Declarant: NN
Family members: (1) NN [declarant], farmer, age lost
(2) —on s. [of declarant] and Senpachoumis, age lost
(3) NN s./d. [of declarant and Senpachnoumis], age lost
(4) NN, age lost
Free non-kin, slaves: None
Verif./photo: Giessen inv. 221; photograph.
Discussion: Opening lost; broken at right (ages lost); broken at bottom, apparently
after end of enumeration of family (there may have been a fifth family member given in line 9).

HOUSEHOLD NO.: 117-Ap-5
***Source:** P.Brem.* 32 = *P.Alex.Giss.* 17 = *SB* X 10633
Prov., Date: Tanyaithis (Apoll.), 6–24/5/119
Stemma:

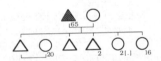

Declarant: Hartbos s. NN
Family members: (1) Hartbos [declarant] s. NN, 65
(2) Hartbos s. Hartbos [declarant] and Tapeeis [no.5],
age lost
(3) Pachoumis s. Hartbos [declarant] and Tapeeis [no.5],
brother of Hartbos [no.2], age lost
(4) Bekis, s. Hartbos [declarant] and Tapeeis [no.5],
brother of Hartbos [no.2], 2
(5) Tapeeis d. Pachopsais, wife of Hartbos [declarant],
age lost
(6) Senorsenouphis d. Hartbos [declarant] and Tapeeis
[no.5], 20+
(7) Senosiris d. Hartbos [declarant] and Tapeeis [no.5],
sister of Senorsenouphis [no.6], 16
(8) Senrophis d. Orsenouphis, wife of Hartbos [no.2], 20

Free non-kin, slaves: None
Verif./photo: Bremen inv. 30; photograph.
Discussion: Complete except for minor damage at right (some ages lost). Senor-senouphis' [no.6] age could have had a second (lost) numeral.

HOUSEHOLD NO.: 117-Ap-6
*Source: *P.Brem.* 33 = *P.Alex.Giss.* 19 = *SB* X 10635 (cf. BL 3.33; *BASP* 27 [1990] 1–2)
Prov., Date: Tanyaithis (Apoll.), 118/9
Stemma:

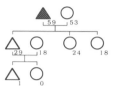

Declarant: [Miusis s. NN]
Family members:
(1) [Miusis (declarant) s. NN], farmer, 59
(2) Pachoumis s. Miusis [declarant] and Senpachompsais (d. Panechates) [no.4], farmer, 29
(3) Pachoumis younger, s. Pachoumis [no.2] and Thatres (d. Hermaios) [no.7], 1
(4) Senpachompsais d. Panechates, wife of Miusis [declarant], 53
(5) Senosiris d. Miusis [declarant] and Senpachompsais [no.4], 24
(6) Senartbos d. Miusis [declarant] and Senpachompsais [no.4], sister of Senosiris [no.5], 18
(7) Thatres d. Hermaios, w. Pachoumis [no.2], 18
(8) Senpachoumis born to Pachoumis [no.2], age lost (probably < 1)

Free non-kin, slaves: None
Verif./photo: Bremen inv. 85; photograph.
Discussion: Broken at end, where names could be lost. Upper left also lost with most of name(s) of declarant(s). [πρ]εσβ(ύτερον) for no.2 is uncertain; [υἱὸ]ν seems possible. The available space is 1.0 cm., suitable for the latter reading, while the former would occupy about 1.5 cm.

HOUSEHOLD NO.: 117-Ap-7
*Source: *P.Giss.* 43 = *P.Alex.Giss.* 14 = *SB* X 10630 (cf. BL 1.171, 3.68)
Prov., Date: Tanyaithis (Apoll.), 15/5/119
Stemma:

Declarant: Harpokration s. Dioskoros (s. Harmais) and Senorsenouphis (d.
    Psenanouphis)
Family members: (1) Harpokration [declarant] s. Dioskoros (s. Harmais)
                and Senorsenouphis (d. Psenanouphis), scribe, 70
            (2) Dioskoros s. Harpokration [declarant] and
                Senpachoumis d. Anompis [no.3], doctor, 17
            (3) Senpachoumis d. Anompis, wife of Harpokration
                [declarant], 39
            (4) Tazbes younger, d. Harpokration [declarant] and
                Senpachoumis [no.3], 15

Free non-kin, slaves: None
Verif./photo: Giessen inv. 9; photograph.
Discussion: Complete. House belongs to Senonnophris d. Harpokration and sib-
    lings.

HOUSEHOLD NO.: 117-Ap-8
*Source: *P.Giss.* 44 = *P.Alex.Giss.* 22 = *SB* X 10638
Prov., Date: Tanyaithis (Apoll.), 118/9
Stemma:

Declarant: Name lost
Family members: (1) NN d. Orsenouphis, 39
            (2) Senpsenchosis d. —phis, 18
            (3) Senpachoumis younger, daughter [of NN and
                Senpsenchosis [no.2]?], 2
Free non-kin: (1) Tatriphis freedw. Tazbes, 36
            (2) Spatala freedw. Senorsenouphis, 35
Slaves: (1) Trontpaisis slave of Senorsenouphis, 3
Verif./photo: Giessen inv. 77; photograph.
Discussion: Broken at top; several names must be lost at start of list, including
    Tazbes (patron of Tatriphis) and Senorsenouphis (owner of Trontpaisis and
    patron of Spatalos) and all males in the household. Broken at bottom, with
    subscription missing.

HOUSEHOLD NO.: 117-Ap-9
*Source: P.Giss.inv. 227 + *P.Brem.* 34 = *P.Alex.Giss.* 15 = *SB* X 10631
Prov., Date: Tanyaithis (Apoll.), 15/5/119
Stemma:

Declarant: Horos s. Pachomos (s. Pachompsais) and Tateathyris
Family members: (1) Horos [declarant] s. Pachomos (s. Pachompsais) and
                                         Tateathyris, age lost
                                     (2) Pachomos, s. Horos [declarant], age lost
                                     (3) Senpatokam[, age lost
Free non-kin, slaves: None
Verif./photo: Giss. inv. 227 + Brem. inv. 67 (photographs).
Discussion: Broken at right, where ages lost; complete otherwise.

HOUSEHOLD NO.: 117-Ar-1
*Source: *P.Corn.* 16.21–38 (cf. *BL* 2.2.49, 3.46, 4.24, 6.31; *BASP* 28 [1991] 19–
    27)
Prov., Date: Arsinoe, 18/3/119
Stemma:

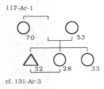

cf. 131-Ar-3

Declarant: Philippiaina d. Zoilos (s. Apollonios) with *kyrios* her husband Ploution
    s. Komon, *katoikos*
Family members: (1) Zois d. Herakleides (s. Sokrates), 53
                                     (2) Sokrates s. Dioskoros and Zois [no.1], 32
                                     (3) Aphrodous d. Dioskoros and Zois [no.1], 33
                                     (4) Aphrodous d. Dioskoros and Zois [no.1], wife of
                                         Sokrates [no.2] her brother, 28
                                     (5) Isarous, paternal aunt of Sokrates et al. [nos. 2–4], 70
Free non-kin, slaves: None
Verif./photo: Michigan, P.Corn. inv. II, 16; seen 9/11/1990.
Discussion: Complete. Philippiaina is declaring the inhabitants of two properties
    she owns but in which she does not reside. This is an extract, but there is no
    indication of any omitted persons. The line numbers are given above for the
    complete text (*BASP* 28 [1991] 19–27); this section is lines 1–18 in the first
    edition. Cf. 131-Ar-3.

HOUSEHOLD NO.: 117-Ar-2
*Source: *P.Fouad* 15 (cf. *BASP* 30 [1993] 41)
Prov., Date: Arsinoe, 119
Stemma:

Declarant: Name lost

Family members: (1) Heron s. Diodoros (s. Ptolemaios) and Thaisarion,
                        idiotes, 32
                        (2) NN s. Diodoros (s. Ptolemaios) and Thaisarion,
                        brother of Heron [no.1], 31 (?)
                        (3) Thaisas d. NN and NN, wife of NN [no.2], 28
                        (4) Dionysios (s. NN [no.2] and Thaisas [no.3]), 2
                        (5) NN (d. NN [no.2] and Thaisas [no.3]), 13
                        (6) Isis (d. NN [no.2] and Thaisas [no.3]), 13

Free non-kin, slaves: None
Verif./photo: Cairo, Société Egyptienne, inv. 37 recto; photograph.
Discussion: Broken at top, with loss of address; at left to a varying degree; and at
     bottom with trivial loss. Declarant registers renters of a house belonging to
     him/her.

HOUSEHOLD NO.: 117-Ar-3
*Source: *P.Brux.* 19 = *SB* V 8263 (cf. *P.Harr.* II, pp. 52–53; *BASP* 30 [1993]
     36–38)
Prov., Date: Arsinoe, 117/8
Stemma:

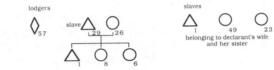

Declarant: Theon
Family members: (1) Theon [declarant], age lost
                        (2) Laberia d. Pasion (s. Pasion) and Alexandra (d.
                        of Pasion), wife of Theon [no.1], 32
Free non-kin: (1) NN, 57
                        (2) Pasion s. Dioskoros [no.1 below] slave of Laberia,
                        and Alexous [no.3 below] d. Hermas, 1
                        (3) Alexous d. Hermas (s. Hermas) and
                        Tasoucharion (d. Syros), wife of Dioskoros the
                        slave (no.1 below), 26
                        (4) Alexous d. Dioskoros (slave of Laberia, no.1
                        below) and Alexous (d. Hermas, no.3 above), 8
                        (5) Taareotis d. Dioskoros (slave of Laberia, no.1
                        below) and Alexous (d. Hermas, no.3 above), 6
Slaves: (1) Dioskoros, slave of Laberia d. Pasion and of
                        Horaiane her sister (equal shares), weaver, 29
                        (2) Dioskoros ἄλλος ("another"), slave of Laberia d.
                        Pasion and of Horaiane her sister (equal shares), 1
                        (3) Isidora slave of Laberia d. Pasion and of Horaiane
                        her sister (equal shares), 49
                        (4) Dioskorous nicknamed Sarapous, slave of Laberia d.
                        of Pasion and of Horaiane her sister (equal shares),
                        23

Verif./photo: P.Brux.inv. E 7360; photograph.

Discussion: Top lost, otherwise almost complete. Ed. describes Laberia as the declarant, but her place in the start of the list of women, after the men, shows that this is not correct. The declarant must have been her husband Theon, who is mentioned in her entry. The first, partly preserved, male entry is that of a renter; Theon and an unknown number of other free males appeared in the lost part of the declaration. This is an extract from the original. The date is inferred but virtually certain. See *P.Harr.* II pp. 52–53 and *BASP* 30 (1993) 36–38 for discussion.

HOUSEHOLD NO.: 117-Ar-4
*Source: *P.Mich.* III 178 (cf. *BL* 7.108–09)
Prov., Date: Bacchias (Arsinoite), 5/5/119
Stemma:

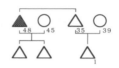

Declarant: Horos s. Horos (s. Horos) and Herieus (d. Menches), public farmer
Family members: (1) Horos [declarant] s. Horos (s. Horos) and Herieus (d. Menches), public farmer, 48
    (2) Tapekysis d. Horos, wife of Horos [declarant], 45
    (3) Horos s. Horos [declarant] and Tapekysis [no.2], age lost
    (4) Horion s. Horos [declarant] and Tapekysis [no.2], age uncertain
    (5) Horion s. Horos (s. Horos) and Herieus (d. Menches), brother of Horos [declarant], 35
    (6) Thenatymis d. Chariton, wife of Horion [no.5], 39
    (7) Horos s. Horion [no.5] and Thenatymis [no.6], 1
Free non-kin, slaves: None
Verif./photo: P.Mich. inv. 106; Pl. V; seen 9/11/1990.
Discussion: Virtually complete. The editors read the age of Horion [no.4] as 1 (α). 30 (λ) is equally possible. The age of Thenatymis [no.6], read by the editor as 31 (λα) and Youtie as 39 (λθ), looks most like 32 (λβ), but the second digit is probably a theta correcting some other letter (maybe beta). See 89-Ar-1 and 103-Ar-8.

HOUSEHOLD NO.: 117-Ar-5
*Source: *BGU* VII 1579
Prov., Date: Kerk(esoucha?) (Arsinoite), 118/9

Stemma:

Declarant: Tnepheros d. Papontos with *kyrios* kinsman Theon s. Aphrodisios
Family members: (1) Tnepheros [declarant] d. Papontos, 30
                        (2) Pnepheros s. Ptollis (s. Pnepheros) and Tnepheros
                            [declarant], 10
                        (3) Aphrodisia d. Ptollis (s. Pnepheros) and Tnepheros
                            [declarant], 8
                        (4) —anion d. Ptollis (s. Pnepheros) and Tnepheros
                            [declarant], age lost
Free non-kin, slaves: None
Verif./photo: Formerly Berlin P. 11489; lost in World War II.
Discussion: Apparently complete, but with no date. The house belongs to
    Pnepheros, the minor son of the declarant.

HOUSEHOLD NO.: 117-Ar-6
*Source: *BGU* VII 1580
Prov., Date: Philadelphia (Arsinoite), 6/6/119
Stemma:

Declarant: NN s. Menches and Sentaos
Family members: (1) NN [declarant] s. Menches and Sentaos, 56
                        (2) T.th— d. Pekeis, wife of NN [declarant], 53
                        (3) Herakles s. NN [declarant] and T.th— [no.2], age lost
                        (4) Ammonarion d. NN [declarant] and T.th— [no.2],
                            age lost
                        (5) Sentaos d. Skammaios, mother of NN [declarant], 75
Free non-kin, slaves: None
Verif./photo: Formerly Berlin P.11496; lost in World War II.
Discussion: Broken at the top; many small lacunae.

HOUSEHOLD NO.: 117-Ar-7
*Source: *BGU* III 706 (cf. *BL* 1.60)#
Prov., Date: Soknopaiou Nesos (Arsinoite), *ca* 118

Stemma:

slaves

of declarant   of declarant's   of declarant's
                mother   brother

Declarant: Harpagathes s. Stotoetis (s. Tesenouphis) and Herieus, priest of the 4th
    tribe
Family members: (1) Harpagathes [declarant] s. Stotoetis (s. Tesenouphis)
                                and Herieus, age lost
                             (2) Thenapynchis d. Stotoetis, wife of Harpagathes
                                [declarant], age lost
                             (3) Stotoetis s. Stotoetis and Thenapynchis [no.2],
                                age lost
                             (4) Pekysis s. Stotoetis (s. Tesenouphis) and Herieus
                                [no.10], brother of Harpagathes [declarant], age lost
                             (5) Horos s. Stotoetis (s. Tesenouphis) and Herieus,
                                brother of Harpagathes [declarant] and Pekysis
                                [no.4], age lost
                             (6) Tapiomis d. P..., wife of Pekysis [no.4], age lost
                             (7) Tapekysis d. Pekysis [no.4] and Tapiomis [no.6],
                                age lost
                             (8) T[d. Pekysis [no.4] and Tapiomis [no.6], age lost
                             (9) Tapiomis d. Tesenouphis, wife of Horos [no.5],
                                age lost
                             (10) Herieus d. Harpagathes (mother of declarant),
                                age lost
Free non-kin: None
Slaves: (1) Isidora slave of Harpagathes [declarant], age lost
                             (2) NN slave (female) of Herieus [no.10], age lost
                             (3) NN slave (female) of Pekysis [no.4], age lost
Verif./photo: Berlin, P.7161; seen 15/4/1991.
Discussion: Broken at left and right, with loss at right of all ages and some names.
    Broken at bottom with possible loss of additional persons. The editor does
    not restore the names of Pekysis (lines 12 and 21) and Herieus (line 4), but
    they appear inescapable, and the listing above assumes the correctness of
    these restorations.

HOUSEHOLD NO.: 117-Ar-8
***Source:** P.Monac.* III 70
Prov., Date: Arsinoe, 6/4/119

Stemma:

Declarant: Philoumene alias Phi[

Family members:	(1) Philoumene alias Phi[[declarant], age lost
Free non-kin:	(1) NN s. NN (s. Herodes) and Diodora, age lost
	(2) NN, wife of NN [no.1], 35
	(3) NN child of NN [no.1] and NN [no.2], age lost
	(4) NN child of NN [no.1] and NN [no.2], age lost
Slaves:	(1) Heraklous alias NN, slave of Philoumene [declarant], age lost

Verif./photo: Munich, P.Graec.Mon. 16; Abb. 18.

Discussion: Broken at top and left; most names and ages are lost, but apparently no complete entries. The four non-kin are renters.

HOUSEHOLD NO.: 117-Ar-9
*Source: *P.Corn.* 16.14–20 (cf. *BASP* 28 [1991] 19–27)
Prov., Date: Arsinoe, 119
Declarant: Name lost
Family members: (1) NN s. NN and Leukarous, *idiotes*, 24
Free non-kin, slaves: None
Verif./photo: Michigan, P.Corn. inv. II, 16; seen 9/11/1990.

Discussion: Mentioned in the introduction to the first edition but not published. This is an extract, most of which is lost at left; its brevity suggests that much was omitted, and it cannot be determined if the original included other persons.

HOUSEHOLD NO.: 117-Ar-10
*Source: *CPR* XV 24
Prov., Date: Arsinoe, 119
Declarant: Hermas s. Diodoros (s. Harpalos) and NN
Family members: (1) Dioskoros s. Didymos
Free non-kin, slaves: None preserved
Verif./photo: Vienna, inv. G 24602; seen 25/4/1991.

Discussion: Broken at bottom and with varying losses at right. Copy of a declaration, appended to a declaration of birth. Hermas declares a property inhabited by renters. The declaration breaks off in the middle of the listing of the first of these.

HOUSEHOLD NO.: 117-Ar-11
*Source: *P.Lond.* inv. 1570b (*Cd'E*, forthcoming)
Prov., Date: Arsinoite, 119 (?)

Stemma:

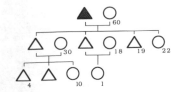

Declarant: Zoilos the elder (?)
Family members: (1) Zoilos the elder [declarant], over 60
                     (2) NN, wife of Zoilos the elder [declarant], 60
                     (3) Harphaesis s. Zoilos the elder [declarant] and
                           NN [no. 2], probably over 30
                     (4) NN wife of Harphaesis [no. 3], 30
                     (5) NN son of Harphaesis [no. 3] and NN [no. 4], 4
                     (6) NN son of Harphaesis [no. 3] and NN [no. 4],
                           < 4
                     (7) NN d. Harphaesis [no. 3] and NN [no.4], 10
                     (8) Satabous s. Zoilos the elder [declarant] and
                           NN [no. 2], age lost (probably in 20s)
                     (9) NN d. Ammonios, wife of Satabous [no. 8], 18
                     (10) NN d. Satabous [no. 8] and NN [no. 9], 1
                     (11) NN s. Zoilos [declarant] and NN [no. 2], 19
                     (12) NN d. Zoilos [declarant] and NN [no. 2], 22
Free non-kin, slaves: None
Verif./photo: London, British Library, inv. 1570b; seen 3/4/1991.
Discussion: Broken at top and left. The provenance is based on the distinctively
    Arsinoite combination of names. The date is inferred, see the publication in
    Cd'E. This is apparently a copy from a register entry derived from a declara-
    tion. Some of the persons listed were included in the lost portion, where still
    others (probably males) may well have been listed. The reconstruction of the
    relationships is in some points very uncertain.

HOUSEHOLD NO.: 117-Ox-1
Source: *P.Oxy.* IV 786 descr. (cf. *BL* 4.60)
Prov., Date: Oxyrhynchos, 25/1/119
Declarants: Ariston s. Apollonios and Didymos s. Didymos
Family members, free non-kin, slaves: None preserved
Verif./photo: Cairo inv. JE 43434; photograph.
Discussion: Only the end is preserved, with all declared persons lost before the
    preserved part. The phrasing of the closing suggests that some persons *were*
    declared.

HOUSEHOLD NO.: 117-Ox-2
Source: P.Oxy. XII 1547#
Prov., Date: Oxyrhynchos, 24/1/119

Stemma:

slaves

◊ 3[.] ○ 3[.]
of declarant? of declarant's wife

Declarant: Petosiris s. Dionysios (s. Petosiris) and Mieus (d. Horos)
Family members: (1) Petosiris [declarant] s. Dionysios (s. Petosiris) and
Mieus (d. Horos), stonecutter, 74
(2) Ti— s. Petosiris [declarant] and Tetoeus (d.
Thoonas), stonecutter, 45
(3) Apollonides s. Petosiris (s. Thoonis) and Tapsois (d.
Paulos), stonecutter, 21
(4) Papontos s. Thoonas (s. Petosiris) and Thaisous (d.
Papontos), brother of Tetoeus [no.5], stonecutter
(currently absent), 57
(5) Tetoeus d. Thoonas (s. Petosiris) and Thaisous, sister
of Papontos [no.4], wife of Petosiris [declarant],
age lost
Free non-kin: None
Slaves: (1) NN (name lost), 3[.]
(2) Thaesis, purchased slave of Tetoeus [no.5], 3[.]
Verif./photo: Cairo, inv. JE 47492; photograph in Ashmolean, seen 5/4/1991.
Discussion: Fairly complete, but extensive minor damage throughout and badly
abraded over much of the surface. We assume that the first-named male (line
16) is the declarant, and that his name is to be restored as the patronymic of
Ti— (line 17). We also restore Tetoeus as the name of the only free female
person registered (line 25). It is not clear what the relationship of Apollonides
[no.3] is to the others. Petosiris declares another house, unoccupied. Another
person is listed in line 32, but the situation is unclear.

HOUSEHOLD NO.: 131-Ar-1
***Source:** BGU* I 132 (cf. *BL* 1.22)
Prov., Date: Arsinoe, 132/3
Stemma:

△ △ △ △
14   9   3   0

Declarant: Name lost
Family members: (1) NN s. NN and NN, 14
(2) Dionas s. NN and NN, 9
(3) Hermes s. NN and NN, 3
(4) Heron s. NN and NN, < 1
Free non-kin, slaves: None preserved
Verif./photo: Berlin, P.1354; seen 16/4/1991.

Discussion: In two columns, apparently an extract or extracts. Col. i is broken at the left and the entire papyrus at the bottom. The relationship of the two is unclear, but a great deal is lost in col. i, which gives no connected sense. It seems best to consider only col. ii, children whose parents were mentioned earlier. All of the children are described as μη(τρὸς) τῆς α(ὐτῆς).

HOUSEHOLD NO.: 131-Ar-2
***Source:** BGU I 182.16–22 (cf. BL 1.24, 3.9, 7.10; BASP 29 [1992] 107–08)
Prov., Date: Arsinoe, 132/3
Declarant: NN d. NN (s. Souchas) and NN with *kyrios* NN s. Diodoros
Family members: (1) NN [declarant] d. NN (s. Souchas) and NN, age lost
Free non-kin, slaves: None preserved
Verif./photo: Berlin, P.7145; seen 12/4/1991.
Discussion: Only the upper part is preserved, breaking off just after καί εἰμι; above it on the papyrus is 145-Ar-6. Broken also at left and right. The identification of the declarant as female is based on the placement of the name Diodoros, which must be part of the name of a *kyrios*, not an ascendant of the declarant.

HOUSEHOLD NO.: 131-Ar-3
***Source:** P.Corn. 16.39–58 (cf. BL 2.2.49, 3.46, 4.24; BASP 28 [1991] 19–27)
Prov., Date: Arsinoe, 22/7/133
Stemma:

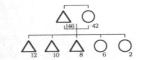

Declarant: Ploution s. Komon (s. Heron) and Ptollarous alias Ptolema (d. Apollonios, *katoikos*)
Family members: (1) Sokrates s. Dioskoros, [46]
                        (2) Aphrodous d. Dioskoros, full sister and wife of
                            Sokrates [no.1], 42
                        (3) Dioskoros s. Sokrates [no.1] and Aphrodous [no.2], 12
                        (4) Onesimos s. Sokrates [no.1] and Aphrodous [no.2], 10
                        (5) Asklas s. Sokrates [no.1] and Aphrodous [no.2], 8
                        (6) Zoidous d. Sokrates [no.1] and Aphrodous [no.2], 6
                        (7) Herais d. Sokrates [no.1] and Aphrodous [no.2], 2
Free non-kin, slaves: None
Verif./photo: Michigan, P.Corn. inv. II, 16; seen 9/11/1990.
Discussion: Complete except for minor damage. Declarant registers renters of a house he owns but does not live in. The age of no.3 cannot be verified in the current condition of the papyrus. Cf. 117-Ar-1.

HOUSEHOLD NO.: 131-Ar-4
***Source:** P.Giss.Univ.Bibl. I 14 (cf. BL 2.2.67, 3.68, 4.34)#
Prov., Date: Apias (Arsinoite), 132/3
Declarant: Saras s. Heras (s. Saras) and Tases (d. Peteusorapis)

Family members: (1) Saras [declarant] s. Heras (s. Saras) and Tases (d. Peteusorapis), age lost

Free non-kin, slaves: None

Verif./photo: P.Giss.Univ.Bibl. inv. 197; photograph.

Discussion: Broken at left and at bottom, with minor losses at both. The household is complete.

HOUSEHOLD NO.: 131-Ar-5

Source: *BGU* I 53 (cf. *BL* 1.12)

Prov., Date: Dionysias (Arsinoite), 24/7/133

Declarant: Ioulia Krispina through *phrontistes* Horos s. Onnophris

Family members, free non-kin, slaves: None

Verif./photo: Berlin, P.6880; seen 15/4/1991.

Discussion: Complete. Only property (two houses with courtyards) is declared, no persons.

HOUSEHOLD NO.: 131-Ar-6

Source: *SB* XII 10842 = *Cd'E* 46 (1971) 120–28 = *P.Tebt.* II 522 descr.

Prov., Date: Ibion Eikosipentarouron (Arsinoite), 4/8/133

Declarant: Herakleides s. Didymos the younger (s. Herodes), former gymnasiarch, member of the 6475, through his *phrontistes* Tyrannos

Family members, free non-kin, slaves: None

Verif./photo: Berkeley, P.Tebt. 522; seen 28/9/1990.

Discussion: Complete at top and bottom, some damage at the sides and scattered throughout. Herakleides lives in Arsinoe; this is a declaration of property in Ibion Eikosipentarouron in which no one is registered.

HOUSEHOLD NO.: 131-Ar-7

Source: *P.Tebt.* II 566 = *Aegyptus* 72 (1992) 64–66 (cf. *Archiv* 6 [1920] 144 and 222)

Prov., Date: Samareia (Arsinoite), 133

Declarant: Ptolemaios s. NN (s. Apollonides), *katoikos*

Family members: None

Free non-kin, slaves: None preserved

Verif./photo: Berkeley, P.Tebt. 566; seen 28/9/1990.

Discussion: Broken at the bottom, just after the indication that no one is registered in the property. In *Archiv* one finds lines 1–2 (p. 144) and 3–4 (p. 222); the full text is published in *Aegyptus*.

HOUSEHOLD NO.: 131-Ar-8

*Source: *P.Bad.* VI 169 (cf. *BL* 8.16)

Prov., Date: Tebtunis (Arsinoite), 132/3

Stemma:

Declarant: Harpochration s. Marepsemis (s. Marsisouchos) and Thenpakebkis (d. —sis), priest

Family members: (1) Harpochration [declarant] s. Marepsemis (s. Marsisouchos) and Thenpakebkis (d. —sis), priest, 66

(2) NN d. —eus (s. Psena[]), wife of Harpochration
[declarant], age lost
Free non-kin, slaves: None preserved
Verif./photo: Heidelberg Universitätsbibliothek, inv. 2077; photograph.
Discussion: Broken at left and below, in middle of list of persons.

HOUSEHOLD NO.: 131-Ar-9
***Source:** BGU* XIII 2220#
Prov., Date: Soknopaiou Nesos? (Arsinoite), 133
Declarant: Apion s. Apion (s. NN), one of the 6475 Hellenes
Family members, free non-kin, slaves: None preserved
Verif./photo: W. Berlin, P.21706; seen 11/4/1991.
Discussion: Fragment from upper left corner of document. It comes from excavations at Soknopaiou Nesos (which there is room to restore in line 3), but editor refrains from giving any provenance except "Fayum." Nothing preserved of the section listing any individuals.

HOUSEHOLD NO.: 131-Ar-10
***Source:** BullAinShams* 1 (1985) 38–40, no.1#
Prov., Date: Theadelphia (Arsinoite), 2/5/133
Stemma:

Declarants: Lykos s. Heras (s. Lykos) and Tasooukis and Deios s. Heras (s. Lykos) and Tasooukis, public farmers
Family members: (1) Lykos [declarant] s. Heras (s. Lykos) and Tasooukis, public farmer, 34
                        (2) Deios [declarant] s. Heras (s. Lykos) and Tasooukis, public farmer, 29
Free non-kin, slaves: None
Verif./photo: Cairo, SR 3049/69; photograph; original not found 2/4/1993.
Discussion: Complete.

HOUSEHOLD NO.: 131-Ar-11
***Source:** P.Graux inv. 937 (cf. *AEPHE* 1931–32, 3–19; *BASP* 30 [1993] 43–45)
Prov., Date: Arsinoe, 133
Stemma:

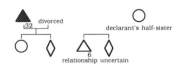

Declarants: Not preserved; two or more members of a family
Family members: (1) Aphrod( ) [declarant, male], 32
                        (2) NN d. NN [no.1] and NN [divorced wife], age lost
                        (3) NN child of NN [no.1] and NN [divorced wife], age lost

(4) Philippos s. Apollonios and ....ion, 6
(5) NN child of Apollonios and ....ion, age lost
(6) Sarapias, d. NN and NN, sister on father's side
of no.1, age lost

Free non-kin, slaves: None preserved
Verif./photo: Paris, Institut de Papyrologie, Sorbonne, P.Graux inv. 937;
photograph; original seen 21/6/1993.
Discussion: Broken at top, bottom, left, and partially at right, with much internal
damage. Some persons are certainly lost. Probably this is a household with
two or three siblings and their (spouses and) children living together.

HOUSEHOLD NO.: 131-Be-1
*Source: *P.Hamb.* I 7 (cf. *BL* 1.193, *BASP* 28 [1991] 29–31)#
Prov., Date: Peptaucha (Berenike), 30/6/132
Stemma:

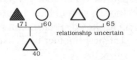

Declarant: Niktathymis s. Papeiris (s. Niktathymis)
Family members: (1) Niktathymis [declarant] s. Papeiris (s. Niktathymis)
and Apollonia, 71
(2) NN d. Piesies, wife of Niktathymis [declarant], 60
(3) Niktathymis s. Niktathymis [declarant] and NN
[no.2], priest, 40
(4) NN alias Samounis s. Archidemos and Taesis, age lost
(5) NN d. Paesis, wife of NN alias Samounis [no.4], 65
Free non-kin, slaves: None
Verif./photo: Hamburg, inv. 68; Tafel IV; photograph.
Discussion: Complete except for scattered damage, especially a strip from the middle part of the left side. γυ(νή) is both times followed by κλω( ), the sense of
which is obscure. No indication is given of the relationship of nos. 4 and 5 to
nos. 1–3.

HOUSEHOLD NO.: 131-He-1
*Source: *P.Oslo* III 98 (cf. *BL* 3.126; 8.229)#
Prov., Date: Herakleopolis, 132/3
Declarant: Semtheus s. Hephaistas (s. Panasneus) and Nemesous (d. Herakleios),
katoikos
Family members: (1) Semtheus [declarant] s. Hephaistas (s. Panasneus) and
Nemesous (d. Herakleios), *katoikos*, 39
Free non-kin, slaves: None
Verif./photo: Oslo; P.Oslo III, pl. IV.
Discussion: Almost complete, with minor damage at foot. Ends of a few lines of a
preceding column with another declaration survive. Cf. 145-He-1.

HOUSEHOLD NO.: 131-He-2
*Source: *P.Bad.* IV 75a (cf. *BL* 2.2.183, *BASP* 27 [1990] 2–3)

Prov., Date: Ankyronpolis (Herakleopolite), 133
Stemma:

Declarant: Petesouchos s. Pisoithis and Thenamenneus
Family members: (1) Petesouchos [declarant] s. Pisoithis and
Thenamenneus, [28]
(2) Tausiris d. Paritis, wife of Petesouchos [declarant], 20
(3) Pnephoros s. Petesouchos [declarant] and Tausiris
[no.2], said to have been born ἐπὶ ξένης, 3
(4) Thenphrokos d. Psenamounis (s. Thenamounis) and
Tausiris [mother of Tausiris no.2, apparently],
50(+)
Free non-kin, slaves: None
Verif./photo: Heidelberg, P.Heid.inv. G 668; photograph.
Discussion: Broken at right and at bottom; no apparent loss of persons. *P.Bad.* IV
75b (145-He-1) gives the declarant's age in the following census, from which
it is restored here. Thenphrokos' age survives as ν[, thus anything from 50–
59.

HOUSEHOLD NO.: 131-He-3
*Source: *P.Bon.* I 18, col. i (cf. *BASP* 28 [1991] 122–23)
Prov., Date: Machor (Herakleopolite), 3–4/133
Stemma:

Declarant: Piathres s. Petechon (s. Piathres) and Soeris
Family members: (1) Piathres [declarant] s. Petechon (s. Piathres) and
Soeris, farmer, 27
(2) Petechon s. ?Piathres and Apychis (?), father of
declarant, 70
Free non-kin, slaves: None
Verif./photo: Bologna, inv. 7; photograph.
Discussion: Broken at left, fragmentary, rubbed and crumpled in the lower part.
Relationship of no.2 apparently not stated in remaining papyrus. The list of
the household is complete.

HOUSEHOLD NO.: 131-He-4
*Source: *P.Bon.* I 18, col. ii (cf. *BL* 7.30, *BASP* 28 [1991] 122–23)
Prov., Date: Machor (Herakleopolite), 3–4/133

Stemma:

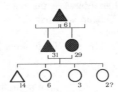

Declarants: Piathres s. Piathres and his children Psois and Thapetemounis
Family members: (1) Piathres [declarant] s. Piathres and NN, 61
  (2) Psois [declarant] s. Piathres [declarant] and Thauetis, 31
  (3) Thapetemounis [declarant] d. Piathres [declarant] and
    Taphel( ), sister and wife of Psois [no.2], 29
  (4) Chath( ) s. Psois [no.2] and Thapetemounis [no.3], 14
  (5) Achorais d. Psois [no.2] and Thapetemounis [no.3], 6
  (6) Thaphe...es d. Psois [no.2] and Thapetemounis
    [no.3], 3
  (7) Thaara.. d. Psois [no.2] and Thapetemounis [no.3], 2
Free non-kin, slaves: None?
Verif./photo: Bologna, inv. 7; photograph.
Discussion: Broken down the middle and fragmentary in lower part. After listing
  no.7, the text appears to go on to registering other property. There are still
  problems in the readings of some of the names. The age of no.7 is not
  certain, but given the order of listing it is probable.

HOUSEHOLD NO.: 131-He-5
Source: *P.Bon.* I 18, col. iii (cf. *BASP* 28 [1991] 122–23)
Prov., Date: Machor (Herakleopolite), 133
Declarant: Herph[aesis?
Family members, free non-kin, slaves: None preserved
Verif./photo: Bologna, inv. 7; photograph.
Discussion: Only the upper left corner preserved.

HOUSEHOLD NO.: 131-Me-1
***Source:** *P.Vindob.Sijp.* 24 (cf. *BL* 5.63; 8.200)
Prov., Date: Memphis, 132
Stemma:

Declarant: Tetanoupis d. Areios (s. Nemesas) and Areia (d. Zoilos), with *kyrios*
  Hierakion s. Petobastis
Family members: (1) Tetanoupis [declarant] d. Areios (s. Nemesas) and
    Areia (d. Zoilos), *arge*, 55

(2) Bochanoupis s. —pion (s. Te—) and Phe— (d.
Dekianos), husband of Tetanoupis [declarant],
age lost
(3) NN s. NN and Tetanoupis [declarant], 33
Free non-kin, slaves: None
Verif./photo: Vienna, inv. G 25852; seen 22/4/1991.
Discussion: Damaged after line 22 and broken at the bottom. Despite the damage it
appears that no.3 is Tetanoupis' son by a father other than no.2, presumably
a previous husband.

HOUSEHOLD NO.: 131-Ox-1
*Source: *PSI* I 53, col. i (cf. *BL* 8.391)
Prov., Date: Oxyrhynchos, 4/12/132
Stemma:

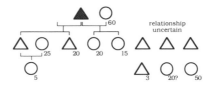

Declarant: Heliodoros s. Heliodoros
Family members: (1) Heliodoros [declarant] s. Heliodoros, age lost
(2) Heliodoros s. Heliodoros [declarant], age lost
(3) NN [male], age lost
(4) NN [male], age lost
(5) NN [male], age lost
(6) NN s. Totes (s. Operos), 3
(7) Dionysios s. Heliodoros and [Tne]phersois,
ἄτεχνος, 20
(8) Ptollous d. Amois (s. Amois) and Theudous, wife of
Heliodoros [declarant], ἄτεχνος, 60
(9) Kleopatra d. Heliodoros [declarant] and Ptollous
[no.8], ἄτεχνος, 20
(10) NN [female] d. Heliodoros [declarant] and
Ptollous [no.8], ἄτεχνος, 15
(11) NN [female] d. Heliodoros (s. Antonios) and Didyme,
ἄτεχνος, 20 (or 2)
(12) NN [female] d. —reus and Teros (d. Gaios),
ἄτεχνος, 50
(13) —is d. Totoes (s. Heleis) and —ia, wife of
Heliodoros s. Heliodoros [no.2], 25
(14) NN [female] d. Heliodoros [no.2] and —is
[no.13], 5
Free non-kin, slaves: None
Verif./photo: Florence, Biblioteca Laurenziana; seen 25/5/1989.
Discussion: Broken at the top, with loss of listings for nos. 1–5 (nos. 1–2
reconstructed from other information in text); some damage at left. The ed.

supposes that no.10 is daughter of Ptollous by another husband, but that is not likely. The two children of Heliodoros and Ptollous whose ages survive are 15 and 20; Dionysios is 20 and has a different mother, and Heliodoros [no.2] is probably around 25 like his wife. [Tne]phersois was probably Heliodoros' first wife, and Ptollous his second; no.10 is probably Heliodoros' daughter, with the surviving text carefully indicating the mother's identity. Age rounding is rampant; no one over 5 has an age not divisible by 5, a fact which makes the existence of two children aged 20 by different mothers less surprising.

HOUSEHOLD NO.: 131-Ox-2
*Source: *PSI* I 53, col. ii
Prov., Date: Oxyrhynchos, 11–12/132
Declarant: Not preserved
Family members: No names preserved; at least one female
Free non-kin, slaves: None preserved
Verif./photo: Florence, Biblioteca Laurenziana; seen 25/5/1989.
Discussion: Only lower left edge preserved with oath and date formulas.

HOUSEHOLD NO.: 131-Ox-3
*Source: *PSI* I 53, col. iii
Prov., Date: Oxyrhynchos, 132/3
Declarant: Sabinos
Family members: (1) Sabinos [declarant], age lost
Free non-kin, slaves: None preserved
Verif./photo: Florence, Biblioteca Laurenziana; seen 25/5/1989.
Discussion: Only lower right corner preserved with oath and date formulas.

HOUSEHOLD NO.: 131-Ox-4
*Source: *PSI* I 53, col. iv
Prov., Date: Oxyrhynchos, 15/11/132
Stemma:

Declarant: Hermogenes s. Eutychides
Family members: (1) Hermogenes [declarant] s. Eutychides, age lost
                        (2) NN [female], age lost
                        (3) Tne[[female], 14 (24 possible but less likely)
                        (4) Didyme sister [of no.3], ἄτεχνος, 3
Free non-kin: None preserved
Slaves: None
Verif./photo: Florence, Biblioteca Laurenziana; seen 25/5/1989.
Discussion: Lower portion preserved with oath and date, but only the end of the listing. Three females were declared.

HOUSEHOLD NO.: 131-Ox-5
*Source: *PSI* I 53, col. v
Prov., Date: Oxyrhynchos, 132/3
Declarant: Germanos

Family members: (1) Germanos [declarant], age lost
Free non-kin, slaves: None preserved
Verif./photo: Florence, Biblioteca Laurenziana; seen 25/5/1989.
Discussion: Small fragment from lower left part of declaration, with part of date and subscription. No information on persons declared.

HOUSEHOLD NO.: 131-Ox-6
*Source: *PSI* I 53, col. vi
Prov., Date: Oxyrhynchos, 132/3
Stemma:

Declarant: Plou[
Family members: (1) Plou[[declarant], information lost
                       (2) NN, age 62
                       (3) NN, age 68
                       (4) NN, age 78
Free non-kin, slaves: None preserved
Verif./photo: Florence, Biblioteca Laurenziana; seen 25/5/1989.
Discussion: Right side, broken at top; impossible to derive information from lines 89–98 (following the entry for no.4), which no doubt contained some persons.

HOUSEHOLD NO.: 131-Ox-7
*Source: *PSI* I 53, col. vii (cf. *BASP* 27 [1990] 12)
Prov., Date: Oxyrhynchos, 28/4/133
Stemma:

relationship uncertain

Declarant: Amois s. Sarapion
Family members: (1) Amois [declarant] s. Sarapion, weaver, age lost
                       (2) Sarapion s. Amois [declarant] and Didyme, weaver, age lost
                       (3) Aphynchis s. Amois [declarant] and Didyme, brother of Sarapion [no.2], age lost
                       (4) Demetr[ia?], age lost
                       (5) NN (female), age lost
Free non-kin, slaves: None preserved
Verif./photo: Florence, Biblioteca Laurenziana; seen 25/5/1989.
Discussion: Broken at top, complete on all other sides but with some large gaps, particularly in lines 116–120, where only a few letters survive. Three men and two women were declared, according to subtotals.

HOUSEHOLD NO.: 131-Ox-8
*Source: *PSI* I 53, col. viii
Prov., Date: Oxyrhynchos, 11–12/132
Declarant: NN d. Kastor, with NN, cousin, as *kyrios*
Family members: (1) NN [declarant] d. Kastor, age lost
Free non-kin, slaves: None preserved
Verif./photo: Florence, Biblioteca Laurenziana; seen 25/5/1989.
Discussion: Only lower part preserved, with declaration and date; some holes. The reading of the patronymic in line 142 as Kastor seems doubtful to me.

HOUSEHOLD NO.: 131-Ox-9
*Source: *PSI* I 53, col. ix
Prov., Date: Oxyrhynchos, 132/3
Declarant: Herieus (?) d. Apoll[
Family members: (1) Herieus (?) [declarant] d. Apoll[, age lost
Free non-kin, slaves: None preserved
Verif./photo: Florence, Biblioteca Laurenziana; seen 25/5/1989.
Discussion: Only the lower left corner preserved, with oath and date. The editor does not read the declarant's name; Ἐριεῦς seems possible to me but not certain.

HOUSEHOLD NO.: 131-Ox-10
*Source: *PSI* I 53, col. x
Prov., Date: Oxyrhynchos, 21/11/132
Stemma:

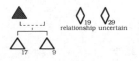

Declarants: Dionysios and Papontos, both ss. Horos
Family members: (1) Dionysios [declarant] s. Horos, age lost
(2) Papontos [declarant] s. Horos, age lost
Free non-kin, slaves: None preserved
Verif./photo: Florence, Biblioteca Laurenziana; seen 25/5/1989.
Discussion: Only lower left corner preserved, with oath and date.

HOUSEHOLD NO.: 131-Ox-11
*Source: *PSI* I 53, col. xi
Prov., Date: Oxyrhynchos, 132/3
Stemma:

Declarant: Name lost; perhaps Tryphon (patronymic of nos. 2 and 3)
Family members: (1) [Tryphon?] [declarant], age lost
(2) NN s. Tryphon and NN (d. Ammonios), weaver, 17

(3) —as, s. Tryphon and NN (d. Ammonios), brother [of
no.2], ἄτεχνος, 9
(4) NN, ἄτεχνος, 19
(5) NN, ἄτεχνος, 29
Free non-kin, slaves: None preserved
Verif./photo: Florence, Biblioteca Laurenziana; seen 25/5/1989.
Discussion: Complete at right, only date and subscription lost at foot, but torn at
right and top. Probably no declared persons are totally lost. A line between
175 and 176 completed the declarant's entry but is ignored by the editor
because all is lost at left. Persons 4 and 5 are listed apparently in a separate
section, and their relationship to the others is not clear. What lines 183–187
contained is still less clear, perhaps just property. The editor read the age of
no.4 as *.θ*; the first letter is iota.

HOUSEHOLD NO.: 131-Ox-12
*Source: *PSI* I 53, col. xii
Prov., Date: Oxyrhynchos, 14/12/132
Declarant: Dioskourides (?)
Family members: (1) Dioskourides (?) [declarant], age lost
Free non-kin, slaves: None preserved
Verif./photo: Florence, Biblioteca Laurenziana; seen 25/5/1989.
Discussion: Small fragment from lower left corner. All persons lost.

HOUSEHOLD NO.: 131-Ox-13
*Source: *PSI* VIII 874, col. i
Prov., Date: Oxyrhynchos, 132/3
Declarants: Onnophris s. Theon (s. Sarapion) and Thermouthion (d. Onnophris);
and Heras s. Horos (s. Horos) and Taamois, *epitropoi* for Anteis and
Taamois, children of Panemgeus (s. Dioskoros) and Tauris (d. Horos); and
Tausoreus d. Panemgeus (s. Dioskoros) and Tauris (d. Horos), sister of the
minors, with her husband Pokkaous s. Pantauchos as *kyrios*
Family members: (1) Anteis s. Panemgeus (s. Dioskoros) and Tauris (d.
Horos), ἄτεχνος, minor, age lost
Free non-kin, slaves: None preserved
Verif./photo: Cairo, Egyptian Museum; photograph seen 26/5/1989.
Discussion: Complete except at bottom and some damage at right. The formula is
odd: no one is said to be registered in the property declared, but the declaration goes on all the same to list Anteis, who is living in another property he
owns jointly with his sisters. It is unclear if Taamois was listed in the lost
portion.

HOUSEHOLD NO.: 131-Ox-14
*Source: *PSI* VIII 874, col. ii
Prov., Date: Oxyrhynchos, 132/3

Stemma:

Declarant: Herodes s. Hermi[ ] (s. Karpounios) and Ese[ ] (d. Apollonios)
Family members: (1) Herodes [declarant] s. Hermi[ ] (s. Karpounios)
                   and Ese[ ] (d. Apollonios), age lost
                   (2) Apollonios alias D[ ], s. Herodes [declarant] and
                   Didyme (deceased), age lost
Free non-kin, slaves: None
Verif./photo: Cairo, Egyptian Museum; photograph seen 26/5/1989.
Discussion: Complete except at bottom and along the right side. Total of males
   given as 2, so no males lost.

HOUSEHOLD NO.: 131-Ox-15
Source: *P.Oxy.* III 480 (cf. *BL* 3.131)#
Prov., Date: Oxyrhynchos, 25/11/132
Declarant: Chairemon s. Chairemon
Family members, free non-kin, slaves: None
Verif./photo: Chicago, Oriental Institute, inv. 8337; seen 7/9/1990.
Discussion: Broken at top; only description of property and conclusion preserved.
   This declaration concerns a house in which no one is registered, and no fam-
   ily members' names were given.

HOUSEHOLD NO.: 131-Ox-16
*Source: *P.Oxy.* XLVII 3336#
Prov., Date: Oxyrhynchos, 11/1/133
Declarant: Stephanos s. Stephanos
Family members: (1) Stephanos [declarant] s. Stephanos, ἄτεχνος, 17
Free non-kin, slaves: None
Verif./photo: Ashmolean; seen 4/4/1991.
Discussion: Complete except at top. No entries are lost.

HOUSEHOLD NO.: 131-Pr-1
*Source: *P.Lond.* II 324.1–24 (p. 63) (cf. *BL* 1.245, 3.93) = *W.Chr.* 208#
Prov., Date: Prosopite (exact place not given), original date not given
Stemma:

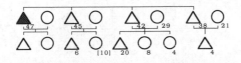

Declarant: Pathermouthis s. Anikos (s. Pathermouthis) and Thaseis, *metallikos*
Family members: (1) Pathermouthis [declarant] s. Anikos (s.
                   Pathermouthis) and Thaseis, *metallikos*, 47

(2) Thaneutis d. Tithoenathymis (s. Herpsaesis), wife of
    Pathermouthis [declarant], age not stated
(3) Thaesis d. Pathermouthis [declarant] and Thaneutis
    [no.2], age not given
(4) Anikos s. Pathermouthis [declarant] and Thaneutis
    [no.2], age not given
(5) Thenthnoupis s. Anikos (s. Pathermouthis) and
    Thaseis (d. Herpaesis), [brother of declarant], 45
(6) Demetrous d. Soterichos and Thamistis, wife of
    Thenthnoupis [no.5], age not given
(7) Thamistis d. Thenthnoupis [no.5] and Demetrous
    [no.6], [10]
(8) Anikos s. Thenthnoupis [no.5] and Demetrous [no.6], 6
(9) Herpaesis s. Anikos (s. Pathermouthis) and Thaseis
    (d. Herpaesis), [brother of declarant], 42
(10) —esies d. Horos and Tertia Capitolina, wife of
    Herpaesis [no.9], 29
(11) Anikos s. Herpaesis [no.9] and —esies [no.10], 20
(12) Thaseis d. Herpaesis [no.9] and —esies [no.10], 8
(13) Tertia d. Herpaesis [no.9] and —esies [no.10], 4
(14) Pantbeus s. Anikos (s. Pathermouthis) and Thaseis
    (d. Herpaesis), [brother of declarant], 38
(15) Thaesis d. Thaubastis (d. Piesies), wife of Pantbeus
    [no.14], 21
(16) Anikos s. Pantbeus [no.14] and Thaesis [no.15], 4

Free non-kin, slaves: None
Verif./photo: London, BL inv. 324; microfilm; original seen 2/4/1991.
Discussion: Copy of a copied extract of a declaration, followed by another includ-
    ing only nos. 5,7, and 8 (145-Pr-1); complete but with scattered damage. The
    date of the cover letter is 24/3/161. Some ages are omitted in this copy; those
    in brackets are computed from ages given in 145-Pr-1. There are some prob-
    lems of identification and age (notably nos. 10 vs. 11). Wilcken resolves
    Καπιτω( ) in no.10 (not resolved by ed.) as Καπίτωνος. This is certainly
    possible, but her father's patronymic is not given, and Tertia often occurs
    with a second name (or as second name). *Metallikos* here probably means
    "quarry worker."

HOUSEHOLD NO.: 145-Ar-1
*Source: *P.Mil.Vogl.* III 193a = *SB* VI 9495.1a
Prov., Date: Tebtunis, 3/7/147
Stemma:

38
13
apator

Declarant: Kroniaina d. Herakles (s. —os) and Thea ..., with br. Herakles as
    kyrios

Family members: (1) Kroniaina [declarant] d. Herakles (s. —os) and
Thea ..., 38
(2) Hero *apator*, d. Kroniaina [declarant], 13
Free non-kin, slaves: None
Verif./photo: Milan, Univ. degli Studi, Istituto di Papirologia, inv. 472; seen
1/6/1989.
Discussion: Complete but scattered damage. We take Κρονιαινης (line 11) to be a
faulty genitive for nominative, not equivalent to Κρονιαινίς (ed.).

HOUSEHOLD NO.: 145-Ar-2
*Source: *P.Mil.Vogl.* III 193b = *SB* VI 9495.1b
Prov., Date: Tebtunis, 18/7/147
Stemma:

Declarant: Tephorsais d. Pasion, with paternal uncle Tourbon s. Herakles as
kyrios
Family members: (1) Tephorsais [declarant] d. Pasion, 29
(2) Herakles s. Onnophris (s. Harmiusis) [divorced husband
of declarant] and Tephorsais [declarant],
Harmiusis, age lost (1 or 2 digits possible)
Free non-kin, slaves: None
Verif./photo: Milan, Univ. degli Studi, Istituto di Papirologia, inv. 472; seen
1/6/1989.
Discussion: Complete, with serious damage to line 4 and scattered holes elsewhere.

HOUSEHOLD NO.: 145-Ar-3
*Source: *P.Mil.Vogl.* III 194a = *SB* VI 9495.2a (cf. *BASP* 27 [1990] 7–8)
Prov., Date: Tebtunis, 146/7
Stemma:

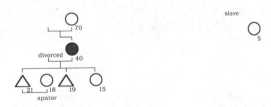

Declarant: Herais d. Protas (s. Orseus), with son Kronion as *kyrios*
Family members: (1) Herais [declarant] d. Protas (s. Orseus), 40
(2) Kronion s. Herakles [divorced husband of declarant] (s.
Kronion s. Amaeis) and Herais [declarant], 21

(3) Protas, s. Herakles [divorced husband of declarant] (s. Kronion s. Amaeis) and Herais [declarant], 19

(4) Achillis, d. Herakles [divorced husband of declarant] (s. Kronion s. Amaeis) and Herais [declarant], 15

(5) Serapias d. Thermion, *apator*, wife of Kronion [no.2], 18

(6) Apias alias Didyme d. Lysimachos gd. Eutychos, mother of Herais [declarant], 70

Free non-kin: None
Slaves: (1) Lampra, 5
Verif./photo: Milan, Univ. degli Studi, Istituto di Papirologia, inv. 700; seen 1/6/1989.
Discussion: Complete. Name of mother of no.5 is very doubtful.

HOUSEHOLD NO.: 145-Ar-4
*Source: *P.Mil.Vogl.* III 194b = *SB* VI 9495.2b (cf. H.C. Youtie, "P.Mil.Vogl. III 194b," *ZPE* 14 [1974] 261–62 = *Scr.Post.* I 115–16 [*BL* 7.120]; *BASP* 27 [1990] 8–9)
Prov., Date: Tebtunis, 146/7
Declarant: Herakleia d. Herakles and Tapetesouchos, with Herakles s. Phomnasis as *kyrios*
Family members: (1) Herakleia [declarant] d. Herakles and Tapetesouchos, age lost
Free non-kin, slaves: None
Verif./photo: Milan, Univ. degli Studi, Istituto di Papirologia, inv. 700; seen 1/6/1989
Discussion: Complete at top and right, some loss at left and slight damage at foot. Herakleia reports that Herakles (and another son? One would suppose that τέκνα referred to sons in light of the following αἰ δὲ θυγατέραις) are registered (separately?), probably with her divorced husband (who is mentioned), while daughters Herakleia and Tapetesouchos are each registered with their own husbands. Youtie rejects ed.'s restorations making *kyrios* be the divorced husband, who is Herakles s. NN alias Areotes. Herakleia's age is presumably 40+ since she has 4 living children, 2 married.

HOUSEHOLD NO.: 145-Ar-5
*Source: *BGU* I 137 (cf. *BASP* 29 [1992] 106–07)
Prov., Date: Arsinoe, 146/7
Stemma:

lodgers   30   slave / of declarant

Declarant: Eudarion alias Eudaimon s. NN (s. Eudaimon) and Thermoutharion
Family members: (1) Eudarion alias Eudaimon [declarant] s. NN (s. Eudaimon) and Thermoutharion, *idiotes*, 30

Free non-kin: (1) NN s./d. NN and NN (d. Euremon) ?, age lost
                      (2) NN s./d. NN and the same, *idiotes*, age lost
                      (3) Aphrodous alias NN, age lost
                      (4) Charidemos, *idiotes*, age lost
Slaves: (1) Epagathos slave of Eudarion [declarant], age lost
Verif./photo: Berlin, P.1333; seen 12/4/1991.
Discussion: Substantial losses at right; broken at bottom. Part of the list of persons lost. The listing second of the slave suggests that there were no more family males declared, but it is impossible to say with certainty if the surviving names are those of family females or of renting males or females; the latter seems more likely given the order, and the explicit mention of *enoikoi* in the initial formula.

HOUSEHOLD NO.: 145-Ar-6
*Source: *BGU* I 182.1–15 (cf. *BL* 1.24, 7.10; *BASP* 29 [1992] 107–08)
Prov., Date: Arsinoe, 19/7/147
Stemma:

Declarant: NN d. Ptolemaios with *kyrios* NN s. Heron
Family members: (1) NN, 5
                      (2) Apion, 2
                      (3) Onesas, age lost
                      (4) NN, d. NN (s. Onesas), wife of NN, age lost
                      (5) Phelon, s. NN and NN [no.4], 5
Free non-kin, slaves: None
Verif./photo: Berlin, P.7145; seen 12/4/1991.
Discussion: Broken at left and right; some damage in the middle. Followed by 131-Ar-2. The description section is very fragmentary and probably included at least two more people. These are renters of the declarant, whose principal residence was declared in another statement.

HOUSEHOLD NO.: 145-Ar-7
Source: *BGU* VII 1581#
Prov., Date: Arsinoe, 22/7/147
Declarant: Didymos slave of Longinia Nemesilla and Longinia Petronilla
Family members, free non-kin, slaves: None
Verif./photo: Berlin,, P.11499; seen 12/4/1991.
Discussion: Broken at top, with loss of address. Didymos declares a half share of a third of a house belonging to his mistresses, who are absent, and in which no one is registered.

HOUSEHOLD NO.: 145-Ar-8
*Source: *P.Corn.* 16.59–80 (cf. *BL* 2.2.49, 3.46, 4.24; *BASP* 28 [1991] 19–27)
Prov., Date: Arsinoe, 147

Stemma:

cf. 131-Ar-3

Declarant: Isidora d. Heron tritos (s. Heron) and Isidora (d. Asklepiades), with *kyrios* her husband Asklepiades s. Asklepiades

Family members: (1) Zoidous [? d. Sokrates and Aphrodous, see 131-Ar-3], age lost [20?]

(2) NN, 5

Free non-kin, slaves: None preserved

Verif./photo: Michigan, P.Corn. inv. II, 16; seen 9/11/1990.

Discussion: Declarant registers renters of house she owns but does not live in. They are listed in column iv, with only the start of lines preserved. Those listed here are only a part of those originally listed. The rest is too fragmentary to allow reconstruction.

HOUSEHOLD NO.: 145-Ar-9
*Source: *P.Meyer* 9 (cf. *BL* 4.50)
Prov., Date: Arsinoe, 8/7/147
Stemma:

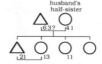

Declarant: Name lost

Family members: (1) Chares s. Atarios (s. Dionysios) and Charition (d. Aphrodisios, *katoikos*), ὑπερετής, [6?]3

(2) Herois d. Atarios (s. Dionysios) and Tertia (d. Didymos, *katoikos*), sister of Chares [declarant] on father's side and his wife, 41

(3) Atarias s. Chares [declarant] and Herois [no.2], 21

(4) Athenarion d. Chares [declarant] and Herois [no.2], sister and wife of Atarias [no.3], 13

(5) Charition alias Theodote d. Chares [declarant], 11

(6) Didyme d. Chares [declarant], age lost

(7) NN s. Dioskoros and Rhodous (d. Dioskoros), *idiotes*, 40

Free non-kin: None

Slaves: (1) NN, female slave of Aphrodisios, age lost

(2) Pasion, called Eutyches, male offspring of NN [no.1], 20

(3) Harpalos, called Nikephoros, male offspring of NN [no.1], 18

(4) Herois, female offspring of NN [no.1], 8

(5) NN, slave, age lost

(6) Isidora alias Hediste, slave, 23
(7) Aphrodous alias Parinous, female offspring of Isidora [no.6], 6
(8) NN, slave, age lost

Verif./photo: Berlin, formerly Neutestamentliches Seminar. The papyri of this collection were destroyed during World War II (information from W. Brashear).

Discussion: Broken at left with substantial loss; complete elsewhere. This is a declaration of renters of a house belonging to the declarant. The free person NN [no.7] may be the Aphrodisios who is the owner of some or all of the slaves. Meyer restored the age of the first family member as [7]3, arguing that ὑπερετής had to mean "over the age for liturgies," which he claimed was 70, rather than "over the age of liability for taxes" (on the grounds that as a *katoikos* he was not liable anyway). This is not correct. In 131-Ar-12 (see Adddenda) there is a ὑπερετής aged 61, which makes it clear that the reference is to the age of liability for taxes. Since a husband-wife age difference of 32 years here would be the highest known, though not by much, we take a restoration of [6]3 to be somewhat more likely than [7]3, but neither is excluded.

HOUSEHOLD NO.: 145-Ar-10
*Source: *P.Ryl.* II 111a#
Prov., Date: Arsinoe, 146/7
Stemma:

Declarant: Didis d. Ptolemaios with *kyrios* her husband Sotas s. Herakleides
Family members: (1) Pasion s. Aphrodisios (s. Heron) and Didarous (d. Dionysios), *idiotes*, 21
            (2) Philadelphos s. Aphrodisios (s. Heron) and Didarous (d. Dionysios), brother of no.1, 19
Free non-kin, slaves: None
Verif./photo: Manchester, John Rylands Library; photograph.
Discussion: Complete. A copy written around 161 of a declaration of renters occupying a house belonging to the declarant.

HOUSEHOLD NO.: 145-Ar-11
Source: *P.Tebt.* II 321
Prov., Date: Arsinoe, 147
Declarant: Heras d. Lysimachos (s. Herodion) and Tamystha, with *kyrios* kinsman Herakleides s. Patron
Family members, free non-kin, slaves: None preserved
Verif./photo: Berkeley, P.Tebt. 321; seen 27/9/1990.
Discussion: Broken at bottom, taking list of persons declared. This is a copy of a declaration for a 2/3 share of a house inhabited by renters of the declarant, not by herself.

HOUSEHOLD NO.: 145-Ar-12
*Source: *BGU* I 95 (cf. *BL* 1.19)#
Prov., Date: Karanis (Arsinoite), 24/7/147

Stemma:

Declarant: Petheus s. Petheus (s. Pnepheros) and Tamystha
Family members:　(1) Petheus [declarant] s. Petheus (s. Pnepheros) and
　　　　　　　　　　　Tamystha, 76
　　　　　　　　　　(2) Aphrodous d. Apis (s. Papontos), wife of Petheus
　　　　　　　　　　　[declarant], 70
　　　　　　　　　　(3) Diodora d. Petheus [declarant] and Aphrodous
　　　　　　　　　　　[no.2], 33
Free non-kin: None
Slaves:　　　　(1) Tasoucharion, slave of Diodora [no.3], 32
Verif./photo: Berlin, P.6868; seen 16/4/1991.
Discussion: Complete except for minor losses. The three female children of
　　Diodora [no.3] are said to be declared by their father (NN s. Petheus) in
　　another declaration. Presumably Diodora is divorced from him.

HOUSEHOLD NO.: 145-Ar-13
Source: *SB* VI 9554,1
Prov., Date: Karanis (Arsinoite), 146/7
Declarant: NN s. Sambathion, as *phrontistes* for NN Gemellus
Family members, free non-kin, slaves: None preserved
Verif./photo: Michigan, inv. 2940; now in Cairo; seen 1/4/1993.
Discussion: Broken at the left and bottom, with loss of any persons declared.

HOUSEHOLD NO.: 145-Ar-14
Source: *SB* VI 9554,2b
Prov., Date: Karanis (Arsinoite), 19/7/147
Declarant: Didyme alias Niliaina
Family members, free non-kin, slaves: None
Verif./photo: Michigan, inv. 4731a, recto col. i; seen 9/11/1990.
Discussion: Broken at top with actual declaration formula lost. Declares a house in
　　which no one is registered.

HOUSEHOLD NO.: 145-Ar-15
Source: *SB* VI 9554,2c
Prov., Date: Karanis (Arsinoite), 7 or 10/7/147
Declarants: My... alias Sarapion, Ptolemaios, and Sarapammon alias Andronikos,
　　all three sons of Ptolemaios alias NN (Paniskos?), *katoikoi*
Family members, free non-kin, slaves: None
Verif./photo: Michigan, inv. 4731a, recto col. ii; seen 9/11/1990.
Discussion: Some loss at right. Declarants are registered in the metropolis; here
　　they declare a vacant lot in Karanis.

HOUSEHOLD NO.: 145-Ar-16
Source: *SB* VI 9554,4
Prov., Date: Karanis (Arsinoite), 24/7/147
Declarant: Longinus Maximus through *phrontistes* Ptolemaios (?) s. Petheus
Family members, free non-kin, slaves: None
Verif./photo: Michigan, inv. 5961; seen 9/11/1990.
Discussion: Broken at top. Declaration of quarter-share of house in Karanis by owner without any mention of persons (nor declaration that there were none). Line 8, the papyrus reads κώμης Καρινίδ(ι) (*sic*).

HOUSEHOLD NO.: 145-Ar-17
*Source: *SB* VI 9554,3
Prov., Date: Mendes (Arsinoite), 23/7/147
Stemma:

Declarant: Sisois s. Orsenouphis (s. Sisois) and Tauris (d. Nemesas)
Family members: (1) Sisois [declarant] s. Orsenouphis (s. Sisois) and Tauris (d. Nemesas), 45
(2) Tepheros d. Mysthes (s. Papontos) and Tenaus, wife of Sisois [declarant], 36
(3) Sisois s. Sisois [declarant] and Tepheros [no.2], age lost
(4) Dioskoros s. Sisois [declarant] and Tepheros [no.2], twin of no.5, 14
(5) Dioskoros s. Sisois [declarant] and Tepheros [no.2], twin of no.4, 14
Free non-kin, slaves: None
Verif./photo: Michigan, inv. 4715a; seen 9/11/1990.
Discussion: Complete. One wonders if the parents actually called the twins Kastor and Polydeukes! Line 3, for Νεμέσεως (ed.), read Νεμεϱᾶτος.

HOUSEHOLD NO.: 145-Ar-18
*Source: *P.Berl.Leihg.* III 52A (ined.)
Prov., Date: Philagris (Arsinoite), 6–7/147
Stemma:

Declarant: Sarapas s. Hatres (s. Papous) and Taes (d. Sarapas)

Family members: (1) Sarapas [declarant] s. Hatres (s. Papous) and Taes (d.
                        Sarapas), 48
                        (2) Sabinos s. Hatres (s. Papous) and Philous, half-
                        brother of Sarapas [declarant], 58
                        (3) Alkes s. Sabinos [no.2] and Herois (d. Apollonios), 16
Free non-kin, slaves: None
Verif./photo: Berlin, P. 11535; seen 17/4/1991.
Discussion: Complete, minor abrasion. There is no indication of what has hap-
pened to the mother of no.3. No.2 is described as released from laographia,
apparently on grounds of disability (he is described as ἐπισινής).

HOUSEHOLD NO.: 145-Ar-19
*Source: *P.Berl.Leihg.* III 52B (ined.)
Prov., Date: Philagris (Arsinoite), 26/6/147
Stemma:

Declarant: Harphesis *apator* s. Thermouthis (d. Harphesis), farmer
Family members: (1) Harphesis [declarant] *apator* s. Thermouthis (d.
                        Harphesis), farmer, 30
                        (2) Hatres *apator* s. Thermouthis (d. Harphesis), brother
                        of Harphesis [declarant], 22
                        (3) Orseus *apator* s. Thermouthis (d. Harphesis), brother
                        of Harphesis [declarant], 20
                        (4) Hermes *apator* s. Thermouthis (d. Harphesis), brother
                        of Harphesis [declarant], 16
                        (5) NN, wife of Harphesis [declarant], 20
                        (6) Heras, *apator* d. Thermouthis (d. Harphesis), sister
                        and wife of Hatres [no.2], 14
                        (7) Ponneis *apator*, d. NN, 16
Free non-kin, slaves: None
Verif./photo: Berlin, P.11535; seen 17/4/1991.
Discussion: Complete but with considerable surface damage. The relationship of
no.7 to the rest of the family is unclear.

HOUSEHOLD NO.: 145-Ar-20
*Source: *P.Amh.* II 74 (cf. *Pap.Lugd.Bat.* V, pp. 118 n.8, 161 [*BL* 3.5]; *BL* 8.4;
    BASP 28 [1991] 13–14)
Prov., Date: Soknopaiou Nesos (Arsinoite), 24/7/147
Stemma:

Declarant: Panephremmis s. Anchophis the elder (s. Panephremmis) and Stotoetis (d. Horos), priest

Family members: (1) Panephremmis [declarant] s. Anchophis the elder (s. Panephremmis) and Stotoetis (d. Horos), priest, 32

(2) Panephremmis s. Anchophis the younger (s. Panephremmis) and Thases (d. Stotoetis), cousin of Panephremmis [declarant], 8

(3) Stotoetis s. Anchophis the younger (s. Panephremmis) and Thases (d. Stotoetis), cousin of Panephremmis [declarant], 1

(4) Thases d. Anchophis the elder (s. Panephremmis) and Stotoetis (d. Horos), sister and wife of Panephremmis [declarant], 2[.]

(5) Stotoetis d. Panephremmis (s. Paous), mother of Panephremmis [declarant?], 55

Free non-kin: (1) Segathis d. Stotoetis the elder (s. Stotoetis) and Thases (d. Satabous), renter, [.]8

Slaves: None

Verif./photo: New York, Pierpont Morgan Library; seen 8/1/1991.

Discussion: Complete except for minor holes. A copy. Of what Panephremmis is Stotoetis [no.5] the mother? The declarant's mother's father was Horos, not Panephremmis; no.2's mother was Thases. The latter is the more serious discrepancy. The editors read her age as 51 and no.1's as 40, rightly queried by Hombert and Préaux; that obstacle to her being the mother of no.1 is now removed. The age-difference, moreover, taken with the difference in names, does seem to exclude her being the mother of 2 and 3. The most probable solution is that her patronymic is given incorrectly in either the initial declaration or her entry.

HOUSEHOLD NO.: 145-Ar-21

Source: *P.Wisc.* I 18 (cf. *BL* 6.71)#

Prov., Date: Theadelphia (Arsinoite), 146/7

Declarants: Apollo(nios?) and Heron the elder and Heron the younger, sons of Apol(lonios?) alias Sokrates

Family members, free non-kin, slaves: None

Verif./photo: Madison, P.Wisc. inv. 46; photograph.

Discussion: Complete but with scattered damage. Declaration of property belonging to the three brothers, in which no one lives.

HOUSEHOLD NO.: 145-Ar-22

*****Source:** *P.Fay.* 319.13–19 (*Aegyptus* 70 [1990] 27–31; cf. *BASP* 30 [1993] 38–40)

Prov., Date: Arsinoite, 147? (document *post* 161)

Stemma:

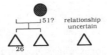

Declarant: Thermoutharion d. NN, with *kyrios* of her son M[

Family members: (1) Thermoutharion [declarant], daughter of *katoikos*, 51?
                        (2) NN s. NN and Thermoutharion [declarant], age lost
                        (3) NN s. (?) NN and Thermoutharion [declarant], 26
                        (4) NN alias NN [m.], age lost (over 14)

Free non-kin, slaves: None

Verif./photo: Cairo, JE 10850; plate in *Aegyptus* (Tav. 1); seen 3/4/93

Discussion: Broken at right, with large loss, and torn at the bottom. This is an excerpt from the original declaration, quoted in an *epikrisis* document of unknown date. See 159-Ar-26 for the preceding declaration in the same document. No. 4 may be another child of the declarant or perhaps some other descendant, such as a child of no.2. Other persons were probably listed in the lost portions of the text.

HOUSEHOLD NO.: 145-Ar-23

*Source: *CPR* VI p. 3 = *P. Vindob. Tand.* 20 + *P. Vindob. Sijp.* 25#

Prov., Date: Arsinoe, 7/7/147

Stemma:

Declarant: Polydeukes s. Sotas (s. Maron) and Heraklous (d. Dioskoros)

Family members: (1) Ptolemaios s. Mystes (s. Pr—) and Theonis (the sister of his father), 4[.]
                        (2) Thaisas alias Thasion d. Dionysios (s. Didymos) and Thasion (the sister of her father), 28
                        (3) Satyros s. Ptolemaios [no.1] and Thaisas [no.2], 6
                        (4) Thaisarion d. Ptolemaios [no.1] and Thaisas [no.2], 3
                        (5) Thasion d. Ptolemaios [no.1] and Thaisas [no.2], 1

Free non-kin, slaves: None

Verif./photo: P. Vindob. G 25.853 + G 73 + G 39.955; Pl. of G 39.955 in *P. Vindob. Tand.*, Pl. X; whole seen 22/4/1991.

Discussion: Complete except for minor holes in the middle.

HOUSEHOLD NO.: 145-Ar-24

*Source: *P. Wisc.* I 36 (cf. *BL* 7.100)#

Prov., Date: Theadelphia (Arsinoite), 9/7/147

Stemma:

Declarant: Sambathion d. Diodoros alias Dioskoros (s. Petesouchos) and Isidora, with *kyrios* her brother Ptolemaios

Family members: (1) Ptolemaios s. Diodoros alias Dioskoros (s.

Petesouchos) and Isidora, brother of Sambathion
[declarant], 35
(2) Dioskoros alias Heron s. Ptolemaios [no.1] and
Anoubiaina alias Achilis, *aste*, 3 or 13
Free non-kin, slaves: None
Verif./photo: Wisconsin, inv. 25; plate; photograph.
Discussion: Dioskoros is Ptolemaios' son by Anoubiaina, who is described as his
wife living with him; but she herself is not declared. Perhaps her legal
residence is in the city of which she had citizen status. Sambathion
presumably lives in other property in Theadelphia, which she lists as her
idia, but she says that she has also registered in Apias, where we know that
Ptolemaios had business interests. Dioskoros alias Heron ceased to live with
his father in 155/6, cf. H.C. Youtie, *ZPE* 23 (1976) 131–38 = *Scriptiunculae
Posteriores* I 375–82, but we do not know what age he was then; either 13 or
23 is possible, and thus either 3 or 13 here, where only the gamma survives.

HOUSEHOLD NO.: 145-Ar-25
Source: *BGU* I 122 (cf. *BASP* 29 [1992] 105)
Prov., Date: Arsinoe, 147
Declarant: Thermoutharion d. M[, with *kyrios* kinsman Sotas s. Dios
Family members, free non-kin, slaves: None preserved
Verif./photo: Berlin, P.1334; seen 12/4/1991.
Discussion: Broken at right and below, with loss of entire list of persons declared.

HOUSEHOLD NO.: 145-He-1
*Source: *P.Bad.* IV 75b = *SelPap* II 312 (cf. *BL* 2.2.183, 3.256, 6.8, 8.15; *BASP*
27 [1990] 2–3)
Prov., Date: Ankyronpolis (Herakleopolite), 10/3/147
Stemma:

Declarant: Petesouchos s. Pisoitis and Thenammeneus
Family members: (1) Petesouchos [declarant] s. Pisoitis and
Thenammeneus, 42
(2) Tausiris d. Pareitis, wife of Petesouchos [declarant], 34
(3) Pnephoros s. Petesouchos [declarant] and Tausiris
[no.2], 17
(4) Psenamounis s. Petesouchos [declarant] and
Tausiris [no.2], 5
(5) Pnephoros ἄλλος ("another") s. Petesouchos
[declarant] and Tausiris [no.2], deceased in the
current year, 9
Free non-kin, slaves: None
Verif./photo: Heidelberg, P.Heid.inv. G 604; plate in Seider, *Paläographie* I 35;
photograph.

Discussion: Complete. Cf. 131-He-2 (*P.Bad.* IV 75a) for this household 14 years earlier.

HOUSEHOLD NO.: 145-He-2
*Source: *P.Corn.* 17 (cf. *BL* 2.2.49, 3.46, 8.90; *BASP* 28 [1991] 27–29)
Prov., Date: Ankyronon (Herakleopolite), 10/3/147
Stemma:

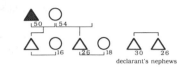

declarant's nephews

Declarant: Serempis s. Patermouthis (s. Siris) and Thenp...
Family members: (1) Serempis [declarant] s. Patermouthis (s. Siris) and
Thenp..., 50
(2) Thenosiris d. Psenosiris, wife of Serempis
[declarant], 54
(3) Patermouthis s. Serempis [declarant] (and
Thenosiris [no.2]?), 2[.]
(4) Thenamounis d. Psenamounis, wife of Patermouthis
[no.3], 16
(5) Taas d. Serempis [declarant] and Tetemouthis,
registered by her husband, age not given
(6) Nouris s. Pnepheros (deceased brother of Serempis
[declarant]) and Thennoupis, 30
(7) Patermouthis s. Pnepheros (deceased brother of
Serempis [declarant]) and Thennoupis, brother of
Nouris [no.6], 26
(8) Pnephoros s. Pnephoros and Thenosiris [no.2], 26
(9) Tamounis d. Ameneus, wife of Pnephoros [no.8], 18
(10) Taphorsois d. Ameneus, sister of Tamounis [no.9],
registered by her husband, age not given
(11) Taas d. Ameneus, sister of Tamounis [no.9],
registered by her husband, age not given
Free non-kin, slaves: None
Verif./photo: Michigan, P.Corn. inv. II, 11; seen 9/11/1990.
Discussion: Two lines missing at the start; lower part damaged at left.

HOUSEHOLD NO.: 145-Hm-1
Source: *SB* VIII 9871 (*Cd'É* 39 [1964] 118–19); cf. *P.Petaus* 14.10n.
Prov., Date: Hermopolis, 146
Declarant: Name lost
Family members, free non-kin, slaves: None preserved
Verif./photo: P.Stras.inv. W.G. 366, seen 14/3/1989.
Discussion: Broken at top, bottom (subscription lost), left, and right; declaration of property in village of Poei; all names of persons lost.

HOUSEHOLD NO.: 145-Ly-1
*Source: *P.Brux.* 20 = *SB* VI 9360
Prov., Date: Lykopolis, 28/8/146
Stemma:

Declarant: Senesneus d. Sou— and Tapnoubchis, with as *kyrios* her father's
brother Ploutogenes s. Apollonios
Family members: (1) Senesneus [declarant] d. Sou— and Tapnoubchis, 40
                       (2) Senpho— d. Pore[- -] and Senesneus [declarant], 21
Free non-kin: (1) Isarous d. Sareus, ὁ[ρφαν]ὴ[ν ?], 8
Slaves: None
Verif./photo: P.Brux.inv. E 7641; Pl. V.
Discussion: Complete except for minor damage.

HOUSEHOLD NO.: 145-Me-1
*Source: *BGU* III 777 (cf. *BL* 1.66)
Prov., Date: Memphis, 145/6
Declarant: Areios
Family members: (1) Areios [declarant], 14
Free non-kin, slaves: None preserved
Verif./photo: Berlin, P.7486; seen 16/4/1991.
Discussion: Broken at top (with declarant's full identity) and bottom (with any
other persons included; but there were probably none, to judge form line 1).
Declarant is a renter in house of Isidoros s. Anoubion alias Pankrates. Cf.
ZPE 75 (1988) 255–56: Is Areios the brother of Melas in 173-Me-1 (9 years
younger than Melas)?

HOUSEHOLD NO.: 145-Oa-1
*Source: *PSI* X 1111
Prov., Date: Trimeithis (Great Oasis), 145/6
Stemma:

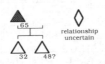

Declarant: Petosiris s. Haryotes (s. Horos) and Sen[os?]iris,
Family members: (1) Petosiris [declarant] s. Haryotes and Sen[os?]iris, gs.
                       Horos, 65
                       (2) Haryotes s. Petosiris and Tapsais, 32
                       (3) Psais s. Petosiris and Tapsais, brother of Haryotes
                       [no.2], 48 (or 28?)

(4) NN s./d. Petosiris, age lost
Free non-kin, slaves: None preserved
Verif./photo: Florence, Biblioteca Laurenziana; seen 25/5/1989.
Discussion: Broken at bottom. No.4 probably not a child of declarant because patronymic given again; any women are lost. For provenance, cf. Calderini-Daris, *Dizionario* s.v. P. J. Sijpesteijn (*per litt.*) reads the age of no. 3 as κη, which would give a normal order.

HOUSEHOLD NO.: 145-Ox-1
*Source: *P.Lond.* inv. 2187 (*Cd'E*, forthcoming)
Prov., Date: Oxyrhynchos, 146/7
Stemma:

Declarant: NN (name lost)
Family members: (1) NN [declarant, male], age lost
                        (2) Alexandra, freedwoman of Heronas, wife of NN [declarant], age lost
                        (3) Dionysia d. NN [declarant] and Alexandra [no.2], 3
Free non-kin, slaves: None
Verif./photo: London, inv. 2187; seen 3/4/1991.
Discussion: Broken at top, with loss only of the first person listed, evidently the declarant, and possibly other males. Dionysia is said to be a twin, but the other child is not listed in the surviving part. It is likely that this was a male and included in the missing portion.

HOUSEHOLD NO.: 145-Ox-2
*Source: *P.Oxy.* I 171 (*P.Oxy.* II, p. 208)
Prov., Date: Oxyrhynchos, *ca* 146
Stemma:

Declarant: Hierax s. Hakoris (s. M...) and Dionysia (d. Hierax), ἀπὸ γυμνασίου
Family members: (1) Hierax [declarant] s. Hakoris (s. M...) and Dionysia (d. Hierax), ἀπὸ γυμνασίου, 66
                        (2) Hierax s. Hierax [declarant] and Alexandra, freedwoman, age lost
                        (3) Theon, relationship unknown (son?), age lost
Free non-kin, slaves: None preserved
Verif./photo: Cambridge, Add.Ms. 4045; photograph.
Discussion: Broken at right with small losses; broken off at bottom, with loss of unknown number of family members.

HOUSEHOLD NO.: 145-Ox-3
***Source:** P.Lond.* inv. 2194 (*Cd'E*, forthcoming)
Prov., Date: Talao (Oxyrhynchite), 20/2/147
Stemma:

Declarant: Dikaiogenes s. Philon and Senherakleia (d. Dikaiogenes)
Family members: (1) Dikaiogenes [declarant] s. Philon and Senherakleia (d.
                Dikaiogenes), ἐπὶ ξένης, 22
Free non-kin: (1) Sarapion alias Eutyches, freedman, 19
Slaves: None
Verif./photo: London, inv. 2194; seen 3/4/1991.
Discussion: Virtually complete; no persons are lost. The property is said to belong
to the declarant's parents, who are however not listed.

HOUSEHOLD NO.: 145-Pr-1
***Source:** P.Lond.* II 324.25–29 (p. 63)
Prov., Date: Prosopite, original date omitted
Stemma:

Declarant: Not stated
Family members: (1) Chentmouphis s. Anikos (s. Pathermouthis) and
                Thaseis (d. Herpaesis), 52 (should be 59, cf.
                131-Pr-1)
            (2) Anikos s. Chentmouphis [declarant] and Demetrous
                (d. Soterichos), 20
            (3) Thamistis d. Chentmouphis [declarant] and Demetrous
                (d. Soterichos), sister of Anikos [no.2], 24
Free non-kin, slaves: None
Verif./photo: London, BL inv. 324; microfilm; original seen 2/4/1991.
Discussion: Copy of a copied extract of a declaration, preceded by another (131-
Pr-1); complete but with scattered damage. The date of the cover letter is
24/3/161. As the editor's note points out, Thamistis is said in the two extracts
to be the full sister of Anikos, thus daughter of Chentmouphis (Thenthnoupis
in 131-Pr-1), but in the cover letter Anikos says she is his sister on the
mother's side, and ἀπάτωρ. In Chentmouphis' age, it seems most likely that
νβ is a copyist's misreading of νθ, since beta and theta can look much alike.

HOUSEHOLD NO.: 159-Ar-1
***Source:** BGU* I 55 ii.1–10 (cf. *BL* 1.12, 3.8)#

Prov., Date: Arsinoe, 24/6/161
Stemma:

Declarant: [Mysthes s. Philon]
Family members: (1) Mysthes [declarant] s. Philon, age lost
                         (2) Mysthes alias Ninnos, s. Mysthes [declarant] and
                             Herais (d. Ammonios, *katoikos*), 33
                         (3) Zosime freedwoman of Ammonarion d. Marion (s.
                             Geoum( )), wife of Mysthes [no.2], 22
                         (4) Ammonios, s. Mysthes [no.2] and Zosime [no.3], 5
                         (5) Didymos, s. Mysthes [no.2] and Zosime [no.3], 4
Free non-kin, slaves: None
Verif./photo: Berlin, P.6914, col. ii; seen 16/4/1991.
Discussion: Column i very fragmentary; it is probably not part of the declaration in
col. ii. Part of the information about nos. 1–2 derives from ii.11–22 (173-Ar-
3). These are extracts from declarations, not originals. The copyist seems not
to have understood his original in places.

HOUSEHOLD NO.: 159-Ar-2
Source: *BGU* I 57 i (cf. *BL* 1.13)#
Prov., Date: Arsinoe, 160/1
Declarants: Thaisarion and Herois dd. Melanas (s. Tryphon), with *kyrios* kinsman
Pammenes s. Sokrates
Family members, free non-kin, slaves: None
Verif./photo: Berlin, P.6938 recto i; seen 12/4/1991.
Discussion: Some damage at left and right, part of date lost at bottom. Declaration
by metropolitan women of village property in Nilopolis of which they own
part-shares and in which no one is registered. Heading is missing: This may
be a copy or a declaration on which the recipient's name was never written.

HOUSEHOLD NO.: 159-Ar-3
Source: *BGU* I 57 ii (cf. *BL* 1.13)
Prov., Date: Arsinoe, 160/1 (?)
Declarant: Sokrates s. Pammenes
Family members, free non-kin, slaves: None
Verif./photo: Berlin, P.6938 recto ii; seen 12/4/1991.
Discussion: Only a small part of left side of declaration preserved. Sokrates is
declaring property in Nilopolis belonging to a woman of whom he is
phrontistes (line 6), with no mention of persons.

HOUSEHOLD NO.: 159-Ar-4
*Source: *P.Berl.Leihg.* I 17#

Prov., Date: Arsinoe, 11/5/161
Stemma:

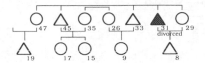

slaves
of declarant's ex-wife

Declarant: Herodes s. Philadelphos (s. Herodes) and Thermoutharion (sister of his
father)

Family members:
    (1) Herodes [declarant] s. Philadelphos (s. Herodes) and
        Thermoutharion, 31
    (2) Sarapion alias Hermias, s. Herodes [declarant] and
        Zoidous (d. Philadelphos) (full sister of declarant),
        his divorced wife, 8
    (3) Ischyrion s. Philadelphos (s. Herodes) and
        Thermoutharion, brother of Herodes [declarant], 45
    (4) Aphrodisios s. Philadelphos (s. Herodes) and
        Thermoutharion, brother of Herodes [declarant], 33
    (5) Thermoutharion d. Philadelphos (s. Herodes) and
        Thermoutharion, sister of Herodes [declarant], 47
    (6) Zoidous d. Philadelphos (s. Herodes) and
        Thermoutharion, sister and divorced wife of
        Herodes [declarant], 29
    (7) Demarion d. Diodoros (s. Polydeukes) and Sambous,
        wife of Ischyrion [no.3], 35
    (8) Helene d. Ischyrion [no.3] and Demarion [no.7], 17
    (9) Didyme d. Ischyrion [no.3] and Demarion [no.7], 15
    (10) Demarion d. Diodoros (s. Polydeukes) and Sambous,
        wife of Aphrodisios [no.4], 26
    (11) Helene d. Aphrodisios [no.4] and Demarion [no.10], 9
    (12) Herodes s. Petermouthis (s. Heron) and
        Thermoutharion [no. 5] (d. Philadelphos), 19

Free non-kin: None

Slaves:
    (1) Palaistrike, slave of Sarapion [no.2], bought from
        Apollonarion d. Chairemon (s. Heron), 33
    (2) Ammonios male offspring of Palaistrike [no.1], slave of
        Sarapion [no.2], bought from Apollonarion d.
        Chairemon (s. Heron), 5

Verif./photo: Berlin inv. 11540 verso; seen 15/4/1991.

Discussion: Copy of a declaration. Complete. Herodes is declaring the inhabitants
of a house belonging to two boys whose guardian he is, who do not live
there. The presence of two homonymous sisters, wives of two brothers, with
each couple having a daughter Helene, is noteworthy.

HOUSEHOLD NO.: 159-Ar-5
*Source: *P.Ryl.* II 111 (cf. *BL* 3.160; *BASP* 28 [1991] 129–32)
Prov., Date: Arsinoe, 161

Stemma:

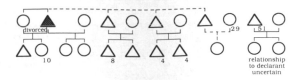

slaves

belonging to declarant 9   belonging to Herois (?)

Declarant: NN
Family members:

(1) NN [declarant], age lost
(2) NN, full sister and divorced wife of declarant, age lost
(3) NN, d. NN [no.1] and NN [no.2], age lost
(4) Didymarion, d. NN [no.1] NN [no.2], 10
(5) NN, wife of NN [declarant], age lost
(6) Tryphaina, d. NN [no.1] and NN [no.5], age lost
(7) NN, d. NN [no.1] and NN [no.5], age lost
(8) NN (male), age lost
(9) NN, wife of NN [no.8], age lost
(10) NN, s. (?) of NN [no.8] and NN [no.9], 8
(11) Dioskoros s. NN [no.8] and NN [no.9], age lost
(12) NN (male), age lost
(13) NN, wife of NN [no.12], age lost
(14) NN, s. NN [no.12] and NN [no.13], 4
(15) NN, s. NN [no.12] and NN [no.13], 4
(16) Heron s. Heron, age lost
(17) —ra, 29
(18) Tasoucharion, age lost
(19) NN (male), 51
(20) NN, wife of NN (no.19), age lost
(21) NN, d. NN (no.19) and NN (no.20), age lost
(22) NN, d. NN (no.19) and NN (no.20), age lost

Free non-kin: None
Slaves:

(1) Nikephoros surnamed Harpalos, slave of declarant, age lost
(2) NN, slave of declarant, age lost
(3) Isiakos alias Amoules, slave of declarant, age lost
(4) Eudaimonis, slave of declarant, 9
(5) Kalokairos, slave of Herois d. Harpokration, age lost

Verif./photo: Manchester, John Rylands Library; photograph.

Discussion: Left side lost, with a loss probably of *ca* 60 letters per line; broken at top. Much is uncertain; some of the families listed could be renters, and it is not entirely clear that all those classified here as slaves are in fact such. See *BASP* 28 (1991) 198–32 for a detailed argument about the reconstruction of the declaration.

HOUSEHOLD NO.: 159-Ar-6
*Source: *SB* X 10219 (*Aegyptus* 46 [1966] 21 no.10) (cf. *BL* 7.216, *BASP* 30 [1993] 49–54)
Prov., Date: Arsinoe, 161
Stemma:

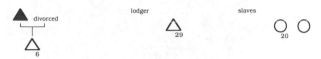

Declarant: Gaius Valerius Apollinarios discharged veteran of Leg. II on behalf of a ward
Family members: (1) Gaius Valerius Apollinarios [declarant], discharged veteran of Leg. II, age lost (at least 40)
(2) Gaius Valerius Capito s. Apollinarios [declarant] and NN (divorced wife of declarant), 6
Free non-kin: (1) Ptolemaios s. Diogenes (s. NN) and Syra (d. Ptolemaios), formerly known as Gaius Valerius Capito, 29
Slaves: (1) Helike, slave of Apollinarios [declarant], age lost
(2) Nike, slave of Apollinarios [declarant], 20
Verif./photo: P.bibl.Univ.Giss.inv. 301; photograph.
Discussion: Broken at left and right, complete at top and bottom. It appears that the non-kin Ptolemaios was first registered in the previous census as Ptolemaios son of M. Anthestius NN, then entered military service as C. Valerius Capito, then was prematurely mustered out and is now known by a purely peregrine name.

HOUSEHOLD NO.: 159-Ar-7
*Source: *BGU* I 54 (cf. *BL* 1.12)#
Prov., Date: Karanis (Arsinoite), 7/7/161
Stemma:

Declarant: Ammonios s. Harpagathos (s. Heras) and Segathis
Family members: (1) Ammonios [declarant] s. Harpagathos (s. Heras) and Segathis, 36
(2) Thaisarion d. Antonios, wife of Ammonios [declarant], 29
(3) Seutharion d. Ammonios [declarant] and Thaisarion [no.2], 9
Free non-kin, slaves: None
Verif./photo: Berlin, P.6881; seen 12/4/1991.
Discussion: Complete. Thaisarion owns the house.

HOUSEHOLD NO.: 159-Ar-8
*Source: *BGU* I 58 (cf. *BL* 1.13; *BASP* 29 [1992] 101–03)
Prov., Date: Karanis (Arsinoite), 161
Stemma:

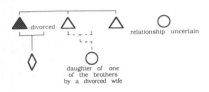

Declarant: Pasoxis s. Pasoxis (s. —sis) and Thi[
Family members: (1) Pasoxis [declarant] s. Pasoxis (s. —sis) and Thi[,
                age lost
             (2) NN s. Pasoxis (s. —sis) and Thi[, brother of Pasoxis
                [declarant], age lost
             (3) Harpalos s. Pasoxis (s. —sis) and Thi[, brother of
                Pasoxis [declarant], age lost
             (4) Thermouthas d. Pt[(s. NN) and Her[, age lost
             (5) NN s./d. Pasoxis [declarant] and Tasoucharion (d.
                NN and Taorsenouphis?), divorced wife of Pasoxis,
                age lost
             (6) Thaisas d. NN (no. 2 or no.3) and NN (d. Noostis),
                divorced wife, age lost
Free non-kin, slaves: None
Verif./photo: Berlin, P.6939; seen 15/4/1991.
Discussion: Broken at right with substantial loss. There were at least two or three
    more persons listed, but only bits of their identification survive, insufficient
    for restoration or description.

HOUSEHOLD NO.: 159-Ar-9
*Source: *BGU* I 154 (cf. *BL* 1.22, 3.8)#
Prov., Date: Karanis (Arsinoite), 17/7/161
Stemma:

Declarant: Herais d. Satabous (s. Phanomgeus) and Tanesneus (d. Pnepheros),
    with *kyrios* her father Satabous
Family members: (1) Herais [declarant] d. Satabous (s. Phanomgeus) and
                Tanesneus (d. Pnepheros), 16
             (2) Satabous s. Phanomgeus (s. Phanomgeus) and Heras
                (d. Esouris), father of Herais [declarant], 44
             (3) Tanesneus d. Pnepheros (s. Petesouchos) and
                Tasoucharion, mother of Herais [declarant], 39

(4) Tasoucharion d. Satabous [no.2] and Tanesneus [no.3],
sister of Herais [declarant], 9

Free non-kin, slaves: None

Verif./photo: Berlin, P.6927; seen 12/4/1991.

Discussion: Damaged at right after line 16. There is no indication why Herais rather than one of her parents is the owner of the half-house in which they live. The declaration also reports two unoccupied houses owned by Tanesneus.

HOUSEHOLD NO.: 159-Ar-10

***Source:** BGU* II 524 (cf. *BL* 1.49; *BASP* 29 [1992] 111–12)

Prov., Date: Karanis (Arsinoite), 160/1

Stemma:

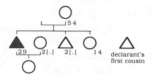

Declarant: Sisois s. Petheus (s. Akousilaos) and Thermouthis (d. —is)

Family members: (1) Sisois [declarant] s. Petheus (s. Akousilaos) and Thermouthis (d. —is), 29

(2) Thermouthis d. Pasoknopaios, wife of Sisois [declarant], 2[.]

(3) Thermouth[d. Sisois [declarant] and Thermouthis [no.2], age lost

(4) Besas s. Petheus (s. Akousilaos) and Thermouthis (d. —is), brother of Sisois [declarant], 2[.]

(5) Teonchonsis (?) d. Petheus (s. Akousilaos) and Thermouthis (d. —is), sister of Sisois [declarant], 14

(6) Sisois s. Onnophris and —this (d. Apollonios), cousin (i.e., son of paternal uncle) of Sisois [declarant], age lost

(7) Thermouthis d. —is, mother of Sisois [declarant], 54

Free non-kin, slaves: None

Verif./photo: Berlin, P.7402; seen 16/4/1991.

Discussion: Complete but with minor damage throughout.

HOUSEHOLD NO.: 159-Ar-11

***Source:** P.Lond.* II 182b (p. 62) (cf. *BASP* 27 [1990] 6–7; *BASP* 30 [1993] 45)

Prov., Date: Karanis (Arsinoite), 160/1

Stemma:

Declarant: Petheus s. Isidoros (s. Petheus) and Taimouthes, 73
Family members: (1) Petheus [declarant] s. Isidoros (s. Petheus) and
                          Taimouthes, 73
                      (2) Isidoros s. Petheus [declarant] and Dideis [no.4], 40
                      (3) Ninnaros alias Ptolemaios s. Isidoros [no.2] and
                          Taonnophris [no.5], 2
                      (4) Dideis d. Isidoros, sister and wife of Petheus
                          [declarant], age lost
                      (5) Taonnophris d. Petheus [declarant] and Dideis [no.4],
                          sister and wife of Isidoros [no.2], age lost
Free non-kin, slaves: None preserved
Verif./photo: London, British Library, BL inv. 182b; microfilm; original seen
    2/4/1991.
Discussion: Damaged at bottom. An extract from the declaration, copied sometime
    before 175. One or more daughters of Isidoros and Taonnophris could be lost
    at the bottom.

HOUSEHOLD NO.: 159-Ar-12
Source: *SB* VI 9554,5 (cf. *BL* 8.350)
Prov., Date: Karanis (Arsinoite), 7–8/161
Declarant: NN alias —nis (female)
Family members, free non-kin, slaves: None
Verif./photo: Michigan, inv. 4731b; seen 9/11/1990.
Discussion: Broken at top and left. Declaration of an unoccupied house.

HOUSEHOLD NO.: 159-Ar-13
*Source: *BGU* I 90 (cf. *BL* 1.17) = I 224 (cf. *BL* 1.27) = I 225 (cf. *BL* 1.27) = II
    410 = II 537 = *P.Grenf.* II 55 (cf. *Aegyptus* 3, 341 f.)
Prov., Date: Soknopaiou Nesos (Arsinoite), 28/7/161
Stemma:

Declarant: Hatres s. Satabous (s. Panephremmis) and Segathis
Family members: (1) Hatres [declarant] s. Satabous (s. Panephremmis) and
                          Segathis, 25
                      (2) Isarion *apator*, d. Tanephremmis (d. Panomieus), wife
                          of Hatres [declarant], 13

(3) Tapetsiris d. Stotoetis (s. Panephremmis) and
Tapetsiris, 12
Free non-kin, slaves: None
Verif./photo: Berlin, P.7024, P.7291, P.6883, P.7828, P.7185; Oxford, Bodleian
MS Gr. class. e.69 (P); all Berlin copies seen 16/4/1991 except P.7828;
P.6883 seen in photograph.
Discussion: Six copies of the same declaration (I 90 and II 537 to *komogram-*
mateus, I 224 and II 410 to *strategos*, I 225 to *laographoi*, *P.Grenf.* II 55 to
basilikos grammateus). Tapetsiris is not identified by any term of relation-
ship, but neither is she called a renter. She could be a first cousin of Hatres.

HOUSEHOLD NO.: 159-Ar-14
*Source: *P.Berl.Leihg.* I 16A#
Prov., Date: Theadelphia (Arsinoite), 27/5/161
Declarant: Apollos
Family members: (1) Apollos [declarant], 3[.] or 4[.]
Free non-kin, slaves: None
Verif./photo: Berlin inv. 11659, col. i; seen 15/4/1991.
Discussion: Broken at top, taking full identification of declarant. Apollos was the
only member of the household.

HOUSEHOLD NO.: 159-Ar-15
*Source: *P.Berl.Leihg.* I 16B
Prov., Date: Theadelphia (Arsinoite), 25/7/161
Declarant: Panephremmis s. Heron (s. Heron) and Tapheus
Family members: (1) Panephremmis [declarant] s. Heron (s. Heron) and
Tapheus, 59
Free non-kin, slaves: None
Verif./photo: Berlin inv. 11659, col. ii; seen 15/4/1991.
Discussion: Complete. The declarant records that he actually lives in a συνοικία
οὐσιακή in Apias.

HOUSEHOLD NO.: 159-Ar-16
*Source: *P.Berl.Leihg.* I 16C = *BullAinShams* 1 (1985) 40–42, no.2 (*SB* XVIII
13289) (cf. *BL* 8.62)
Prov., Date: Theadelphia (Arsinoite), 31/7/161
Declarant: Horion *apator* s. Tapheus
Family members: (1) Horos [declarant] *apator* s. Tapheus, 33
Free non-kin, slaves: None
Verif./photo: Berlin inv. 11659, col. iii (seen 15/4/1991); Cairo, SR 3049/73
(photograph; original not found 3/4/1993).
Discussion: Virtually complete in both Berlin and Cairo copies. It is notable that
the declarant refers to himself once as Horion, once as Horos. He actually
lives in a συνοικία οὐσιακή in the Arsinoite village of Pelousion.

HOUSEHOLD NO.: 159-Ar-17
*Source: *P.Berl.Leihg.* I 16D (cf. *BL* 8.62)
Prov., Date: Theadelphia (Arsinoite), 31/7/161
Declarant: Apynchis the elder, s. Orseus (s. Apynchis) and Thenapynchis

Family members: (1) Apynchis the elder [declarant], s. Orseus (s.
Apynchis) and Thenapynchis, 27
Free non-kin, slaves: None
Verif./photo: Berlin inv. 11659, col. iv; seen 15/4/1991.
Discussion: Complete. The declarant records that he actually lives in the epoikion
of Theon at Ptolemais Drymou.

HOUSEHOLD NO.: 159-Ar-18
Source: *P.Berl.Leihg.* I 16E
Prov., Date: Theadelphia (Arsinoite), 4/8/161
Declarant: Harphaesis s. Osis (s. Harphaesis) and ..ais
Family members: No names preserved
Free non-kin, slaves: None preserved
Verif./photo: Berlin inv. 11659, col. v; seen 15/4/1991.
Discussion: Large middle section missing with name(s) of person(s) declared,
probably only Harphaesis, who no doubt lives elsewhere.

HOUSEHOLD NO.: 159-Ar-19
*Source: *BGU* XI 2089 = *BullAinShams* 1 (1985) 46–50, nos. 5–6# (*SB* XVIII
13294)
Prov., Date: Arsinoite, 25/6–24/7/161
Declarant: Taseis d. Mysthes (s. Ision), with *kyrios* Horion s. Kastor
Family members: (1) Taseis [declarant] d. Mysthes (s. Ision), 44
Free non-kin, slaves: None
Verif./photo: W. Berlin, P.21631 (seen 11/4/1991); Cairo, SR 3049/72 and
3049/74 (photograph; originals seen 3/4/1993).
Discussion: Berlin: complete at left and bottom, damaged at top and at right.
Cairo: Two copies, one addressed to the *strategos* (complete), the other to
the *basilikos grammateus* (damaged throughout). Omar gives a revised ver-
sion of *BGU* XI 2089.2–6 at *BullAinShams* 1 (1985) 50.

HOUSEHOLD NO.: 159-Ar-20
*Source: *P.Lond.* III 843 (p. 28) (cf. *BL* 1.274, 3.94; *BASP* 28 [1991] 125)
Prov., Date: Arsinoite (Soknopaiou Nesos?), 13/1/161
Stemma:

Declarant: NN
Family members: (1) NN [declarant], 41
(2) Thases d. Pakysis (s. Orsenouphis), wife of NN
[declarant], 35
(3) Thases, d. NN [declarant] and Thases [no.2], 12
(4) Stotoetis d. NN [declarant] and Thases [no.2], 8
Free non-kin, slaves: None
Verif./photo: London, British Library, inv. 843; seen 2/4/1991.

Discussion: Only the bottom survives, but apparently no one is lost. Line 11 contains the personal name Thenosiris with the age 9, but it is not clear what the relationship to the preceding is. The declarant's age is not quite certain.

HOUSEHOLD NO.: 159-Ar-21
*Source: *P.Tebt.* II 481, ii (see *Aegyptus* 72 [1992] 67–71)
Prov., Date: Talei (Arsinoite), 25/4/161
Stemma:

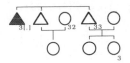

Declarant: Sansneus s. NN (s. Patunis) and NN (d. Sansneus), public farmer
Family members: (1) Sansneus [declarant] s. NN (s. Patunis) and NN (d. Sansneus), public farmer, 3[.]
      (2) Apollonios, s. NN (s. Patunis) and NN (d. Sansneus), brother of Sansneus [declarant], age lost
      (3) Sochotes, s. NN (s. Patunis) and NN (d. Sansneus), brother of Sansneus [declarant], 33
      (4) NN, wife of Apollonios [no.2], 32
      (5) Tamystha (?) d. Apollonios [no.2] and NN [no.4], age lost
      (6) NN d. Hatres and Sarapous, wife of Sochotes [no.3], age lost
      (7) NN d. Sochotes [no.3] and NN [no.6], age lost
      (8) Sarapous d. Sochotes [no.3] and NN [no.6], 3
Free non-kin, slaves: None
Verif./photo: Berkeley, P.Tebt. 481; seen 27/9/1990; photograph.
Discussion: Broken at right, otherwise complete. The age of no.7 is presumably greater than 3.

HOUSEHOLD NO.: 159-Ar-22
*Source: *P.Tebt.* II 481, i (see *Aegyptus* 72 [1992] 67–71)
Prov., Date: Talei (Arsinoite), 29/4/161
Stemma:

Declarant: Heron s. NN, public farmer
Family members: (1) Heron s. NN, public farmer, age lost
      (2) NN d. NN and Thermouthas, probably wife of declarant, age lost
Free non-kin, slaves: None preserved
Verif./photo: Berkeley, P.Tebt. 481; seen 27/9/1990; photograph.
Discussion: The ends of a few lines.

HOUSEHOLD NO.: 159-Ar-23
*Source: *BGU* XIII 2221#
Prov., Date: Soknopaiou Nesos (Arsinoite), 160/1
Declarant: Stotoetis the elder, s. Pakysis and Stotoetis (d. Onnophris), priest of the 1st tribe of Soknopaios
Family members: (1) Stotoetis the elder [declarant], s. Pakysis and Stotoetis (d. Onnophris), age lost
Free non-kin, slaves: None preserved
Verif./photo: W. Berlin, P.21751; seen 11/4/1991.
Discussion: Broken at left and below, just after listing Stotoetis; other persons are lost.

HOUSEHOLD NO.: 159-Ar-24
Source: *BGU* XIII 2222#
Prov., Date: Arsinoite, 161
Declarant: Anchopis
Family members, free non-kin, slaves: None
Verif./photo: W. Berlin, P.21910; seen 11/4/1991.
Discussion: Broken at top (taking the full identification of the declarant), minor damage at left. No persons are declared, only property belonging to Anchopis and to his daughter Thases, in which no one is registered. A Demotic docket stands on the verso.

HOUSEHOLD NO.: 159-Ar-25
*Source: *BullAinShams* 1 (1985) 42–45, nos. 3–4#
Prov., Date: Theadelphia (Arsinoite), 30/6/161
Declarant: Tephorsais d. Pabous, with *kyrios* her kinsman Kastor s. Sarapion
Family members: (1) Tephorsais [declarant] d. Pabous, 48
Free non-kin, slaves: None
Verif./photo: Cairo, SR 3049/71 and 3049/70; photographs; originals seen 3/4/1993.
Discussion: Both complete; two versions of the same declaration, one addressed to the *strategos* and the other to the *basilikos grammateus*.

HOUSEHOLD NO.: 159-Ar-26
*Source: *P.Fay.* 319.20–26 (*Aegyptus* 70 [1990] 27–31; cf. *BASP* 30 [1993] 38–40)
Prov., Date: Arsinoe, 161 (document *post* 161)
Stemma:

Declarant: NN s. or gs. Akousilaos alias Mystharion
Family members: (1) NN s. or gs. Akousilaos alias Mystharion [declarant], age lost
  (2) NN, full sister and wife of NN [declarant], age lost

(3) Sarapion alias Leontas, s. NN [declarant] and
   NN [no.2], 23
(4) NN s. NN [declarant] and NN [no.2], tailor?, age lost
(5) Herois d. NN [declarant] and NN [no.2], age lost

Free non-kin, slaves: None
Verif./photo: Cairo, JE 10850; plate in *Aegyptus* (Tav. 1); seen 3/4/93.
Discussion: Broken at right, with large loss, and torn at the bottom. This is an excerpt from the original declaration, quoted in an *epikrisis* document of unknown date. See 145-Ar-22 for the following declaration in the same document. There may have been other persons listed in the lost portions of the text.

HOUSEHOLD NO.: 159-Hm-1
*Source: *SB* VIII 9869a (*Cd'É* 39 [1964] 111–14)#
Prov., Date: Hermopolis, 28/9/160
Declarant: NN s. —emgeus
Family members: NN [declarant] s. —emgeus, 20 (?)
Free non-kin, slaves: None
Verif./photo: P.Stras.inv.gr. 35, seen 14/3/1989
Discussion: Broken at left, some damage at right and bottom. Declaration of house and one person.

HOUSEHOLD NO.: 159-Hm-2
*Source: *SB* VIII 9869b (*Cd'É* 39 [1964] 114–15)
Prov., Date: Hermopolis, 160
Stemma:

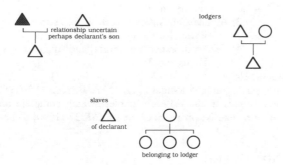

Declarant: NN
Family members: (1) NN [declarant], age lost
                        (2) Hermapollon, relative of NN [declarant], age lost
                        (3) Dios, son of NN [declarant], age lost
Free non-kin: (1) Eudaimon, age lost
                        (2) Dionysarion, wife of Eudaimon [no.1], age lost
                        (3) Boubastous, daughter of Eudaimon [no.1] and
                            Dionysarion [no.2], age lost
Slaves: (1) Nikephoros, slave of NN [declarant], age lost
                        (2) Demetria, slave of Eudaimon [non-kin no.1], age lost

    (3) Lamprous, female offspring of Demetria [slave of
      Eudaimon (non-kin no.1)], age lost
    (4) Techosous, female offspring of Demetria [slave of
      Eudaimon (non-kin no.1)], age lost
    (5) Stephanous, female offspring of Demetria [slave of
      Eudaimon (non-kin no.1)], age lost

Verif./photo: P.Stras.inv.gr. 35, seen 14/3/1989.

Discussion: Broken at right and bottom. Fragment of date at bottom indicates that
  no persons are lost. A name in line 9, Dionysios, in genitive, cannot be
  placed in syntax; Hermapollon, Boubastous, and Dionysarion are mentioned
  again in lines 20–22 in an uncertain context.

HOUSEHOLD NO.: 159-Hm-3

*Source: *P.Oslo* III 99 (cf. *BL* 3.126) = P.Mich.inv. 158A–B (*SymbOsl* 65 [1990]
  139–45) (cf. *BASP* 27 [1990] 9–10)

Prov., Date: Alabanthis (Hermopolite), 1–2/161

Stemma:

Declarant: Paesis s. Nebteichis (d. Pachomis), *hyperetes*

Family members: (1) Paesis [declarant] s. Nebteichis, *hyperetes*, 72
        (2) Horos s. Paesis [declarant] and Athenais alias Kinna
          [no.3], minor, 8
        (3) Athenais alias Kinna d. Besis (s. Harpechis), wife of
          Paesis [declarant], 57
        (4) Tereus d. Paesis [declarant] and Athenais alias
          Kinna [no.3], 40

Free non-kin, slaves: None

Verif./photo: Oslo; photograph. Michigan, inv. 158A–B, seen 11/9/1990.

Discussion: Various losses in the different copies, which complete one another.
  For the filiation of Paesis, provenance, see *BASP* 27 [1990] 9–10 (and reject
  BL 8.229).

HOUSEHOLD NO.: 159-Me-1

*Source: *P.Lond.* III 915 (p. 26) (cf. *BL* 1.274, 8.181)

Prov., Date: Memphis, 159/160

Stemma:

Declarant: Apollonios s. Harphaesis alias Hephaistion and Thermouthis, *argos*

Family members: (1) Apollonios [declarant] s. Harphaesis alias Hephaistion
        and Thermouthis, *argos*, 37

(2) Soterichos s. Apollonios [declarant] and Ptolema (d.
Archosis), 5

Free non-kin, slaves: None

Verif./photo: London, British Library, inv. 915; seen 2/4/1991.

Discussion: Complete except for minor damage. The declarant and son are renters
in a house belonging to Sarapion s. Sarapion. Apollonios describes Ptolema
as "long divorced" from him.

HOUSEHOLD NO.: 159-Me-2

*Source: *P.Rain.Cent.* 59 (cf. *BL* 8.286)

Prov., Date: Memphis, 7–8/160

Stemma: see 159-Me-1

Declarant: Herakleides s. Apollonios (s. Harphaesis alias Hephaistion) and
Taur[—] d. Hathres

Family members: (1) Herakleides [declarant] s. Apollonios (s.
Harphaesis alias Hephaistion) and Taur[—] (d.
Hathres), 14

Free non-kin, slaves: None

Verif./photo: P.Vindob. G 39999; Pl. 69.

Discussion: Complete except for small holes. Declarant is a renter in house of
Sarapion s. Sarapion (s. Hartotes). Cf. *P.Lond.* III 915, 159-Me-1, in which
the declarant's father Apollonios files his own declaration as living in the
same house. Bingen notes in his commentary this Memphite characteristic of
having children past the age of fiscal majority file separate returns even
though living in the same household.

HOUSEHOLD NO.: 159-Me-3

*Source: *P.Monac.* III 71#

Prov., Date: Memphis, 159/160

Declarant: Papontos s. Psosnaus and Artemis

Family members: (1) Papontos [declarant] s. Psosnaus and Artemis, *argos*,
age lost

Free non-kin, slaves: None preserved

Verif./photo: Munich, P.Monac.inv. 25; Abb. 20.

Discussion: Appended to a cover letter dated 4.3.164. A declaration of Papontos
and his family in the house which they rent (cf. *ZPE* 75 [1988] 255–56), it
breaks off after the start of the list of persons. The preliminaries indicate that
at least two family members were declared. A fragment contains part of the
oath.

HOUSEHOLD NO.: 159-Ox-1

Source: *P.Rein.* II 93

Prov., Date: Oxyrhynchos, 159/160

Declarant: Harpaesis s. Thonas (s. Harpaesis) and Thaesis (d. Thonis), *hierotek-
ton* of Athena Thoeris etc.

Family members, free non-kin, slaves: None listed

Verif./photo: Paris, Institut de Papyrologie, inv. 2105; photograph.

Discussion: Broken at bottom with list of any persons declared. A copy, not
original, with perhaps some abbreviation. Concerns property in the village of
Mouchinor formerly belonging to declarant's mother.

HOUSEHOLD NO.: 173-Ar-1
Source: *P.Stras.* IV 268#
Prov., Date: Philadelphia, 174/5
Declarant: Lucius Poplius (Publius) Isidoros
Family members, free non-kin, slaves: None
Verif./photo: P.Stras.inv. W.G. 349, seen 14/3/1989.
Discussion: Complete except at left. Only a declaration by Isidoros of property belonging to ? his mother and managed by him; no persons declared.

HOUSEHOLD NO.: 173-Ar-2
*Source: *P.Flor.* III 301 (cf. *BL* 3.57)
Prov., Date: Soknopaiou Nesos, 29/8/175
Stemma:

Declarant: Mesoeris s. Tesenouphis (s. Satabous?) and Segathis (d. Tesenouphis), priest of the 3rd tribe of Soknopaios
Family members: (1) Mesoeris [declarant] s. Tesenouphis (s. Satabous?) and Segathis (d. Tesenouphis), priest, 22
　　　　　　　　(2) Satabous younger, son of Mesoeris [declarant] and his divorced wife Stotoetis d. Stotoetis (his sister on mother's side, age 26), age lost
　　　　　　　　(3) Tesenouphis (?), son of Mesoeris [declarant] and his divorced wife Stotoetis d. Stotoetis, age lost
　　　　　　　　(4) Tesenouphis (?? younger), son of Mesoeris [declarant] and his divorced wife Stotoetis d. Stotoetis, age lost
Free non-kin, slaves: None
Verif./photo: Florence, Biblioteca Laurenziana; seen 25/5/1989.
Discussion: Complete except at left and some losses at lower right, affecting mainly the list of the children. This listing is somewhat uncertain, since declarant apparently botched the formula (cf. 11n.) and most of information about the children is damaged. Tesenouphis can be masculine or feminine.

HOUSEHOLD NO.: 173-Ar-3
*Source: *BGU* I 55 ii.11–22 (cf. *BL* 1.12–13, 3.8, 4.3)#
Prov., Date: Arsinoe, 25/8/175
Stemma:

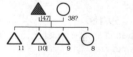

Declarant: Mysthes alias Ninnos s. Mysthes (s. Philon) and Herais (d. Ammonios, *katoikos*)

Family members: (1) Mysthes alias Ninnos [declarant] s. Mysthes (s.
                      Philon) and Herais (d. Ammonios, *katoikos*), [47]
                      (2) Zosime freedwoman of Ammonarion d. Marion, 38
                      (3) NN, s. Mysthes [declarant] and Zosime [no.2], 11
                      (4) Dioskoros s. Mysthes [declarant] and Zosime
                      [no.2], [10]
                      (5) NN, s. Mysthes [declarant] and Zosime [no.2], 9
                      (6) Isidora d. Mysthes [declarant] and Zosime [no.2], 8
Free non-kin, slaves: None
Verif./photo: Berlin, P.6914; seen 16/4/1991.
Discussion: Broken at right with some loss. A copy. The editor restores Mysthes'
   age as 59, but he was 33 in the previous census (lines 1–10, 159-Ar-1).
   Zosime was 22 in that one; that number or 38 here must be in error. In that
   declaration sons aged 5 and 4 are declared; if still alive now, they are no
   longer living at home.

HOUSEHOLD NO.: 173-Ar-4
Source: *BGU* I 119 (cf. *BL* 1.21)
Prov., Date: Arsinoe, 26/8/175
Declarant: NN alias Ammonios, tax-exempt *hieronikes*
Family members, Free non-kin, Slaves: None
Verif./photo: Berlin, P.1351; seen 15/4/1991.
Discussion: Broken at top and left, with loss of most information. This was a
   declaration of part of a house belonging to the declarant in which no one was
   registered.

HOUSEHOLD NO.: 173-Ar-5
*Source: *BGU* I 123 (cf. *BL* 2.2.14, 3.8)#
Prov., Date: Arsinoe, 175
Declarant: Tamystha d. Theon (s. Demetrios) with *kyrios* her kinsman —onios s.
   Theon
Family members: (1) Demetrios s. NN (s. Dionysios) and NN, *idiotes*,
                      age lost
Free non-kin, slaves: None
Verif./photo: Berlin, P.1338; seen 16/4/1991.
Discussion: Broken at left, right, and bottom. Declaration of a single renter of
   property belonging to the declarant.

HOUSEHOLD NO.: 173-Ar-6
Source: *BGU* I 127
Prov., Date: Arsinoe, 23/8/175
Declarant: Name lost
Family members, free non-kin, slaves: None preserved
Verif./photo: Berlin, P.1339; seen 16/4/1991.
Discussion: A fragment from the bottom of a declaration, with loss at upper right.

HOUSEHOLD NO.: 173-Ar-7
*Source: *BGU* I 298
Prov., Date: Arsinoes Kome (Arsinoite), 175

Stemma:

Declarant: Dionysios s. Chairemon and Tapheros
Family members: (1) Dionysios [declarant] s. Chairemon and Tapheros, 48
                (2) Ammon[arion?] d. Dionysios [declarant] and ?,
                age lost
Free non-kin, slaves: None preserved
Verif./photo: Berlin, P.1353; seen 15/4/1991.
Discussion: Broken at bottom with loss of any persons other than these two. We do not know what to make of the curious μη(τρὸς) μὴ γραπ[τῆς ? of Ammon[arion].

HOUSEHOLD NO.: 173-Ar-8
***Source:** BGU I 59 (cf. BL 1.13)
Prov., Date: Karanis (Arsinoite), 175
Stemma:

Declarant: Diodora d. NN (s. Petheus) and NN, through *phrontistes*
Family members: (1) Diodora [declarant] d. NN (s. Petheus) and NN, 6[.]
                (2) Tasoucharion d. NN, age lost
Free non-kin, slaves: None
Verif./photo: Berlin, P.6940; seen 15/4/1991.
Discussion: Complete at top, bottom, and left, but about two thirds are lost at right. Probably at least two persons were declared between Diodora and Tasoucharion; Ptolla in line 20 may be the patronymic of one. It is not certain that Tasoucharion was a family member.

HOUSEHOLD NO.: 173-Ar-9
***Source:** BGU II 447 = I 26 (cf. BL 1.46, 3.13, 8.27; BASP 29 [1992] 111)
Prov., Date: Karanis (Arsinoite), 26/11/174
Stemma:

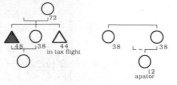

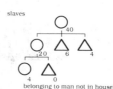

Declarant: Ptollas s. Sabeinos (s. Ptolemaios) and Vettia (d. Vettius)
Family members: (1) Ptollas [declarant] s. Sabeinos (s. Ptolemaios) and
 Vettia (d. Vettius), 48
 (2) Harpokras s. Sabeinos (s. Ptolemaios) and Vettia (d.
 Vettius), brother of Ptollas [declarant], ἐν
 ἀναχωρήσι, 44
 (3) Ptolemais d. Sabeinos (s. Ptolemaios) and Vettia (d.
 Vettius), sister and wife of Ptollas [declarant], 38
 (4) Vettia d. Ptollas [declarant] and Ptolemais [no.3],
 age lost
 (5) Vettia d. Vettius, mother of Ptollas [declarant], 72
 (6) Soeris d. Ptolemaios (s. Pnepheros) and NN (d.
 Ptolemaios), 38
 (7) Taos d. Ptolemaios (s. Pnepheros) and NN (d.
 Ptolemaios), 38
 (8) Xanaris *apator* d. Taos [no.7], 12
Free non-kin: (1) Sarapias, freedwoman of Valerius Aphrodisios, soldier
 of Cohors I Eq. (brother of nos. 6 and 7), 30 (?)
Slaves: (1) Kopr[eia], slave of Sempronius Herminos (eques Alae
 Maur.), 40
 (2) Sarapias female offspring of Kopr[eia] [no.1], 20
 (3) Dioskoros offspring of Kopr[eia] [no.1], 6
 (4) Polydeukes nicknamed Eros, offspring of Kopr[eia], 4
 (5) Didyme, offspring of Sarapias [no.2], 4
 (6) Kastor offspring of Sarapias [no.2], 2 months
Verif./photo: Berlin, P.6906; seen 12/4/1991.
Discussion: Complete but with numerous small lacunae. It seems possible that
either Valerius Aphrodisios, the patron of Sarapias the freedwoman, or
Sempronius Herminos (owner of the slaves) was the husband as well as the
brother of Taos and hence the actual father of Xanaris [no.8]; since as a
soldier they could not marry, she would be officially fatherless (cf. Youtie,
Hommages Préaux). Soeris and Taos are stated to be twins; they are called
kin, συγγενεῖς, of the declarant. They cannot be the declarant's half-sisters,
as neither parent is identical.

HOUSEHOLD NO.: 173-Ar-10
*Source: *SB* VI 9573 (*Eos* 48.3 [1957] 155)#
Prov., Date: Karanis (Arsinoite)
Stemma:

Declarant: Petronia Gaia
Family members: (1) Petronia Gaia [declarant], age lost
 (2) Petronia Gemella, sister of Petronia Gaia [declarant],
 age lost
Free non-kin, slaves: None
Verif./photo: Berlin, former P.Ibscher inv. 10; now P.18018; seen 16/4/1991.

Discussion: Complete except at bottom, where broken before details of persons given. Petronia Gaia calls herself acting without *kyrios* under Roman law. The declaration included children, number and ages unknown.

HOUSEHOLD NO.: 173-Ar-11
*Source: *BGU* I 302 (cf. *BL* 3.10; *BASP* 29 [1992] 108–10)
Prov., Date: Arsinoite, 175
Stemma:

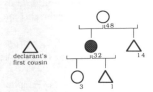

Declarant: Methe d. Panameus (s. Aurelius) and Thaumastes with *kyrios* kinsman
]phis s. Aurelius
Family members: (1) Methe [declarant] d. Panameus (s. Aurelius) and
Thaumastes (d. Orseus), 32
(2) The[d. NN and Methe [declarant], 3
(3) Nouma s. Tithoes (s. Panameus) and Methe
[declarant], 1
(4) Her[s. NN and Thaumastes [no.5], half-brother of
Methe [declarant], 14
(5) Thaumastes d. Orseus and NN, mother of Methe
[declarant] and of Her[[no.4], 48
(6)]phis s. Aurelius (s. Orseus) and Tephorsais, nephew
of Thaumastes, age lost
Free non-kin, slaves: None
Verif./photo: Berlin, P.1834; seen 12/4/1991.
Discussion: Broken at right and damaged throughout. See *BASP* 29 (1992) 108–10
for the reconstruction of the family.

HOUSEHOLD NO.: 173-Ar-12
Source: *BGU* XIII 2223 (cf. *BL* 8.55)
Prov., Date: Arsinoe, 24–29/8/175
Declarant: Sarapion, *phrontistes*, on behalf of Isidora alias Harpokratiaina, d. C.
Iulius Gemellus, *aste*
Family members, free non-kin, slaves: None declared
Verif./photo: W. Berlin, P.25138; Pl. VI.
Discussion: Broken at top, minor damage at right. This is only a declaration of
property in which no one is registered, since the declarant has already
reported herself in another document. Isidora is an *aste*, citizen of one of the
Greek cities.

HOUSEHOLD NO.: 173-Ar-13
*Source: *BGU* XIII 2224, i = *ZPE* 9 (1972) 245–51, i (cf. *BL* 8.55)
Prov., Date: Arsinoe, 175
Declarant: Sarapion s. Deios (s. NN) and Isarous

Family members: (1) Sarapion [declarant] s. Deios (s. NN) and Isarous,
idiotes, age lost
Free non-kin, slaves: None preserved
Verif./photo: W. Berlin, P.21879, frag. a; seen 11/4/1991.
Discussion: Broken at bottom and at right; breaks just after giving name of
declarant as a person registered. Col. 65 of a *tomos synkollesimos*.

HOUSEHOLD NO.: 173-Ar-14
Source: *BGU* XIII 2224, ii (cf. *BL* 7.25) = *ZPE* 9 (1972) 245–51, ii
Prov., Date: Arsinoe, 175
Declarant: Pasion alias NN, *katoikos*, on behalf of two freedmen who are his
charges: Neilos freedman of NN alias Nikandros, Antinoite, and Sarapias
freedwoman of Mysthas alias NN (s. Mystharion)
Family members, free non-kin, slaves: None declared
Verif./photo: W. Berlin, P.21879, frag. b; seen 11/4/1991.
Discussion: Broken at right and bottom; another declaration reported the freed-
women, this one just concerning their property. Col. 66 of a *tomos synkollesimos*.

HOUSEHOLD NO.: 173-Ar-15
***Source:** *SB* XVI 12288, i.1–10 (reed. R. S. Bagnall-K. A. Worp, *Archiv für
Papyrusforschung* 39 [1994], forthcoming)
Prov., Date: Arsinoe, 26/8/175
Stemma:

Declarant: Gaion s. Akousilaos
Family members: (1) Gaion [declarant], s. Akousilaos, age lost
(2) Thaubarion d. Sarapion (s. Zoilos) and Sarapias
(d. NN), wife of Gaion [declarant], 19
(3) Ploution s. Gaion [declarant] and Thaubarion [no.2], 3
(3) Horion s. Gaion [declarant] and Thaubarion [no.2], 1
Free non-kin, slaves: None
Verif./photo: E. Berlin, P. 13357, seen 15/4/1991 + (W. Berlin), P.21383 frag.
b; photograph of reunited papyrus.
Discussion: Broken at top, minor damage elsewhere. A copy. Another text follows
on the same sheet, and this and two other sheets are glued together (the back
being reused as a unit). The father's presence is reconstructed from the formula; his name appears in the second text.

HOUSEHOLD NO.: 173-Ar-16
***Source:** P.Berol.inv. 1342 + 1345, col. i (*Archiv* 39 [1993] 22)
Prov., Date: Arsinoe, 175
Stemma:

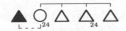

Declarant: Herakleides s. Chairemon (s. Chairemon) and NN, *katoikos*
Family members: (1) Herakleides [declarant] s. Chairemon (s. Chairemon)
                and NN, age lost
            (2) Didym( ) (?), wife (?) of Herakleides [declarant], 24
            (3) Pasion brother of Didyme, age lost
            (4) NN brother of Didyme, 24
            (5) Sara[pion?], brother of Didyme, age lost
Free non-kin, slaves: None
Verif./photo: Berlin, inv. P.1342+1345; seen 19/4/1991.
Discussion: The combined fragments are still missing text at left and below, as
    well as along the upper part of the right edge; it is also possible that a line is
    missing at the start. Column ii is 173-Ar-17. The declarant is registering
    property which belongs to a woman of whom he is *phrontistes*, probably
    named Didyme d. Sarapion, an *aste* (i.e., citizen of one of the Greek cities of
    Egypt). Too much is lost to ensure the precise reconstruction of the
    household. No.2 may be the ward Didyme, but the traces preceding the name
    do not suggest that.

HOUSEHOLD NO.: 173-Ar-17
Source: P.Berol.inv. 1342+1345, col. ii (*Archiv* 39 [1993] 21)
Prov., Date: Arsinoe, 175
Declarant: Not preserved
Family members, free non-kin, slaves: None preserved
Verif./photo: Berlin, inv. P.1342+1345; seen 19/4/1991.
Discussion: For column i, see 173-Ar-16. This second column is only the left
    edge of a declaration of an inhabited property.

HOUSEHOLD NO.: 173-Ar-18
*Source: P.Berol.inv. 1349 (*Archiv* 39 [1993] 24)
Prov., Date: Arsinoe, 28/8/175
Stemma:

▲ △
17 41

Declarant: Not preserved
Family members: (1) NN (male) [declarant], 17
            (2) NN s. Peteeus (?), 41
Free non-kin, slaves: None
Verif./photo: Berlin, inv. P.1349; seen 19/4/1991.
Discussion: Broken at top and left, with only the lower right-hand corner
    preserved and slight remains of another declaration preserved at the right.
    The relationship of no.2 to no.1 is unclear; perhaps his guardian?

HOUSEHOLD NO.: 173-Ar-19
*Source: P.Berol.inv. 1350 (*Archiv* 39 [1993] 25)
Prov., Date: Arsinoe, 175
Declarant: NN d. Isidoros alias Klo[(*katoikos*) and Ammonarion, with her father
    as *kyrios*
Family members: (1) NN [declarant] d. Isidoros alias Klo[(*katoikos*)
                and Ammonarion, age lost

Free non-kin, slaves: None preserved
Verif./photo: Berlin, inv. P.1350; seen 19/4/1991.
Discussion: Broken apparently on all sides, but probably without any loss of text at top. The section in which persons were listed is almost entirely lost. The date is inferred (see ed.). The declarant speaks of registering "myself and mine," so at least two additional family members were included.

HOUSEHOLD NO.: 173-Ar-20
*Source: P.Berol.inv. 1355 (*Archiv* 39 [1993] 26)
Prov., Date: Arsinoe, 175
Declarant: NN d. Heron and NN
Family members: (1) Pt[, age lost
Free non-kin, slaves: None preserved
Verif./photo: Berlin, inv. P.1355; seen 19/4/1991.
Discussion: Fragment of the upper part of a declaration, broken at both sides with substantial loss at left. The date is inferred (see ed.). This is a declaration of lodgers, the names and ages of whom are represented only by brief traces in lines 8–13; there were probably two or three of them.

HOUSEHOLD NO.: 173-Me-1
*Source: *BGU* III 833 = *W.Chr.* 205
Prov., Date: Memphis, 1/10/174
Stemma:

Declarant: Melas s. Areios and Kaleis
Family members: (1) Melas [declarant] s. Areios and Kaleis, 51
                         (2) Melas s. Melas [declarant] and Tesagris, 1
                         (3) Tnephremphis d. Melas [declarant] and Herieus, 17
Free non-kin, slaves: None
Verif./photo: Berlin, P.7097; sent to Münster in 1907, but no longer to be found; probably destroyed in World War II.
Discussion: Complete. The declarant and his two children by different wives (neither wife declared here) are renters in the house of another (cf. *ZPE* 75 [1988] 255–56). Cf. 145-Me-1 for a possible brother of the declarant.

HOUSEHOLD NO.: 173-Me-2
*Source: *P.Lond.* III 919b (p. 28) (cf. *BL* 1.274)
Prov., Date: Memphis, 175
Declarant: Tyrannos
Family members: (1) Tyrannos [declarant], 28
Free non-kin, slaves: None
Verif./photo: London, BL inv. 919b; microfilm; original seen 2/4/1991.
Discussion: Broken at top and bottom. The declarant and sole person declared is a renter. His full self-description is lost.

HOUSEHOLD NO.: 173-Me-3
*Source: *SPP* XX 11 (cf. *BL* 3.236, 8.461)#
Prov., Date: Moithymis (Memphite), 23/7/174
Stemma:

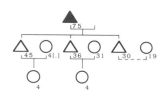

Declarant: Peteamounis s. Peteamounis and Tamasis, *nekrotaphos*
Family members:　　(1) Peteamounis [declarant] s. Peteamounis and Tamasis,
　　　　　　　　　　　　nekrotaphos, 75
　　　　　　　　　　(2) Ammonas s. Peteamounis [declarant] and Senamounis
　　　　　　　　　　　　(deceased), *nekrotaphos*, 45
　　　　　　　　　　(3)]is d. Isas, wife of Ammonas [no.2], 4[.]
　　　　　　　　　　(4) NN d. Ammonas [no.2] and Isis [no.3], 4
　　　　　　　　　　(5) Horos s. Peteamounis [declarant] and Senamounis,
　　　　　　　　　　　　brother of Ammonas [no.2], *nekrotaphos*, 36
　　　　　　　　　　(6) Taoris d. Horos, wife of Horos [no.5], *arge*, 31
　　　　　　　　　　(7) Amounis d. Horos [no.5] and Taoris [no.6], 4
　　　　　　　　　　(8) NN s. Peteamounis [declarant] and Senamounis,
　　　　　　　　　　　　brother of Ammonas [no.2] and Horos [no.5],
　　　　　　　　　　　　nekrotaphos, 30
　　　　　　　　　　(9) —asis d. Pasion (s. Horos) and Ammonarion, *arge*, 19
Free non-kin, slaves: None
Verif./photo: Vienna, inv. G 2011; seen 22/4/1991.
Discussion: Small losses at left, otherwise complete. It is not clear if no.9 is the
　　wife of no.8; there is a small lacuna at this point. Sijpesteijn (*BL* 8.461) sug-
　　gests reading the alpha of no. 6's age as the start of ἄσ[ημος] instead as part
　　of her age, but I do not see the basis for this (physical condition is mentioned
　　only sporadically here).

HOUSEHOLD NO.: 173-Pr-1
*Source: *P.Brux.* I 1 (cf. *BASP* 28 [1991] 15–16)
Prov., Date: Theresis (Prosopite), 21/6/174
Declarant: Sarapion s. Aranchis
Family members:　　(1) Sarapion [declarant] s. Aranchis, 18 (?)
Free non-kin, slaves: None
Verif./photo: P.Brux.inv. E.7616 recto, i; Pl. I; photograph.
Discussion: Complete except for strip along left edge, but the middle section where
　　individuals were listed is badly damaged, including missing fibers, so that no
　　entries concerning persons survive completely and clearly. Sarapion was
　　probably the only person declared. The reading of his age is probable but not
　　certain, cf. *BASP* 28 (1991) 15–16.

HOUSEHOLD NO.: 173-Pr-2
*Source: *P.Brux.* I 2 (cf. *BASP* 28 [1991] 15–16)
Prov., Date: Theresis (Prosopite), 24/6/174
Declarant: Harmachis s. Nektheros, gs. Thamounis (f.)
Family members: (1) Harmachis [declarant] s. Nektheros (s.
                   Thamounis [f.]) and Thermouthis (d.
                   Harmachis), age lost
Free non-kin, slaves: None
Verif./photo: P.Brux.inv. E.7616 recto, ii; Pl. I; photograph.
Discussion: Complete except for minor holes and loss at right where the declara-
    tion is glued to the next one; age is lost at right (not indicated by editor).

HOUSEHOLD NO.: 173-Pr-3
*Source: *P.Brux.* I 3
Prov., Date: Thelbonthon Siphtha (Prosopite), 19/7/174
Stemma:

Declarants: Therothbechis and Therobasthis, daughters of Peteesis alias Athas (s.
    Hephaistion) and Taartysis (d. Pnepheros)
Family members: (1) Athas s. Tithoes alias Athas (s. Hephaistion) and
                   Taartysis (d. Pnepheros), 56
                   (2) Therothbechis [declarant] d. Tithoes alias Athas (s.
                   Hephaistion) and Taartysis (d. Pnepheros), sister
                   of Athas [no.1], 44
                   (3) Therobasthis [declarant] d. Tithoes alias Athas (s.
                   Hephaistion) and Taartysis (d. Pnepheros), sister
                   of Athas [no.1], 48
Free non-kin: None
Slaves: (1) Areios offspring of Thermouthion, 28
                   (2) Pathermouthis offspring of Thaubarous, 18
Verif./photo: P.Brux.inv. E.7616 recto, iii; Pl. I; photograph.
Discussion: Complete. Problems posed by fact that the sisters call their father
    Peteesis alias Athas in lines 3 and 33–34 but Tithoes alias Athas in 18; also
    both their mother and their father's mother are called Taartysis d. Pnepheros.
    Perhaps the latter information is an error.

HOUSEHOLD NO.: 173-Pr-4
*Source: *P.Brux.* I 4
Prov., Date: Thelbonthon Siphtha (Prosopite), 19/7/174
Stemma:

Declarant: Thremmemphis d. Sarapion, with her mother Soeris d. Perpheis as *phrontistria*
Family members: (1) Soeris d. Perpheis (s. Phounsis) and Thapsaipis
(d. Potamon), 47
(2) Thremmemphis [declarant] d. Sarapion (s.
Petos) and Soeris [no.1], 10
Free non-kin, slaves: None
Verif./photo: P.Brux.inv. E.7616 recto, iv; Pl. 56 in O. Montevecchi, *La papirologia* (Turin 1973; 2nd ed. Milan 1988); photograph.
Discussion: Complete. The daughter is the owner of the property, coming to her from her (evidently deceased) father, hence the declarant. But the mother actually submits the declaration.

HOUSEHOLD NO.: 173-Pr-5
***Source:** P.Brux. I 5
Prov., Date: Thelbonthon Siphtha (Prosopite), 19/7/174
Stemma:

Declarant: Pantbeus s. Phibis
Family members: (1) Pantbeus [declarant] s. Phibis the younger (s.
Pnepheros) and Thasachmounis (d.
Pnepheronphis), 69
(2) Taapollos d. Orsenouphis and Taaronnesis, wife of
Pantbeus [declarant], 52
(3) Isidoros s. Pantbeus [declarant] and Taapollos
[no.2], 3
(4) Pkouthis s. Pantbeus [declarant] and Thaesis (d.
Perpheis), 35
(5) Thermouthis d. Nemesas (s. Tithoes) and
Tatithoes, wife of Pkouthis [no.4], 16
(6) Phibis s. Pantbeus [declarant] and Taapollos
[no.2], 21
(7) Thermouthis d. Pantbeus [declarant] and Taapollos
[no.2], wife of Phibis [no.6], 13
(8) Taaronnesis d. Pantbeus [declarant] and Taapollos
[no.2], 24
Free non-kin, slaves: None
Verif./photo: P.Brux.inv. E.7616 recto, v; Pl. II; photograph.
Discussion: Complete.

HOUSEHOLD NO.: 173-Pr-6
Source: P.Brux. I 6
Prov., Date: Thelbonthon Siphtha (Prosopite), 19/7/174
Declarant: Athas s. Pnepheros

Family members, free non-kin, slaves: None
Verif./photo: P.Brux.inv. E.7616 recto, vi; Pl. II; photograph.
Discussion: Complete. Declares property in which no one lives.

HOUSEHOLD NO.: 173-Pr-7
*Source: *P.Brux.* I 7
Prov., Date: Thelbonthon Siphtha (Prosopite), 19/7/174
Stemma:

Declarant: Thapsois d. Pnepheros (s. Herakleides)
Family members: (1) Thapsois [declarant] d. Pnepheros (s.
  Herakleides) and Thermouthis (d. Psosnaus), 47
  (2) Hierakion alias Horos, s. Petos (husband of
  Thapsois), 55
  (3) Sarapammon s. Hierakion [no.2] and Thapsois
  [declarant], 6
  (4) Psosnaus s. Hierakion [no.2] and Thapsois
  [declarant], 3
Free non-kin, slaves: None
Verif./photo: P.Brux.inv. E.7616 recto, vii; photograph.
Discussion: Complete.

HOUSEHOLD NO.: 173-Pr-8
*Source: *P.Brux.* I 8
Prov., Date: Thelbonthon Siphtha (Prosopite), 19/7/174
Declarant: Pnepheros freedman of Phimouis
Family members: (1) Pnepheros [declarant] freedman of Phimouis, son of
  Thamounis (d. Aphrodit(e?)), 70
Free non-kin, slaves: None
Verif./photo: P.Brux.inv. E.7616 recto, viii; photograph.
Discussion: Complete.

HOUSEHOLD NO.: 173-Pr-9
Source: *P.Brux.* I 9
Prov., Date: Thelbonthon Siphtha (Prosopite), 19/7/174
Declarants: Pantbeus s. Eudaimon (s. Orsenoupis [s. Petos]), and Thermouthis d.
  Petos (s. Petsiris)
Family members, free non-kin, slaves: None
Verif./photo: P.Brux.inv. E.7616 recto, ix; photograph.
Discussion: Complete. Apparently Pantbeus and his great-aunt declare their three-
  fifths of property coming from his grandfather = her brother Orsenoupis, in
  which no one lives. Unlike eds., we take Eudaimon as patronymic rather
  than as a second name for Pantbeus.

HOUSEHOLD NO.: 173-Pr-10
Source: P.Brux. I 10 (cf. *BASP* 28 [1991] 16–17)
Prov., Date: Thelbonthon Siphtha (Prosopite), 19/7/174
Stemma:

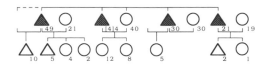

Declarants: Pantbeus s. Petos, Tithoennesis s. Petos, Haronnesis s. Petos, and
Phalakres s. Petos

Family members:
    (1) Pantbeus [declarant] s. Petos (s. Pnepheros) and
        Thaeies (d. Psenamounis), 49
    (2) Theros d. Ammonios (s. Hephaistion) and
        Taphibichis, wife of Pantbeus [no.1], 21
    (3) Petos s. Pantbeus and Thapsathis (d. Petos), 10
    (4) Ammonios s. Pantbeus [no.1] and Theros [no.2], 5
    (5) Taphibichis d. Pantbeus [no.1] and Theros [no.2], 4
    (6) Thaeies d. Pantbeus [no.1] and Theros [no.2], 2
    (7) Tithoennesis [declarant] s. Petos and
        Thaeiees, < 4 > 4
    (8) Serathes d. Petos and Thaeies, sister and wife of
        Tithoennesis [no.7], 40
    (9) Theros d. Tithoennesis [no.7] and Serathes [no.8], 12
    (10) Thapsathis d. Tithoennesis [no.7] and Serathes
        [no.8], 8
    (11) Phalakres [declarant] s. Petos (s. Pnepheros)
        and Thaeies (d. Psenamounis), 30
    (12) Taartysis d. Saiphis (s. Pnepherontithoes) and
        Achilleis, wife of Phalakres [no.11], 30
    (13) Nouatis d. Phalakres [no.11] and Thermouthis (d.
        of Pnepheros), 5
    (14) Haronnesis [declarant] s. Petos (s. Pnepheros)
        and Thaeies (d. Psenamounis), 21
    (15) Thanibichis d. Herpaesis and Thsenamounis, wife
        of Haronnesis [no.14], 19
    (16) Herpaesis s. Haronnesis [no.14] and Thanibichis
        [no.15], 2
    (17) Thsenamounis d. Haronnesis [no.14] and
        Thanibichis [no.15], 1

Free non-kin, slaves: None
Verif./photo: P.Brux.inv. E.7616 recto, x; photograph.
Discussion: Complete. The order in which the brothers are given and his wife's
age support the supposition that the scribe has simply omitted a mu in the age
of no.7.

HOUSEHOLD NO.: 173-Pr-11
*Source: *P.Brux.* I 11 (cf. *BASP* 28 [1991] 17–19)
Prov., Date: Thelbonthon Siphtha (Prosopite), 19/7/174
Stemma:

Declarant: Harendotes s. Pantbeus (s. Pnepheros)
Family members: (1) Serathes d. Phimouis and Aphrodite, 48
                (2) Harendotes [declarant] s. Pantbeus (s.
                     Pnepheros) and Serathes [no.1], 15
Free non-kin, slaves: None
Verif./photo: P.Brux.inv. E.7616 recto, xi; Pl. III; photograph.
Discussion: Complete. See *BASP* 28 (1991) 17–19 for a detailed discussion of this
    text. The property was formerly that of Pantbeus, the (probably dead) father
    of Harendotes, whose mother is listed first even though he is the nominal
    declarant.

HOUSEHOLD NO.: 173-Pr-12
*Source: *P.Brux.* I 12
Prov., Date: Thelbonthon Siphtha (Prosopite), 19/7/174
Declarants: Thesies and Thermouthis daughters of Pnephero( ) (s. Phal( ))
Family members: (1) Thounonsis d. Pnepheros and Theros, 54
Free non-kin, slaves: None
Verif./photo: P.Brux.inv. E.7616 recto, xii; Pl. III; photograph.
Discussion: Complete. As no relationship between the single occupant of the
    noubis and lot, owned by the declarants, and the latter is given, the occupant
    is presumably not a relative but a renter.

HOUSEHOLD NO.: 173-Pr-13
*Source: *P.Brux.* I 13 (cf. Bingen, *Cd'E* 47 [1972] 231–35; *BL* 7.31–32)
Prov., Date: Thelbonthon Siphtha (Prosopite), 19/7/174
Stemma:

Declarants: Pantbeus s. Hartysis (s. Pnepherotithoes), Stoetis his sister, and
    Thapeis and Thanibechis daughters of Peebos
Family members: (1) Pantbeus [declarant] s. Hartysis (s.
                       Pnepherotithoes) and Thsontithoes (d.
                       Pnepherotithoes), 40

(2) Pnepherotithoes s. Pantbeus [declarant] and
Stotoetis d. Pnepherotithoes, 16
(3) Thapeis d. Peebos (s. Pnepheros) and
Hierakiaina (d. Harphichis), 13

Free non-kin, slaves: None
Verif./photo: P.Brux.inv. E.7616 recto, xiii; Pl. III; photograph.
Discussion: Complete. P.Brux. gives a stemma, based on Bingen's arguments, showing the three non-resident declarants (sister and two nieces of Pantbeus). Thapeis [no.3] is of uncertain relationship to the other two residents; she is not the Thapeis who figures among the declarants.

HOUSEHOLD NO.: 173-Pr-14
*Source: *P.Brux.* I 14
Prov., Date: Thelbonthon Siphtha (Prosopite), 19/7/174
Stemma:

Declarant: Tatithoes d. Petephnouthis
Family members: (1) Tatithoes [declarant] d. Petephnouthis and
Taertysis (d. Harphbichis), 60
(2) Thermouthis d. Pnepheros (s. Pnepheros) and
Tatithoes [declarant], 20

Free non-kin, slaves: None
Verif./photo: P.Brux.inv. E.7616 recto, xiv; photograph.
Discussion: Complete. Tatithoes calls herself γυνή, translated by Nachtergael as "veuve"; the point of the term is the contrast with θυγάτηρ, as Thermouthis is called. Cf. *P.Brux.* I 4 for a parallel.

HOUSEHOLD NO.: 173-Pr-15
*Source: *P.Brux.* I 15
Prov., Date: Thelbonthon Siphtha (Prosopite), 19/7/174
Stemma:

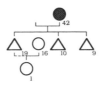

Declarant: Thermouthion d. Tantbeus
Family members: (1) Thermouthis [declarant] d. Tantbeus, 42
(2) Tithoennesis s. Pnepheros and Thermouthis
[declarant], 19

(3) Areia d. Hierakion the freedman of
Pnepherontithoes s. Saiphis, 16
(4) Thermouthis d. Areia [no.3], 1
(5) Perpheis s. Pnepheros (s. Tithoes) and
Thermouthis [declarant] (d. Tantbeus), 10
(6) Dionysios s. Pnepheros (s. Tithoes) and
Thermouthis [declarant] (d. Tantbeus), 9

Free non-kin, slaves: None
Verif./photo: P.Brux.inv. E.7616 recto, xv; photograph.
Discussion: Complete. Nachtergael shows no.2 as the son of the declarant by a
first husband Pnepheros s. Tithoennesis, and nos.5–6 as her sons by a second husband Pnepheros s. Tithoes. This seems an unnecessary multiplication
of husbands; all three can perfectly well be by Pnepheros s. Tithoes. He also
shows Areia [no.3] as the wife of Tithoennesis [no.2], something not stated
by the declaration; nor does the declaration call Thermouthis [no.4] the
daughter ἐξ ἀμφοτέρων (as with Dionysios, no.6).

HOUSEHOLD NO.: 173-Pr-16
Source: *P.Brux.* I 16#
Prov., Date: Thelbonthon Siphtha (Prosopite), 19/7/174
Declarants: Pantbeus and Tithoenesis and Palakres and Haronnesis, all sons of
Petos s. Pnepheros
Family members, free non-kin, slaves: None
Verif./photo: P.Brux.inv. E.7616 recto, xvi; photograph.
Discussion: Complete. They declare properties in which no one is registered. The
same declarants appear in 173-Pr-10.

HOUSEHOLD NO.: 173-Pr-17
***Source:** *P.Brux.* I 17
Prov., Date: Thelbonthon Siphtha (Prosopite), 20/7/174
Stemma:

Declarant: Ammonios s. Amenneus
Family members: (1) Ammonis [declarant] s. Amenneus (s.
Harnektotes) and Smithis (d. Harnektotes), 47
(2) Smithis d. Harnektotes and Therepsois, mother of
Ammonis [declarant], 69
Free non-kin, slaves: None
Verif./photo: P.Brux.inv. E.7616 recto, xvii; photograph.
Discussion: Complete.

HOUSEHOLD NO.: 173-Pr-18
Source: *P.Brux.* I 18
Prov., Date: Thelbonthon Siphtha (Prosopite), 19/7/174
Declarants: Kallinikos and Osarapollon and Areia, all children of Apollonios, and
Heraklas and Kallinikos both sons of Asklepiades

Family members, free non-kin, slaves: None
Verif./photo: P.Brux.inv. E.7616 recto, xviii; photograph.
Discussion: Complete except losses along right margin. Declare property in which no one is registered.

HOUSEHOLD NO.: 187-An-1
*Source: *P.Oxy.* VIII 1110 (cf. *BL* 1.332, 3.134, 7.135, 8.241)
Prov., Date: Antinoopolis, 187/8
Stemma:

slaves

$\Diamond \underset{28}{\triangle}\triangle\underset{22}{\triangle}\triangle \quad \underset{[.]6}{\Diamond}\underset{22}{\bigcirc\triangle} \quad \underset{4}{\Diamond} \quad \underset{19}{\Diamond} \quad \bigcirc\underset{12}{\bigcirc}\underset{24}{\Diamond}$

Declarant: Dioskourides s. Zoilos (s. Dioskourides)
Family members:　　(1) Dioskourides [declarant] s. Zoilos (s. Dioskourides), 2[.]
　　　　　　　　　　　(2) ?NN, d.? Zoilos gd.? Zoilos [prob. wife of Dioskourides (declarant)], age lost
Free non-kin: None
Slaves:　　　　　(1) NN, age lost
　　　　　　　　　　(2) Narkissos, 28
　　　　　　　　　　(3) Horos, age lost
　　　　　　　　　　(4) Pamonthis, 22
　　　　　　　　　　(5) Paulemis alias Paulinus, age lost
　　　　　　　　　　(6) NN, [.]6
　　　　　　　　　　(7) Ploution, 22
　　　　　　　　　　(8) Didymos, age lost
　　　　　　　　　　(9) NN, offspring of Sarapias, 4
　　　　　　　　　　(10) NN, 19
　　　　　　　　　　(11) Sarapias, age lost
　　　　　　　　　　(12) (?P)inarous alias Peina, 12
　　　　　　　　　　(13) NN, 24
Verif./photo: Bodl. Ms. Gr. Class. e 100 (P); photograph.
Discussion: Many lacunae; minimum of about 20 letters lost at left, probably with some slaves lost. Broken at bottom; only date and subscription lost there. For the declarant, see the discussion of D. Hagedorn, *P.Köln* III 143.9–11n. He suggests that the Zoilos s. Zoilos of line 11 is the declarant's brother. But the persons declared later in the text are in the nominative, and Zoilos therefore cannot be among them. (This person could also be in the accusative; but not the genitive). Rather, Zoilos must be the father of the person declared. In that event it is unlikely (though not impossible) that he is the declarant's brother. We have adopted with hesitation the editors' view that this is the declarant's wife.

HOUSEHOLD NO.: 187-An-2
*Source: *PSI* XII 1227 (cf. *BL* 3.229, 6.185, 8.408)
Prov., Date: Antinoopolis, 12/8/188

Stemma:

lodger

38
freedman of declarant's fat

slaves

Declarant: Valerius alias Philantinoos s. Philantinoos alias Nilammon (s. Herakleides)

Family members: (1) Valerius alias Philantinoos [declarant] s. Philantinoos, 24

(2) Didyme d. Lysimachos alias Didymos (s. Herakleides), wife of Valerius alias Philantinoos [declarant], 21

Free non-kin: (1) Sarapion, freedm. of Philantinoos alias Nilammon [father of declarant], 38

Slaves: (1) Diodora, 42

(2) Koprias, male offspring of Diodora [no.1], 15 (uncertain; 8 is possible)

Verif./photo: Florence, Biblioteca Laurenziana; seen 25/5/1989.

Discussion: Virtually complete. Recto has accounts; this is a copy of the original, made on the verso. Spouses are perhaps first cousins. This belongs to the archive of *P.Fam.Tebt.*, cf. 187-Ar-19.

HOUSEHOLD NO.: 187-Ar-1
Source: *P.Stras.* V 313 (cf. *BASP* 27 [1990] 11)
Prov., Date: Arsinoe, 25/5/189
Declarant: Tasoucharion
Family members, free non-kin, slaves: None
Verif./photo: P.Stras.inv.gr. 1221(b), seen 14/3/1989.
Discussion: Broken at right. Declaration only of property. It is not clear what the relationship of names in lines 6–7 is to the declarant; Taorsenouphis in 6 is feminine, in accusative. Whose metronymic (line 7) is not clear.

HOUSEHOLD NO.: 187-Ar-2
*Source: *P.Flor.* I 102 + *P.Prag.* I 17 (= *SB* III 6696); cf. *Tyche* 5 [1990] 200; *BASP* 27 [1990] 13; *ZPE* 77 (1989) 224, 225–26
Prov., Date: Soknopaiou Nesos (Arsinoite), 188/9
Stemma:

Declarant: Stotoetis s. Anchophis the younger (s. Panephremis) and Thases, priest of the 3rd tribe of Soknopaios

Family members: (1) Stotoetis [declarant] s. Anchophis the younger (s. Panephremis) and Thases, priest, 43
(2) Taouetis d. Stotoetis the elder (s. Pakysis) and Herieus, wife of Stotoetis [declarant], 43 (corr. from 41?)
(3) Panephremis s. Stotoetis [declarant] and Taouetis [no.2], age lost
(4) Th[, d.? of Stotoetis [declarant] and Taouetis [no.2], age lost
(5) Thases d. Stotoetis [declarant] and Taouetis [no.2], 6

Free non-kin, slaves: None

Verif./photo: Right half in Florence, Biblioteca Laurenziana; seen 25/5/1989; left half in Prague, plate in *P.Prag.* pl. XXIII.

Discussion: Virtually complete with two halves except for minor losses in the middle. See L. Vidman, *ZPE* 77 (1989) 225–26 for combination.

HOUSEHOLD NO.: 187-Ar-3
*Source: *P.Laur.* III 66
Prov., Date: Philadelphia (Arsinoite), 188/9
Declarant: NN s. Sabinos, from the metropolis
Family members, free non-kin: None
Slaves: (1) Isidora, 25
(2) NN, age lost
(3) —aktike, 33 (very uncertain)
(4) Thermouthas, age lost

Verif./photo: Florence, Biblioteca Laurenziana; seen 25/5/1989; *P.Laur.* III, pl. LVI.

Discussion: Broken at left and an abraded, almost blank, strip along a join down the middle. A declaration only of property, including probably four slaves (no.2 is not certain, posited for the size of the lacuna) belonging to Nemesilla.

HOUSEHOLD NO.: 187-Ar-4
*Source: *BGU* I 115 i = *W.Chr.* 203#
Prov., Date: Arsinoe, 189
Stemma:

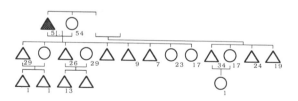

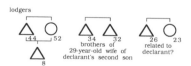

lodgers

Declarant: Herodes s. Heron (s. Herakleides) and Eirene
Family members: (1) Herodes [declarant] s. Heron (s. Herakleides) and
                               Eirene, weaver, 5[.]
                           (2) Eirene d. Heron (s. Herakleides) and Eirene, sister
                               and wife of Herodes [declarant], 54
                           (3) Heron s. Herodes [declarant] and Eirene [no.2],
                               weaver (?), 29
                           (4) Neilos s. Herodes [declarant] and Eirene [no.2],
                               goldsmith, 26
                           (5) Sarapion s. Herodes [declarant] and Eirene [no.2],
                               age lost
                           (6) Herakleides s. Herodes [declarant] and Eirene [no.2], 9
                           (7) Euporas s. Herodes [declarant] and Eirene [no.2], 7
                           (8) NN d. Herodes [declarant] and Eirene [no.2], 23
                           (9) Neilliaina d. Herodes [declarant] and Eirene [no.2],
                               wife of Heron [no.3], age lost
                           (10) Thaisarion d. Herodes [declarant] and Eirene [no.2],
                               17
                           (11) Herodes s. Heron [no.3] and Neilliaina [no.9], 1
                           (12) Tryphon s. Heron [no.3] and Neilliaina [no.9], 1
                           (13) Thermoutharion d. Kastor (s. Heron) and Isidora,
                               wife of Neilos [no.4], 29
                           (14) NN s. Neilos [no.4] and Thermoutharion [no.13], 13
                           (15) Heron s. Neilos [no.4] and Thermoutharion [no.13],
                               age lost
                           (16) Heron s. [Herakleides] [deceased brother of
                               declarant] and Eirene, cloth-beater, 34
                           (17) Apion s. [Herakleides] [deceased brother of
                               declarant] and Eirene, workman, 24
                           (18) Herakleides s. [Herakleides] [deceased brother of
                               declarant] and Eirene, goldsmith, 19
                           (19) Thaisarion d. [Herakleides] [deceased brother of
                               declarant] and Eirene, wife of Heron [no.16], 17
                           (20) Syra d. Heron [no.16] and Thaisarion [no.19], 1
Free non-kin: (1) Neilos s. Demetrios (s. NN) and Thaisarion, donkey-
                               driver, 44
                           (2) Eirene d. Demetrios (s. NN) and Thaisarion, sister
                               and wife of Neilos [no.1], 52
                           (3) Kastor s. Neilos [no.1] and Eirene [no.2], 8
                           (4) Heron s. Kastor (s. Heron) and Isidora, brother of
                               Thermoutharion [kin no.13], cloth-beater, 34
                           (5) Melanas s. Kastor (s. Heron) and Isidora, brother of
                               Thermoutharion [kin no.13], gardener, 32
                           (6) Heron s. Herakleides (s. Heron) and Didyme,
                               workman, 26
                           (7) NN d. Herakleides (s. Heron) and Didyme, sister of
                               Heron [no.6], 23
Slaves: None
Verif./photo: Berlin, P.1326, col. i; seen 15/4/1991.

Discussion: Damaged at left, and smaller holes throughout. The persons listed under "non-kin" are described as renters by the declarant, but some of them are in fact related; quite possibly all were kin. The possible confusion in such a household can be seen in the presence of two 34-year old ῥαβδισταί named Heron, or two Eirenes in their early 50s! Kin nos. 11 and 12 are described as twins.

HOUSEHOLD NO.: 187-Ar-5
*Source: *BGU* I 115 ii = *W.Chr.* 203 (cf. *BL* 3.8)#
Prov., Date: Arsinoe, 24/6/189
Declarant: Sarapammon s. Apollonios (s. NN) and Didymarion, *katoikos*
Family members: (1) Sarapammon [declarant] s. Apollonios (s. NN) and
                                      Didymarion, *katoikos*, 70
Free non-kin: None
Slaves: (1) Aunes, slave of Sarapammon [declarant], age lost
Verif./photo: Berlin, P.1326, col. ii; seen 15/4/1991.
Discussion: Broken at right with significant loss. Lines 16–22 are occupied with a list of Aunes' former owners. Lines 23–25 record that the declarant's daughter Didymarion is registered by her husband Achilleus s. Apollonios along with their children Valerius and NN in another amphodon.

HOUSEHOLD NO.: 187-Ar-6
*Source: *BGU* I 116 i#
Prov., Date: Arsinoe, 28/8/189
Declarant: Horigenes s. Isidoros
Family members: (1) Melas s. Heraklas (s. Zenas) and NN, workman (?) age
                                      lost (probably 18 or 28)
Free non-kin, slaves: None
Verif./photo: Berlin, P.1327, col. i; seen 15/4/1991.
Discussion: Broken at left with considerable loss (nearly all restored). The one person declared is presumably a renter of the two-thirds of a house owned by the declarant and its sole occupant.

HOUSEHOLD NO.: 187-Ar-7
*Source: *BGU* I 116 ii (cf. *BL* 8.19)
Prov., Date: Arsinoe, 28/8/189
Stemma:

Declarant: Ision s. Patron alias Patalos (s. Demetrios) and Chousarion, *katoikos*
Family members: (1) Ision [declarant] s. Patron alias Patalos (s. Demetrios)
                                      and Chousarion, *katoikos*, workman, 17
                                  (2) Herois d. Patron alias Patalos (s. Demetrios) and
                                      Chousarion, sister of Ision [declarant], 14
Free non-kin, slaves: None
Verif./photo: Berlin, P.1327, col. ii; seen 15/4/1991.
Discussion: Complete except for minor holes. Ision does not declare Herois as his wife.

HOUSEHOLD NO.: 187-Ar-8
*Source: *BGU* I 117 (cf. *BL* 8.19; *BASP* 29 [1992] 103–04)
Prov., Date: Arsinoe, 20/8/189
Stemma:

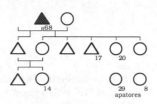

Declarant: Dioskoros s. NN (s. Herakleides)
Family members: (1) Dioskoros [declarant] s. NN (s. Herakleides),
                                farmer, 68
                     (2) Thaisarion, ?freedwoman of Thaisarion d. Souchas (s.
                                Mysthes) and Heraklous, wife of Dioskoros
                                [declarant], age lost
                     (3) Horion s. Dioskoros [declarant] and Thaisarion
                                [no.2], farmer, age lost
                     (4) NN s. Dioskoros [declarant] and Thaisarion [no.2],
                                scribe, 17
                     (5) Satornilos s. Dioskoros [declarant] and Sarapous (d.
                                Horion), farmer, age lost
                     (6) Harpokratiaina d. Dioskoros [declarant] and
                                Thaisarion [no.2], wife of Satornilos [no.5],
                                age lost
                     (7) Satornilos s. Satornilos [no.5] and Harpokratiaina
                                [no.6], age lost
                     (8) Satornila d. Satornilos [no.5] and Harpokratiaina
                                [no.6], 14
                     (9) Artemidora alias ?Dioskorous, d. Dioskoros [declarant]
                                and Thaisarion [no.2], 20
                     (10) Tasoucharion d. Dioskoros [declarant] (and
                                Thaisarion [no.2]), age lost
                     (11) Than[apator (female), 29
                     (12) Sarapous apator, 8
Free non-kin, slaves: None
Verif./photo: Berlin, P.1328; seen 16/4/1991.
Discussion: Substantial loss at right, small holes at left and elsewhere. Complete
    top and bottom.

HOUSEHOLD NO.: 187-Ar-9
*Source: *BGU* I 118 i (cf. *BL* 1.21; *BASP* 29 [1992] 104)
Prov., Date: Arsinoe, 189

Stemma:

Declarant: Nemesilla alias Kyrilla
Family members: (1) Nemesilla alias Kyrilla [declarant], 39
                          (2) NN, son of NN and Nemesilla alias Kyrilla
                              [declarant], 16
                          (3) NN, child of Nemesilla, age lost
Free non-kin: (1) —don (male), 54
Slaves: (1) Bithyne, 28
                          (2) NN, offspring of Rhodine, age lost
Verif./photo: Berlin, P.1329, col. i; seen 16/4/1991.
Discussion: Only the right-hand part preserved, with about three-quarters lost to
        the left. Broken also at top. The household certainly contained more persons
        than can now be recovered.

HOUSEHOLD NO.: 187-Ar-10
*Source: *BGU* I 118 ii (cf. *BL* 1.21)
Prov., Date: Arsinoe, 26/5/189
Stemma:

Declarants: Mysthes, ropemaker, and Tamystha
Family members: (1) Mysthes [declarant], ropemaker, 36
                          (2) Tamystha [declarant], sister of Mysthes [no.1], 49
                          (3) Kyrilla d. Chaireas (s. Herakleides s. Dionysios) and
                              Tamystha [no.2], 10
Free non-kin, slaves: None
Verif./photo: Berlin, P.1329, col. ii; seen 16/4/1991.
Discussion: Broken at top, and with minor losses elsewhere. Kyrilla's father is
        Tamystha's divorced husband. Mysthes acts as Tamystha's *kyrios*.

HOUSEHOLD NO.: 187-Ar-11
*Source: *BGU* I 118 iii (cf. *BL* 1.21)#
Prov., Date: Arsinoe, 5–6/189
Stemma:

Declarant: Chaireas, woolwasher
Family members: (1) Chaireas [declarant], woolwasher, 54
        (2) Dioskoria d. An[(s. Sarapion) and Thotarion alias
            Sarapias, wife of Chaireas [declarant], 34
        (3) —domias s. Chaireas [declarant] and Dioskoria [no.2],
            15
        (4) —rios s. Chaireas [declarant] and Dioskoria [no.2], 9
        (5) Chaireas s. Chaireas [declarant] and Dioskoria [no.2],
            age lost
        (6) Dioskor[s./d. Chaireas [declarant] and Dioskoria
            [no.2], age lost
Free non-kin, slaves: None
Verif./photo: Berlin, P.1329, col. iii; seen 16/4/1991.
Discussion: Broken at top and at right, with large losses. The sex of nos. 3 and 4
is assumed to be masculine from their placement before Chaireas. It is pos-
sible that one more child is lost in the lacuna at the end.

HOUSEHOLD NO.: 187-Ar-12
*Source: *BGU* I 120
Prov., Date: Arsinoe, 21/8/189
Stemma:

Declarant: Name lost
Family members: (1) Didymos s. Sarapion (s. Souchas) and Helene, 21
        (2) Thermoutharion d. Sarapion (s. Souchas) and Helene,
            sister and wife of Didymos [no.1], age lost
        (3) Klaudios s. Didymos [no.1] and Thermoutharion
            [no.2], under 1 (born in current year)
        (4) NN s./d. Didymos [no.1] and Thermoutharion [no.2],
            age lost
Free non-kin, slaves: None
Verif./photo: Berlin, P.1330; seen 16/4/1991.
Discussion: Broken at top and some damage at right. No.4 is probably a daughter,
since (s)he is listed after a son just born in the current year.

HOUSEHOLD NO.: 187-Ar-13
*Source: *BGU* I 124 (cf. *BL* 1.22, 8.19)#
Prov., Date: Arsinoe, 189
Stemma:

Declarant: NN s. Chaireas (s. NN) and Thaisarion alias Theano, priest of
Petesouchos

Family members:		(1) NN [declarant] s. Chaireas (s. NN) and Thaisarion
			alias Theano, priest of Petesouchos, 36
		(2) Thais d. Ptolemaios (s. Harpokration) and Thaisarion
			alias Ch[, 23
		(3) NN, female
Free non-kin, slaves: None
Verif./photo: Berlin, P.1358; seen 12/4/1991.
Discussion: Broken at top, bottom, and upper and lower left. Apparently from an
	extract from a register rather than a declaration itself (cf. line 10). Apart
	from the priest, who is apparently the declarant, only the females are
	extracted from the declaration. The relationship of no.2 to the declarant is not
	clear, and nothing can be said about no.3 except that the name Theano fig-
	ured somewhere in her entry. More persons may have been listed.

HOUSEHOLD NO.: 187-Ar-14
*Source: *BGU* I 126
Prov., Date: Arsinoe, 189
Declarant: Herakleides s. Am[(s. NN) and —lous (daughter of *katoikos*)
Family members:		(1) Herakleides [declarant] s. Am[(s. NN) and —lous
			(daughter of *katoikos*), age lost
Free non-kin, slaves: None preserved
Verif./photo: Berlin, P.1352+1340; seen 16/4/1991.
Discussion: Broken at right and below with loss of all listed persons except the
	declarant.

HOUSEHOLD NO.: 187-Ar-15
*Source: *BGU* I 128 i
Prov., Date: Arsinoe, 189
Stemma:

⭕ △ ⭕ △

10
relationships uncertain

slaves

Declarant: Name lost
Family members:		(1) Thermoutharion
		(2) Tourbon (m.)
		(3) Apia, 10
		(4) Tourbon (m.)
Free non-kin: None preserved
Slaves:		(1) —lla, 36
		(2) NN offspring of —lla [no.1], age lost
Verif./photo: Berlin, P.1332, col. i; seen 16/4/1991.
Discussion: Broken except at right. The list of family members is partial and
	uncertain.

HOUSEHOLD NO.: 187-Ar-16
***Source:** BGU* I 128 ii#
Prov., Date: Arsinoe, 189
Stemma:

Declarant: Herakleides, linenweaver
Family members: (1) Herakleides [declarant], linenweaver, age lost
                   (2) NN, perhaps wife and sister of Herakleides
                       [declarant], age lost
Free non-kin, slaves: None preserved
Verif./photo: Berlin, P.1332, col. ii; seen 16/4/1991.
Discussion: Broken at top, right, and bottom. Both family and renters were evidently declared, but they are mostly lost.

HOUSEHOLD NO.: 187-Ar-17
Source: *BGU* I 129#
Prov., Date: Arsinoe, 189
Declarant: Name lost
Family members, free non-kin, slaves: None preserved
Verif./photo: Berlin, P.1341; seen 16/4/1991.
Discussion: Broken at top, right, and bottom. The declarant declared at least himself or herself.

HOUSEHOLD NO.: 187-Ar-18
***Source:** BGU* I 138 (cf. *BL* 4.3)#
Prov., Date: Arsinoe, 189
Stemma:

Declarant: Apion s. Harpokration (s. NN) and Sarapous
Family members: (1) Deios s. Heron the younger (s. Kapiton alias NN) and
                       Besous (freedwoman of Hermione d. Didas),
                       katoikos, 31
                   (2) Soterichos s. Deios (s. Triadelphos) and NN, 72
                   (3) NN s. Soterichos [no.2] and Melanous, farmer, 43
                   (4) Protas s. Ze[(s. NN alias Matrone[) and]phis, farmer,
                       age lost
                   (5) NN s. Ptolemaios (s. NN) and Segathis, 20
                   (6) Harpokration s. NN (s. Sotas), age lost
Free non-kin, slaves: None
Verif./photo: Berlin, P.1331; seen 16/4/1991.
Discussion: Broken at left (small loss), right (larger loss), and bottom (in the middle of the list of persons). Apion declares a house belonging to him, with its renters. Enough information is lost that the interrelationships of most of the

renters cannot be determined, and it is possible that some of them are non-kin.

HOUSEHOLD NO.: 187-Ar-19
Source: *P.Fam.Tebt.* 44.13–22#
Prov., Date: Arsinoe, 189
Declarants: Valerius alias Philantinoos and Philantinoos alias Herodes sons of Philantinoos alias Neilammon (s. Herakleides)
Family members, free non-kin, slaves: None
Verif./photo: London, BL inv. 1914A; seen 2/4/1991.
Discussion: Broken at right and damaged below; copy of an original declaration. Though the end is damaged, it appears that only property is declared, not any inhabitants. Cf. 187-An-2.

HOUSEHOLD NO.: 187-Ar-20
*Source: P.Lond.inv. 1914B (*P.Fam.Tebt.* p. 152)
Prov., Date: Arsinoe
Declarant: Not given
Family members: Herakles Maximos mentioned
Free non-kin, slaves: None
Verif./photo: London, BL inv. 1914B; seen 3/4/1991.
Discussion: Fragments mentioned, not published. Said to be written in the same hand as 187-Ar-19 (*P.Fam.Tebt.* 44, BL inv. 1914A). The fragments seem too small and scattered to yield any connected sense or usable data.

HOUSEHOLD NO.: 187-Ar-21
Source: *PSI* ined. (Calderini, 15 n.2)
Prov., Date: Arsinoe
Declarant:Not known
Family members; Free non-kin; Slaves: Not known
Verif./photo: Not seen
Discussion: So far not able to be identified in Florence.

HOUSEHOLD NO.: 187-Ar-22
*Source: *P.Tebt.* II 322 (= *Sel.Pap.* II 313) (cf. *BL* 3.242, 4.97; *JJurPap* 21 [1991] 7–8)
Prov., Date: Arsinoe, 27/8/189
Stemma:

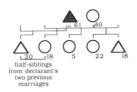

half-siblings
from declarant's
two previous
marriages

Declarant: Achilleus s. Apollonios (s. Lourios alias Apollonios), *katoikos*

Family members: (1) Pasigenes s. Theon (s. Eutyches), donkeydriver, 61
(2) Eutyches s. Pasigenes [no.1] and Apollonous [d.
Herodes], 30
(3) Herakleia d. Kronion (freedman of Didymos s.
Heron), wife of Pasigenes [no.1], 40
(4) Thasis d. Pasigenes [no.1] and Herakleia [no.3], 5
(5) Sabeinos s. Sabeinos (s. Kronion) and Herakleia
[no.3], woolcarder, 18
(6) Sarapias d. Sabeinos (s. Kronion) and Herakleia
[no.3], 22
(7) Tapesouris d. Pasigenes [no.1] and Isidora, sister on
the father's side and wife of Eutyches [no.2], 18

Free non-kin, slaves: None

Verif./photo: Berkeley, P.Tebt. 322; seen 27/9/1990.

Discussion: Complete. Achilleus, who is himself registered in another declaration, declares a property belonging to him and renters living in it. This family consists of Pasigenes' children by two previous marriages, his wife Herakleia's by a previous marriage, and their daughter together.

HOUSEHOLD NO.: 187-Ar-23
*Source: *P.Tebt.* II 504 (see *Aegyptus* 72 [1992] 71–74)
Prov., Date: Arsinoite, 24/8/189
Stemma:

Declarants: Heliodoros s. NN and Taesies (?), and his sister Aretina

Family members: (1) Heliodoros [declarant] s. NN and Taesies (?), age lost
(2) Aretina d. NN and Taesies (?), full sister and wife of
Heliodoros [declarant], age lost
(3) Aretion s. Heliodoros [declarant] and Aretina [no.2],
age lost
(4) NN s. Heliodoros [declarant] and Aretina [no.2],
age lost
(5) Artemidoros (?), age lost
(6) NN, 20
(7) Sarap[[sex unknown], age lost
(8) Sarapias [female], 34
(9) —ammon [male], age lost

Free non-kin, slaves: None

Verif./photo: Berkeley, P.Tebt. 504; seen 28/9/1990; photograph.

Discussion: About two-thirds is lost at the right, except at the bottom, where the right part is preserved; the other margins are preserved. Some entries are probably lost. The relationships (if any) of nos. 5–9 to the declarant are unknown, and it is possible that they are renters or slaves.

HOUSEHOLD NO.: 187-Ar-24
*Source: *BGU* I 60 (cf. *BL* 1.13)
Prov., Date: Karanis (Arsinoite), 189
Declarant: —archos s. Apollonios (s. NN) and NN (d. Herakles)
Family members:　　(1) —archos [declarant] s. Apollonios (s. NN) and NN (d. Herakles), 61
Free non-kin, slaves: None preserved
Verif./photo: Berlin, P.6954; seen 16/4/1991.
Discussion: Broken at left, right, and bottom, leaving only a small strip; persons declared other than the declarant are lost.

HOUSEHOLD NO.: 187-Ar-25
Source: *BGU* II 430
Prov., Date: Karanis (Arsinoite), 189
Declarant: Name lost
Family members, free non-kin, slaves: None preserved
Verif./photo: Berlin, P.7438; seen 12/4/1991.
Discussion: Broken at bottom with loss of all useful information.

HOUSEHOLD NO.: 187-Ar-26
*Source: *BGU* XI 2018 (cf. Youtie, *ZPE* 9 [1972] 133–37 = *Scr.Post.* I 61–65; *BASP* 29 [1992] 113–14)
Prov., Date: Karanis (Arsinoite), 188/9
Stemma:

Declarant: Petsoraipis s. Hatres (s. Imouthes) and Soeris (d. Phanomgeus)
Family members:　　(1) Petsoraipis [declarant] s. Hatres (s. Imouthes)
　　　　　　　　　　　and Soeris (d. Phanomgeus), 57
　　　　　　　　　　(2) Soeris d. Petsoraipis [declarant] and Tapetheus, 13
　　　　　　　　　　(3) Ptolemais, kin, *apator*, 25
　　　　　　　　　　(4) Tkoll—, kin, *apator*, 15
　　　　　　　　　　(5) Thaesis, kin, *apator*, 4
Free non-kin, slaves: None preserved
Verif./photo: W. Berlin, P.21514; seen 11/4/1991.
Discussion: Complete at right and much of left; damaged at top, at lower left, and at bottom, evidently with no loss of entries of persons. Multiple properties declared. Youtie rejects the editor's notion that the ἀπάτορες may have been children of Tapetheus, since her name is not connected to them. They are perhaps children of a deceased sibling of Petsoraipis or of some more distant relative. It seems likely enough that all three come from the same relationship.

HOUSEHOLD NO.: 187-Ar-27
Source: *P.Mich.* VI 370
Prov., Date: Karanis (Arsinoite), 9/8/189
Declarant: Sarapion s. Esouris
Family members, free non-kin, slaves: None
Verif./photo: Michigan, inv. 2977, now in Cairo; photograph seen 9/11/1990.
Discussion: Complete with minor damage along folds. This declaration registers properties owned by an Antinoite woman for whom Sarapion is *phrontistes* and by her children, but no persons living in any of them.

HOUSEHOLD NO.: 187-Ar-28
*Source: *BGU* XI 2090#
Prov., Date: Soknopaiou Nesos (Arsinoite), 7–8/189
Stemma:

Declarant: NN s. NN (s. Stotoetis) and NN, priest of Soknopaios
Family members: (1) NN [declarant] s. NN (s. Stotoetis) and NN,
                              priest of Soknopaios, 43
                         (2) NN d. NN [declarant], age lost
Free non-kin, slaves: None preserved
Verif./photo: W. Berlin, P.21649; seen 11/4/1991.
Discussion: Broken at left, some damage at right, complete top and bottom. At least two other persons were declared, but nothing can be made of the remnants of these entries.

HOUSEHOLD NO.: 187-Ar-29
*Source: *P.Rein.* I 46 (cf. *BL* 1.386)
Prov., Date: Soknopaiou Nesos (Arsinoite)
Stemma:

Declarant: Stotoetis d. Paouetis (s. Stotoetis) and Thases, through her father Paouetis as *phrontistes*
Family members: (1) Stotoetis [declarant] d. Paouetis (s. Stotoetis) and
                              Thases, 36
                         (2) Tapiepis d. Sotas and Stotoetis [declarant], 13
                         (3) Teseuris d. NN and Stotoetis [declarant], 4
Free non-kin, slaves: None

Verif./photo: Paris, Institut de Papyrologie, inv. 2048; photograph.
Discussion: Complete with small lacunae.

HOUSEHOLD NO.: 187-Ar-30
*Source: *P.Berl.Leihg.* I 15# (cf. *BL* 8.62)
Prov., Date: Tebtunis (Arsinoite)
Stemma:

Declarant: Isidora d. Orses the elder (s. Orses) and Heras (d. Paeus), with *kyrios*
Pakebkis s. Aunes (s. Ornophris)
Family members: (1) Isidora [declarant] d. Orses the elder (s. Orses) and
                           Heras (d. Paeus), 60
Free non-kin: None
Slaves: (1) Philoumene, slave of Isidora [declarant], 45
                          (2) Dioskorous, offspring of Philoumene [no.1], slave of
                              Isidora [declarant], 8
                          (3) Athenarion, offspring of Philoumene [no.1], slave of
                              Isidora [declarant], 4
                          (4) Elephantine offspring of Demetria, slave of Isidora
                              [declarant], 20
                          (5) Eudaimonis offspring of Elephantine, slave of Isidora
                              [declarant], 5
                          (6) Isarous offspring of Elephantine, slave of Isidora
                              [declarant], 1
                          (7) Helene, slave of Isidora [declarant], runaway, 68
                          (8) Ammonarion, slave of Isidora [declarant], runaway,
                              42
                          (9) Herakleia, slave of Isidora [declarant], runaway, 38
Verif./photo: Berlin, P.13988; seen 15/4/1991.
Discussion: Complete, with small holes. Duplicate in P.Lond.inv. 1899 verso (unpublished; nearly complete, seen 3/4/1991), which confirms that Isidora's
age has no second digit. Nos. 8 and 9 may be offspring of no.7, given the
age differential and the fact that they seem to have escaped together, but that
is not said explicitly.

HOUSEHOLD NO.: 187-Ar-31
Source: *P.Tebt.* II 518 (see *Aegyptus* 72 [1992] 74–79)
Prov., Date: Arsinoite, 28/8/189
Declarants: Herodes alias Liberalis and Triamallos alias Tyrannos s. Herodes,
katoikos, sitometrosakkophoros
Family members, free non-kin, slaves: None
Verif./photo: Berkeley, P.Tebt. 518; seen 28/9/1990; photograph.
Discussion: Broken at left. Only property is declared, in which no one lives.

HOUSEHOLD NO.: 187-Ar-32
*Source: *SB* XIV 11355 (*CIMGL* 6 [1971] 10–13)
Prov., Date: Arsinoe, 188/9
Stemma:

Declarant: Didymos s. Kallinikos (s. Didymos) and Taphorsais
Family members: (1) Didymos [declarant] s. Kallinikos (s. Didymos)
                and Taphorsais, *idiotes*, age lost
            (2) Sarapias d. Sabeinos (s. Kronion) and
                Eudaimonis, wife of Didymos [declarant], 43 (46
                also possible)
            (3) Didymos, s. Didymos [declarant] and Hermiaine
                apator, daughter of Herois, his divorced wife, 10
Free non-kin: None
Slaves: (1) Eurepos, offspring of NN, slave of Didymos
                [declarant], 32 (age very uncertain)
            (2) Ammon, offspring of NN, slave of Didymos
                [declarant], 29
            (3) NN, offspring of Tapaeis, [.]9
            (4) Alexandria, 29 (somewhat uncertain)
            (5) NN, female
            (6) NN, female
            (7) NN, male
Verif./photo: Copenhagen, P.Hafn.inv. 24; Pl. in *CIMGL*.
Discussion: A copy of the declaration. Complete except at left, where there is a
    varying loss. Declarant notes that his son Xenophon by his divorced wife
    NN, an Antinoite (a different person from the mother of Didymos [no.3]
    above), is registered with his mother in Antinoopolis, and that her children
    by her divorced husband (not the declarant) are registered with their father.
    He thus has two divorced wives living (and she two divorced husbands). He
    also mentions a half share of two slaves, Isis alias Memphis and her son
    Sarapammon (age 6); the context is fragmentary, but they are apparently resi-
    dent elsewhere. He states (line 17) that there are 7 slaves in his household.
    This piece is connected to *P.Fam.Tebt.*, esp. no.48 (202/3), whence
    Sarapias' name is restored. Her age there (57) agrees with 43 here. Cf.
    Sijpesteijn-Worp, *BASP* 14 (1977) 145–47 (*BL* 8.370) on the back and on the
    family.

HOUSEHOLD NO.: 187-Ar-33
*Source: *SB* XIV 11268 (*Aegyptus* 54 [1974] 18) (cf. *ZPE* 20 [1976] 40)
Prov., Date: Arsinoe, 28/8/189
Declarant: NN s. Didymos
Family members: (1) Syros s. Pasion (s. NN) and Philoutos, farmer, 33
Free non-kin, slaves: None
Verif./photo: P.Med.inv. 13; Pl. V.

Discussion: Complete except upper left and scattered holes. NN has filed another declaration for himself; this one concerns a third of a house rented out to a single lodger. Tens digit dotted, but reading is virtually certain.

HOUSEHOLD NO.: 187-Ar-34
*Source: *BGU* XIII 2225 = *ZPE* 9 (1972) 251–55
Prov., Date: Arsinoe, 189
Stemma:

Declarant: Sarapias d. Eirenaios (s. Maron) and Isarion, with as *kyrios* her kinsman Heron s. NN
Family members: (1) Sarapias [declarant] d. Eirenaios (s. Maron) and
                       Isarion, age lost
                       (2) NN alias Sarapias, daughter of Sarapias [declarant],
                       age lost
Free non-kin: (1) NN s. NN and Apollonia, [14?]
                       (2) Herm[, age lost
Slaves: None preserved
Verif./photo: W. Berlin, P.21880; seen 11/4/1991.
Discussion: Three fragments, together missing the centers of most lines, the right ends of most lines, and the bottom, breaking off in the middle of listing persons. The ed. restores the daughter's name as Isarion and age as 22 on the basis of the appearance of an Isarion alias Sarapias, age 25, in *SB* VI 9618, but this seems insufficient. The restoration of the age of non-kin no. 1 is based on (partly restored) information that he underwent *epikrisis* in year 28, i.e. 187/8.

HOUSEHOLD NO.: 187-Ar-35
Source: P.Berol.inv. 1335 (*Archiv* 39 [1993] 27)
Prov., Date: Arsinoe, 189
Declarant: Taorseus alias He[d. NN and NN (d. Herakleides)
Family members, Free non-kin, Slaves: None preserved
Verif./photo: Berlin, inv. P. 1335; seen 19/4/1991.
Discussion: Column ii of a multicolumn roll; broken at right and below. The ends of lines of column i to the left belong to a similar declaration. The declarant, registered herself in another declaration, is here declaring renters of a property she owns.

HOUSEHOLD NO.: 187-Ar-36
*Source: P.Berol.inv. 1336 (*Archiv* 39 [1993] 26)
Prov., Date: Arsinoite, 189
Stemma:

Declarant: Not preserved
Family members: (1) NN [declarant], male, age lost
(2) NN
Free non-kin: (1) NN, lodger, male, age lost
Slaves: None preserved
Verif./photo: Berlin, inv. P. 1336; seen 19/4/1991.
Discussion: A fragment, broken at top, bottom, and left. Enough survives to show that the declarant registered himself, one or more family members, and one renter.

HOUSEHOLD NO.: 187-Ar-37
*Source: *P.Hamb.* III 203
Prov., Date: Arsinoe, 20/8/189
Declarant: Ptolemaios s. Sarapion
Family members: (1) Ptolemaios s. NN (s. Chairemon) and Herois,
workman, 19
Free non-kin, slaves: None
Verif./photo: Pl. VII.
Discussion: Complete except at right and scattered damage. The declarant has registered in another declaration and is registering a lodger (despite "lodgers" in line 9).

HOUSEHOLD NO.: 187-Hm-1
*Source: *P.Lond.* III 923 (6) (Van Minnen, forthcoming)
Prov., Date: Hermopolis, 188/9
Stemma:

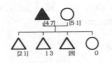

cf. 215-Hm-1, 215-Hm-2

Declarant: Hermaios alias Pathotes s. Achilleus (s. Hermaios) and Eudaimonis alias Tisois (d. Nearchos)
Family members: (1) Hermaios alias Pathotes s. Achilleus (s. Hermaios)
and Eudaimonis alias Tisois (d. Nearchos), [47]
(2) Hermeinos alias Moros s. Hermaios alias Pathotes
[declarant] and Souerous (d. Kastor) [no.5], [21]
(3) Isidoros s. Hermaios alias Pathotes [declarant]
and Souerous (d. Kastor) [no.5], 13
(4) Theognostos alias Moros s. Hermaios alias Pathotes
[declarant] and Souerous (d. Kastor) [no.5], [8]
(5) Souerous d. Kastor, wife of Hermaios alias Pathotes
[declarant], [51]
(6) Isidora d. Hermaios alias Pathotes [declarant]
and Souerous (d. Kastor) [no.5], < 1
Free non-kin, slaves: None
Verif./photo: London, British Library, inv. 923 (6); seen 3/4/1991.

Discussion: Broken at left and with minor damage at right. Some ages restored from other evidence; for the family cf. 215-Hm-1 with *ZPE* 76 (1989) 213–18 and 229-Hm-1.

HOUSEHOLD NO.: 187-Me-1
*Source: *BGU* XI 2019 (cf. *BASP* 29 [1992] 114–15)
Prov., Date: Moithymis (Memphite), 20/9/188
Stemma:

Declarant: Herakleia freedwoman of Senamounis d. Petesouchos
Family members: (1) Herakleia [declarant], freedwoman of Senamounis d.
                  of Petesouchos, 45
                  (2) Senamounis, *apator*, daughter of Herakleia
                  [declarant], *arge*, 20
                  (3) Tastoous, *apator*, daughter of Herakleia [declarant], 12
Free non-kin: None
Slaves: (1) Thermouthis, slave of Herakleia [declarant], 15
Verif./photo: W. Berlin, P.21516; seen 11/4/1991.
Discussion: Complete, but with some of the bottom lines unreadable (no material loss). Col. ii contains the remains of another declaration to the same officials from the same year, but only part has been deciphered; the portion containing any persons is not preserved.

HOUSEHOLD NO.: 187-Ox-1
Source: *P.Oxy.* XXXVI 2762
Prov., Date: Oxyrhynchos, 188/9
Declarant: Apollonios s. Dioskoros (s. Apollonios) and Meithous
Family members, free non-kin, slaves: None preserved
Verif./photo: Oxford, Ashmolean; seen 4/4/1991.
Discussion: Broken at the bottom, with loss of all entries of persons.

HOUSEHOLD NO.: 187-Ox-2
Source: *P.Oxy.* XXXVI 2800
Prov., Date: Oxyrhynchos, 188/9
Declarant: Theon s. Pausirion (s. Sarapion alias Pausirion) and Eudaimonis alias Apia
Family members, free non-kin, slaves: None preserved
Verif./photo: Oxford, Ashmolean; seen 4/4/1991.
Discussion: Broken at bottom and at the right of some lines. At left are remnants of four lines with bits of another declaration (only a mention of the prefects remains).

HOUSEHOLD NO.: 187-Ox-3
*Source: *P.Princ.* III 129 i (cf. *P.Oxy.* XXXVI 2762 introd.; *BASP* 28 [1991] 125–29)
Prov., Date: Oxyrhynchos, 189
Stemma:

Declarants: Teteuris d. —thous and Taapol( ) and her sister NN d. NN and NN
Family members: (1) Teteuris [declarant] d. —thous and Taapol( ), 25
                        (2) NN [declarant] d. NN and NN, sister of no.1, 22
Free non-kin, slaves: None
Verif./photo: Princeton, GD 7928B, col. i; seen 26/2/1991.
Discussion: Broken at top, left, and bottom. Text of i 3–10 (introductory part) by Rea given in *P.Oxy.* XXXVI 2762 introd., full text in *BASP* 28 [1991] 126–27. The household is completely preserved. No.2 is probably the daughter of the same father but not of the same mother, but that is not certain.

HOUSEHOLD NO.: 187-Ox-4
*Source: *P.Princ.* III 129 ii (cf. *BL* 3.151–52; *BASP* 28 [1991] 125–29)
Prov., Date: Oxyrhynchos, 189
Stemma:

Declarant: NN d. Panomgeus and Taesis (d. Apollos), with *kyrios* Paous s. Harmiusis
Family members: (1) NN [declarant] d. Panomgeus and Taesis (d. Apollos), 32
                        (2) NN d. NN [declarant]?, 3
                        (3) NN d. NN [declarant]?, 10
Free non-kin, slaves: None
Verif./photo: Princeton, GD 7928B, col. ii; seen 26/2/1991.
Discussion: Broken at left and top. The household is apparently completely preserved, but damage at the crucial point makes it unclear exactly who is declared. The first person is almost certainly the declarant, and it appears that the two following persons are daughters. But they are in inverse age order, and the description of them is evidently more complex than one would expect.

HOUSEHOLD NO.: 187-Ox-5
Source: *P.Harr.* I 71 (cf. *BL* 3.78, *P.Oxy.* XXXVI 2762 introd.)
Prov., Date: Ision Panga (Oxyrhynchite), 188/9
Declarants: Horion s. Apollonios (s. Horion alias L—) and his cousin Horion s. Myros, and perhaps a third person, both or all former *exegetai*

Family members, free non-kin, slaves: None
Verif./photo: Birmingham, Selly Oak, inv. 199a; photograph.
Discussion: Broken at right in parts. The declarants register property (mainly vacant lots) in which no one is registered.

HOUSEHOLD NO.: 187-Ox-6
Source: *P.Oxy.* LVIII 3918
Prov., Date: Tanais (Oxyrhynchite), 188/9
Declarant: Sarapion alias Eusebes s. Sarapion, tribe and deme Matideios/Thesmophoreios (in Antinoopolis)
Family members, free non-kin, slaves: None
Verif./photo: Ashmolean; seen 4/4/1991.
Discussion: Complete except at bottom; no one was registered in this property owned by an Antinoite.

HOUSEHOLD NO.: 201-Ar-1
*Source: *P.Stras.* IV 257; cf. *P.Stras.* IV, p. 190 (*BL* 5.140–41)#
Prov., Date: Tebtunis, 203
Stemma:

Declarant: Thenpestsokis d. Petesouchos and Tasoucharion, with her son Ptolemaios s. Pathotes as *kyrios*
Family members: (1) Thenpetesouchos [declarant] d. Petesouchos and Tasoucharion, 59
                   (2) Ptolemaios s. Pathotes alias Heron (s. Orsenouphis) and Thenpetesouchos [declarant], 33
                   (3) Tolis alias Helledora, *apator*, relative?, 54
                   (4) Tasous daughter of Horion and Thaubarion, wife of Ptolemaios [no.2], 35
                   (5) Ptollous, daughter of Ptolemaios [no.2] and Tasous [no.4], born in the present year (202/3)
Free non-kin: None
Slaves: (1) Thermouthis female offspring of Tyche, slave of Thenpetesouchos, 8
Verif./photo: P.Stras.inv.gr. 1154, seen 14/3/1989.
Discussion: Broken at bottom, minor damage elsewhere; declares property also, and names of inhabitants of second house may be lost.

HOUSEHOLD NO.: 201-Ar-2
*Source: *PSI* X 1147 (cf. *BL* 6.185)
Prov., Date: Tebtunis, 202/3

Stemma:

Declarant: Pakebkis s. Pakebkis alias Zosimos (s. Pakebkis) and NN, priest of the Temple of Soknebtunis alias Kronos and Isis and Sarapis and Harpokrates

Family members: (1) Pakebkis [declarant] s. Pakebkis alias Zosimos (s. Pakebkis) and NN, priest, age lost

(2) Thaesis d. NN (s. NN) and Isidora, wife of Pakebkis [declarant], age lost

(3) NN s. Pakebkis [declarant] and NN, his deceased wife and the full sister of Thaesis [no.2], priest, age lost

Free non-kin: None

Slaves: (1) Eudaimonis, age lost

(2) NN offspring of Eudaimonis, age lost

Verif./photo: Florence, Biblioteca Laurenziana; seen 25/5/1989.

Discussion: All margins preserved, but there are large gaps in the center and right lower parts. There may be a slave preceding Eudaimonis and perhaps another child of Eudaimonis, but this cannot be determined. Pakebkis is exempt from capitation taxes, but whether for age or priesthood is not said.

HOUSEHOLD NO.: 201-Ar-3

Source: *SB* XII 11150 (*SIFC* 43 [1971] 155)

Prov., Date: Tebtunis, 202/3

Declarant: Sarapias d. Patermouthis (s. Kronion) and Taorses, from the metropolis, with Herakleides her full brother as *kyrios*

Family members, free non-kin, slaves: None

Verif./photo: Florence, Istituto Papirologico, inv. 340; seen 25/5/1989.

Discussion: Complete except at bottom, but up to that point the declarant has listed only a house in Tebtunis in which no one is registered.

HOUSEHOLD NO.: 201-Ar-4

Source: *BGU* XI 2091 (cf. *BL* 7.24)

Prov., Date: Arsinoe, 203

Declarant: Maron s. Hermias

Family members: None

Free non-kin: Plural *enoikoi*.

Slaves: None

Verif./photo: W. Berlin, P.21612; seen 11/4/1991.

Discussion: Broken at left and below, with loss of all entries. The declarant is himself registered in another declaration; this one is only for renters of another property.

HOUSEHOLD NO.: 201-Ar-5

*Source: *BGU* XIII 2226 = *ZPE* 9 (1972) 255–58

Prov., Date: Arsinoe, 203

Stemma:

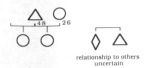

relationship to others
uncertain

Declarant: NN through Heroninos s. Pasion (s. NN) and Helene, *katoikos*,
phrontistes

Family members: (1) Heroninos s. Pasion, *katoikos*, wineseller [agent of
declarant], 48
(2) Sabina d. Her[, wife of Heroninos [no.1], 26
(3) NN, d. Heroninos [no.1] and Sabina [no.2],
age lost
(4) NN, d. Heroninos [no.1] and Sarapias, age lost
(5) NN?, age lost
(6) Apollonios?, age lost

Free non-kin: None

Slaves: None preserved

Verif./photo: W. Berlin, P.21881; seen 11/4/1991.

Discussion: Broken at top and bottom; in two fragments, with some loss in the
middle of all lines and some loss at right; breaks off in the middle of listing
persons. Nos. 5 and 6 are the children of the same person, but it is unknown
of whom. The *phrontistes* and his family are described as *enoikoi* of the
owners, who apparently are in Alexandria.

HOUSEHOLD NO.: 201-Ar-6

*Source: *P.Fam.Tebt.* 48 (cf. *BL* 3.104, 6.67, 7.96)#

Prov., Date: Arsinoe, 202/3

Stemma:

slaves of 57-year-old woman

Declarants: Valerius alias Philantinoos and Philantinoos alias Herodes, sons of
Philantinoos alias Neilammon, and Valerius alias Philantinoos s. Sarapam-
mon alias Nilammon, and Philosarapis and Herakleides both sons of
Lysimachos

Family members: (1) Neilos s. Patron (s. Didymos) and Sarapias, weaver, 50
(2) Eudaimonis surnamed Kale, wife of Neilos [no.1], 44
(3) Helene d. Neilos [no.1] and Eudaimonis [no.2],
declared with her husband Philosarapis in
Antinoopolis, age not given
(4) Sarapias d. Sabeinos (s. Kronion) and Eudaimonis, 57
(5) Tyrannis alias Isidora d. Sarapias [no.4], registered
with her father Philantinoos alias Herodes in
Antinoopolis, age not given [14 or more]

Free non-kin: None

Slaves: (1) Elpis slave of Sarapias, 26
                     (2) Sarapammon offspring of Isis alias Memphis, slave of
                     Sarapias (half-share), 20
Verif./photo: London, BL inv. 1902; seen 2/4/1991.
Discussion: Complete but with many small holes. The persons are renters of the
     property belonging to the declarants. Neilos and Eudaimonis are the parents-
     in-law of one of the owners, Sarapias the ex-wife of another owner. The
     owners declare two persons who were also declared elsewhere; where they
     were actually resident is not clear.

HOUSEHOLD NO.: 201-Ar-7
Source: *BGU* I 158#
Prov., Date: Herakleia (Arsinoite)
Declarant: Taonnophris d. Stotoetis (s. Stotoetis) and Taphiamis (d. Satabous)
Family members, free non-kin, slaves: None preserved
Verif./photo: Berlin, P.7086; seen 12/4/1991.
Discussion: Broken at bottom before list of persons. The date is based on the
     strategos; *BL* 1.23 wrongly suggests 138 as date.

HOUSEHOLD NO.: 201-Ar-8
*Source: *BGU* I 97 = *W.Chr.* 204#
Prov., Date: Karanis (Arsinoite), 203
Stemma:

Declarant: Herois d. Kastor (s. Onnophris) and Taorsenouphis, through the hus-
     band of her daughter, Longinos alias Zosimos s. Leonides
Family members: (1) Herois [declarant] d. Kastor (s. Onnophris) and
                         Taorsenouphis, 50
                     (2) Soeris d. Heron (s. Ptolemaios) and Herois
                         [declarant], 21
                     (3) Gaia d. Longinos alias Zosimos and Soeris [no.2], 1
Free non-kin, slaves: None
Verif./photo: Berlin, P.6856; seen 15/4/1991.
Discussion: Complete with minor holes. Herois declares herself, her daughter, and
     her granddaughter, but not her son-in-law, even though she makes the
     declaration through him. Cf. 201-Ar-9.

HOUSEHOLD NO.: 201-Ar-9
*Source: *BGU* II 577 (cf. *BL* 1.54)#
Prov., Date: Karanis (Arsinoite), 21/4/203

Stemma:

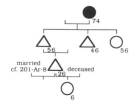

Declarant: Tasoucharion d. Heras (s. Petsiris) and Artemis, with *kyrios* her son
   Leonides s. Ptollas (s. Leonides)
Family members: (1) Tasoucharion [declarant] d. Heras (s. Petsiris) and
                  Artemis, 74
               (2) Leonides s. Ptollas (s. Leonides) and Tasoucharion
                  [declarant], 56
               (3) Longinos alias Zosimos s. Leonides [no.2] and Gaia
                  (d. Longinos), 26
               (4) Gaia alias Tapesis d. Longinos [no.3] and Tapesis
                  (deceased wife), 6
               (5) NN s. Ptollas (s. Leonides) and Tasoucharion
                  [declarant], full brother of Leonides [no.2], 46
               (6) NN d. Ptollas (s. Leonides) and Tasoucharion
                  [declarant], full sister of Leonides [no.2] and NN
                  [no.5], 56
Free non-kin, slaves: None
Verif./photo: Berlin, P.6974; seen 12/4/1991.
Discussion: Damaged at left and at bottom corners, with smaller gaps throughout.
   Longinos alias Zosimos also occurs in *BGU* I 97 (201-Ar-8) as the father of a
   one-year old daughter by Soeris (one of the persons declared there), but he is
   not living in that household. There is no indication of divorce in that docu-
   ment either.

HOUSEHOLD NO.: 201-Ar-10
*Source: *P.Tebt.* II 480 (see *Aegyptus* 72 [1992] 79–82)
Prov., Date: Tebtunis (Arsinoite), 203
Stemma:

Declarant: Thenpetsokis d. Petesouchos and Tasoucharion, with *kyrios* her son
   Ptolemaios s. NN

Family members: (1) Thenpetsokis [declarant] d. Petesouchos and
            Tasoucharion, 54
         (2) Ptolemaios s. NN and Thenpetsokis [declarant],
            locksmith, 33
         (3) Helene d. Petesouchos, sister of Thenpetsokis
            [declarant], 54
         (4) Taorseus d. Helene [no.3], wife of Ptolemaios
            [no. 2] 35
         (5) NN child of Ptolemaios [no.2] and Taorseus
            [no.4], < 1 (born in the current year)
         (6) NN child of Ptolemaios [no.2] and Taorseus
            [no.4], < 1 (born in the current year)
Free non-kin: None
Slaves: (1) Thermoutharion sl. of Thenpetsokis [declarant], 8
         (2) Protous, slave of Taorseus [family no. 4] age lost
Verif./photo: Berkeley, P.Tebt. 480; seen 27–28/9/1990; photograph.
Discussion: Essentially complete, but much text effaced, especially on the left side.

HOUSEHOLD NO.: 201-Ar-11
Source: *P.Diog.* 21
Prov., Date: Arsinoite (?), 203
Declarant: Name lost
Family members, free non-kin, slaves: None preserved
Verif./photo: London, British Library, inv. 2530B.
Discussion: Small fragment, with only the end of the description of the property
    and part of the date, written in red ink. No information survives about any of
    the people declared.

HOUSEHOLD NO.: 201-Ar-12
*Source: *P.Lond.* II 452.9–13 (p. 65) (cf. *BL* 1.245, *BASP* 28 [1991] 123–24)
Prov., Date: Arsinoite, 202/3
Stemma:

reconstruction uncertain

Declarant: Not preserved
Family members: (1) NN s. NN (s. NN) and Thatres (d. Pakysis), priest,
            age lost
         (2) Thases d. Satabous (s. Panomieus) and Tases, wife of
            no.1?, 16
         (3) NN s./d. NN [no.1] and Thases [no.2], 3
Free non-kin, slaves: None
Verif./photo: London, British Library inv. 452; seen 3/4/1991.
Discussion: See *BASP* 28 [1991] 123–24 for this text. This is an extract; the inter-
    relationship of the parties is not certain but a deduction from the order in
    which they are given.

HOUSEHOLD NO.: 201-Ox-1
*Source: *P.Oxy.* XII 1548 (cf. *BL* 6.102)
Prov., Date: Oxyrhynchos, 202/3
Stemma:

Declarant: Ploution s. Ploution (s. Ploution) and Tapsois
Family members:　(1) Ploution [declarant] s. Ploution (s. Ploution) and
　　　　　　　　　　　Tapsois, ἄτεχνος, 48
　　　　　　　　　(2) Tapsois alias Eudaimonis d. Ploution [declarant],
　　　　　　　　　　　living with her husband Apollonios, ἄτεχνος, 20
　　　　　　　　　(3) Gaiane d. Ploution [declarant], ἄτεχνος, 15
Free non-kin: None
Slaves:
　　　　　　　　　(1) Dioskoros slave of Ploution [declarant], ἄτεχνος, [.]8
　　　　　　　　　(2) Aphrodite surnamed Isidora, slave of Tapsois alias
　　　　　　　　　　　Eudaimonis [kin no.2], living with her owner,
　　　　　　　　　　　ἄτεχνος, 13
　　　　　　　　　(3) Taeros slave of Ploution [declarant] and his brothers
　　　　　　　　　　　and others, ἄτεχνος, 35
　　　　　　　　　(4) Taepimachos slave of Ploution [declarant] and his
　　　　　　　　　　　brothers and others, offspring of Taeros [no.3], 9
Verif./photo: Rochester; photo in Ashm., seen 5/4/1991.
Discussion: Broken at bottom in middle of oath formula.

HOUSEHOLD NO.: 201-Ox-2
Source: *P.Oxy.* VIII 1111, col. i
Prov., Date: Memertha (Oxyrhynchite), 202/3
Declarant: Didyme d. Kephalon and Didyme, with *kyrios* Heliodoros s. Dionysios
Family members, free non-kin, slaves: None preserved
Verif./photo: Bodleian, Bodl. MS.Gr.Class. f 90 (P); photograph.
Discussion: Broken at bottom in middle of property description.

HOUSEHOLD NO.: 201-Ox-3
*Source: *P.Oxy.* VIII 1111, col. ii (cf. *BL* 1.332, 3.134)
Prov., Date: Memertha (Oxyrhynchite), 202/3
Stemma:

Declarant: Admetos s. Herakles and T[
Family members: (1) Admetos s. Herakles and Tapontos, gf. of declarant,
                          deceased
                         (2) Herakles s. Admetos [no.1] and NN, f. of declarant,
                          deceased
                         (3) Admetos [declarant] s. Herakles [no.2] (s. Admetos
                          [no.1]) and T[, ἄτεχνος, age lost
                         (4) Mieus s. Herakles [no.2] and T[, brother of Admetos
                          [declarant], age lost
Free non-kin, slaves: None preserved
Verif./photo: Bodleian, Bodl. MS.Gr.Class. f 90 (P); photograph.
Discussion: Broken at top with full identification of declarant and at bottom in the
middle of list of persons. Broken at right with loss of all ages. The first two
persons declared are followed by the phrase ὃν δηλ(ῶ) τετελ(ευτηκέναι); the
editors take these to refer to the mother's father, pointing out that "they can
hardly refer to the persons named in ll. 9 and 12, since it is the rule for the
name of the person making the return to stand first." But it is equally the
rule that statements of this kind refer to the person entered, not to persons
not involved in the declaration at all. Moreover, the earlier part of the
declaration shows precisely that the father and father's father were the
previous owners of the property. Despite ἔτι πάλα[ι, the deaths may have
been comparatively recent (ἔτι π[άλαι is possible in line 11 also).

HOUSEHOLD NO.: 215-An-1
*Source: *P.Rein.* I 49 = *W.Chr.* 207 (cf. *BL* 1.386, 8.288; *BASP* 30 [1993] 46–
49)
Prov., Date: Antinoopolis, 215/6
Stemma:

still married?

Declarants: Aur. Thermoutharion d. Aur. Aline (d. NN the elder, freedm. of
Ptolemaios s. Euangelianos) and her children M. Aur. Eudaimon alias Bes-
odoros, minor and Aur. Maria alias Basileia, minor, through their father
Aur. Besarion s. Eudaimon
Family members: (1) Aur. Thermoutharion [declarant] d. Aur. Aline (d.
                          NN the elder, freedm. of Ptolemaios s.
                          Euangelianos), age not given,
                         (2) M. Aur. Eudaimon alias Besodoros [declarant], s. Aur.
                          Besarion (s. Eudaimon) and Aur. Thermoutharion
                          [no. 1], minor, age not given
                         (3) Aur. Maria alias Basileia [declarant], d. Aur.
                          Besarion (s. Eudaimon) and Aur. Thermoutharion
                          [no. 1], minor, age not given
Free non-kin, slaves: None
Verif./photo: Paris, Institut de Papyrologie, inv. 2051; photograph; original seen
21/6/1993.

Discussion: Virtually complete but with numerous small lacunae. An odd formula, declaring property but not ages. See *BASP* 30 [1993] 46–49 for discussion.

HOUSEHOLD NO.: 215-Ar-1
*Source: *P. Oslo* II 25
Prov., Date: Karanis (Arsinoite), 217
Stemma:

Declarant: Aur. Achillas s. Ptolemaios (s. Chairemon) and Tauris
Family members: (1) Aur. Achillas [declarant] s. Ptolemaios (s. Chairemon) and Tauris, 35
   (2) Aurelia Tauris, mother of Achillas [declarant], 60
Free non-kin, slaves: None
Verif./photo: Oslo; photograph.
Discussion: Complete.

HOUSEHOLD NO.: 215-Ar-2
*Source: *SPP* II p. 29 no.3, i (cf. *BL* 7.254)#
Prov., Date: Soknopaiou Nesos (Arsinoite), 28/8/217
Stemma:

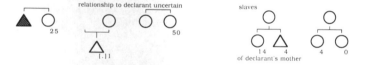

Declarant: Aur. Tesenouphis s. Stotoetis (s. Tesenouphis) and Tha[, priest
Family members: (1) Aur. Tesenouphis [declarant] s. Stotoetis (s. Tesenouphis) and Tha[, priest, age lost
   (2) Tases d. Stotoetis (s. Tesenouphis) and Tha[, sister of Tesenouphis [declarant], 25
   (3) NN s. Herieus (s. Tesenouphis) and Segathis, [.]1
   (4) Segathis d. Harpagathos (s. Sataboutos), mother of NN [no.3?], age lost
   (5) Taouetis d. Satabous, age lost
   (6) Ta.ases d. Satabous (s. NN) and NN (d. Stotoetis), 50
Free non-kin: None
Slaves:
   (1) NN, slave of Th[[mother of declarant], age lost
   (2) Taesis, female offspring of NN [no.1], slave of Th[[mother of declarant], 14
   (3) Orsenouphis, male offspring of NN [no.1], slave of Th[[mother of declarant], 4
   (4) NN, slave, age lost
   (5) Ta[, (female) offspring of NN [no.4], slave, 4

(6) Taseus, female offspring of NN [no.4], slave, < 1
(born in year 24)

Verif./photo: Vienna, inv. G 24555; seen 22/4/1991.

Discussion: Left half lost, as well as the right edge. The list given here of persons
is probably incomplete, and their interrelationships are impossible to establish
in several cases.

HOUSEHOLD NO.: 215-Ar-3
*Source: *SPP* II p. 29 no.3, ii (cf. *BL* 3.233, 7.254)
Prov., Date: Soknopaiou Nesos (Arsinoite), 28/8/217
Stemma:

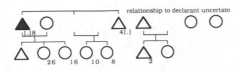

Declarant: Aur. Pa[s. NN (s. Satabous) and NN (d. Herieus), priest
Family members: (1) Aur. Pa[[declarant] s. NN (s. Satabous) and NN (d.
                   Herieus), priest, [.]8
             (2) NN d. NN (s. Stotoetis) and Tapekysis, wife of Pa[
                   [declarant], age lost
             (3) NN s. Pa[[declarant] and NN [no.2], age lost
             (4) Tases d. Pa[[declarant] and NN [no.2], 26
             (5) Tasisois d. Pa[[declarant] and NN [no.2], 16
             (6) Tanephremmis d. NN [deceased brother of
                   declarant], 10
             (7) Stotoetis d. NN [deceased brother of declarant], 8
             (8) Segathis, age lost
             (9) NN [prob. female], age lost
             (10) Herieus s. NN (s. Satabous) and NN (d. Herieus),
                   full brother of Pa[[declarant], 4[.]
             (11) Harpagathes s. Harpagathes (s. Stotoetis) and
                   Tanephremmis, age lost
             (12) Satabous s. Harpagathes [no.11]?, 2
             (13) Thaisarion d. Harpagathes [no.11]?, age lost
Free non-kin: None
Slaves: (1) Taseus, 49
             (2) S[, offspring of Taseus [no.1], 34
             (3) NN, offspring of Taseus [no.1], 13
             (4) Taseus, offspring of Taseus [no.1], 10
             (5) Thermouthis, offspring of Taseus [no.1], age lost

Verif./photo: Vienna, inv. G 24555; seen 22/4/1991.

Discussion: Large gap in the middle, amount not easy to establish with certainty in all cases. A number of uncertainties about relationships of the persons listed, particularly with the slaves.

HOUSEHOLD NO.: 215-Ar-4
*Source: *SPP* II p. 30 no.3, iii (cf. *BL* 1.407, 7.255)
Prov., Date: Soknopaiou Nesos (Arsinoite), 28/8/217
Stemma:

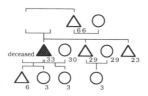

Declarant: Aur. Stotoetis s. Panephremmis and Taphiomis (d. Satabous), priest
Family members:
    (1) Aur. Stotoetis [declarant] s. Panephremmis (s. Stotoetis) and Taphiomis (d. Satabous), priest, 33
    (2) Tanephremmis d. Stotoetis and Se[, wife of Stotoetis [declarant], 30
    (3) Herieus d. Stotoetis [declarant] and Tanephremmis [no.2], 3
    (4) Pabous s. Stotoetis [declarant] and his deceased wife Ta[, 6
    (5) Taphiomis d. Stotoetis [declarant] and his deceased wife Ta[, 3
    (6) Pabous s. Panephremmis and Taphiomis (d. Satabous), brother of Stotoetis [declarant], 29
    (7) Amoun s. Panephremmis and Taphiomis (d. Satabous), brother of Stotoetis [declarant], 23
    (8) Tanephremmis d. Pekysis and Taouetis, wife of Pabous [no.6], 29
    (9) Taphiomis d. Pabous [no.6] and Tanephremmis [no.8], 3
    (10) Stotoetis s. Stotoetis (s. Satabous) and Taoues, brother of the father of Stotoetis [declarant], priest, 66
    (11) Taouetis wife of Stotoetis [no.10], age lost

Free non-kin, slaves: None
Verif./photo: Vienna, inv. G 24555; seen 22/4/1991.
Discussion: Losses at left and right and large holes in the center toward the bottom.

HOUSEHOLD NO.: 215-Ar-5
*Source: *SPP* II p. 30 no.3, iv (cf. *BL* 7.255)
Prov., Date: Soknopaiou Nesos (Arsinoite), 28/8/217

Stemma:

Declarant: Aur. Panephremmis s. Pekysis (s. Stotoetis) and Taoues (d. Stotoetis), priest

Family members: (1) Aur. Panephremmis [declarant] s. Pekysis (s. Stotoetis) and Taoues (d. Stotoetis), priest, 36

(2) Taphiomis d. Pakysis alias Sisois, wife of Panephremmis [declarant], 34

(3) Taoues d. Stotoetis, mother of Panephremmis [declarant], 54

Free non-kin, slaves: None
Verif./photo: Vienna, inv. G 24555; seen 22/4/1991.
Discussion: Complete except for minor gaps.

HOUSEHOLD NO.: 215-Ar-6
*Source: *SPP* II p. 31 no.3, v
Prov., Date: Soknopaiou Nesos (Arsinoite), 28/8/217
Stemma:

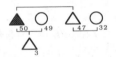

Declarant: Aur. Panephremmis s. Satabous (s. Herieus) and Segathis (d. Horos), priest

Family members: (1) Aur. Panephremmis [declarant] s. Satabous (s. Herieus) and Segathis (d. Horos), priest, 50

(2) Tapekysis d. Stotoetis (s. Satabous), wife of Panephremmis [declarant], 49

(3) Herieus s. Panephremmis [declarant] and Tapekysis [no.2], 3

(4) Satabous s. Satabous (s. Herieus) and Segathis (d. Horos), brother of Panephremmis [declarant], 47

(5) Taouetis d. Onnophris and Taphiomis, wife of Satabous [no.4], 32

Free non-kin, slaves: None
Verif./photo: Vienna, inv. G 24555; seen 22/4/1991.
Discussion: Complete.

HOUSEHOLD NO.: 215-Ar-7
*Source: *P.Lond.* II 452.4–8 (p. 65) (cf. *BL* 1.245, 8.178–79; *BASP* 28 [1991] 123–24)
Prov., Date: Arsinoite, March–April (?) 217

Stemma:

Declarant: Name lost
Family members: (1) NN s. Pabous (s. Panomieus) and NN, age lost
(2) NN d. NN (s. NN) and NN, wife of NN [no.1], age lost
(3) NN s./d. NN [no.1] and NN [no.2], age lost
(4) NN s./d. NN [no.1] and NN [no.2], age lost
Free non-kin, slaves: None
Verif./photo: London, BL inv. 452; seen 2/4/1991.
Discussion: Broken at left. This is an excerpt, cf. *BASP* 28 (1991) 123–24.

HOUSEHOLD NO.: 215-Ar-8
Source: *P.Tebt.* II 446 (cf. *BL* 1.428; see *Aegyptus* 72 [1992] 82–84)
Prov., Date: Arsinoite (found at Tebtunis, but filed in Arsinoe), 216/7
Declarant: Aurelia Protous, *apator*, d. Syra
Family members, free non-kin, slaves: Not preserved
Verif./photo: Berkeley, P.Tebt. 446; seen 28/9/1990; photograph.
Discussion: Only the beginning is preserved, with the name of the declarant.

HOUSEHOLD NO.: 215-He-1
*****Source:** *SPP* II, p. 26–27, no.1 (cf. *BL* 1.407, 8.433)#
Prov., Date: Herakleopolis, 7–8/217
Stemma:

lodgers
80   freedwoman
of 80-year-old
lodger

Declarant: Aur. Herakl[
Family members: (1) Aur. Herakl[[declarant], age lost
(2) [?Askl]epia d. Herakleios and Herakl[, wife of
Herakl[[declarant], age lost
(3)]s alias Herakleides s. Herakl[[declarant] and
[?Askl]epia [no.2], in school, 12 (13 in current
year)
(4) Aur. Theodoros alias Herakleios, s. Herakl[
[declarant] and [?Askl]epia [no.2], in school, 9 (10
in current year)
(5) Aur. Tastoous alias Isidora, d. Herakl[[declarant] and
[?Askl]epia [no.2], 7
Free non-kin: (1) Aur. Atrainis s. Atrainis and Ancharous alias Prot[, 80
(2) Aur. Korintia, freedwoman of Atrainis [no.1],

age lost
Slaves: None
Verif./photo: Vienna, inv. G 25799; *ZPE* 65 (1986) Taf. IIb; seen 22/4/1991.
Discussion: Broken at top, left, and bottom. The full identification of the declarant and the beginning of the list of persons are lost. Kin nos. 1–2 are reconstructed from information given elsewhere. The ages of kin nos. 3–4 are given as of current year in the declaration.

HOUSEHOLD NO.: 215-He-2
*Source: *SPP* II, p. 27–28, no.2 = *W.Chr.* 209 (cf. *BL* 3.233, 8.433–34)#
Prov., Date: Ankyronpolis (Herakleopolite), 217
Stemma:

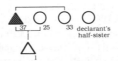

Declarant: Aur. Pareitis s. Horos and Thenpachnoubis
Family members: (1) Pareitis [declarant] s. Horos and Thenpachnoubis, 37
    (2) NN, wife of Pareitis [declarant], 25
    (3) NN s. Pareitis [declarant] and NN [no.2], 1
    (4) Tamounis d. Horos and Thenpachnoubis, sister of Pareitis [declarant], 33
    (5) Thenpachnoubis d. Horos and Thenphatres, sister on father's side of Pareitis [declarant] and Tamounis [no.4], age lost
Free non-kin, slaves: None
Verif./photo: Vienna, inv. G 24861; seen 22/4/1991.
Discussion: Broken at left (large losses in lower part) and below. The heading is an acknowledgment by nos. 4 and 5 of a copy of an extract from a declaration submitted by Pareitis, which is then appended.

HOUSEHOLD NO.: 215-He-3
*Source: *P.Oxy.* XXXIII 2671#
Prov., Date: Leonidou (Herakleopolite [?]), 216/7
Stemma:

Declarant: Aurelius Menches s. Horos and Taseus
Family members: (1) Aurelius Menches [declarant] s. Horos and Taseus, 60 (or 61–69)

(2) Aurelius Horos s. Menches [declarant] and
    Theonilla, 32
(3) Th[—] d. Achilleus and Taaphynchis, wife of Aur.
    Horos [no.2], 31
(4) Ps[—] s. Aur. Horos [no.2] and Th[—] [no.3], 4
(5) Nechthenibis alias —, s. Menches [declarant] and
    Theonilla, 29
(6) Tsenatis d. Menches [declarant] and Theonilla, 19

Free non-kin: (1) Horos alias ..mes, son of Isidora (below, no.1),
                          freedman, age lost
Slaves: (1) Isidora slave of Menches [declarant], age lost
                      (2) NN female offspring of Isidora [no.1], age lost (and
                          status also lost)

Verif./photo: Ashm.; seen 4/4/1991.
Discussion: Complete except at bottom, where an entry or more have been lost.
    The declaration also records that Taseus, another daughter of Horos [no.2],
    has died (age at death not stated). The declarant's age may or may not have
    had a second digit; there are no traces of one. The entry about Horos alias
    ..mes is very uncertain of reading and interpretation.

HOUSEHOLD NO.: 215-Hm-1
*Source: *P.Lond.* III 935 (p. 29) (cf. *BL* 1.274, 3.95, 6.62; *ZPE* 76 [1989] 213
    n.4)
Prov., Date: Hermopolis, 12/3/217
Stemma:

declarant   declarant
of 215-Hm-1   of 215-Hm-2
          48 36   30

Declarant: Aur. Hermeinos alias Moros s. Hermaios alias Pathotes (s. Achilleus)
    and Souerous (d. Kastor)
Family members: (1) Aur. Hermeinos alias Moros [declarant] s. Hermaios
                           alias Pathotes (s. Achilleus) and Souerous (d.
                           Kastor), 49
                        (2) Aur. Theognostos alias Moros s. Hermaios alias
                           Pathotes (s. Achilleus) and Souerous (d. Kastor),
                           brother of Hermeinos [declarant], 36
Free non-kin, slaves: None
Verif./photo: London, BL inv. 935; microfilm; original seen 3/4/1991.
Discussion: Complete. The date as given by the scribe is in 216, but the editor
    points out that one would expect 217, as in 215-Hm-2; cf. *BL* 6.62 for the
    scribal error. Cf. also 215-Hm-2. For the family at an earlier stage, see 187-
    Hm-1; later, cf. 229-Hm-1.

HOUSEHOLD NO.: 215-Hm-2
*Source: *P.Lond.* III 936 (p. 30) (cf. *BL* 1.274, 3.95; *ZPE* 76 [1989] 213–18)
Prov., Date: Hermopolis, 16/3/217
Stemma: see 215-Hm-1
Declarant: Aur. Dioskorous d. Hermaios alias Pathotes and Souerous (d. Kastor),
    with presence of her brother and husband Theognostos alias Moros

Family members: (1) Aur. Dioskorous [declarant] d. Hermaios alias
Pathotes and Souerous (d. Kastor), 30
Free non-kin, slaves: None
Verif./photo: London, BL inv. 936; microfilm; original seen 2/4/1991.
Discussion: Cf. 215-Hm-1 for the declaration of Dioskorous' husband and brother
as a resident of his brother Hermeinos' household.

HOUSEHOLD NO.: 215-Hm-3
***Source:** P.Mil. I 37 = SB X 10437 (cf. BL 7.102, 8.206)
Prov., Date: Hermopolis, 216/7
Stemma:

 slaves

Declarant: Aurelia Demetria d. NN (s. Horion) and Eudaimonis, with *kyrios* Aur.
E.[....] s. Agathos Daimon, (s. ?Theonermeinos), her [kinsman]
Family members: (1) Aurelia Demetria [declarant] d. NN (s. Horion) and
Eudaimonis, 72
Free non-kin: None
Slaves: (1) NN, offspring of Ploteina her slave, 34
(2) —nos alias Beryllos, surnamed Xenophon, male
offspring of NN alias Hermione her slave, 28
Verif./photo: Milan, Castelli Collection, inv. 58; Pl. XV in *P.Mil.*
Discussion: Very fragmentary at top, broken at left and bottom (only end of sub-
scription lost). Declarant refers to another declaration, possibly of property
only but perhaps including other persons; she owns more than one house.
We do not accept the correction to line 10 proposed in *BL* 8.206.

HOUSEHOLD NO.: 215-Ox-1
Source: *P.Oxy.* XLVII 3347
Prov., Date: Oxyrhynchos, 216/7
Declarant: Titus Flavius Hermeinos (?), spurius, son of Flavia Tamerylla
Family members, free non-kin, slaves: None preserved
Verif./photo: Ashmolean; seen 4/4/1991.
Discussion: Complete except at bottom, where it is broken before declaration of
any persons.

HOUSEHOLD NO.: 229-Ar-1
Source: *BGU* I 125 (cf. *BL* 7.10)
Prov., Date: Arsinoe, 6–8/231 (?)
Declarant: Aur. NN
Family members, free non-kin, slaves: None preserved
Verif./photo: Berlin, P.1348; seen 15/4/1991.
Discussion: Broken at bottom and right, some loss at left. Entire list of persons
declared is lost; since the declarant says that he registered in another declara-
tion, this is probably a list of renters of a property he owns. For the date,
which is based on an uncertain reading of the *strategos*' name, see Bastianini
and Whitehorne, *Strategi*, 38.

HOUSEHOLD NO.: 229-Ar-2
*Source: *BGU* III 971.8–15 (cf. *BASP* 29 [1992] 112–13)
Prov., Date: Arsinoe, 6–8/231 (?)
Stemma:

cf. 243-Ar-4

Declarant: Aur. Ammonios s. Doras (s. Ptolemaios)
Family members:　(1) Aur. Ammonios [declarant] s. Doras (s. Ptolemaios), 48
　　　　　　　　　　(2) Thermoutharion *apator* d. Thermoutharion, wife of
　　　　　　　　　　　　Ammonios [declarant], age lost
　　　　　　　　　　(3) NN d. Ammonios [declarant] and Thermoutharion
　　　　　　　　　　　　[no.2], age lost
Free non-kin, slaves: None
Verif./photo: Berlin, P.7171; seen 15/4/1991.
Discussion: Broken at left and right. A copy in a later petition. For the date, which
　　　depends on the *strategos*, see Bastianini and Whitehorne, *Strategi*, 38. Some
　　　names are restored from other parts of the petition and the declaration 243-
　　　Ar-4 which follows on the papyrus.

HOUSEHOLD NO.: 229-He-1
Source: *P.Heid.* 244 (cf. *Cd'E* 39 [1964] 168–71; *Proc. XII Congr.* 390 n.8; *BL*
　　　8.149)
Prov., Date: Herakleopolite, 230/1
Declarant: Titus Aelius Sarapammon, veteran leg. II Traian.
Family members, free non-kin, slaves: None preserved
Verif./photo: Heidelberg, inv. Gr. 52; Tafel VIc
Discussion: Broken at left and bottom, before any list of persons; also some
　　　damage at right. Given that this is a Roman citizen, it is possible that only
　　　property was declared. But that is not in any case an invariable rule. The text
　　　must be read in the reedition by Bingen in *Cd'E*.

HOUSEHOLD NO.: 229-Hm-1
*Source: *P.Lond.* III 946 (p. 31) (cf. *BL* 1.274, 3.95, *Proc. XII Congr.* 389–90;
　　　ZPE 76 [1989] 213–18)#
Prov., Date: Hermopolis, 12/5/231
Stemma:

Declarant: Aur. Theognostos alias Moros s. Hermaios alias Pathotes (s. Achilles)
　　　and Souerous (d. Kastor)
Family members:　(1) Aur. Theognostos alias Moros [declarant] s. Hermaios
　　　　　　　　　　　alias Pathotes (s. Achilles) and Souerous (d.
　　　　　　　　　　　Kastor), [50]

(2) Aur. Dioskorous d. Hermaios alias Pathotes (s.
Achilles) and Souerous (d. Kastor), sister of
Theognostos [declarant], 44

Free non-kin, slaves: None

Verif./photo: London, BL inv. 946; microfilm; original seen 3/2/1991.

Discussion: Very much mutilated, with losses at lower left, right center, and throughout. In the previous census Theognostos, though called Dioskorous' husband, was declared in the house of his brother Hermeinos (215-Hm-1), while Dioskorous declared her own house (215-Hm-2). The editor restored the age as 64 on the basis of a false reading in 215-Hm-1 (q.v.). Partial copies are found in *P.Stras.* VI 573 and in *P.Lond.* III 947 I i descr.

HOUSEHOLD NO.: 229-Hm-2

*Source: *P.Lond.inv.* 1157 recto (a) (cf. *Proc. XII Congr.* 390–92) (*Cd'E*, forthcoming)

Prov., Date: Alabastrine (Hermopolite), 20/5/231

Stemma:

Declarant: Aurelius Harendotes s. Pytakis

Family members: (1) Aur. Harendotes [declarant] s. Pytakis (s.
Harendotes), priest, 57
(2) Dionysios s. —chis and NN, priest, 6
(3) NN alias NN s. Aur. Harendotes [declarant] and
Taeus, priest, 8

Free non-kin, slaves: None

Verif./photo: London, British Library, inv. 1157 recto (a); seen 3/2/1991, 1/12/1993.

Discussion: Broken at left, and the surface obscured or abraded. Only partial transcript in Parsons' article. The first child's name is partly lost, but the patronymic is not Harendotes. No female members of the household are declared, and we cannot securely reconstruct the family history nor know why the younger child, evidently not the declarant's son, is listed before the older child.

HOUSEHOLD NO.: 229-Ly-1

*Source: *SPP* II, p. 31 (cf. *BL* 8.434)

Prov., Date: Lykopolis, 229/230

Declarant: Aur. Didyme d. Sarapion (s. Pathermoites), with *kyrios* granted to her by the prefect's office, Aur. Lykaon alias Sarapion

Family members, free non-kin, slaves: None

Verif./photo: Vienna, inv. G 19796; seen 22/4/1991.

Discussion: Broken at top and bottom, slight damage at left and lower right. This is a supplementary declaration to the *strategos* and *basilikos grammateus* correcting an error made in ignorance concerning the ownership of a 6-year-old male slave, whom she declared although he actually belonged to another.

HOUSEHOLD NO.: 229-Ox-1
Source: *PSI* X 1112 (cf. *BL* 3.228, 4.90, 6.184, 8.406)
Prov., Date: Oxyrhynchos, 7–8/231
Declarant: Aur. Di.. alias Theon s. N......
Family members, free non-kin, slaves: None
Verif./photo: Florence, Biblioteca Laurenziana; seen 25/5/1989.
Discussion: Complete except minor losses at sides. Declares no individuals in full, not even the declarant. Those previously registered are stated to have died and been released from capitation taxes.

HOUSEHOLD NO.: 229-Ox-2
Source: *P.Oxy.* XLII 3077 (cf. *Proc. XII Congr.Pap.* 397)
Prov., Date: Oxyrhynchos, 229/230
Declarants: Aurelii Matres (?) s. NN and Dieus, and NN
Family members: Names lost; presumably the declarants themselves
Free non-kin, slaves: None preserved
Verif./photo: Ashmolean; seen 4/4/1991. This is listed by Nachtergael as *P.Oxy.* ined. from the citation in *Proc. XII Congr.Pap.* 397.
Discussion: Broken at right and at bottom, taking the names of all persons registered.

HOUSEHOLD NO.: 243-Ar-1
*Source: *P.Flor.* I 5 (cf. *BL* 1.134, 3.55, 7.49; *BASP* 27 [1990] 4–5)
Prov., Date: Arsinoe, 244/5
Stemma:

Declarant: Aur. Thermoutharion d. Ammonios alias Herakleides and Ptolemais alias Laodita?
Family members: (1) Aur. Thermoutharion [declarant] d. Ammonios alias Herakleides and Ptolemais alias Laodita?, 27
(2) Koprei[os] s. Thermoutharion [declarant], age lost
(3) —on, s. Thermoutharion [declarant], 6
Free non-kin, slaves: None preserved
Verif./photo: Florence, Biblioteca Laurenziana; seen 25/5/1989.
Discussion: Complete at top and right, some loss at left and broken at the bottom in the middle of the list of persons declared. Other persons were listed, with a total (not readable) in line 20.

HOUSEHOLD NO.: 243-Ar-2
*Source: *P.Prag.* I 18 = *SB* I 4299
Prov., Date: Arsinoe, 7–8/245
Stemma:

Declarant: Aurelius Aphrodisios alias Euporas s. Neilogenes
Family members: (1) Dioskoros s. Zoilos (s. Her—) and Theano,
                      katoikos, salaried linen-weaver, 30
                   (2) Aurelia Sambous d. Spo— and P—, age lost
                   (3) Aurelia NN daughter of Dioskoros [no.1] and
                      Sambous [no.2], age lost
Free non-kin, slaves: None
Verif./photo: P.Prag. Gr. I 34; Pl. XXIII.
Discussion: Complete except at right. Declarant is registered in another declaration; this one concerns another property and its renters.

HOUSEHOLD NO.: 243-Ar-3
*Source: *BGU* IV 1069 recto (cf. *BL* 3.17)#
Prov., Date: Arsinoe, 244/5
Stemma:

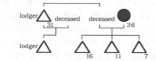

Declarant: Aur. Syra d. Apollonios (s. NN) and Herais (d. Alkimos), acting
    without *kyrios*
Family members: (1) Aur. Syra [declarant] d. Apollonios (s. NN) and
                      Herais (d. Alkimos), 36
                   (2) Aur. Sarapammon s. Ploutammon (s. Sarapammon [s.
                      Ninnaros] and Demetrous) [deceased husband of
                      declarant] and Syra [declarant], linenweaver, 16
                   (3) Apollonios s. Ploutammon (s. Sarapammon [s.
                      Ninnaros] and Demetrous) [deceased husband of
                      declarant] and Syra [declarant], 11
                   (4) Ammonios s. Ploutammon (s. Sarapammon [s.
                      Ninnaros] and Demetrous) [deceased husband of
                      declarant] and Syra [declarant], 7
Free non-kin: (1) Aur. Ninnos, s. Sarapammon (s. Ninnaros) and
                      Demetrous, brother of Aur. Ploutammon [deceased
                      husband of declarant], linenweaver, 31
                   (2) A[s. Aur. Ninnos [no.1] and Aur. Isidora (d. A[)
                      [deceased wife of Aur. Ninnos], age lost
Slaves: None
Verif./photo: Formerly Berlin, Ersatz Ehnas; since 1907 in Cairo Museum, SR
    2937 = J. 39459; seen 3/4/1993.
Discussion: Broken at bottom; some loss at left. This is a copy. The two persons
    classified as "renters" by the declarant are in fact related by marriage.

HOUSEHOLD NO.: 243-Ar-4
*Source: *BGU* III 971.16–21 (*BASP* 29 [1992] 112–13)
Prov., Date: Arsinoe, 6–8.245 (?)

Stemma:

Declarant: Thermoutharion *apator* d. Thermoutharion
Family members: (1) Thermoutharion [declarant] *apator* d.
Thermoutharion, age lost
(2) NN minor son of Ammonios (s. Doras) and
Thermoutharion [declarant], age lost
Free non-kin, slaves: None preserved
Verif./photo: Berlin, P.7171; seen 15/4/1991.
Discussion: Broken at left, right, and below. A copy of the declaration included in a petition. For date, which depends on *strategos*, see Bastianini and Whitehorne, *Strategi*, 38. The previous declaration for this household, 229-Ar-2, included Thermoutharion's now deceased husband Ammonios and a daughter of unknown age. We cannot tell if the latter figured also in this declaration or was now married and living elsewhere.

HOUSEHOLD NO.: 243-Ox-1
*Source: *P.Flor.* I 4 = *W.Chr.* 206 (cf. *BL* 4.29, *BASP* 27 [1990] 3)
Prov., Date: Oxyrhynchos, 4–5/245
Stemma:

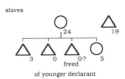

Declarants: Aurelii Petsiris and Aphynchis sons of Aphynchis (s. Petsiris) and
Taaphynchis
Family members: (1) Aur. Petsiris [declarant] s. Aphynchis (s. Petsiris)
and Taaphynchis, ἄτεχνος, 27
(2) Aur. Aphynchis [declarant] s. Aphynchis (s. Petsiris)
and Taaphynchis, 26
Free non-kin: None
Slaves: (1) Silbanos, slave of Aphynchis [no.2], ἄτεχνος, 19
(2) Mouses, slave of Aphynchis [no.2], offspring of slave
Sinthonis, ἄτεχνος, 3 (probable reading)
(3) Markos, slave of Aphynchis [no.2], offspring of slave
Sinthonis, ἄτεχνος, in his 1st year
(4) Markos the younger, manumitted slave, [?offspring of
Sinthonis], age not given
(5) Sinthonis, slave of Aphynchis, ἄτεχνος, 24
(6) Eirene, slave of Aphynchis, offspring of slave

Sinthonis, 5
Verif./photo: Florence, Biblioteca Laurenziana; seen 25/5/1989.
Discussion: Complete. The younger Markos [no.4] apparently has been freed; the
start of line 24 does not contain his age. See *BASP* 27 [1990] 3.

HOUSEHOLD NO.: 243-Ox-2
Source: *P.Heid.* IV 299
Prov., Date: Oxyrhynchos, 244/5
Declarant: Aur. Herakleides alias Claudius NN, s. NN (s. Sarapodoros),
Alexandrian, member of the hiera synodos
Family members, free non-kin, slaves: None preserved
Verif./photo: Heidelberg, inv. G 961; Tafel VI.
Discussion: Two fragments. The declarant registers apparently a house in the
quarter of Tegmenouthis.

HOUSEHOLD NO.: 243-Ox-3
Source: *P.Oxy.* L 3565
Prov., Date: Oxyrhynchos, 5/4/245
Declarant: Aurelius Aniketos s. Ploutarchos, councillor
Family members, free non-kin, slaves: None
Verif./photo: Ashmolean; seen 4/4/1991.
Discussion: Complete. A return of property in the village of Ision Panga in which
no one is registered.

HOUSEHOLD NO.: 257-Ar-1
***Source:** *SPP* II p. 32 (cf. *BL* 1.407; *BASP* 30 [1993] 54–56)
Prov., Date: Arsinoe, 28/8/259
Stemma:

Declarant: Aur. Helene d. Sarapammon (s. Dioskoros)
Family members: (1) Aur. Helene [declarant] d. Sarapammon (s.
Dioskoros), 38
(2) Koprios s. NN and Helene [declarant], 5
(3) Marinos s. NN and Helene [declarant], 1
Free non-kin, slaves: None
Verif./photo: Vienna, inv. G 25757; seen 22/4/1991.
Discussion: Broken at left along most of the length. It is unknown if the father of
the children was dead or divorced from Helene at the time of the declaration.
Another child might have been declared in line 10 in the lacuna.

HOUSEHOLD NO.: ???-An-1
Source: *P.Col.* X 269 (P.Col.inv. 420b)
Prov., Date: Antinoopolis, 2/3c
Declarant, family members, free non-kin, slaves: Not preserved
Verif./photo: Columbia, P.Col.inv. 420b; seen.

Discussion: Broken at left and just below the address.

HOUSEHOLD NO.: ???-Ar-1
*Source: *BGU* I 130 (cf. *BL* 1.22, 3.8)#
Prov., Date: Apias (Arsinoite), 2/3c.
Declarant: Serenos s. Deios (s. Heron)
Family members: (1) Serenos [declarant] s. Deios (s. Heron), age lost
Free non-kin, slaves: None preserved
Verif./photo: Berlin, P.1346; seen 19/4/1991.
Discussion: Broken at left and below, with some loss at right. Breaks off before
      list of persons, but preserving indication that declarant was one of persons
      listed, i.e. it was his household.

HOUSEHOLD NO.: ???-Ar-2
*Source: *BGU* I 131 (cf. *BL* 4.3; *BASP* 29 [1992] 106)
Prov., Date: Arsinoite, 3c. (215, 229, 243, or 257)
Stemma:

Declarant: Kopreia d. Hatres (?) and —ion, acting without *kyrios*
Family members: (1) Kopreia [declarant] d. Hatres (?) and —ion, age lost
                 (2) NN d. Kopreia [declarant] by former husband Aurelius
                     NN, age lost
Free non-kin, slaves: None preserved
Verif./photo: Berlin, P.1347; seen 15/4/1991.
Discussion: Broken at left, right, and bottom, with loss of all but a thin strip.
      Several further persons may have been declared, but not enough remains to
      reconstruct anything of their identity.

HOUSEHOLD NO.: ???-Ar-3
*Source: *P.Lond.* III 1119b (p. lviii) (Calderini, *La composizione della famiglia*
      57–59 = *SB* IV 7284; Bagnall, *Cd'E*, forthcoming)
Prov., Date: Soknopaiou Nesos (Arsinoite), 2c
Stemma:

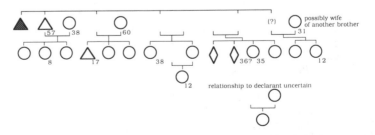

Declarant: NN
Family members: (1) NN alias Th[[declarant] s. Panephremmis, age lost
                    (2) NN, brother of NN [declarant], 57
                    (3) NN, wife of NN [no.2], 38
                    (4) NN d. NN [no.2] and NN [no.3], age lost
                    (5) Thases d. NN [no.2] and NN [no.3], 8
                    (6) Aaou—, d. NN [no.2] and NN [no.3], age lost
                    (7) Thermoutharion wife of]oteros, 31
                    (8) NN d.]oteros and Thermoutharion [no.7], age lost
                    (9) Tekiasis d.]oteros and Thermoutharion [no.7], 12
                    (10) Taphiomis d. Stotoetis, wife of NN, deceased
                            brother [of declarant], 60
                    (11) Pakysis s. NN (deceased brother) and Taphiomis
                            [no.10], 17
                    (12) Tympanthes d. NN (deceased brother) and
                            Taphiomis [no.10], age lost
                    (13) NN d. Tourbon (deceased brother) and Taphiomis
                            [no.10], age lost
                    (14) Thaesis d. Tourbon (deceased brother) and
                            Herieus, 38
                    (15) Tapakysis d. Tourbon (deceased brother) and
                            Herieus, age lost
                    (16) Tekiasis d. Tapakysis [no.15], 12
                    (17) NN s./d. Tathous, deceased sister, age lost
                    (18) NN s./d. Tathous, deceased sister, 36 (?)
                    (19) Taneph— d. Tathous, deceased sister (?), 35
                    (20) Taouetis, d. Tathous, deceased sister (?), age lost
                    (21) Tan— (female), age lost
                    (22) Tanephremmis d. Tan— [no.20], age lost
Free non-kin, slaves: None
Verif./photo: London, BL inv. 1119b; microfilm; seen 3/4/1991.
Discussion: Broken at bottom, damaged at top, right and here and there through the body. The text given by Calderini is a very preliminary transcript by Bell. This is listed as of unknown provenance, but the names point unmistakably to Soknopaiou Nesos. The editor mistakenly read the age of no.11 as *ιη*. Another brother,]oteros, may have figured in a lacuna somewhere.

HOUSEHOLD NO.: ???-Ar-4
Source: P.Berol.inv. 1343 (*Archiv* 39 [1992] 28)
Prov., Date: Arsinoe, 175 or 189
Declarant: None preserved
Family members, free non-kin, slaves: None preserved
Verif./photo: Berlin, inv. P.1343; seen 19/4/1991.
Discussion: A small fragment from the bottom of a declaration, with some loss at right. Only a description of property remains.

HOUSEHOLD NO.: ???-Ar-5
*Source: P.Berol.inv. 1361 (*Archiv* 39 [1993] 28)
Prov., Date: Arsinoe, 2c

Stemma:

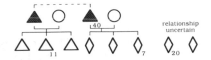

Declarants: Names lost (probably two brothers)
Family members: (1) NN [declarant], age lost
                         (2) NN, wife of NN [no.1], age lost
                         (3) NN s. NN [no.1] and NN [no.2], age lost
                         (4) NN ?s. NN [no.1] and NN [no.2], 11
                         (5) Souchion, ?s. NN [no.1] and NN [no.2], age lost
                         (6) NN [declarant], 40
                         (7) Ant[(?), wife of NN [no.6], age lost
                         (8) NN child of NN [no.6] and Ant[[no.7], age lost
                         (9) NN child of NN [no.6] and Ant[[no.7], age lost
                         (10) NN child of NN [no.6] and Ant[[no.7], 7
                         (11) NN, relationship unknown, 20
                         (12) Sara[, relationship unknown, age lost
Free non-kin, slaves: None
Verif./photo: Berlin, inv. P.1361; seen 19/4/1991.
Discussion: Fragment, broken on all sides, of what is apparently a household con-
     taining two brothers, their wives, and their children. So much is lost that the
     age and sex of most of the children is impossible to recover, and each couple
     may have had one or two more than given here.

HOUSEHOLD NO.: ???-Me-1
*Source: *P.Cair.Preis.* 10 (cf. *BL* 5.22; *ZPE* 80 [1990] 219–20)
Prov., Date: Memphis, 146 or 160
Stemma:

Declarant: Protas
Family members: (1) Protas [declarant], 33
                         (2) Nemesion s. Protas [declarant], 3
Free non-kin, slaves: None
Verif./photo: Cairo; plate in *P.Cairo-Preisigke Plates*, pl.10.
Discussion: Broken at the top.

HOUSEHOLD NO.: ???-Ox-1
Source: *P.Amst.* I 30
Prov., Date: Oxyrhynchos, 2c. (middle)
Declarant: Not preserved
Family members, free non-kin, slaves: Not preserved

Verif./photo: P.Amst.inv. 108. Pl. XIV.
Discussion: Fragment broken above and below.

HOUSEHOLD NO.: ???-Ox-2
*Source: *P.Col.* X 262 (P.Col.inv. 465)
Prov., Date: Oxyrhynchos, 146 or 160
Stemma:

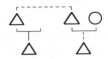

Declarant: Not preserved
Family members: (1) Dionysios alias Kom..., age lost
     (2) Dionysios s. Dionysios [no.1] and NN, age lost
     (3) Pausiris alias Ptollas, age lost
     (4) Didymos, age lost
     (5) Thaisous d. A— and NN, wife of Pausiris alias
     Ptollas [no.3], age lost
Free non-kin, slaves: None
Verif./photo: Columbia, P.Col.inv. 465; seen.
Discussion: Broken at top and at right. No persons are lost. The persons declared
 may represent a family of renters, or perhaps more than one family; some
 were registered in different amphoda in previous censuses.

HOUSEHOLD NO.: ???-XX-1
Source: *P.Erl.* 38
Prov., Date: Unknown, 2c.
Declarant: Claudia NN, on behalf of her son NN, through *kyrios* Claudius
 Germanus alias NN
Family members, free non-kin, slaves: None preserved
Verif./photo: Erlangen, inv. 101; photograph.
Discussion: Broken above and at right, with only the subscriptions preserved. This
 may be a declaration only of property if these are Roman citizens.

Addendum

The following households come from documents that became available to us only
after this book was in page proof.

HOUSEHOLD NO.: 117-Ar-12
Source: *ZPE* 98 (1993) 283-91 col. ii.42-60 (cf. Bagnall, forthcoming)
Prov., Date: Arsinoe, 119

Stemma:

slaves

Declarant: Kronous d. Maron (s. Maron) and Kronous
Family members: (1) Apronios s. Marcus (s. Apronios), deceased cavalry-
                        man, and Kronous, *idiotes*, *laographoumenos*, 48
                        (2) Apronios alias Pasinikos s. Apronios [no. 1] and
                        Ammonous (d. Heron), 8
                        (3) Kronous [declarant] d. Maron (s. Maron) and
                        Kronous, mother of Apronios [no. 1], 64
                        (4) Ammonous d. Heron (s. Aunes), wife of Apronios
                        [no. 1], 36
                        (5) Sempronia d. Apronios [no. 1] and Ammonous
                        [no. 4], 20
                        (6) Kronia d. Apronios [no. 1] and Ammonous [no. 4], 17
Free non-kin: None
Slaves: (1) Dioskoros slave of Apronios [family no. 1], 4
                        (2) Pantagathos slave of Apronios [family no. 1], 2
                        (3) Dioskorous slave of Apronios [family no. 1], 33
Verif./photo: P.Mich. inv. 5806; plate XVIb
Discussion: Extract from the εἰκονισμός of the census of 117/8, quoted in a dossier
of documents (including a cession of real property) compiled for an unknown
reason at a subsequent date. The names have, as is normal in a register, been
rearranged from the order of the original declaration, such that males are
listed in descending order of age, then females. In the original declaration,
Kronous (here no. 3) would as declarant have come first. For this household
fourteen years later, see 131-Ar-12. The name of Kronous' mother is given
differently in the two declarations; the editor takes Kronous here to be an
error. Kronia (no. 6) is called Kroniaina in 131-Ar-12.

HOUSEHOLD NO.: 131-Ar-12
Source: *ZPE* 98 (1993) 283-91 col. i.23-41 (cf. Bagnall, forthcoming)
Prov., Date: Arsinoe, 133
Stemma:

Declarant: Kronous d. Maron (s. Maron) and Pra.ous
Family members: (1) Apronios s. Marcus (cavalryman) and Kronous
                        [declarant], ὑπερετής, released from laographia, 61
                        (2) Apronios alias Pasinikos s. Apronios [no. 1]

and Ammonous [no. 4], ἐπικεκριμένος, 21
(3) Kronous [declarant] d. Maron (s. Maron) and
Pra.ous, mother of Apronios [no. 1], 78
(4) Ammonous d. Heron (s. Aunes), wife of Apronios
[no. 1], 60
(5) Kroniaina d. Apronios [no. 1] and Ammonous
[no. 4], 31

Free non-kin: None
Slaves: None
Verif./photo: P.Mich. inv. 5806; plate XVIb
Discussion: Extract from the εἰκονισμός of the census of 131/2, quoted in a dossier
of documents (including a cession of real property) compiled for an unknown
reason at a subsequent date. The names have, as is normal in a register, been
rearranged from the order of the original declaration, such that males are
listed in descending order of age, then females. In the original declaration,
Kronous (here no. 3) would as declarant have come first. Another daughter
of Apronios and Ammonous, Sempronia, was declared to have been married
to Marcus Valerius Rufus, a centurion of a chort. For this household fourteen
years earlier, see 117-Ar-12. The difference in ages recorded is 14 for two
people, 13 for two, and 24 (probably an error for 14) for one.

HOUSEHOLD NO.: 131-Ar-13
Source: *ZPE* 98 (1993) 283-91 col. ii.61-88
Prov., Date: Arsinoe, 133
Stemma:

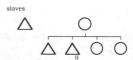

Declarant: Sempronia
Family members: (1) Gaius Sempronius Diogenes, *spurius*, s. Sempronia
Akousarion, *epikekrimenos*, age lost
(2) Sempronia Akousarion [declarant], mother of
Gaius Sempronius Diogenes [no. 1], 57

Free non-kin: None
Slaves: (1) Crescens, slave of Sempronia Akousarion [declarant],
formerly of her and of Gaius Sempronius [family
no. 1] and of Marcus Sempronius, age lost
(2) Kallistos, slave of Sempronia Akousarion,
offspring of Hediste, age not given
(3) Heron, slave of Sempronia Akousarion,
offspring of Hediste, 9
(4) Hediste, slave of Sempronia Akousarion,
formerly of her deceased brother Gaius
Sempronius Priscus, age not given
(5) Serapias, slave of Sempronia Akousarion, offspring of
Hediste [no. 4], age not given

(6) Thermoutharion alias Arsinoe, slave of
Sempronia Akousarion, offspring of Hediste
[no. 4], age not given

Verif./photo: P.Mich. inv. 5806; plate XVIb

Discussion: Extract from the εἰκονισμός of the census of 131/2, quoted in a dossier of documents (including a cession of real property) compiled for an unknown reason at a subsequent date. The names have, as is normal in a register, been rearranged from the order of the original declaration, such that males are listed in descending order of age, then females. In the original declaration, Sempronia Akousarion (here no. 2) would as declarant have come first. Ages were not given for the slaves, except for Crescens and Heron, because they are stated to have been included in another declaration by those who owned the remaining shares of them, probably the Gaius and Marcus Sempronius mentioned in lines 68-69. Cf. 117-Ar-12 and 131-Ar-12 for the other texts in this dossier.

HOUSEHOLD NO.: 159-Ar-27
Source: P.Cair. inv. SR 3049/75 (unpublished)
Prov., Date: Theadelphia, 19/6/161
Stemma:

Declarant: Taorseus *apator* d. NN (d. Herakleides), with *kyrios* her kinsman Didymos s. Horos
Family members: (1) Taorseus [declarant] d. NN (d. Herakleides), age lost
          (2) NN d. Taorseus [declarant], age lost
Free non-kin: None
Slaves: Multiple, entries not surviving
Verif./photo: Photograph.
Discussion: Declaration with the central part, containing the list of persons, largely destroyed; otherwise nearly complete.

Minor corrections to census texts

BGU I 54	Line 3, Σεγᾷθ[ι]ς (*BL* 1.12) > Σεγάθ[ιο]ς Lines 10-11, 'Αν | τῶνο[ς (*BL* 1.12) > 'Αν | των[ί]ο[υ
BGU I 55	Line 4, pap. has Πτολ( ). Γεουμθας: Γεουμ( ) perhaps a patronymic, followed by θυγ( ), with υ < α. Intended must have been θυγ(ατρὸς) κατοίκ(ου). The copyist probably did not understand his original here. Line 7, pap. does have καὶ αὐτ(οὺς) .[
BGU I 57	Line 1, there are traces of a letter above this line, probably a number for this sheet in a *tomos*.
BGU I 58	Line 15, Θερωκ[.]ντ > Θερμουθᾶν ..[Line 20, Ταο[.]..[> perhaps Ταο[ρ]σεν[ούφεως
BGU I 95	Lines 20-21, καὶ τῇ 'Αφροδοῦτι ο[ἰκία ...] | κωι ψιλὸς τόπ[ος (cf. *BL* 1.19) > καὶ τῇ 'Αφροδοῦτι ἐ[ν τῇ] | κώμῃ ψιλὸς τόπ[ος
BGU I 97	Line 16, θυγατρεὶ > θυγατρί μο(υ) Line 19, ὀλ(...) > ὅλ(ης) Line 21, π[. . . . . .]ν > perhaps τῇ[ν ἀδελφή]ν
BGU I 115 i	Line 7, (ἐτῶν) ν (*W. Chr.* 203) > (ἐτῶν) ν[. (as ed.pr.; space exists)

Line 8, ...].ν > perhaps γέρδι]ον; (ἐτῶν) κε
(*W. Chr.* 203) > (ἐτῶν) κϛ (as ed.pr.)

BGU I 115 ii = *W. Chr.* 203 Line 23, Wilcken did not restore ὑπὸ τ[οῦ
ἀνδρός], but since the children are said to
be ἐξ ἀλλ(ήλων), it seems inescapable.
Line 29, Παῦνι . > Παῦνι λ̄

BGU I 116   Line i.14, ..ν͞γ (ἐτῶν) .. > perhaps ἐργ(άτης)
(ἐτῶν) .η (first digit is iota or kappa)

BGU I 119   Line 2,]μαι >]. καὶ
Lines 4-5, ἐνοίκ(ων) | [. . . . . . . > ἐν οἷς
| [οὐδεὶς ἀπογρ(άφεται).

BGU I 123   Lines 4-5, ἀπὸ τῆς μη[τρο] | [πόλεω]ς κ. . . .
. . μερῶν. (cf. *BL* 3.8) > ἀπὸ
ἀμφό[δο(υ)] | [Χηνοβο]σκίων ἑτέρων.

BGU I 124   Line 4,]ρμ..νου > perhaps γεγ]ραμμένου

BGU I 128   Line ii.10, λινόυφος .[.... > λινόυφος
λ[αογρ(αφούμενος) (?)

BGU I 129   Line 7, [..].ρσιον > [συμ]πόσιον
Line 14, [. . . . . > ε[ἰμὶ δὲ

BGU I 130   Line 1, στ]ρ(ατηγῷ) is certain (a basilikos
grammateus of Themistos and Polemon
did not exist).
Line 2, πα]ρὰ (*BL* 3.8) is wrong: pap. has].ε
before Σερήνου

BGU I 138   Line 3, restoring Γυμ]ν[ασίου (*BL* 4.3) leaves a
gap of 11-13 letters to be filled; ed.'s
Διο]ν[υσίου τόπων fills the gap better.

BGU I 154   Line 16, λθ > λθ (theta certain; λ ex μ,
apparently)

BGU I 158   Line 8, Ταφιάμεως [καὶ ? Σ]αταβ- >
Ταφιάμεως Ϲαταβ- (there is no room for
καί)

BGU II 430   Line 5, κ]ώμη[ς] ..[... > κ]ώμης παρὰ ....[

BGU II 447	Line 14, ἐλαιουργίας > ἐλαιουργ(ίου) καὶ Line 16, γ̅ ι̅η̅ > γ̅ ι̅ε̅
BGU II 577	Line 15, (ἐτῶν)‾. > (ἐτῶν) ν̅ζ̅
BGU III 706	Line 15, τ[αύ]της > Τ[.].[.]σης (fem. name)
BGU III 971	Line 19, τῶν κ..[... > ἐν ᾧ κατο(ικῶ) [
BGU IV 1069	Line 10, Αὐρήλιον Σαραπάμμωνα > Αὐρηλίους <Σ>αραπάμμωνα
BGU VIII 1581	Line 19, Ἐπειφὶ ι̅η̅ > Ἐπεὶφ κ̅η̅
BGU XI 2088	Lines 8-9, ἐμαυτὸν	[? καὶ τοὺς ἐμοὺς > ἐμαυτόν τε καὶ τοὺς	[ἐμοὺς Line 12, ὑπὸ γόνυ δεξιὸν > ὑπὸ γόνυν δεξιὸν
BGU XI 2089	Line 3, ...ς > Ἰσίωρος
BGU XI 2090	Line 12,].μι. . . . .[- - - >] (ἐτῶν) μ̅γ̅· θυγατέρ[α
BGU XIII 2220	Date: 133 Line 1, καὶ [δεῖνι > καὶ [Ἑρμαίωι (cf. Bastianini-Whitehorne 120) Line 7, Ἀσκλη[> Ἀσκληπ̣[Line 9, καὶ [τῷ > καὶ τ̣[ῷ
BGU XIII 2221	Lines 7-8, ἐ̣[μα]υτ̣	[όν > ἐ̣[μ]α̣υ	[τόν
BGU XIII 2222	Line 6, ἐν αἷς οἰκ[εῖ καὶ] > ἐν αἷς οὐδ̣[είς]
CPR VI, p.3	Line 12, (ἐτῶν) μη > (ἐτῶν) κη.
P.Berl.Leihg. I 15	Line 5, Ἡρ̣ᾷτ̣ρ[ς] > Ἡρᾶτος Line 17, ξ[.] > ξ
P.Berl.Leihg. I 16A	Line 14, (ἐτῶν) λ[.] > (ἐτῶν) .[(mu also possible)
P.Berl.Leihg. I 17	Line 20, (ἔτους) α̅ .εω( ) τῶν β̄ Καισάρων > (ἔτους) α- ὅλω(ν) τῶν β̄ Καισάρων (cf. Kalén's note; ὅλων = here ἀμφοτέρων)
P.Brux. I 16	Line 2, the papyrus actually reads Βαλακρήους.

P.Cairo SR 3049/72	Lines 3-4, Μύστ(ου) | τοῦ Ἰσῶτος > Μύσθ(ου) | τοῦ Ἰσίωγος
P.Cairo SR 3049/74	Lines 3-4, Μύστου | τοῦ Ἰσῶτος > Μύσθου | τοῦ Ἰσίωγος
P.Fam.Tebt. 44	Line 17, ἥμ(ισυ) > η' (1/8) Line 19, τὸ ἕτερον (?)] > ἄλλον] Line 20, ἥμισυ > η' (1/8) Line 21,]ταγεισιν >]σταλεισιν
P.Fam.Tebt. 48	Line 6, ἥμ(ισυ) > (ἥμισυ) (written S) Line 9, ἥμ(ισυ) > ξο (1/64); κη L [[..ρ..]] {ἔτους} > κηS [[.....]] ἔτους Line 15, Ἑλένη, ῇ > Ἑλένην (read Ἑλένη) Line 17, Εὐδαιμ[ο]γίδο(ς) > Εὐδαιμ[ο]γίδος
P.Giss.Univ.Bibl. I 14	Line 5, Πεσηρᾶ > τοῦ Ἡρᾶ Line 15, (ἐτῶν) .. ἄσ]η[μ](ος) ἀρτρ(κόπος) > [(ἐτῶν) .. οὐλ]ὴ ὀφ(ρυὶ) ἀριστ(ερῷ)
P.Hamb. I 7	Lines 14 and 17, read κλω( ) ἄση(μον).
P.Lond. II 324.1-24 (p.63)	Line 7, read Ἐρψαήσεως. Line 17, [........]εσης > [. .].[.].[.]εσ`ι´ης Line 34, (ἐτῶν) κδ > (ἐτῶν) κ̄δ̄
P.Lond. III 919b (p.28)	Line 1, restoration of ἀπογράφομαι is wrong; the word will have appeared earlier in the formula. Cf. 915.
P.Lond. III 1119a (p.25)	Line 4, ὑπ]αρχ( ) is correct (cf. *BL* 3.96, 4.44) Line 5,]εν >]ς ἐν
P.Lond. III 1221 (p.24)	Line 22, [ὡς] (ἐτῶν) μ > ὡ[ς] (ἐτῶν) μγ
Pap.Lugd.Bat. XIII 12	Lines 7-8, read καὶ τοὺς | ἐμοὺς εἰς τὴν τοῦ διελ(ηλυθότος)
P.Mich. III 177	Line 13, read ἐμαυτό(ν) τε καί.
P.Monac. III 71	Line 15, read παρὰ <Πα> ποντῶτος.

P.*Oslo* III 98   Line 13, for ed. Σενθέως read Σεμθέως.
Immediately following, υἱο(ῦ), omitted by
ed. In line 24, read Σεμθεύς.

P.*Oxy.* II 255 = W.*Chr.* 201 There is enough blank space below the right
part of line 7 on the upper fragment to
show that ὧν εἶναι stood in its left-hand
part, with the remainder blank (it cannot
have stood in line 7, where there is room
only for the two letters shown in the
text). Line 22, for ἔ]ξ <ω> read
παρὲ]ξ, as proposed in *P.Oxy.Hels.*
10.22n. (the space is sufficient).

P.*Oxy.* II 256.12   For]ρησκ( ) read] τῆς κ(αὶ), the kappa being
written as superscript.

P.*Oxy.* III 480   Line 10, the editors' προγ(εγραμμένην) is correct (against *BL* 3.131 προκ(ειμένην));
line 2, probably read τ(οῦ) for α[ὑ(τοῦ)]
(ed.).

P.*Oxy.* XII 1547   Line 24, (γίν.) σώ(ματα) δ > (γίν.) ἄνδ(ρες) δ
Line 27, Thaesis' age stands on the edge of a
lacuna and should be read λ[(.)].

P.*Oxy.* XXXIII 2671   Line 12, Τεϲνᾶτεις > Τσενᾶτεις

P.*Oxy.* XLII 3077   Line 10,])ϲμερ[.]... > (fraction)]' μέρ[ο]ς ..

P.*Oxy.* XLVII 3336   Line 15, [.]. . . . . . . > ὧν εἶναι

P.*Oxy.Hels.* 10   Line 3, Ἡφαιστᾶτ⟦ιων⟧ος >
Ἡφαιστ⟦ατος⟧ίωνος
Line 6, [ʽΗ]φαιϲτᾶ[τος] > [ʽΗ]φαιϲτί[ωνος]
Line 15, Ἡφαιϲτᾶ[τος > Ἡφαιϲτίω[νος

P.*Rein.* I 46   Line 15, Ταπιεμις > Ταπιέπις
Line 16, Τεϲαυριν > Τεσεῦριν

P.*Ryl.* II 111a   In line 14, resolve ἀπεγρά(φησαν) or
ἀπεγρά(ψαντο); the subject of the verb is
the persons declared, not the declarant.
Cf., e.g., *P.Fouad* 15.12, where the third

person middle is written out.

P.Stras. IV 257

Lines 12-13, read perhaps τὸν
πρ[ο] | γεγραμμένον, written in the compressed fashion of προγεγραμμένη in line 12. Line 13, Τῶλις can be read.

P.Stras. IV 268

Lines 5-6, read μη | [τρὶ .].μ. .ρουτ[ι] ?

P.Vindob.Sijp. 24

Line 6, κυρί(ου) > κυρίο(υ)
Line 21, προγεγραμ`μ´(ένου) >
προγεγραμμένο(ν) `μ(ου)´
Line 22, Βυχανοῦπιν > Βοχανοῦπιν (P.J. Sijpesteijn in Vienna copy of volume)
Line 23, read [. . . .]πίωνος Τε. .
Line 26, read υἱόν] μου ἐκ . . . .[
Line 28, read (ἐτῶν)] λγ οὐ(λὴ) γόνα(τι)
ἀρισ(τέρῳ)

P.Wisc. I 18

Line 5, read νεωτ(έρου); 8, read αἰθ(ρίου); 10, read [θ (ἔτους) Ἀντων(ίνου) το(ῦ) κυρ(ίου)] κατ᾽ οἰκ(ίαν) ἀπογρα(φήν).

P.Wisc. I 36

Line 15, (ἐτῶν) κε > (ἐτῶν) λε
Line 18, (ἐτῶν) γ > (ἐτῶν) [(.)]γ

SB VI 9573

Line 7, Γεμέλλν (read Γεμέλλαν) >
Γεμέλλαν

SB VIII 9869a

Line 8, read [ἐμαυτὸν . . . .]νεμγεως.
The age is very uncertain; one cannot exclude (e.g.) ν or ις. There is a left vertical stroke and part of a curved stroke at right.

SB XIV 11577

Line 10, (ἐτῶν) ι. > (ἐτῶν) ε

SPP II, p.27

Line 1, read]ρ..ος [
Line 2, read]ληπιᾳ Ἡρακλείου μητ(ρὸς)
.Ἡρακλε[είας
Line 7, there are 2-3 additional characters before (ἐτῶν) ι
Line 10, before (ἐτῶν) π read ... λαογρ( )

SPP II, p.28

Line 8, ἐξσ<υν>κολλησίμων (*W. Chr.* 209)
> ἐξ συνκολλησίμων
Line 12, κώμ[ης] > κωμ[ο]γ[ρ(αμματεῖ)]
Line 18, read [τῆς κώμ(ης)·] ε[ἴ]μι δὲ ὁ
[Α]ὐρήλιος Παρεῖτις (cf. *BL* 3.233)
Line 19, read [καὶ ἡ γυνὴ NN   ]..[.] Ἀσκ[λ.
. . . .] (ἐτῶν) κε
Line 22, read ἀδελφ]ῇ (cf. *BL* 3.233)

SPP II, pp.29-31

i.10, read] θ[υ]γατ[έ]ρα Τα[ου]ῆτιν
Σατᾳβρ[ῦ]τ[ο]ς τοῦ .[
i.13, read] καὶ ταύτης ἔγγον[α] Ταῆσ[ι]ν
(ἐτῶν) ιδ
i.14-15, read ἔ]γγονον Τ)α...[. (ἐτῶν)] δ καὶ
Τασεῦν γεννη[θεῖσαν] τῷ | [κδ (ἔτους)

SPP XX 11

Line 20, [Ἰ]σιν Ἰσᾶτος ἀργ(ὴν) (ἐτῶν) μ > [.
. .]. ιν Ἰσᾶτος ἀργ(ὴν) (ἐτῶν) μ[(.)]

BullAinShams 1 (1985) 38-40, no.1 Line 3, Ἡρᾷ appears to be complete,
rather than editor's Ἡρα( ).

BullAinShams 1 (1985) 42-45, nos. 3-4 Read the father's name as
Παβοῦτος rather than editor's Παμοῦτος.
The kinsman's patronymic appears to be
Σαραπίωνος instead of editor's Συρίωνος,
although written with *Verschleifung*.
no. 5.3 and no. 6.3, Μύστ(ου) / Μύστου >
Μύσθ(ου) / Μύσθου
no. 5.4 and no. 6.4, Ἰσωτος > Ἰσίωνος

Concordance of publications
and household numbers

Publication	Household Number
BGU I 26	173-Ar-9
BGU I 53	131-Ar-5
BGU I 54	159-Ar-7
BGU I 55 ii.1-10	159-Ar-1
BGU I 55 ii.11-22	173-Ar-3
BGU I 57 i	159-Ar-2
BGU I 57 ii	159-Ar-3
BGU I 58	159-Ar-8
BGU I 59	173-Ar-8
BGU I 60	187-Ar-24
BGU I 90	159-Ar-13
BGU I 95	145-Ar-12
BGU I 97	201-Ar-8
BGU I 115 i	187-Ar-4
BGU I 115 ii	187-Ar-5
BGU I 116 i	187-Ar-6
BGU I 116 ii	187-Ar-7
BGU I 117	187-Ar-8
BGU I 118 i	187-Ar-9
BGU I 118 ii	187-Ar-10
BGU I 118 iii	187-Ar-11
BGU I 119	173-Ar-4
BGU I 120	187-Ar-12
BGU I 122	145-Ar-25
BGU I 123	173-Ar-5
BGU I 124	187-Ar-13
BGU I 125	229-Ar-1
BGU I 126	187-Ar-14
BGU I 127	173-Ar-6

BGU I 128 i	187-Ar-15
BGU I 128 ii	187-Ar-16
BGU I 129	187-Ar-17
BGU I 130	???-Ar-1
BGU I 131	???-Ar-2
BGU I 132	131-Ar-1
BGU I 137	145-Ar-5
BGU I 138	187-Ar-18
BGU I 154	159-Ar-9
BGU I 158	201-Ar-7
BGU I 182.1-15	145-Ar-6
BGU I 182.16-22	131-Ar-2
BGU I 224	159-Ar-13
BGU I 225	159-Ar-13
BGU I 298	173-Ar-7
BGU I 302	173-Ar-11
BGU II 410	159-Ar-13
BGU II 430	187-Ar-25
BGU II 447	173-Ar-9
BGU II 524	159-Ar-10
BGU II 537	159-Ar-13
BGU II 577	201-Ar-9
BGU III 706	117-Ar-7
BGU III 777	145-Me-1
BGU III 833	173-Me-1
BGU III 971.8-15	229-Ar-2
BGU III 971.16-21	243-Ar-4
BGU IV 1069 recto	243-Ar-3
BGU VII 1579	117-Ar-5
BGU VII 1580	117-Ar-6
BGU VII 1581	145-Ar-7
BGU XI 2018	187-Ar-26
BGU XI 2019	187-Me-1
BGU XI 2088	75-Ar-1
BGU XI 2089	159-Ar-19
BGU XI 2090	187-Ar-28
BGU XI 2091	201-Ar-4
BGU XIII 2220	131-Ar-9
BGU XIII 2221	159-Ar-23
BGU XIII 2222	159-Ar-24
BGU XIII 2223	173-Ar-12
BGU XIII 2224, i	173-Ar-13

BGU XIII 2224, ii	173-Ar-14
BGU XIII 2225	187-Ar-34
BGU XIII 2226	201-Ar-5
CPR VI, p.3	145-Ar-23
CPR XV 24	117-Ar-10
P.Alex.Giss. 14	117-Ap-7
P.Alex.Giss. 15	117-Ap-9
P.Alex.Giss. 16	117-Ap-1
P.Alex.Giss. 17	117-Ap-5
P.Alex.Giss. 18	117-Ap-2
P.Alex.Giss. 19	117-Ap-6
P.Alex.Giss. 20	117-Ap-3
P.Alex.Giss. 21	117-Ap-4
P.Alex.Giss. 22	117-Ap-8
P.Amh. II 74	145-Ar-20
P.Amst. I 30	???-Ox-1
P.Bad. IV 75a	131-He-2
P.Bad. IV 75b	145-He-1
P.Bad. VI 169	131-Ar-8
P.Berl.Leihg. I 15	187-Ar-30
P.Berl.Leihg. I 16A	159-Ar-14
P.Berl.Leihg. I 16B	159-Ar-15
P.Berl.Leihg. I 16C	159-Ar-16
P.Berl.Leihg. I 16D	159-Ar-17
P.Berl.Leihg. I 16E	159-Ar-18
P.Berl.Leihg. I 17	159-Ar-4
P.Berl.Leihg. III 52A	145-Ar-18
P.Berl.Leihg. III 52B	145-Ar-19
P.Berol. inv. 1335	187-Ar-35
P.Berol. inv. 1336	187-Ar-36
P.Berol. inv. 1342+1345, i	173-Ar-16
P.Berol. inv. 1342+1345, ii	173-Ar-17
P.Berol. inv. 1343	???-Ar-4
P.Berol. inv. 1349	173-Ar-18
P.Berol. inv. 1350	173-Ar-19
P.Berol. inv. 1355	173-Ar-20
P.Berol. inv. 1361	???-Ar-5
P.Bon. I 18, col. i	131-He-3
P.Bon. I 18, col. ii	131-He-4
P.Bon. I 18, col. iii	131-He-5
P.Brem. 32	117-Ap-5
P.Brem. 33	117-Ap-6

P.Brem. 34	117-Ap-9
P.Brux. I 1	173-Pr-1
P.Brux. I 2	173-Pr-2
P.Brux. I 3	173-Pr-3
P.Brux. I 4	173-Pr-4
P.Brux. I 5	173-Pr-5
P.Brux. I 6	173-Pr-6
P.Brux. I 7	173-Pr-7
P.Brux. I 8	173-Pr-8
P.Brux. I 9	173-Pr-9
P.Brux. I 10	173-Pr-10
P.Brux. I 11	173-Pr-11
P.Brux. I 12	173-Pr-12
P.Brux. I 13	173-Pr-13
P.Brux. I 14	173-Pr-14
P.Brux. I 15	173-Pr-15
P.Brux. I 16	173-Pr-16
P.Brux. I 17	173-Pr-17
P.Brux. I 18	173-Pr-18
P.Brux. I 19	117-Ar-3
P.Brux. I 20	145-Ly-1
P.Cair.Preis. 10	???-Me-1
P.Col. X 262	???-Ox-2
P.Col. X 269	???-An-1
P.Col.inv. 8	11-Ar-1
P.Col.inv. 420b	???-An-1
P.Col.inv. 465	???-Ox-2
P.Corn. 16.1-13	103-Ar-3
P.Corn. 16.14-20	117-Ar-9
P.Corn. 16.21-38	117-Ar-1
P.Corn. 16.39-58	131-Ar-3
P.Corn. 16.59-80	145-Ar-8
P.Corn. 17	145-He-2
P.Diog. 21	201-Ar-11
P.Erl. 38	???-XX-1
P.Fam.Tebt. 44.13-22	187-Ar-19
P.Fam.Tebt. 48	201-Ar-6
P.Fay. 319.13-19	145-Ar-22
P.Fay. 319.20-26	159-Ar-26
P.Flor. I 4	243-Ox-1
P.Flor. I 5	243-Ar-1
P.Flor. I 102	187-Ar-2

P.Flor. III 301	173-Ar-2
P.Fouad 15	117-Ar-2
P.Giss. 43	117-Ap-7
P.Giss. 44	117-Ap-8
P.Giss.inv. 227	117-Ap-9
P.Giss.Univ.Bibl. I 14	131-Ar-4
P.Graux inv. 937	131-Ar-11
P.Grenf. II 55	159-Ar-13
P.Hamb. I 7	131-Be-1
P.Hamb. I 60	89-Hm-1
P.Hamb. III 203	187-Ar-37
P.Harr. I 70	75-Ar-2
P.Harr. I 71	187-Ox-5
P.Heid. III 244	229-He-1
P.Heid. IV 298	103-Ar-14
P.Heid. IV 299	243-Ox-2
P.Laur. III 66	187-Ar-3
P.Lond. II 182b	159-Ar-11
P.Lond. II 324.1-24	131-Pr-1
P.Lond. II 325.25-29	145-Pr-1
P.Lond. II 452.4-8	215-Ar-7
P.Lond. II 452.9-13	201-Ar-12
P.Lond. II 476a	103-Ar-5
P.Lond. III 843	159-Ar-20
P.Lond. III 915	159-Me-1
P.Lond. III 919b	173-Me-2
P.Lond. III 923 (6)	187-Hm-1
P.Lond. III 935	215-Hm-1
P.Lond. III 936	215-Hm-2
P.Lond. III 946	229-Hm-1
P.Lond. III 947 I i descr.	229-Hm-1
P.Lond. III 1119a	103-Ar-6
P.Lond. III 1119b	???-Ar-3
P.Lond. III 1221	103-Ar-11
P.Lond. inv. 1157 recto	229-Hm-2
P.Lond. inv. 1570b	117-Ar-11
P.Lond. inv. 1914B	187-Ar-20
P.Lond. inv. 2187	145-Ox-1
P.Lond. inv. 2194	145-Ox-3
P.Lond. inv. 2196	61-Ar-1
P.Meyer 9	145-Ar-9
P.Mich. III 176	89-Ar-1

P.Mich. III 177	103-Ar-8
P.Mich. III 178	117-Ar-4
P.Mich. VI 370	187-Ar-27
P.Mich. IX 537	103-Ar-9
P.Mich. XV 693	103-Ar-13
P.Mich.inv. 158A-B	159-Hm-3
P.Mil. I 3	11-Ar-1
P.Mil. I 37	215-Hm-3
P.Mil.Vogl. III 193a	145-Ar-1
P.Mil.Vogl. III 193b	145-Ar-2
P.Mil.Vogl. III 194a	145-Ar-3
P.Mil.Vogl. III 194b	145-Ar-4
P.Monac. III 70	117-Ar-8
P.Monac. III 71	159-Me-3
P.Oslo II 25	215-Ar-1
P.Oslo III 98	131-He-1
P.Oslo III 99	159-Hm-3
P.Oxf. 8	103-Ar-7
P.Oxy. I 171	145-Ox-2
P.Oxy. II 254	19?-Ox-1
P.Oxy. II 255	47-Ox-1
P.Oxy. II 256	33-Ox-1
P.Oxy. II 361	75-Ox-1
P.Oxy. II, p.208	145-Ox-2
P.Oxy. III 480	131-Ox-15
P.Oxy. IV 786	117-Ox-1
P.Oxy. VIII 1110	187-An-1
P.Oxy. VIII 1111, col. i	201-Ox-2
P.Oxy. VIII 1111, col. ii	201-Ox-3
P.Oxy. XII 1547	117-Ox-2
P.Oxy. XII 1548	201-Ox-1
P.Oxy. XXXIII 2671	215-He-3
P.Oxy. XXXVI 2762	187-Ox-1
P.Oxy. XXXVI 2800	187-Ox-2
P.Oxy. XLII 3077	229-Ox-2
P.Oxy. XLVII 3336	131-Ox-16
P.Oxy. XLVII 3347	215-Ox-1
P.Oxy. L 3565	243-Ox-3
P.Oxy. LVIII 3918	187-Ox-6
P.Oxy.Hels. 10	33-Ox-2
P.Prag. I 17	187-Ar-2
P.Prag. I 18	243-Ar-2

P.Princ. III 129 i	187-Ox-3
P.Princ. III 129 ii	187-Ox-4
P.Rain.Cent. 59	159-Me-2
P.Rein. I 46	187-Ar-29
P.Rein. I 49	215-An-1
P.Rein. II 93	159-Ox-1
P.Ryl. II 111	159-Ar-5
P.Ryl. II 111a	145-Ar-10
PSI I 53, col. i	131-Ox-1
PSI I 53, col. ii	131-Ox-2
PSI I 53, col. iii	131-Ox-3
PSI I 53, col. iv	131-Ox-4
PSI I 53, col. v	131-Ox-5
PSI I 53, col. vi	131-Ox-6
PSI I 53, col. vii	131-Ox-7
PSI I 53, col. viii	131-Ox-8
PSI I 53, col. ix	131-Ox-9
PSI I 53, col. x	131-Ox-10
PSI I 53, col. xi	131-Ox-11
PSI I 53, col. xii	131-Ox-12
PSI VIII 874, col. i	131-Ox-13
PSI VIII 874, col. ii	131-Ox-14
PSI IX 1062	103-Ar-1
PSI X 1111	145-Oa-1
PSI X 1112	229-Ox-1
PSI X 1136	103-Ar-2
PSI X 1147	201-Ar-2
PSI XII 1227	187-An-2
PSI ined.	187-Ar-21
P.Stras. IV 257	201-Ar-1
P.Stras. IV 268	173-Ar-1
P.Stras. V 313	187-Ar-1
P.Stras. VI 573	229-Hm-1
P.Tebt. II 321	145-Ar-11
P.Tebt. II 322	187-Ar-22
P.Tebt. II 446	215-Ar-8
P.Tebt. II 480	201-Ar-10
P.Tebt. II 481, ii	159-Ar-21
P.Tebt. II 481, i	159-Ar-22
P.Tebt. II 504	187-Ar-23
P.Tebt. II 518	187-Ar-31
P.Tebt. II 522	131-Ar-6

P.Tebt. II 566	131-Ar-7
P.Vindob.Sijp. 24	131-Me-1
P.Vindob.Sijp. 25	145-Ar-23
P.Vindob.Tand. 20	145-Ar-23
P.Wisc. I 18	145-Ar-21
P.Wisc. I 36	145-Ar-24
SB I 4299	243-Ar-2
SB I 5661	33-Ar-2
SB III 6696	187-Ar-2
SB IV 7284	???-Ar-3
SB V 8263	117-Ar-3
SB VI 9360	145-Ly-1
SB VI 9495.1a	145-Ar-1
SB VI 9495.1b	145-Ar-2
SB VI 9495.2a	145-Ar-3
SB VI 9495.2b	145-Ar-4
SB VI 9554, 1	145-Ar-13
SB VI 9554, 2b	145-Ar-14
SB VI 9554, 2c	145-Ar-15
SB VI 9554, 3	145-Ar-17
SB VI 9554, 4	145-Ar-16
SB VI 9554, 5	159-Ar-12
SB VI 9572	61-Ar-1
SB VI 9573	173-Ar-10
SB VI 9639	103-Ar-4
SB VIII 9869a	159-Hm-1
SB VIII 9869b	159-Hm-2
SB VIII 9871	145-Hm-1
SB X 10219	159-Ar-6
SB X 10437	215-Hm-3
SB X 10630	117-Ap-7
SB X 10631	117-Ap-9
SB X 10632	117-Ap-1
SB X 10633	117-Ap-5
SB X 10634	117-Ap-2
SB X 10635	117-Ap-6
SB X 10636	117-Ap-3
SB X 10637	117-Ap-4
SB X 10638	117-Ap-8
SB X 10759	33-Ar-1
SB XII 10788B	61-Ox-1
SB XII 10842	131-Ar-6

SB XII 11150	201-Ar-3
SB XIV 11268	187-Ar-33
SB XIV 11355	187-Ar-32
SB XIV 11577	103-Ar-9
SB XIV 12110	89-At-1
SB XVI 12288, i.1-10	173-Ar-15
SB XVIII 13289	159-Ar-16
SB XVIII 13294	159-Ar-19
SB XVIII 13324	75-Ar-2
SPP II p.26-27 no.1	215-He-1
SPP II p.27-28 no.2	215-He-2
SPP II p.29 no.3, i	215-Ar-2
SPP II p.29 no.3, ii	215-Ar-3
SPP II p.30 no.3, iii	215-Ar-4
SPP II p.30 no.3, iv	215-Ar-5
SPP II p.30 no.3, v	215-Ar-6
SPP II p.31	229-Ly-1
SPP II p.32	257-Ar-1
SPP XX 11	173-Me-3
SPP XXII 32	103-Ar-10
CPJud. II 430	103-Ar-6
CPJud. III 485	89-Hm-1
Pap.Lugd.Bat. XIII 12	103-Ar-12
SelPap II 312	145-He-1
SelPap II 313	187-Ar-22
W.Chr. 201	47-Ox-1
W.Chr. 203	187-Ar-4, 187-Ar-5
W.Chr. 204	201-Ar-8
W.Chr. 205	173-Me-1
W.Chr. 206	243-Ox-1
W.Chr. 207	215-An-1
W.Chr. 208	131-Pr-1
W.Chr. 209	215-He-2
Aegyptus 46 (1966) 21 no.10	159-Ar-6
Aegyptus 54 (1974) 18	187-Ar-33
Aegyptus 70 (1990) 27-31	145-Ar-22, 159-Ar-26
Aegyptus 72 (1992) 64-66	131-Ar-7
Aegyptus 72 (1992) 67-71	159-Ar-21
Aegyptus 72 (1992) 67-71	159-Ar-22
Aegyptus 72 (1992) 71--74	187-Ar-23
Aegyptus 72 (1992) 74-79	187-Ar-31
Aegyptus 72 (1992) 79-82	201-Ar-10

Aegyptus 72 (1992) 82-84	215-Ar-8
Archiv 39 (1993) 22	173-Ar-16
Archiv 39 (1993) 23	173-Ar-17
Archiv 39 (1993) 24	173-Ar-18
Archiv 39 (1993) 25	173-Ar-19
Archiv 39 (1993) 26	173-Ar-20
Archiv 39 (1993) 26	187-Ar-36
Archiv 39 (1993) 27	187-Ar-35
Archiv 39 (1993) 28	???-Ar-5
Archiv 39 (1993) 28	???-Ar-6
BASP 7 (1970) 87-98	61-Ox-1
BASP 28 (1991) 19-27	103-Ar-3, 117-Ar-9
BASP 28 (1991) 125-29	187-Ox-3, 187-Ox-4
BASP 30 (1993) ##	257-Ar-1
BullAinShams 1 (1985) 38-40 no.1	131-Ar-10
BullAinShams 1 (1985) 40-42 no.2	159-Ar-16
BullAinShams 1 (1985) 42-45 nos.3-4	159-Ar-25
BullAinShams 1 (1985) 46-50 nos. 5-6	159-Ar-19
Calderini, *La composizione* 57-59	???-Ar-3
Cd'E 39 (1964) 111-14	159-Hm-1
Cd'E 39 (1964) 114-15	159-Hm-2
Cd'E 39 (1964) 118-19	145-Hm-1
Cd'E 39 (1964) 168-71	229-He-1
Cd'E 46 (1971) 120-28	131-Ar-6
CIMGL 6 (1971) 10-13	187-Ar-32
Eos 48.3 (1957) 155	173-Ar-10
GRBS 32 (1991) 255-65	11-Ar-1
JEA 52 (1966) 135-37	61-Ar-1
Proc. XII Congr. 390-92	229-Hm-2
SIFC 43 (1971) 155	201-Ar-3
SymbOsl 65 (1990) 139-45	159-Hm-3
ZPE 5 (1970) 18	33-Ar-1
ZPE 9 (1972) 245-51, i	173-Ar-13
ZPE 9 (1972) 245-51, ii	173-Ar-14
ZPE 9 (1972) 251-55	187-Ar-34
ZPE 9 (1972) 255-58	201-Ar-5
ZPE 21 (1976) 209	103-Ar-9
ZPE 25 (1977) 137	89-At-1

Statistical methods

At various points in this book, we use statistical methods to test theories about data derived from the census returns. The nature and purpose of these techniques are described in all standard introductions to statistics; we recommend R. E. Kirk, *Statistics: An Introduction* (3d ed.; 1990), to which we refer below. As a rule, these tests are easily performed either on a statistical calculator or with a computer statistics program.

Common to many statistical tests is a predetermined confidence level that indicates the degree of confidence one uses in accepting or rejecting a given hypothesis (Kirk, pp. 426–446). For data of the kind this book examines, the usual confidence level is 95 percent. If a test indicates significance at a higher than 95 percent confidence level, the statistical odds are less than one in 20 that the result is fortuitous.

Measures of dispersion

In Chapter 6, Section 2, we examine the gap in age between spouses for 78 cases attested in the census returns, where the gap is defined as the husband's age minus the wife's. The average (or arithmetic mean) of the attested gaps is simply their sum divided by the number in the sample (Kirk, pp. 84–87): in this instance, 7.53 years.

However, this average is not meaningful unless we also know the degree of typical dispersion about the mean, that is, the extent to which the attested figures normally vary from the average. The usual measurement of this dispersion is the standard deviation (Kirk, pp. 119–123), an easily determined statistic that measures dispersion by construing the attested figures as a normal bell curve; about 68 percent of the attested cases should lie within one standard deviation of the mean. For the statistics on age gap, the standard deviation is about 7.82, meaning that husbands are usually between 0 and 15 years older than their wives; and in fact, 56 of the 78 cases (or 72 percent) do fall within one standard deviation of the mean.

But Figure 6.3 shows that the distribution of age gaps is actually very asymmetrical, or "skewed"; husbands are closer in age to their wives than the mean implies, and the apex (or "mode") of the curve is around three to four years. Kirk describes various ways to describe and measure such asymmetry (pp. 54–57, 140–143). One good indicator that the data are skewed is the median age gap, which is 6 years: well below the mean.

This descriptive technique can also be used for subgroups of the sample. For instance, the twenty marriages between close kin have a mean age gap of 5.4 years with a standard deviation of 6.8; this dispersion is much narrower than for the 58 non–kin marriages, which have a mean of 8.3 with a standard deviation of 8.1. A statistical test, called the t–test (Kirk, pp. 378–381), indicates fairly high probability that these differences are significant. On the other hand, the means and standard deviations for age gaps in village and metropolitan marriages are virtually identical.

Single sample: population proportion

In a random sample from a much larger population, a proportion p_s has a certain characteristic; the remainder does not. Sampling, however, introduces possible error if what we seek to determine is p for the larger population. Granted p_s for the sample, how can we determine the likeliest range of p for the larger population?

One statistical means to answer this question is the z test (Kirk, pp. 355–358, 361–362), a test that is fairly easily calculated. We use this test in, for instance, Chapter 5, Section 1, when we discuss the possible sex ratios consistent with the sex ratios attested in the census returns; here the proportion of males in the various samples is p_s. The census returns have 530 males out of 1010 persons whose sex can be identified; hence p_s is 0.525. The z test indicates that, at 95 percent confidence, the sample proportion is consistent with a population proportion of males between 0.494 and 0.556. The sex ratio of the population is therefore likely to fall in a very wide range from 98 to 125.

As would be anticipated, the z test yields a wider range of p for the population when the sample is small than when it is large, and a wider range when the predetermined confidence level is higher than when it is lower. Although none of our samples meets statistical tests for true randomness (see Kirk, pp. 262–265), they may at least approach the random, at any rate if there is no reason to suspect major bias in the sample.

Two samples: difference between population proportions

The z test can also be applied when samples from two different populations have distinct proportions p_1 and p_2. Here one problem is to determine the likelihood that the two populations also have different proportions. The z test is sensitive not only to the size of the two samples and the predetermined confidence level, but also to the gap between the two sample proportions; it proceeds by establishing whether we should accept or reject the "null" hypothesis that, on the evidence of the two samples, the larger populations had the same proportion p (Kirk, pp. 372–373).

We use this test, for example, at the end of Chapter 6, Section 1, when discussing whether, in complete or nearly complete returns, the different proportions of married women among all free women aged 15 to 25 indicate that village women married earlier than metropolitan women. The z test indicates that even though the proportions of married women in the two samples are very different (0.543 as against 0.391), the sample sizes are too small to permit rejection of the "null" hypothesis; this means that both village and metropolitan women *could* be marrying at about the same rate. A larger sample is needed in order to settle the question.

Multiple independent samples: the chi-square test

Pearson's chi-square test looks not at proportions, but at the actual number of occurrences of discretely classified phenomena in one or more samples (Kirk, pp. 532–548). An example, discussed in Chapter 3, Section 3, is the number of simple as against complex households in villages and metropoleis, respectively; but the chi-square test can also be used to examine more than one variable and more than two samples, and so is more flexible than the z test. The chi-square test has many statistical uses, but we normally employ it to determine the likelihood that the proportions of the discrete sample phenomena are likely to be different in two or more populations.

The chi-square test yields a value for the tested data; this value becomes larger as the discrepancy increases between proportions of the tested variables, but the test is also sensitive to the size of the samples. Each chi-square test is associated with a specified number of degrees of freedom; this number is calculated from the number of rows and columns in the tested data, according to the formula $df = (r - 1)(c - 1)$. The resulting chi-square value can then be tested by comparing it with the significant values associated with given degrees of freedom and levels of confidence; all statistical manuals contain a table of these values (e.g., Kirk, pp. 658–659). If the calculated chi-square value is higher than the table value for a given confidence level, then the test indicates that the difference in samples is significant at the predetermined confidence level.

For instance, in the example given above, the chi-square value obtained by comparing simple and complex households (54/41 in villages, 53/19 in metropoleis) is 5.003, with one degree of freedom. Since the corresponding table value, at 95 percent confidence, is 3.841, the test indicates that the different proportions of complex and simple households in the two populations are probably real; complex households were in fact more common in villages than in metropoleis.

However, when, as in this case, there is only one degree of freedom, a technical correction, called Yates's correction for continuity, is used in calculating the chi-square value (Kirk, pp. 537–538). This correction lowers the calculated chi-square value to 4.301, still higher than 3.841 and therefore still significant at a 95 percent confidence level. If the five Cambridge types are disaggregated and compared for villages and metropoleis, the outcome is less striking because the sample is so small; but there are still about three chances in four that village and metropolitan household structures are different.

Co-variance: linear regression

Regressions are an important means for testing the strength of association between two sets of figures, their "covariance," over a tested range (Kirk, pp. 162–170, 202–217). A regression computes the best fitting line through the two sets of figures, and then measures, through a statistic called the coefficient of determination (r^2), the extent to which one variable can be "explained" through the other. Although we make little overt use of regressions, they often underlie statements in our text. For instance, Table 6.1 suggests that the age-specific age gap between husbands and wives drifts aberrantly downward as women grow older, but moves sharply upward as men age. A regression confirms that the trend in the male data is real, even though the extent of co-variance is not especially high because of the normal wide dispersion in age gaps. On the other hand, there is no measurable covariance at all between the marital age gap and the age of wives, and the attested differences in the means for various female age groups may therefore well result from chance.

Tables A-D

Table A. *Persons with exact ages in the census returns*

Age	Females			Males			Uncertain sex			All persons		
	Vill	Met	All	Vill	Met	All	Vill	Met	All	Vill	Met	All
0	3	1	4	1	4	5	2	-	2	6	5	11
1	5	2	7	8	10	18	-	-	-	13	12	25
2	3	2	5	4	2	6	-	-	-	7	4	11
3	8	3	11	5	6	11	1	-	1	14	9	23
4	9	-	9	6	4	10	-	1	1	15	5	20
5	3	4	7	4	5	9	-	2	2	7	11	18
6	3	3	6	5	6	11	-	-	-	8	9	17
7	-	2	2	1	2	3	-	1	1	1	5	6
8	10	6	16	3	6	9	-	-	-	13	12	25
9	2	2	4	3	7	10	-	-	-	5	9	14
10	6	3	9	3	4	7	-	-	-	9	7	16
11	1	1	2	-	4	4	-	-	-	1	5	6
12	7	1	8	-	2	2	-	-	-	7	3	10
13	6	4	10	-	2	2	1	-	1	7	6	13
14	4	5	9	4	4	8	-	-	-	8	9	17
15	4	3	7	1	3	4	-	-	-	5	6	11
16	8	-	8	3	4	7	-	-	-	11	4	15
17	-	5	5	3	6	9	-	-	-	3	11	14
18	6	2	8	2	5	7	-	-	-	8	7	15
19	3	1	4	4	5	9	-	2	2	7	8	15
20	8	7	15	5	6	11	1	1	2	14	14	28
21	4	2	6	4	6	10	-	-	-	8	8	16
22	1	4	5	3	1	4	-	-	-	4	5	9
23	-	5	5	1	1	2	-	-	-	1	6	7
24	2	2	4	-	4	4	-	1	1	2	7	9

Table A (continued)

Age	Females			Males			Uncertain sex			All persons		
	Vill	Met	All	Vill	Met	All	Vill	Met	All	Vill	Met	All
25	6	3	9	1	1	2	-	-	-	7	4	11
26	1	5	6	4	3	7	-	-	-	5	8	13
27	-	1	1	2	1	3	-	-	-	2	2	4
28	-	4	4	2	3	5	-	-	-	2	7	9
29	6	5	11	5	4	9	2	1	3	13	10	23
30	5	2	7	5	3	8	-	-	-	10	5	15
31	3	-	3	1	4	5	-	-	-	4	4	8
32	5	1	6	3	5	8	-	-	-	8	6	14
33	3	2	5	5	5	10	-	-	-	8	7	15
34	2	1	3	2	2	4	1	2	3	5	5	10
35	7	4	11	5	-	5	-	-	-	12	4	16
36	3	2	5	3	3	6	1	-	1	7	5	12
37	-	-	-	1	1	2	-	-	-	1	1	2
38	7	2	9	1	1	2	-	-	-	8	3	11
39	5	1	6	-	1	1	-	-	-	5	2	7
40	4	2	6	3	2	5	-	-	-	7	4	11
41	-	1	1	1	1	2	-	-	-	1	2	3
42	2	2	4	2	-	2	-	-	-	4	2	6
43	1	2	3	2	2	4	-	-	-	3	4	7
44	3	2	5	4	1	5	-	-	-	7	3	10
45	3	-	3	3	2	5	-	-	-	6	2	8
46	-	-	-	1	2	3	-	-	-	1	2	3
47	2	1	3	3	2	5	-	-	-	5	3	8
48	5	-	5	5	4	9	-	-	-	10	4	14
49	2	2	4	1	1	2	-	-	-	3	3	6
50	2	1	3	2	2	4	-	-	-	4	3	7
51	1	1	2	-	2	2	-	-	-	1	3	4
52	1	1	2	2	-	2	-	-	-	3	1	4
53	2	1	3	-	-	-	-	-	-	2	1	3
54	7	1	8	-	2	2	-	-	-	7	3	10
55	1	1	2	2	-	2	-	-	-	3	1	4
56	1	-	1	3	1	4	-	-	-	4	1	5
57	1	1	2	3	2	5	-	-	-	4	3	7
58	-	-	-	1	-	1	-	-	-	1	-	1
59	1	-	1	2	-	2	-	-	-	3	-	3

Table A (continued)

Age	Females			Males			Uncertain sex			All persons		
	Vill	Met	All	Vill	Met	All	Vill	Met	All	Vill	Met	All
60	6	1	7	1	-	1	-	-	-	7	1	8
61	-	-	-	2	1	3	-	-	-	2	1	3
62	-	-	-	-	1	1	-	1	1	-	2	2
63	-	-	-	-	1	1	-	-	-	-	1	1
64	-	-	-	-	-	-	-	-	-	-	-	-
65	1	1	2	2	-	2	-	-	-	3	1	4
66	-	-	-	2	1	3	-	-	-	2	1	3
67	-	-	-	-	-	-	-	-	-	-	-	-
68	1	-	1	-	1	1	-	1	1	1	2	3
69	1	-	1	1	-	1	-	-	-	2	-	2
70	3	1	4	3	1	4	-	-	-	6	2	8
71	-	-	-	1	-	1	-	-	-	1	-	1
72	1	1	2	1	1	2	-	-	-	2	2	4
73	-	-	-	1	-	1	-	-	-	1	-	1
74	1	-	1	-	1	1	-	-	-	1	1	2
75	1	-	1	1	-	1	-	-	-	2	-	2
76	-	-	-	1	-	1	-	-	-	1	-	1
77	-	-	-	-	-	-	-	-	-	-	-	-
78	-	-	-	-	-	-	-	1	1	-	1	1
79	-	-	-	-	-	-	-	-	-	-	-	-
80	-	-	-	-	1	1	-	-	-	-	1	1
Total	211	126	337	169	181	350	9	14	23	389	321	710
Unc. age	70	75	145	76	114	190	12	27	39	158	216	374
Total	281	201	482	245	295	540	21	41	62	547	537	1084

Table B. *Incidence of marriage*

		Females			Males	
Age	All	Marr.	Ex-marr.	All	Marr.	Ex-marr.
10	5	-	-	7	-	-
11	2	-	-	4	-	-
12	7	-	-	2	-	-
13	9	3	-	2	-	-
14	7	1	-	6	-	-
15	5	-	-	3	-	-
16	7	4	-	6	-	-
17	5	1	-	8	-	-
18	7	6	-	5	-	-
19	4	3	-	8	1	-
20	9	4	-	7	-	1
21	5	4	-	10	7	-
22	4	1	-	3	1	1
23	2	-	-	2	-	-
24	4	1	-	3	1	-
25	6	4	-	2	2	-
26	2	2	-	6	3	-
27	-	-	-	3	-	-
28	3	3	-	2	1	-
29	8	5	2	7	4	-
30	6	5	1	8	6	-
31	3	3	-	4	2	2
32	4	2	2	5	3	-
33	3	-	2	10	6	1
34	3	3	-	4	1	-
35	9	6	2	5	3	-
36	3	1	2	5	4	-
37	-	-	-	2	1	1
38	8	3	1	2	1	-
39	3	3	-	1	-	-
40	5	2	2	5	2	1

Table B (continued)

(Free persons in complete or nearly complete households)						
	Females				Males	
Age	All	Marr.	Ex-marr.	All	Marr.	Ex-marr.
41	1	1	-	1	1	-
42	2	1	1	2	2	-
43	3	3	-	2	2	-
44	4	2	-	5	3	1
45	2	1	-	5	4	-
46	-	-	-	3	2	-
47	3	1	2	5	4	-
48	4	-	2	6	3	2
49	2	1	1	2	1	-
50	1	-	1	4	4	-
51	1	1	-	1	-	1
52	2	2	-	2	1	1
53	3	2	1	-	-	-
54	8	2	4	1	1	-
55	2	1	1	2	1	1
56	1	-	-	4	2	1
57	2	1	1	3	1	1
58	-	-	-	1	-	1
59	1	-	1	2	1	-
60	6	2	3	1	-	1
61	-	-	-	2	1	-
62	-	-	-	1	-	1
63	-	-	-	1	1	-
64	-	-	-	-	-	-
65	1	1	-	1	1	-
66	-	-	-	1	1	-
67	-	-	-	-	-	-
68	-	-	-	1	1	-
69	1	-	1	1	1	-
70	4	1	2	4	1	2
71	-	-	-	1	1	-

Table B (continued)

Age	Females				Males		
	All	Marr.	Ex-Marr.		All	Marr.	Ex-Marr.
72	2	-	1		1	1	-
73	-	-	-		1	1	-
74	1	-	1		1	1	-
75	1	-	1		1	-	1
76	-	-	-		1	1	-
77	-	-	-		-	-	-
78	-	-	-		-	-	-
79	-	-	-		-	-	-
80	-	-	-		1	-	-
Total	206	93	38		218	94	21

(Free persons in complete or nearly complete households)

Table C. *Incidence of fertility*

Age of maternity			Age of paternity	
Age	All	Slaves	Age	All
9	1	-	13	1
10	-	-	17	2
11	-	-	18	3
12	-	-	19	2
13	1	-	20	2
14	-	-	21	2
15	7	2	22	2
16	7	1	23	3
17	11	1	24	2
18	11	-	25	5
19	11	2	26	3
20	13	2	27	2
21	7	1	28	11
22	9	-	29	7
23	8	-	30	10
24	6	2	31	5
25	15	-	32	5
26	7	1	33	9
27	10	1	34	7
28	9	1	35	4
29	9	-	36	6
30	9	-	37	4
31	5	-	38	4
32	4	-	39	8
33	5	-	40	1
34	5	1	41	3
35	5	-	42	2
36	4	2	43	5
37	6	1	44	4
38	3	-	45	4
39	3	1	46	1
40	5	-	47	3
41	4	1	48	4
42	-	-	49	5
43	2	-	50	2
44	2	-	51	2
45	2	-	52	2
46	1	-	53	1

Table C (continued)

	Age of maternity			Age of paternity	
Age	All	Slaves		Age	All
47	1	-		55	2
48	-	-		56	2
49	2	-		63	1
50	-	-		64	1
51	1	-		66	1
Total	211	20		Total	154

Table D. *Slave ages*

Age	Females			Males			Uncertain sex			All persons		
	Vill	Met	All	Vill	Met	All	Vill	Met	All	Vill	Met	All
0	1	-	1	1	1	2	-	-	-	2	1	3
1	1	-	1	-	1	1	-	-	-	1	1	2
2	-	-	-	-	-	-	-	-	-	-	-	-
3	1	-	1	-	1	1	-	-	-	1	1	2
4	3	-	3	2	-	2	-	1	1	5	1	6
5	2	1	3	-	1	1	-	-	-	2	2	4
6	-	1	1	1	1	2	-	-	-	1	2	3
7	-	-	-	-	-	-	-	-	-	-	-	-
8	3	1	4	-	-	-	-	-	-	3	1	4
9	-	1	1	-	-	-	-	-	-	1	-	1
10	1	-	1	-	1	1	-	-	-	1	1	2
11	-	-	-	-	-	-	-	-	-	-	-	-
12	-	1	1	-	-	-	-	-	-	-	1	1
13	-	1	1	-	-	-	1	-	1	1	1	2
14	1	-	1	-	-	-	-	-	-	1	-	1
15	1	-	1	-	1	1	-	-	-	1	1	2
16	-	-	-	-	-	-	-	-	-	-	-	-
17	-	-	-	-	-	-	-	-	-	-	-	-
18	-	-	-	1	1	2	-	-	-	1	1	2
19	-	-	-	-	1	1	-	1	1	-	2	2
20	2	1	3	-	2	2	-	-	-	2	3	5
21	-	-	-	-	-	-	-	-	-	-	-	-
22	-	1	1	-	1	1	-	-	-	-	2	2
23	-	2	2	-	-	-	-	-	-	-	2	2
24	-	1	1	-	-	-	-	1	1	-	2	2
25	1	-	1	-	-	-	-	-	-	1	-	1
26	-	1	1	-	-	-	-	-	-	-	1	1
27	-	-	-	-	-	-	-	-	-	-	-	-
28	-	1	1	1	2	3	-	-	-	1	3	4
29	-	1	1	-	2	2	-	-	-	-	3	3
30	-	-	-	-	-	-	-	-	-	-	-	-
31	-	-	-	-	-	-	-	-	-	-	-	-
32	1	-	1	-	1	1	-	-	-	1	1	2
33	1	1	2	-	-	-	-	-	-	1	1	2
34	-	-	-	-	-	-	1	1	2	1	1	2

Table D (continued)

Age	Females			Males			Uncertain sex			All persons		
	Vill	Met	All	Vill	Met	All	Vill	Met	All	Vill	Met	All
35	-	1	1	-	-	-	-	-	-	-	1	1
36	-	1	1	-	-	-	-	-	-	-	1	1
37	-	-	-	-	-	-	-	-	-	-	-	-
38	1	-	1	-	-	-	-	-	-	1	-	1
39	-	-	-	-	-	-	-	-	-	-	-	-
40	1	-	1	-	-	-	-	-	-	1	-	1
41	-	-	-	-	-	-	-	-	-	-	-	-
42	1	1	2	-	-	-	-	-	-	1	1	2
45	1	-	1	-	-	-	-	-	-	1	-	1
49	1	1	2	-	-	-	-	-	-	1	1	2
68	1	-	1	-	-	-	-	-	-	1	-	1
Total	25	19	44	6	17	23	2	4	6	33	40	73
Unc. age	11	13	24	-	11	11	2	8	10	13	32	45
Total	36	32	68	6	28	34	4	12	16	46	72	118

Bibliography

Acsádi, G. T., "Age: Some Problems of Reporting Errors," in *Family and Marriage in Some African and Asiatic Countries* (ed. S. S. Huzayyin and G. T. Acsádi; Cairo, 1976) 22-50

Bagnall, R. S., "The Beginnings of the Roman Census in Egypt," *GRBS* 32 (1991) 255-265

Bagnall, R. S., *Egypt in Late Antiquity* (Princeton, 1993)

Barclay, G. W., A. J. Coale, M. A. Stoto, and T. J. Trussell, "A Reassessment of the Demography of Traditional Rural China," *Population Index* 42 (1976) 606-635

Barker, D., "Some Findings from the Census Returns of Roman Egypt," *Ancient Society: Resources for Teachers* 15 (1985) 138-147

Biezunska-Malowist, I., *L'esclavage dans l'Egypte romaine* II (Wroclaw, 1977)

Boak, A. E. R., "Egypt and the Plague of Marcus Aurelius," *Historia* 8 (1959) 248-250

Bowman, A. K., *Egypt after the Pharaohs, 332 BC-AD 640* (Oxford, 1986)

Bowman, A. K., and D. W. Rathbone, "Cities and Administration in Roman Egypt," *JRS* 82 (1992) 107-127

Bradley, K. R., *Discovering the Roman Family: Studies in Roman Social History* (New York, 1991)

Braunert, H., *Die Binnenwanderung: Studien zur Sozialgeschichte Ägyptens in der Ptolemäer- und Kaiserzeit* (Bonn, 1964)

Coale, A. J., "Age Patterns of Marriage," *Population Studies* 25 (1971) 193-214

Coale, A. J., and P. Demeny, *Regional Model Life Tables and Stable Populations* (2d ed.; New York, 1983)

Coale, A. J., and T. J. Trussell, "Model Fertility Schedules: Variations in the Age Structure of Childbearing in Human Populations," *Population Index* 40 (1974) 185-258

Connell, J., B. Dasgupta, R. Laishley, and M. Lipton, *Migration from Rural Areas: The Evidence from Village Studies* (Delhi, 1976)

Cox, P. R., *Demography* (5th ed.; Cambridge, 1976)

Determinants of Fertility in Developing Countries vols. I-II (ed. R. A. Bulatao and R. D. Lee; New York, 1983)

The Decline of Fertility in Europe (ed. A. J. Coale and S. C. Watkins; Princeton, 1986)

Dixon, S., *The Roman Family* (Baltimore, 1992)

Duncan-Jones, R., "Age-Rounding in Greco-Roman Egypt," *ZPE* 33 (1979) 169-177

Duncan-Jones, R., *Structure and Scale in the Roman Economy* (Cambridge, 1990)

East Asian History, see *Family and Population in East Asian History*

Egitto e storia antica dall' ellenismo all' età araba: bilancio di un confronto (ed. L. Criscuolo and G. Geraci; Bologna, 1989)

The Estimation of Recent Trends in Fertility and Mortality in Egypt (National Research Council, Committee on Population and Demography, Report no. 9; 1982)

The European Experience of Declining Fertility, 1850—1970: The Quiet Revolution (ed. J. R. Gillis, L. A. Tilly, and D. Levine; Cambridge, Mass., 1992)

Family and Population in East Asian History (ed. S. B. Hanley and A. P. Wolf; Stanford, 1985)

Family Forms in Historic Europe (ed. R. Wall, J. Robin, and P. Laslett; Cambridge, 1983)

Family History at the Crossroads: A Journal of Family History Reader (ed. T. Haraven and A. Plakans; Princeton, 1987)

The Family in Italy from Antiquity to the Present (ed. D. I. Kertzer and R. P. Saller; New Haven, 1991)

Flandrin, J.-L., *Families in Former Times: Kinship, Household and Sexuality* (trans. R. Southern; Cambridge, 1979)

Flinn, M. W., *The European Demographic System, 1500-1820* (Baltimore, 1981)

Gallant, T. W., *Risk and Survival in Ancient Greece: Reconstructing the Rural Domestic Economy* (Stanford, 1991)

Goldsmith, R. W., "An Estimate of the Size and Structure of the National Product of the Early Roman Empire," *Review of Income and Wealth* 30 (1984) 263-288

Goody, J., *The Oriental, the Ancient and the Primitive: Systems of Marriage and the Family in the Pre-Industrial Societies of Eurasia* (Cambridge and New York, 1990)

Hajnal, J., "Age at Marriage and Proportions Marrying," *Population Studies* 7 (1953) 111-136

Hanson, A. E., "The Keeping of Records at Philadelphia in the Julio-Claudian Period and the 'Economic Crisis under Nero'," *Proc. XVIII Int. Congr. Pap.* II (Athens, 1988) 261-277

Hasan, A. F., "Age at First Marriage and Fertility in Egypt, 1984," in *Studies in African and Asian Demography* (Cairo Demographic Centre; Cairo, 1989) 281-308

Henry, L., "Some Data on Natural Fertility," *Eugenics Quarterly* 8 (1961) 81-91

Herlihy, D., and C. Klapisch-Zuber, *Tuscans and Their Families: A Study of the Florentine Catasto of 1427* (New Haven, 1985), condensed from *Les Toscans et leurs familles: une étude du catasto florentin de 1427* (Paris, 1978)

Histoire de la population française vols. I-IV (ed. J. Dupâquier *et al.*, 1988)

Hobson, D. W., "House and Household in Roman Egypt," *YClS* 28 (1985) 211-229

Hollingsworth, T. H., *Historical Demography* (Ithaca, NY, 1969)

Hombert, M., and C. Préaux, *Recherches sur le recensement dans l'Egypte romaine (P. Bruxelles inv. E. 7616)* (Leiden, 1952)

Hopkins, K., "Brother-Sister Marriage in Roman Egypt," *Comparative Studies in Society and History* 22 (1980) 303-354

Hopkins, K., "Graveyards for Historians," in *La mort, les morts et l'au-delà*, ed. F. Hinard; Caen, 1987) 113-126

Household and Family in Past Time (ed. P. Laslett; Cambridge, 1972)

India's Historical Demography: Famine, Disease and Society (ed. T. Dyson; London, 1989)

Kertzer, D. I., "Household History and Sociological Theory," *Annual Review of Sociology* 17 (1991) 155-179

Keyfitz, N., *Applied Mathematical Demography* (2d ed.; New York, 1985)

Lewis, N., *Life in Egypt under Roman Rule* (Oxford, 1983)

Littman, R. J., and M. L. Littman, "Galen and the Antonine Plague," *AJPh* 94 (1973) 243-355

Livi-Bacci, M., *Population and Nutrition: An Essay on European Demographic History* (trans. T. Croft-Murray; Cambridge, 1991)

Livi-Bacci, M., *A Concise History of World Population* (trans. C. Ipsen; Cambridge, MA, 1992)

McEvedy, C., and R. Jones, *Atlas of World Population History* (New York, 1978)

Marcus, A., *The Middle East on the Eve of Modernity: Aleppo in the Eighteenth Century* (New York, 1989)

Marriage and Remarriage in Populations of the Past (ed. J. Dupâquier et al.; London, 1981)

Modrzejewski, J., "Die Geschwisterehe in der hellenistischen Praxis und nach römischem Recht," *ZRG* 81 (1964) 52-82

Montevecchi, O., "Il censimento romano d'Egitto. Precisazioni," *Aevum* 50 (1976) 72-84

Nathanson, C. A., "Sex Differences in Mortality," *Annual Review of Sociology* 10 (1984) 191-213

Newell, C., *Methods and Models in Demography* (New York, 1988)

Nicolet, C., *Space, Geography, and Politics in the Early Roman Empire* (Ann Arbor, 1991)

Omran, A. R., *Egypt: Population Problems & Prospects* (Chapel Hill, 1973)

Parkin, T. G., *Demography and Roman Society* (Baltimore, 1992)

Pestman, P. W., *Marriage and Matrimonial Property in Ancient Egypt: A Contribution to Establishing the Legal Position of the Woman* (Leiden, 1961)

Pomeroy, S. B., *Women in Hellenistic Egypt: From Alexander to Cleopatra* (New York, 1984)

Pomeroy, S. B., "Women in Roman Egypt: A Preliminary Study Based on Papyri," *ANRW* II.10.1 (Berlin, 1988) 708-723

Population Française, see *Histoire de la population française*

Rathbone, D. W., "Villages, Land and Population in Graeco-Roman Egypt," *PCPhS* 216, n.s. 36 (1990) 103-142

Rathbone, D. W., *Economic Rationalism and Rural Society in Third-Century A.D. Egypt* (Cambridge, 1991)

Rathbone, D. W., "Egypt, Augustus and Roman Taxation," *Cahiers du Centre G. Glotz* 4 (1993) 81-112

Riddle, J. M., *Contraception and Abortion from the Ancient World to the Renaissance* (Cambridge, MA, 1992)

Ruggles, S., *Prolonged Connections: The Rise of the Extended Family in Nineteenth-Century England and America* (Madison, WI, 1987)

Russell, J. C., "Late Ancient and Medieval Population," *Transactions of the American Philosophical Association* 48.3 (Philadelphia, 1958)

Salmon, P., *Population et dépopulation dans l'empire romain* (Brussels, 1974)

Shaw, B., "Brother-Sister Marriage in Graeco-Roman Egypt," *Man* 27 (1992) 267-299

Shryock, H. S., and J. S. Siegel, *The Methods and Materials of Demography* (4th rev. pr.; Washington, 1980)

Sidler, N., *Zur Universalität des Inzesttabu: eine kritische Untersuchung der These und der Einwände* (Stuttgart, 1971)

Sijpesteijn, P. J., "Theognostos alias Moros and His Family," *ZPE* 76 (1989) 213-218

Straus, J. A., "L'esclavage dans l'Egypte romaine," *ANRW* II.10.1 (Berlin, 1988) 841-911

Taubenschlag, R., *The Law of Greco-Roman Egypt in the Light of the Papyri* (2d ed.; Warsaw, 1955)

Treggiari, S., *Roman Marriage: "Iusti Coniuges" from the Time of Cicero to the Time of Ulpian* (Oxford, 1991)

United Nations, *Manual X: Indirect Techniques for Demographic Estimation* (Dept. of International Economic and Social Affairs, *Population Studies*, no. 81; New York, 1983)

Visaria, P. M., *The Sex Ratio of the Population of India* (*Census of India 1961*, 1, monograph 10; New Delhi, 1971)

Wallace, S. L., *Taxation in Egypt from Augustus to Diocletian* (Princeton and London, 1937)

Weiss, K. H., *Demographic Models for Anthropology, American Antiquity* 38.2, Pt. II, *Memoirs* no. 27 (Washington, 1973)

Willigan, J. D., and K. A. Lynch, *Sources and Methods of Historical Demography* (New York, 1982)

Wrigley, E. A., *People, Cities and Wealth: The Transformation of Traditional Society* (Oxford, 1987)

Wrigley, E. A., and R. S. Schofield, *A Population History of England, 1541-1871: A Reconstruction* (rev. pb. ed., Cambridge, Mass., 1989; first pub. 1981)

Yaukey, D., *Demography: The Study of Human Population* (New York, 1985)

Youtie, H. C., "ΑΠΑΤΟΡΕΣ: Law vs. Custom in Roman Egypt," in *Hommages à C. Préaux* (Brussels, 1975) 723-740, reprinted in H. C. Youtie, *Scriptiunculae Posteriores* I (Bonn, 1981) 17-34

Index

Titles available in paperback are marked with an asterisk

Reviews

B. J. Malina, RelSRv 21/3
(1995) 230.

L. L. Grabbe, SOTS Booklist
(1995) 123.